SUPPLEMENTATION AND THE STUDY OF THE HEBREW BIBLE

Program in Judaic Studies
Brown University
Box 1826
Providence, RI 02912

BROWN JUDAIC STUDIES

Edited by

Mary Gluck
David C. Jacobson
Maud Mandel
Saul M. Olyan
Rachel Rojanski
Michael L. Satlow
Adam Teller
Nelson Vieira

Number 361
SUPPLEMENTATION AND THE STUDY
OF THE HEBREW BIBLE

edited by
Saul M. Olyan and Jacob L. Wright

SUPPLEMENTATION AND THE STUDY OF THE HEBREW BIBLE

edited by
Saul M. Olyan and Jacob L. Wright

Brown Judaic Studies
Providence, Rhode Island

© 2018 Brown University. All rights reserved.

No part of this work may be reproduced or transmitted in any form or by any means, electronic or mechanical, including photocopying and recording, or by means of any information storage or retrieval system, except as may be expressly permitted by the 1976 Copyright Act or in writing from the publisher. Requests for permission should be addressed in writing to the Rights and Permissions Office, Program in Judaic Studies, Brown University, Box 1826, Providence, RI 02912, USA.

Library of Congress Cataloging-in-Publication Data

Names: Olyan, Saul M., editor.
Title: Supplementation and the study of the Hebrew Bible / edited by Saul M. Olyan and Jacob L. Wright.
Description: Providence : Brown Judaic Studies, 2018. | Series: Brown Judaic studies ; Number 361 | Includes bibliographical references and index.
Identifiers: LCCN 2018001754 (print) | LCCN 2018007962 (ebook) | ISBN 9781946527066 (ebk) | ISBN 9781946527059 (pbk : alk. paper) | ISBN 9781946527073 (hbk : alk. paper)
Subjects: LCSH: Bible. Old Testament—Criticism, interpretation, etc.
Classification: LCC BS1171.3 (ebook) | LCC BS1171.3 .S87 2018 (print) | DDC 221.6/6—dc23
LC record available at https://lccn.loc.gov/2018001754

Printed on acid-free paper.

Contents

Abbreviations vii

Introduction
   Saul M. Olyan and Jacob L. Wright xi

Part 1: Psalms and Lyrical Literature

Supplementation in Psalms: Illustrations from Psalm 145
   Marc Z. Brettler 3

Textual Supplementation in Poetry: The Song of Hannah
as a Test Case
   Reinhard G. Kratz 21

Part 2: Narrative Texts of the Pentateuch

Genre Conventions and Their Implications for
Composition History: A Case for Supplementation in Exodus 16
   Angela Roskop Erisman 53

Joseph and the Egyptian Wife (Genesis 39):
A Case of Double Supplementation
   Thomas Römer 69

Part 3: Deuteronomistic Historical Narrative

Outbidding the Fall of Jerusalem: Redactional
Supplementation in 2 Kings 24
   Konrad Schmid 87

The Evolution of the Gideon Narrative
   Jacob L. Wright 105

Part 4: Prophetic Anthologies

"Biblicist Additions" or the Emergence of Scripture
in the Growth of the Prophets
Anja Klein. 125

Fire and Worms: Isaiah 66:24 in the Context of Isaiah 66
and the Book of Isaiah
Saul M. Olyan 147

Part 5: Legal Texts

Making a Case: The Repurposing of "Israelite Legal
Fictions" as Post-Deuteronomic Law
Sara J. Milstein. 161

Supplementing Leviticus in the Second Temple Period:
The Case of the Wood Offering in 4Q365 Fragment 23
Christophe Nihan 183

Index of Passages 205

Index of Subjects 216

Abbreviations

AAWG.PH	Abhandlungen der Akademie der Wissenschaften zu Göttingen: Philologisch-historische Klasse
AB	Anchor Bible
AfOB	Archiv für Orientforschung: Beiheft
AOAT	Alter Orient und Altes Testament
AR	*Archiv für Religionswissenschaft*
ATANT	Abhandlungen zur Theologie des Alten und Neuen Testaments
ATD	Das Alte Testament deutsch
AYBRL	Anchor Yale Bible Reference Library
BBB	Bonner biblische Beiträge
BBET	Beiträge zur biblischen Exegese und Theologie
BCOTWP	Baker Commentry on the Old Testament Wisdom and Psalms
BdH	La Bible dans l'histoire
BETL	Bibliotheca Ephemeridum Theologicarum Lovaniensium
BEvT	Beiträge zur evangelischen Theologie
Bib	*Biblica*
BibInt	*Biblical Interpretation*
BKAT	Biblischer Kommentar, Altes Testament
BN	*Biblische Notizen*
BThSt	Biblisch-theologische Studien
BZAW	Beihefte zur Zeitschrift für die alttestamentliche Wissenschaft
BWANT	Beiträge zur Wissenschaft vom Alten und Neuen Testament
CBET	Contributions to Biblical Exegesis and Theology
CBQ	*Catholic Biblical Quarterly*
CBQMS	Catholic Biblical Quarterly Monograph Series
CBSC	Cambridge Bible for Schools and Colleges
Conc(D)	*Concilium* (German)
CurBR	*Currents in Biblical Research*
DJD	Discoveries in the Judaean Desert
DSD	*Dead Sea Discoveries*
ECC	Eerdmans Critical Commentary
EHS.T	Europäische Hochschulschriften, Theologie

FAT	Forschung zum Alten Testament
FB	Forschung zur Bibel
FIOTL	Formation and Interpretation of Old Testament Literature
FOTL	Forms of the Old Testament Literature
FRLANT	Forschungen zur Religion und Literatur des Alten und Neuen Testaments
GAT	Grundrisse zum Alten Testament
HACL	History, Archaeology, and Culture of the Levant
HB	Hebrew Bible
HBS	History of Biblical Studies
HCOT	Historical Commentary on the Old Testament
HK	Göttinger Handkommentar zum Alten Testament
HKAT	Handkommentar zum Alten Testament
HS	*Hebrew Studies*
HSM	Harvard Semitic Monographs
HSS	Harvard Semitic Studies
HThKAT	Herders Theologischer Kommentar zum Alten Testament
HUCA	*Hebrew Union College Annual*
ICC	International Critical Commentary
JAOS	*Journal of the American Oriental Society*
JBL	*Journal of Biblical Literature*
JHebS	*Journal of Hebrew Scriptures*
JNES	*Journal of Near Eastern Studies*
JQR	*Jewish Quarterly Review*
JSJSup	Journal for the Study of Judaism in the Persian, Hellenistic, and Roman Period Supplement Series
JSOTSup	Journal for the Study of the Old Testament Supplement Series
JSPSup	Journal for the Study of the Pseudepigrapha, Supplement Series
JSSMS	Journal of Semitic Studies Monograph Series
KHC	Kurzer Hand-Commentar zum Alten Testament
MT	Masoretic Text
NBL	*Neues Bibel-Lexikon*, ed. Manfred Görg and Bernard Lang (Zurich: Benziger, 1988–)
NETS	*A New English Translation of the Septuagint*, ed. Albert Pietersma and Benjamin G. Wright (New York: Oxford University Press, 2007)
NICOT	New International Commentary on the Old Testament
NMES	Near and Middle East Series
NRSV	New Revised Standard Version
OBL	Orientalia et biblica Lovaniensia
OBO	Orbis Biblicus et Orientalis
OED	*Oxford English Dictionary*

Or	*Orientalia*
OTL	Old Testament Library
OTS	Old Testament Studies
OtSt	Oudtestamentische studiën
PÄ	Probleme der Ägyptologie
PEQ	*Palestine Exploration Quarterly*
RB	*Revue biblique*
RBS	Resources for Biblical Study
SBA	Stuttgarter biblische Aufsatzbände
SBS	Stuttgarter Bibelstudien
SBT	Studies in Biblical Theology
SBTS	Sources for Biblical and Theological Study
SEÅ	*Svensk exegetisk årsbok*
SESJ	Schriften der Finnischen Exegetischen Gesellschaft
SJ	Studia Judaica
SKG.G	Schriften der Königsberger Gelehrten Gesellschaft. Geisteswissenschaftliche Klasse
SSEJC	Studies in Scripture in Early Judaism and Christianity
SSN	Studia Semitica Neerlandica
STDJ	Studies on the Texts of the Desert of Judah
TB	Theologische Bücherei
TGl	*Theologie und Glaube*
THAT	*Theologisches Handwörterbuch zum Alten Testament*, ed. Ernst Jenni, 2 vols. (Munich: Kaiser, 1971–1976)
ThW	Theologische Wissenschaft
UTB	Uni-Taschenbücher
VT	*Vetus Testamentum*
VTSup	Supplements to Vetus Testamentum
VWGth	Veröffentlichungen der Wissenschaftlichen Gesellschaft für Theologie
WBC	Word Biblical Commentary
WC	Westminster Commentaries
WMANT	Wissenschaftliche Monographien zum Alten und Neuen Testament
WUNT	Wissenschaftliche Untersuchungen zum Neuen Testament
ZABR	*Zeitschrift für altorientalische und biblische Rechtsgeschichte*
ZAW	*Zeitschrift für die alttestamentliche Wissenschaft*
ZTK	*Zeitschrift für Theologie und Kirche*

Introduction

Saul M. Olyan and Jacob L. Wright

> Then Jeremiah took another scroll
> and gave it to the scribe Baruch ben Neriah,
> who wrote on it at Jeremiah's dictation all the words of the scroll
> that King Jehoiakim of Judah had burned in the fire.
> And many similar words were added to them.
> —Jer 36:32[1]

Jeremiah 36 depicts the Judean king, on one cold day in the winter of 605 BCE, destroying the scroll of Jeremiah's prophecies by casting it piece by piece into the brazier burning before his throne. In response, Jeremiah and Baruch are said to prepare a new scroll containing all the words of the destroyed one. The account concludes with an oft-overlooked remark from the narrator: "And many similar words were added to them" (ועוד נוסף עליהם דברים רבים כהמה). Regardless of whether the scroll to which these additions were allegedly made ever existed, the statement suggests that the author of Jer 36 and his original audience were familiar with the phenomenon of supplementation. It also raises important questions about any supplemented text: Who might have been responsible for the additions? When and why were they added to the text? And can the contemporary reader distinguish between the older words and supplements to them?

The essays in the present volume, originating from a symposium at Brown University in May 2016, investigate the same kinds of questions posed by this verse from Jeremiah, but they do so from the perspective of a wide range of biblical texts. Such texts include not only prophetic writings but also psalms and other lyrical texts, prose narratives, and legal materials. Against the tendency in some circles to bracket the Pentateuch and view its compositional history as *sui generis*, the volume demonstrates that no section of the biblical corpus escaped the hands of readers who added "many similar words" to the texts they received.

Our interest in the phenomenon of supplementation takes us back to the beginnings of modern biblical criticism and the succession of formi-

---

[1]. Trans. Jacob Wright.

dable scholars who set their sights on the origins of the Pentateuch, which became the center of attention for many generations of biblical criticism. Johann Gottfried Eichhorn's *Einleitung in das Alte Testament* from 1783 analyzed the Pentateuch in terms of just two running sources. The compiler who synthesized these sources proceeded in his task with "sacred reverence" (*heilige Ehrfurcht*), resisting any urge to refine the formulation of his inherited texts as he deftly wove them into a rich narrative-legal tapestry.[2] Yet Eichhorn recognized that his theory could not fully account for the Torah's complexity, and thus he assigned considerable space to interpolations.

To do justice to the text's complexity, subsequent analyses multiplied the number of running sources as well as "fragments" from these sources. Karl David Ilgen, known as the founder of the "Older Documentary Hypothesis," explained the origins of Genesis in 1798 as a combination of not fewer than seventeen writings transmitted in three separate sources.[3] Along with other proponents of the "Fragment Hypothesis," Wilhelm M. L. de Wette argued that the "Jehovist" had reworked the "Elohim source," integrating in the process an array of oral and written materials.[4] Similarly, K. H. Graf postulated a narrative substratum that a later author heavily revised and supplemented; the most extensive of the supplements included the exilic insertion of the book of Deuteronomy into an older Hexateuch and the postexilic addition of the materials that belonged to what is now known as the P source.[5]

Graf paved the way for Abraham Kuenen and Julius Wellhausen to formulate the definitive form of the "Four-Source (or Newer) Documentary Hypothesis," and both scholars relied heavily in their theory mak-

---

2. Johann Gottfried Eichhorn, *Einleitung in das Alte Testament* (Leipzig: Weidmann, 1783). For this citation, including the quotation, see Konrad Schmid, "Von der Diaskeuase zur nachendredaktionellen Fortschreibung: Die Geschichte der Erforschung der nachpriesterschriftlichen Redaktionsgeschichte des Pentateuch," in *The Post-Priestly Pentateuch: New Perspectives on Its Redactional Development and Theological Profiles*, ed. Federico Giuntoli and Konrad Schmid, FAT 101(Tübingen: Mohr Siebeck, 2015), 1–18, here 2 n. 8. This essay has recently been published in English translation ("Post-Priestly Additions in the Pentateuch: A Survey of Scholarship," in *The Formation of the Pentateuch: Bridging the Academic Cultures of Europe, Israel, and North America*, ed. Jan C. Gertz et al., FAT 111 [Tübingen: Mohr Siebeck, 2016], 589–604).

3. As pointed out by Thomas Römer, "Zwischen Urkunden, Fragmenten und Ergänzungen: Zum Stand der Pentateuchforschung," *ZAW* 125 (2013): 2–24, here 4. Ilgen's work is *Die Urkunden des ersten Buchs von Moses in ihrer Urgestalt*, vol. 1 of *Die Urkunden des jerusalemischen Tempelarchivs in ihrer Urgestalt* (Halle: Hemmerde und Schwetschke, 1798), cited by Römer.

4. Römer, "Zwischen Urkunden," 5. Wilhelm Martin Leberecht De Wette, *Beiträge zur Einleitung in das Alte Testament*, 2 vols. (Halle: Schimmelpfennig, 1806–1807), cited by Römer.

5. Römer, "Zwischen Urkunden," 6. K. H. Graf, "Die sogenannte Grundschrift des Pentateuch," *Archiv für die wissenschaftliche Erforschung des Alten Testaments* 1 (1869): 466–77, cited by Römer.

ing on the assumption that later readers amplified the received sources with substantial supplements that cannot be assigned to any of the four sources. Wellhausen insisted that the composition of the Pentateuch was not complete with the compilation of sources (JE and P) and emphasized throughout his *Composition* that he was presenting a heavily simplified version of his views, that the literary process was much more complicated, and that the Supplementary Hypothesis must be given a place in any theory.[6]

In formulating their views on the supplementation of the combined pentateuchal sources, both Kuenen and Wellhausen appealed to the role of the "Diaskeuasten." Long used in classical philology to describe the editors who amplified the poetic texts they transmitted, the term was introduced to biblical studies by Julius Popper, a scholar who had a major impact on our theories even if he has been largely forgotten today.[7] In his study of Exodus, Popper demonstrated the exegetical character of the "Amplifikationen" that he isolated and argued that the additions in the Samaritanus and Septuagint must be viewed as part of the same activity of "Diaskeuase" that fashioned the final form of the Pentateuch transmitted in rabbinic Judaism.[8]

In the scholarship that followed Keunen and Wellhausen, we can witness, as Konrad Schmid has recently shown, a tendency to downplay the creativity of those who combined the sources and supplemented them in various ways.[9] The case is especially apparent in the work of Hermann Gunkel and Martin Noth. Yet, while both sought to diminish significantly the contribution of the compiler, they did not hesitate to admit that noteworthy additions continued to be made after the combination of the sources. In the words of Gunkel, "With this is the activity of the redactor in Genesis concluded as a whole. But in the details, the work ('Diaskeuase') on the text continued much longer."[10] Thus, earlier generations of critics

---

6. Julius Wellhausen, *Die Composition des Hexateuchs und der historischen Bücher des Alten Testaments*, 3rd ed. (Berlin: Reimer, 1899), 207: "Der Einfachheit wegen abstrahire ich meistens davon, dass der literarische Process in Wirksamkeit complicirter gewesen ist und die sogenannte Ergänzungshypothese in untergeordneter Weise doch ihre Anwendung findet." For this citation and quotation, see Schmid, "Von der Diaskeuase," 3 and n. 11.

7. Wellhausen honored Popper in his writing as the "gelehrte Rabbi," as Schmid notes ("Von der Diaskeuase," 4, citing *Die Composition des Hexateuchs*, 146). On Popper, see further Schmid, "Von der Diaskeuase," 3–6; and Ran HaCohen, *Reclaiming the Hebrew Bible: German-Jewish Reception of Biblical Criticism*, SJ 56 (Berlin: de Gruyter, 2010), 137–41, the latter cited by Schmid. On Popper's influence on Kuenen, see Schmid, "Von der Diaskeuase," 5.

8. Schmid, "Von der Diaskeuase," 4–5; Julius Popper, *Der biblische Bericht über die Stiftshütte: Ein Beitrag zur Geschichte der Composition und Diaskeue des Pentateuch* (Leipzig: Hunger, 1862).

9. Schmid, "Von der Diaskeuase," 5-7.

10. Trans. Jacob Wright. The original reads: "Damit ist im allgemeinen die Tätigkeit der Redaktoren an der Genesis abgeschlossen. Aber im einzelnen geht die Arbeit ('Diaskeuase')

acknowledged the role of supplementation in the development of the Pentateuch, even if it was not their primary focus.

Interest in the phenomenon of supplementation has waned in some quarters of contemporary North American scholarship. In 2006, John Van Seters published his broadside against the "editor," and it has been positively received among "Neo-Documentarians."[11] Members of this group have worked over the past decade to revitalize interest in the Four Source theory, and, in doing so, they have gone even further than Gunkel and Noth in their curtailment of the role of the final redactor, viewing him essentially as a compiler and insisting that the Pentateuch as we know it is mainly a result of an "almost mechanical" juxtaposition of the sources.[12] The isolation of these sources should be our primary concern, since the finished form of the Pentateuch, as analyzed by this group of interpreters, is an "incoherent" text resulting from the compiler's formalistic mode of assembling his sources.[13] Although Neo-Documentarians acknowledge the presence of "post-compilational redactional activity" of various sorts in the text, this is neither attributed to the compiler, nor is it of particular interest to these scholars.[14]

Meanwhile, European scholarship has continued to pursue its long-standing concern with the earliest precursors to the biblical texts, but beginning in the 1970s it turned its attention to the process by which these

---

am Text noch lange weiter." See Hermann Gunkel, *Genesis*, HKAT 1.1 (Göttingen: Vandenhoeck & Ruprecht, 1901), XCIX. For this quotation, see Schmid, "Von der Diaskeuase," 6.

11. John Van Seters, *The Edited Bible: The Curious History of the "Editor" in Biblical Criticism* (Winona Lake, IN: Eisenbrauns, 2006). Joel Baden characterizes this work as "an extensive and valuable history of the concept of the 'editor' in biblical scholarship" (*The Composition of the Pentateuch: Renewing the Documentary Hypothesis* [New Haven: Yale University Press, 2012], 316 n. 1).

12. For a brief introduction to the work of this group, see Baden, "The Re-Emergence of Source Criticism: The Neo-Documentary Hypothesis," http://www.bibleinterp.com/articles/bad368008.shtml (2012). For a more detailed treatment, see, e.g., Baden, *Composition of the Pentateuch*; and Jeffrey Stackert, *A Prophet like Moses: Prophecy, Law, and Israelite Religion* (New York: Oxford University Press, 2014), esp. 19–26. For examples of the compiler's rare interventions, see Baden, *Composition of the Pentateuch*, 221–24. For the characterization of the compiler as "almost mechanical" in his work, see Baden, "Re-Emergence of Source Criticism." Stackert characterizes the compiler as "working with a consistent method" characterized by several "principles" (*Prophet like Moses*, 21).

13. For the final form of the Pentateuch as "incoherent" or "incomprehensible," see, e.g., Baden, "Re-Emergence of Source Criticism"; and Stackert, *Prophet like Moses*, 22.

14. Stackert, *Prophet like Moses*, 21 on "post-compilational redactional activity." See also Baden, who states, "Literary activities that do not participate in the process of combining the source documents—glosses, secondary additions, theological revisions—these are not part of the compiler's work, and are not attributed to the compiler" ("Re-Emergence of Source Criticism"). See similarly his comments in *Composition of the Pentateuch*, 248: "The Documentary Hypothesis does not deny that each source has a history, nor does it deny that the Pentateuch itself has a history after the compilation of the documents. It is a restricted answer to a restricted question."

texts achieved the unity and coherence evinced in their final forms.[15] This renewed interest in the final forms of texts, and in the gradual process of "Fortschreibung" that gave rise to them, notably did not take its cue from the older research on the Pentateuch reviewed above but rather from the analysis of prophetic writings, especially from Walther Zimmerli's monumental Ezekiel commentary (published in fascicles from 1955 to 1969).[16] During the same period, scholars such as Michael Fishbane and James L. Kugel in North America sought to map the dynamics of inner-biblical exegesis, a phenomenon that included textual expansions and reworking of various sorts evidenced across the biblical corpus.[17] In short, scholarship in both North America and Europe have begun to identify and explore compositional phenomena such as supplementation that contributed to the final form of the biblical text across the canon.

The present volume represents an attempt to contribute to the further development of a pan-biblical compositional perspective by significantly advancing our understanding of the role of supplementation in the development of the Hebrew Bible as a whole. It explores the phenomenon of supplementation in four sections, organized by literary type: Psalms and Lyrical Literature (Brettler, Kratz); Narrative Texts of the Pentateuch (Erisman, Römer); Deuteronomistic Historical Narrative (Schmid, Wright); Prophetic Anthologies (Klein, Olyan); and Legal Texts (Milstein, Nihan).[18] Each essay is an original contribution to the study of supplementation, and, taken together, the ten studies demonstrate clearly just how common, variegated, and significant the phenomenon of supplementation in the Hebrew Bible is. Supplementation may be found in minor additions to a text intended to aid pronunciation, fill in abbreviations, or clarify ambiguous syntax (Brettler). It may also be observed in far more elaborate changes such as the introduction of larger interpolations within

---

15. For more in depth discussion of this turn in the 1970s, see further Schmid, "Von der Diaskeuase," 7–8.

16. Walther Zimmerli, *Ezechiel 1–48*, 2 vols., BKAT 13.1–2 (Neukirchen-Vluyn: Neukirchener Verlag, 1969).

17. E.g., Michael Fishbane, *Biblical Interpretation in Ancient Israel* (Oxford: Clarendon, 1985); and James L. Kugel, "Early Interpretation: The Common Background of Late Forms of Biblical Exegesis," in James L. Kugel and Rowan A. Greer, *Early Biblical Interpretation*, LEC 3 (Philadelphia: Westminster, 1986), 13–106. Fishbane speaks of "exegetical supplements" in his treatment (e.g., 528–29). On inner-biblical exegesis and supplementation, see Reinhard Gregor Kratz, "Innerbiblische Exegese und Redaktionsgeschichte im Lichte empirischer Evidenz," in *Das Judentum im Zeitalter des Zweiten Tempels*, FAT 42 (Tübingen: Mohr Siebeck, 2013), 126–56.

18. The ordering of the essays is somewhat arbitrary and obviously not driven by canonical concerns. Brettler's essay is placed first mainly because in it the author attempts to map types of supplementation in Psalm 145 as well as the reasons for it in a useful way, providing an entry into thinking systematically about the phenomenon in its various permutations.

a work of prose (Wright, Schmid, Römer, Erisman), in a prophetic text (Klein, Olyan), or in a legal text (Milstein, Nihan). Supplementation also includes the addition of an introduction, a conclusion, or an introductory and concluding framework to a particular text, whether lyrical, legal, prophetic, or narrative (Kratz, Brettler, Milstein, Olyan) or the augmentation of a poetic text by adding internal refrains (Brettler). It may also be found in the reworking of older legal texts to produce new legislation, as in the case of 4Q365 23 (Nihan) or, famously, the slave laws of Exod 21:2–6 and Deut 15:12–18.

How do scholars identify supplements and how do they unravel the growth of a text that has experienced supplementation? In order to identify a supplement, one might appeal to the stylistic distinctiveness of a text or passage, as does Römer with regard to Gen 39. Scholars frequently point to evidence of a tight connection linking sections of text on either end of what appears to be a supplement, as does Wright on Judg 8:28, which follows 8:18–21 smoothly, suggesting that 8:22–27 is intrusive, or Schmid on 2 Kgs 24:1 and 5, which flow well if uninterrupted by 24:2–4. A passage might be identified as supplementary if it draws on other passages in a creative way to produce a new text (Kratz, Nihan, Milstein) or if it seems to stand alone, with the narrative in which it is embedded making no reference whatsoever to it (Römer on the larger Joseph story in relation to Gen 39). Supplements may themselves be supplemented, sometimes several times, as the examples of Gen 39 and Isa 66:15–24 show. On occasion, external evidence points to supplementation, as in the case of Judg 6:7–10, missing in 4QJudg^a (Wright) or the refrains of MT Ps 145, missing in the LXX (Kratz).

Reconstructing the stages in the growth of a supplemented text is often very challenging, and it is not unusual for scholars to acknowledge the limits of what we can know (Erisman, Wright, Olyan). In order to unravel the growth of such a text, scholars often focus on tracking dependency: upon which particular texts is a supplement dependent or, put differently, which particular texts does it assume through allusion or citation? A case in point is Isa 66:24, universally acknowledged to be a late addition to the series of supplements that round out the book of Isaiah (66:15–24). Olyan argues that 66:24 depends on 66:15–16, 22–23 and 1:28; that it may assume 66:14 and 14:11; and that there is no evidence it knows of 66:17 or 18–21, given that it does not engage the content of these verses. Thus, Isa 66:24 must postdate 66:15–16, 22–23 and 1:28 but not necessarily 66:17 or 18–21, which may be earlier or later. We simply do not know enough about the stages in the growth of Isa 66:15–24 to decide. Thus, tracking textual dependency does not always provide us with all that we seek to know about the stages of a supplemented text's growth, although it can tell us something of value, as the example of Isa 66:24 illustrates.

Supplementation may have a variety of functions, including but not limited to the following: It may correct perceived errors in a text, as in 11QPsᵃ v. 3, in which a scribe apparently adds a letter to a word in order to correct his own error (Brettler); it may change the focus of a text, as does the framing of the Song of Hannah, which shifts the emphasis of the poem from Yhwh's actions and abilities to the fate of a particular individual—the king—and that of his enemies (Kratz); it may forge connections with texts elsewhere, as does Isa 66:24, which alludes to Isa 1:28 through its mention of transgressors against Yhwh (Olyan), or Isa 41:21, which alludes unmistakably to Exod 15:13 and 16 in its evocation of a "New Exodus" (Klein). Supplementation may contemporize a text for a new context, as the example of the Ashrei prayer demonstrates (Brettler); it may address perceived ambiguities in a passage by means of clarification, as in Isa 66:17, which tells us who exactly are the offenders of 66:15–16 (Olyan); it may create symmetry or harmony as in 11QPsᵃ v. 4, which renders a singular verb as a plural to produce agreement (Brettler). Supplementation may add details to a text or elaborate on its content, as in Ezek 38–39, a pericope that elaborates extensively on Yhwh's promise in Ezek 36:22 to take action to sanctify his profaned name (Klein); it may transform the representation of a literary character, even radically, as in the case of Gideon, who goes from being a skilled warrior to a fearful farmer in need of constant reassurance from Yhwh, a transformation that brings Yhwh's power into relief (Wright). A second example of character transformation by means of supplementation is the case of Joseph, who becomes a model of loyalty and chastity through the addition of Gen 39 to the Joseph story (Römer). Supplementation may fill in perceived gaps, as does the wood offering in 4Q365 (Nihan); it may better integrate new material into an extant work, as does the introductory frame in Deut 17:2–7 with regard to what Milstein calls "Israelite Legal Fictions" (ILFs). In all of these examples, supplementation might be described as a creative and "strategic" (Nihan) activity, with one or more functions.

In his contribution to this volume, Brettler asks whether we can identify types of supplementation that are peculiar to particular literary genres. This is a very apt question that we can only begin to address here. Certainly the addition of refrains to psalms or other poetic texts seems peculiar to lyrical literature by definition, while supplementation intended to transform the character of a literary figure such as Gideon (Wright) or Joseph (Römer) seems at first blush to be a phenomenon of narrative specifically. In contrast, adding introductions, conclusions or introductory and concluding frames is a characteristic of supplementation throughout a range of literary genres (e.g., narrative, poetry, law). Similarly, the tendency of supplements in psalms and other poetic compositions to pursue theological interests (Kratz) is not unique to lyrical literature, as examples from narrative (Schmid, Wright), legal texts (Milstein), and prophetic materials (Klein, Olyan) show. Thus, this book has much to say about supplementation in relation to different genres, yet a detailed investigation of this question is clearly a desideratum for future research.

Can supplementation be viewed as a diachronic phenomenon? Klein's essay makes a striking case for change over time in the nature of the supplementation she identifies in prophetic collections, which she relates to the emergence of an idea of scripture. Whether her insight regarding "dynamic" supplementation in prophetic anthologies might be more broadly attested in other parts of the Hebrew Bible is an exciting question for the coming studies of supplementation that this volume promises—hopes—to inspire.

I

Psalms and Lyrical Literature

Supplementation in Psalms: Illustrations from Psalm 145

MARC Z. BRETTLER
Duke University

Introduction

In contrast to Professor Kratz's following paper, which offers an overview of supplementation in poetic texts, I will focus on supplementation through the lens of a single composition: Psalm 145. I have chosen this psalm for several reasons:

1. It is well known and not especially difficult: thus, it is possible to deal with issues of supplementation without getting bogged down with side issues.[1]

2. Much of the psalm is found in the Great Psalms Scroll from Qumran, 11QPs^a (11Q5).[2] The Qumran version of Ps 145 differs in many ways from the MT, likely in many cases supplementing a text that was close to the MT—this is true in general of 11QPs^a in relation to the MT. Thus, it is an ideal case study for discussing supplementation. In particular, with its differences of many types, it illustrates different types of supplementation and

---

I would like to thank Mr. Lenin Prado, Mr. Cody David, and Ms. Lara Haft for their helpful comments on this paper, and the members of the Biblical Colloquium for their helpful reactions to a slightly different version of this paper.

1. See esp. the recent treatment of this psalm in Reinhard G. Kratz, "'Blessed Be the Lord and Blessed Be His Name Forever': Psalm 145 in the Hebrew Bible and in the Psalms Scroll 11Q5," in *Prayer and Poetry in the Dead Sea Scrolls and Related Literature: Essays in Honor of Eileen Schuller on the Occasion of Her 65th Birthday*, ed. Jeremy Penner, Ken M. Penner, and Cecilia Wassen; STDJ 98 (Leiden: Brill 2012), 229–43.

2. The most recent comprehensive study of this scroll is Ulrich Dahmen, *Psalmen- und Psalter-Rezeption im Frühjudentum: Rekonstruktion, Textbestand, Struktur und Pragmatik der Psalmenrolle 11QPs^a aus Qumran*, STDJ 49 (Leiden: Brill, 2003), which should be supplemented by Eva Jain, *Psalmen oder Psalter? Materielle Rekonstruktion und inhaltliche Untersuchung der Psalmenhandschriften aus der Wüste Juda*, STDJ 109 (Leiden: Brill, 2014), 158–77, and David Wilgren, "Like a Garden of Flowers: A Study in the Formation of the 'Book' of Psalms" (PhD diss., Lund, 2016), 103–8, 121–30.

thus is especially useful in attempts to categorize this phenomenon. Additionally, in places it is shorter than the MT, and thus may also offer opportunities to discuss the phenomenon that is the opposite of supplementation, which might be called shrinkage, diminution, reduction, loss, subtraction, abbreviation, downsizing, or truncating. We cannot automatically assume that, when we have two versions of the "same" text, one shorter and one longer, that the shorter is the more original. This needs to be determined on a case-by-case basis, since a later version of a text may preserve early, short readings. The scholarly consensus, however, suggests that 11QPs[a] knows a version close to the MT, and its plusses vis-à-vis the MT should be viewed as additions, unless specific evidence suggests the contrary.[3]

3. Psalm 145 is used in the Jewish liturgy. It is typically named after its new first word, אשרי,[4] and is recited twice in the morning (שחרית) and afternoon (מנחה) prayers. In its liturgical form, MT Ps 145 is supplemented by an introduction (Ps 84:5; 144:15) and conclusion (Ps 115:18) from the canonical Psalter. I believe that the type of supplementation that it undergoes in this later period is also useful for understanding supplementation within the MT Psalter.

Even though particular empirical models have come under question and critique in some recent scholarship,[5] I believe that looking at three forms of Ps 145 offers a useful empirical model for understanding supplementation in the Psalter. I will explore this by examining MT Ps 145, Qumran Ps 145 as found in 11QPs[a] (that psalm is not attested in any of the other Psalm manuscripts among the scrolls), and the Jewish liturgical version. In offering this comparison, I am well aware of the debate about whether 11QPs[a] is a biblical scroll or a liturgical text; the answer to this question, as far as I can tell, does not affect my argument. (I would just say that I follow those who argue that it is best to avoid the term *biblical text* in reference to Qumran scrolls in general.[6]) Nor is it relevant that the

---

3. This is the thesis of Dahmen, *Psalmen- und Psalter-Rezeption*; see also the remarks of Kratz, "'Blessed Be the Lord,'" 236–37.

4. See Lawrence A. Hoffman, *My People's Prayer Book: Traditional Prayers, Modern Commentaries*, 10 vols. (Woodstock, VT: Jewish Lights, 1997–2007), 3:122.

5. See esp. Seth L. Sanders, "What If There Aren't Any Empirical Models for Pentateuchal Criticism?," in *Contextualizing Israel's Sacred Writings: Ancient Literacy, Orality, and Literary Production*, ed. Brian B. Schmidt, AIL 22 (Atlanta: Society of Biblical Literature, 2015), 281–304; and Jan Joosten, "Empirical Evidence and Its Limits: The Use of the Septuagint in Retracing the Redaction History of the Hebrew Bible," n.p., https://www.academia.edu/23990395/EMPIRICAL_EVIDENCE_AND_ITS_LIMITS._The_Use_of_the_Septuagint_in_Retracing_the_Redaction_History_of_the_Hebrew_Bible.

6. On this issue most broadly, see now Eugene Ulrich, *The Dead Sea Scrolls and the Developmental Composition of the Bible*, VTSup 169 (Leiden: Brill, 2015); he discusses 11QPs[a] on 194–99. See also William Yarchin, "Were the Psalms Collections at Qumran True Psalters?," *JBL* 134 (2015): 775–89; Wilgren, "Like a Garden of Flowers"; and Eva Mroczek, *The Literary Imagination in Jewish Antiquity* (New York: Oxford University Press, 2016).

liturgical אשרי prayer is postbiblical—it is still a version of the psalm and, as such, sheds light on the issue of supplementation. The liturgical אשרי exists in many variants and coalesced in the form that is now used in the Ashkenazi prayer books only in the Middle Ages,[7] but that Ashkenazi edition is sufficient for making the points I would like to adduce.[8]

I would like to admit two problems at the outset. First of all, I am not sure how to define *supplementation*.[9] I will be maximalistic in my definition, relying on *OED*, which indicates that "supplementation" is a recent, mid-nineteenth-century word: "the actions of supplementing."[10] *Supplement* is an older word that was, appropriately enough, first attested in Wycliffe's Bible translation (of Mark 2:21). The beginning of the first definition in *OED* is, "Something added to supply a deficiency,"[11] a definition that others may find too broad, in part because it sidesteps the issue of how deliberate or subconscious such an addition might be. I do not, however, see how we might determine such deliberateness.

In looking into supplementations, the words of Emanuel Tov in an article on the related issue of glosses are especially pertinent: "Upon investigating this topic one realizes time and again how complex the issues are, not only with regard to a definition of what actually constitutes a gloss and an interpolation."[12] He also notes, "Interpolations were not only inserted into texts in the course of the textual transmission, but similar additions must have been made at an earlier stage, that of the literary development of the biblical books."[13] Here Tov points out, as he and others have done elsewhere, that issues such as supplementation are both a lower-critical and a higher-critical issue, and that it is often impossible to distinguish between these two phenomena, as an earlier generation often did in a facile fashion. Moreover, as observed above, it is difficult in some cases to know if a short text has been supplemented, or a longer text

---

7. See Reuven Kimelman, "*Ashre*: Psalm 145 and the Liturgy," *Proceedings of the Rabbinical Assembly* 54 (1992): 121 n. 4.

8. The various different supplementations do show, quite helpfully, that the same composition may be supplemented differently by different editors.

9. In line with the symposium and this volume, this is the term that I use; I leave it to others to explore if this is the most suitable term and how it might differ from other terms such as insertion, expansion, explication, and accretion.

10. OED online, http://www.oed.com.resources.library.brandeis.edu/view/Entry/194630?redirectedFrom=supplementation#eid, s.v. "supplementation," n.

11. *OED* online, http://www.oed.com.resources.library.brandeis.edu/view/Entry/194624?rskey=1jwdpw&result=1&isAdvanced=false#eid, s.v. "supplement," n. 1. It is noteworthy that the Latin *supplere* means "to fill up, complete."

12. Emanuel Tov, "Glosses, Interpolations, and Other Types of Scribal Additions in the Text of the Hebrew Bible," in *Language, Theology, and the Bible: Essays in Honour of James Barr*, ed. Samuel E. Balentine and John Barton (Oxford: Clarendon, 1994), 40–66, here 40.

13. Ibid., 58.

condensed. The small corpus that I am examining will offer ample opportunities to explore these issues.[14]

Preliminary Evidence from MT Psalm 145 and 11QPs[a], Verse 1

Psalm 145:1 introduces some of the problems involved in defining and subcategorizing supplementation; after exploring that verse, I will organize material from the rest of the psalm into various categories reflecting types of supplementation.

The MT of verse 1 reads:

תהלה לדוד ארוממך אלוהי המלך ואברכה שמך לעולם ועד

The Qumran version reads:

תפלה לדויד ארוממכה יְהֹוָה אלוהי המלך ואברכה שמכה לעולם ועד ברוך יהוה וברוך שמו לעולם ועד.

The Qumran text contains several orthographic expansions—namely, the longer forms of the name דויד, of the pronominal suffixes attached to the verb ארוממכה and to the noun שמכה. Each of these represents a form of later Hebrew writing that was known at Qumran but which has no bearing on meaning.[15] These secondary, longer forms are in some sense "supplementing"—they are added to correct a perceived deficiency of sorts—to return to the *OED* definition—and they prevent readers from misreading each of these words, and thus misinterpreting the verse. These three examples illustrate the most minimal type of supplementation on the continuum of types of supplementation.

The next two examples from this verse are more complex. The MT of the first word of the psalm is תהלה, while 11QPs[a] reads תפלה. At first, this seems to be a scribal error or a variation, though I do not know of other

---

14. It is striking that these issues have not been examined more systematically in works such as William P. Brown, ed., *The Oxford Handbook of the Psalms* (Oxford: Oxford University Press, 2014) and Nancy L. deClaissé-Walford, *The Shape and Shaping of the Book of Psalms: The Current State of Scholarship*, AIL 20 (Atlanta: Society of Biblical Literature, 2014). It seems that the field is currently focusing on collections within the Psalter rather than on how individual psalms were formed and re-formed. This tendency is reflected in Erich Zenger, ed., *The Composition of the Book of Psalms*, BETL 138 (Leuven: Peeters, 2010), and to some extent in Peter W. Flint and Patrick D. Miller, eds., *The Book of Psalms: Composition and Reception*, VTSup 99 (Leiden: Brill, 2005).

15. Elisha Qimron, *The Hebrew of the Dead Sea Scrolls*, HSS 29 (Atlanta: Scholars Press, 1986), 19 (100:32), 23 (100:7); and now Eric D. Reymond, *Qumran Hebrew: An Overview of Orthography, Phonology, and Morphology*, RBS 76 (Atlanta: Society of Biblical Literature, 2014), 35–43 (§3.2).

cases where the letters *heh* and *peh,* which are not similar in any of the scripts, interchange.[16] I suspect instead that this difference reflects early supplementation; it is one of many cases in the Hebrew Bible where an abbreviation has been filled in. The more original text was ת לדוד, and when abbreviations went out of fashion, this ת was filled out differently in two different traditions. Although such abbreviations are not found in the Dead Sea Scrolls, substantial evidence supports the idea that they existed at an early point in the copying of biblical texts.[17] Thus, both the MT and 11QPs[a] readings likely reflect supplementation.[18]

The tetragrammaton in v. 1, which is erased by the superlinear and infralinear dots,[19] presents a quandary—is it worth considering erased words in discussions of supplementation? On the one hand, their "erasure" suggests that they should be excluded, but, on the other hand, their initial presence suggests that they are worthy of some discussion. I include this case of Ps 145:1 in 11QPs[a], which likely reflects a tradition that was later corrected to proto-MT.

It is initially difficult to figure out if the reading יהוה אלוהי, unique among the versions, is a supplementation or if it is the more original reading, with the MT and the other witnesses reflecting a shortened text. With the tetragrammaton, the verse (excluding the superscription, which should not be counted for "metrical" considerations) is very long, suggesting that it is secondary; but, with the tetragrammaton, both parts of the verse are better balanced in terms of length or syllables. But should meter or balance be used in this and other psalms to determine supplementation?[20] Given that the metrical evidence does not resolve the issue of textual priority, it is unlikely that ארוממכה יהוה אלוהי המלך is the more original reading, since this longer reading is found in no other witnesses. Thus, the longer version in (pre-erased) 11QPs[a] more likely indicates supplementation rather than deletion.

This case likely reflects a very common type of supplementation: supplementation based on parallel texts. Here, two parallels of different types

---

16. In theory, this could reflect an early oral variant, but the other cases of likely abbreviations in this psalm that cannot be explained similarly suggest that abbreviations are certainly reflected in the variants between 11QPs[a] and the MT and are likely present here.

17. Emanuel Tov, *Textual Criticism of the Hebrew Bible*, 3rd ed. (Minneapolis: Fortress, 2012), 238–39, with literature there.

18. Other scholars see this difference as deriving not from abbreviations that were filled in differently but from other textual phenomena; see, e.g., Dahmen, *Psalmen- und Psalter-Rezeption*, 196–97.

19. For this practice, see Emanuel Tov, *Scribal Practices and Approaches Reflected in the Texts Found in the Judean Desert*, STDJ 54 (Leiden: Brill, 2004), 193–94.

20. This should likely be a psalm-by-psalm judgment—some psalms seem to be balanced "metrically," while others are not. We should not expect all psalms, written by many people in many eras and places, to agree in terms of meter or (a term I prefer) balance.

are relevant: (1) the phrase or formula יהוה אלוהי is found thirty-nine times in the MT, eleven of which are in Psalms; and (2) in Ps 99:5 and 9, the root רום is followed by the tetragrammaton and אלהים with a pronominal suffix (רוממו יהוה אלהינו), which may have influenced the divine names that appeared in our psalm after ארוממך. The influence of parallel texts is an important component of supplementation.

The addition of ברוך יהוה וברוך שמו לעולם ועד clearly deserves to be discussed under supplementation. 11QPs^a is the only textual witness to this phrase, and it is unlikely that it was original. (This refrain is found after every verse as well.) The closest biblical parallel to this formula is the Late Biblical Hebrew doxology in Ps 72:18–19:[21]

ברוך יהוה אלהים אלהי ישראל עשה נפלאות לבדו
וברוך שם כבודו לעולם וימלא כבודו את כל הארץ אמן ואמן

Similar doxologies are found in medieval Jewish and Karaite prayers, perhaps suggesting some continuity with 11QPs^a—such formulae are often transmitted orally.[22] The addition of this formula may reflect a new liturgical setting for the psalm, perhaps even a call-and-response or antiphonal setting.[23] This cannot be proven, though Ezra 3:11 suggests that such types of recitation did exist.[24]

The Evidence from MT Psalm 145 and 11QPs^a: Verses 2–21

The types of supplementation found in the first verse continue throughout the psalm. The refrain ברוך יהוה וברוך שמו לעולם ועד is repeated

---

21. On the date of these doxologies, see Avi Hurvitz, *The Transition Period in Biblical Hebrew: A Study in Post-Exilic Hebrew and its Implications for the Dating of Psalms* (Jerusalem: Bialik Institute, 1972), 170–171 (Hebrew).

22. On the rabbinite formulae, see Naftali Weider, "Baruch hu' uvaruch shemo—Its Origin, Time-Period, and Variants" [in Hebrew], in *Studies in Rabbinic Literature, Bible and Jewish History*, ed. Y. Gilat, Ch. Levine, and Z. Rabinowitz (Ramat Gan: Bar-Ilan University Press, 1982), 277–90; and among the Karaites, see Sidney B. Hoenig, "The Qumran Liturgic Psalms," *JQR* 57 (1967): 327–32, here 328.

23. See, e.g., Hoenig, "Qumran Liturgic Psalms"; M. H. Goshen-Gottstein, "The Psalms Scroll (11 QPs^a): A Problem of Text and Canon," *Textus* 5 (1966): 22–33, here 29, and the scholars cited in Kratz, "'Blessed Be the Lord,'" 239–40. Kratz disputes the liturgical significance of this refrain. At the minimum, the observations of Michael Chyutin ("The Redaction of the Qumranic and the Traditional Book of Psalms as a Calendar," *RevQ* 63 [1994]: 367–95) that this refrain "gives the psalm in the Scroll version a greater ritual resonance and importance," seems reasonable.

24. On congregational responses in the postexilic period, see, e.g., John W. Kleinig, *The LORD's Song: The Basis, Function and Significance of Choral Music in Chronicles*, JSOTSup 156 (Sheffield: JSOT Press, 1993), 95–96; and Nissim Amzallag, "Praise or Antiphonal Singing? The Meaning of להודות Revisited," *HS* 56 (2015): 115–28.

after each verse.²⁵ Further, the text offers a large number of cases, in each verse that has an MT parallel,²⁶ where supplementary letters are added to nudge the reader toward the correct pronunciation; these are too numerous to list.

It is also quite possible that the psalm offers other cases of early abbreviations that have been supplemented differently. This best explains the difference in v. 2 between MT בכל and the (illogical, highly problematic) ברוך—an initial ב was filled in differently in different texts. This may also explain the difference in v. 18 between MT באמת and (the equally possible) 11QPsᵃ's באמונה—each may derive from the abbreviation באמ or בא. In some ways, some early biblical texts may have been more of *aides-memoire*²⁷ than full texts. This was in many ways true until vocalization marks were introduced and is certainly the case in a small number of Cairo Geniza biblical texts that abbreviate the text drastically, using סירוגין form.²⁸

The comparison between the MT and 11QPsᵃ versions offers several other types of supplementation, which I list from more minor to major.

One simple type of supplementation is when a scribe corrects his own error by adding a letter. This is seen clearly in 11QPsᵃ in several places, for example, in v. 3, where the scribe adds a *mem*, correcting the impossible ומהולל to והולל.²⁹

On several occasions, it seems that words are added to disambiguate the syntax. This is most clear in v. 21, where the MT's ויברך כל בשר שם קדשו became 11QPsᵃ's ויברך כול בשר את שם קודשו; this added את makes sure that the reader will not understand בשר as in construct with שם קדשו. The superlinear addition of את in v. 15 is similar.³⁰

In other cases, it is possible that minor additions were made to increase

---

25. See below for a discussion of v. 18, where the refrain appears twice.
26. The *nun* verse in 11QPsᵃ has no parallel in the MT.
27. For this phrase, see recently Peter and Charlotte Vardy, *Bible Matters* (London: SCM, 2015), 32; for greater details, see James Barr, "Reading a Script without Vowels," anthologized in *Bible and Interpretation: The Collected Essays of James Barr*, ed. John Barton, 3 vols. (Oxford: Oxford University Press, 2014), 3:332–51, as well as several of his articles at the beginning of that volume that deal with how the versions read the unpointed text.
28. See, e.g., Ernst Würthwein, *The Text of the Old Testament: An Introduction to the Biblia Hebraica*, trans. Erroll F. Rhodes, 2nd ed. (Grand Rapids: Eerdmans, 1995), 170, with illustration on 171.
29. Based on the paleography, it is likely that the same scribe who made the error corrected it. For other cases, see the addition in v. 2 of וברוך, and the added *waw* in נוחז in v. 15. For more on this, see the brief discussion in Tov, *Scribal Practices*, 222–23.
30. The addition of אתה in 11QPsᵃ in v. 16 initially seems similar, though this case is more complex because the adjacent words את אתה offer the possibility of either haplography or dittography. In this case, it is likely that the longer 11QPsᵃ reflects the more original version. See BHS, and note that without אתה this verse half is short. Thus, the MT likely arose by haplography; for a different view, see Frank-Lothar Hossfeld and Erich Zenger, *Psalms 3: A Commentary on Psalms 101–150*, Hermeneia (Minneapolis: Fortress, 2011), 593.

the parallelism within the psalm. For example, in the first colon of v. 4, the MT reads ישבח, while 11QPs[a] reads ישבחו. The 11QPs[a] reading brings this colon in line with the second half of the verse (וגבורתיכה יגידו) and with the following verses, which, when using a third person subject, have a third person plural, not a singular, subject.[31] This is a type of harmonizing supplementation.

The second part of v. 21 in the MT reads ויברך כל בשר שם קדשו לעולם ועד, while 11QPS[a] reads ויברך כול בשר את שם קודשו. The two words לעולם ועד overload the B part of the verse, and I agree with *BHS* and others that they are secondary.[32] It seems likely that these words were added from v. 1, (ואהללה שמך לעולם ועד) (and v. 2, ואברכה שמך לעולם ועד) to round out the psalm, to create an *inclusio*. If correct, then *inclusio*s elsewhere in the Bible may be secondary, the result of supplementation.

As is well known, the MT lacks a *nun* verse, which is present in 11QPs[a]. It is highly likely that the original composition contained a *nun* verse.[33] The *nun* verse found in 11QPs[a] (and similarly in the LXX, the Peshitta, and Kenicott MS 142) is secondary.[34] Quite problematically, it uses אלוהים rather than the tetragrammaton; אלוהים by itself is used nowhere else as a proper noun in the psalm.[35] Tetragrammaton avoidance is well known at Qumran and elsewhere, and the use of אלוהים suggests that this verse is secondary.[36] The B part of the Qumran verse exactly repeats v. 17b. Such exact repetitions are found nowhere in the psalm and are stylistically inappropriate to it. These two pieces of evidence suggest, decisively in my mind, that this verse, in this form, is secondary; it might even be called, following Patrick W. Skehan, a "clumsy repair."[37]

---

31. It is likely that in the following v. 5, 11QPs[a]'s הדר כבוד הודכה ידברו is more original than the MT's הדר כבוד הודך ודברי. See Dahmen, *Psalmen- und Psalter-Rezeption*, 198.

32. So, e.g., Hermann Gunkel, *Die Psalmen*, HKAT (Göttingen: Vandenhoeck & Ruprecht, 1926), 611. The observation of James A. Sanders (*The Psalms Scroll of Qumran Cave 11 [11QPs[a]]*, DJD 4 [Oxford: Clarendon, 1965], 38), "N.B.: לעולם ועד are the last words of the Q refrain!" is striking but irrelevant. These two words are likely secondary to the development of the MT, and their similarity to the last two words of the refrain are likely an accident.

33. For a contrary argument, see Reuven Kimelman, "Psalm 145: Theme, Structure, and Impact," *JBL* 113 (1994): 37–58, here 49–50.

34. So, e.g., Kratz, "'Blessed Be the Lord,'" 235; see the arguments adduced in Kimelman, "Psalm 145," 50. Contrast, e.g., James VanderKam and Peter Flint, *The Meaning of the Dead Sea Scrolls: Their Significance for Understanding the Bible, Judaism, Jesus, and Christianity* (San Francisco: HarperSanFrancisco, 2002), 123–24; and Peter Flint, *The Dead Sea Psalms Scroll and the Book of Psalms*, STDJ 17 (Leiden: Brill, 1997), 234–35.

35. It is used in v. 1 as a common noun.

36. See the unpublished paper of Jamie Bryson, "Scribal Practices for Writing the Divine Name in the Dead Sea Scrolls: A New Model."

37. P. W. Skehan, "Qumran and Old Testament Criticism," in *Qumrân: Sa piété, sa théologie et son milieu*, ed. M. Delcor, BETL 46 (Gembloux: Duculot, 1978), 163–82, here 171.

Another case where a mistake is instructive is in 11QPsª in v. 18. That verse reads:

קרוב יהוה וברוך שמו לעולם ועד יקראוהו באמונה ברוך יהוה וברוך שמו לעולם ועד.

The scribe has copied the first two words, and then the presence of the tetragrammaton made him think that he was in the middle of the formula ברוך יהוה וברוך שמו לעולם ועד, so he continued writing the formula, penning after the tetragrammaton the words וברוך שמו לעולם ועד, yielding a verse that makes no sense.[38] This is an important reminder that supplementation can be accidental, or at least subconscious, and can in some cases be identified by the resultant problematic text.

As noted above, it is unlikely that the psalm was composed without a *nun* verse. This suggests a complicated but very plausible process of textual loss and supplementation. The psalm originally contained a *nun* verse, although its wording cannot be reconstructed. It was lost accidentally during transmission—even if one purpose of acrostic poems was to assure proper textual transmission,[39] verses and letters got lost, as attested in other biblical acrostics.[40] One scribe realized that the acrostic was broken and fixed it by supplementation, creating a verse that could fit. Thankfully, like the forger of the Yehoash inscription, it fit much too well and thus may be recognized as secondary, as a supplement.[41]

A final case of supplementation is found in 11QPsª at one of the places where supplements are typically expected—the very end. Sadly, the bottom of the Psalms Scroll has rotted away. The last readable words after the end of MT v. 21 (minus לעולם ועד, discussed above) and the expected refrain are זאת לזכרון. Most scholars believe that this was the beginning of a supplement that continued for several more lines.[42] This supplement likely originated at Qumran or in a related community; זכרון never appears in Psalms, and the Qumran texts, including poetic liturgical texts, use the

---

38. To complicate matters, the words לכל קראיו לכל אשר also fell out in 11QPsª.

39. This is one of the arguments frequently made about the purpose or one of the purposes of acrostics; the best survey of the function of acrostics remains Norman K. Gottwald, *Studies in the Book of Lamentations*, SBT 14 (London: SCM, 1954), 23–32.

40. See esp. what is often called the "broken acrostic" in Nah 1.

41. For this criterion concerning the Yehoash inscription, see most recently Ed Greenstein, "The So-Called Jehoash Inscription: A Post Mortem," http://asorblog.org/2016/02/03/the-so-called-jehoash-inscription-a-post-mortem/: "At least three-quarters of the inscription is composed of (sometimes misread and misinterpreted) phrases from the Bible—an extraordinary number, which gives the impression of cobbling together, not original writing."

42. See, e.g., Patrick W. Skehan, "A Liturgical Complex in 11QPsª," *CBQ* 35 (1973): 195–205, here 196. I do not see the merit of his suggestion (195) that זאת לזכרון was a coda to a previous group of psalms, rather than just to Ps 145. More recently, Dahmen reconstructs six missing lines between זאת לזכרון (line 17) and the beginning of Ps 154 (line 24) (*Psalmen- und Psalter-Rezeption*, 87); line 23 was most likely blank.

term.⁴³ We will probably never know what the missing text said, but nevertheless it is a clear example of supplementation at the end of a psalm. It likely did not add poetic verses to the psalm itself, but seems to have been some sort of dedication or explanation of the psalm's use, somewhat similar to the superscriptions found in many psalms.

MT Ps 145 and the Jewish *Ashrei* Prayer

As noted above, the Jewish *ashrei* prayer is comprised of the MT of Ps 145 supplemented by three other verses from Psalms:

Ps 84:5   אשרי יושבי ביתך עוד יהללוך סלה

Ps 144:15   אשרי העם שככה לו אשרי העם שיהוה אלהיו

Ps 145

Ps 115:18   ואנחנו נברך יה מעתה ועד עולם הללו יה

Supplementation is most natural at the beginning and/or the end of literary works, in part for technical reasons. It is easiest to add to a manuscript at its beginning or end, or in a blank line that is meant to divide units in a composition.⁴⁴

Even if Ps 145 had not been an acrostic (which is so helpful when looking for supplementation since it is easy to see verses that do not fit the alphabetic pattern⁴⁵), a careful reader would have noticed that the two initial and one final verse in the Jewish *ashrei* prayer are supplementary. The first two lines, which would make sense at the beginning of a psalm or perhaps after a brief musical notation such as מזמור לדוד, precede Ps 145:1, תהלה לדוד, but are highly problematic in their current context. Furthermore, the jump from the plural יושבי in the first line and the reference to העם (twice!) in the second is quite jarring before the first two verses of the psalm, where the poet speaks in first person singular (ארוממך ... ואברכה). The ending supplement is equally jarring; the psalm's final section refers to humans in the third person, ויברך כל בשר, while Ps 115:18 is in the first

---

43. See, e.g., 1QHª IX, 26. On the זכרון at Qumran, see Lidija Novakovic, "זכר," in *Theologisches Wörterbuch zu den Qumrantexten*, ed. Heinz-Josef Fabry and Ulrich Dahmen, 3 vols. (Stuttgart: Kohlhammer, 2011), 1:846–48.

44. Tov, *Scribal Practices*, 146–48.

45. In general, methods of closure are key for evaluating if a verse at the beginning or end of a psalm is secondary. See, most recently, Gary A. Rendsburg, "Marking Closure," *VT* 66 (2016): 280–313, who neglects, however, the important study of Chris Wyckoff, "Have We Come Full Circle Yet? Closure, Psycholinguistics, and the Problems of Recognition with the *Inclusio*," *JSOT* 30 (2006): 475–505, as well as Wyckoff, "Poetic and Editorial Closure in the Book of Psalms: A Discourse Analytic Perspective" (PhD diss., Brandeis University, 2005).

person plural, opening ואנחנו נברך—nowhere else in the psalm does anyone speak in the first person plural.

It is difficult to date these additions.[46] Already b. Ber. 4b refers to this composition as *ashrei*, but some later sources refer to it as תהלה לדוד, suggesting that the supplementation with these initial verses was not universal in the post-talmudic period.[47] It took a long time for the additions of these three verses to become standard in the liturgy, with some rites adding up to eleven verses before the psalm.[48]

These two initial verses change the psalm's meaning, turning it into a welcome to the בית, now the synagogue rather than the temple.[49] The final verse, despite its first person plural perspective, blends in extremely well.[50] Its opening words ואנחנו נברך יה in this new context pick up on the previous verse's ויברך כל בשר, while מעתה ועד עולם, part of the new conclusion of the psalm, picks up the (original) second verse of the psalm, לעולם ועד.[51] The final מעתה ועד עולם הללו יה picks up on the initial עוד יהללוך סלה, forming a new *inclusio* of sorts. Together, these supplements at the beginning and end turn a psalm that was a hymn of the individual into a psalm of the community, from "I" to "we."

Psalm 145: Types of Supplementation

This detailed study of three forms of Ps 145 suggests that supplementation—namely, "something added to supply a deficiency," exists in many forms and to many degrees. Using the examples adduced above, I would suggest tentatively the following continuum from most minor to most significant types of supplementation.[52] This list initially focuses on mechanics; it is followed by a synthesis that reflects on the goals of supplementation. There are examples of supplemention where

- More full (plene) spelling is introduced to assure that a word is pronounced correctly.[53]

---

46. The final addition is found also in the medieval manuscript Kenicott 147, but this probably reflects liturgical influence on a biblical manuscript.
47. Kimelman, "Ashre," 121 n. 4.
48. Ibid.
49. Ibid., 114.
50. See Adele Berlin, "The Rhetoric of Psalm 145," in *Biblical and Related Studies Presented to Samuel Iwry*, ed. Ann Kort and Scott Morschauser (Winona Lake, IN: Eisenbrauns, 1985), 17–22, here 21–22.
51. For other possible reasons for this choice, see Kimelman, "Ashre," 114–15.
52. Others may opt to arrange this material differently.
53. Most, but not all, more plene spellings may be explained this way; in some cases added vowel letters reflect particular spelling practices and do not disambiguate words.

- Abbreviations are filled in so that the reader will not fill them in incorrectly. The different ways that various textual witnesses filled in likely abbreviations show how necessary this type of supplementation was. (These first two types of supplementation, unlike those that follow, do not change the pronunciation of the text.)
- A missing letter, changing the meaning, was added—this reflects the supplementer's desire to transmit a more correct text.
- Adding a word, typically a particle, disambiguates a phrase, to make sure that its syntax is properly understood.
- A composition is harmonized, for example, changing a third person masculine singular verb to third person masculine plural in order to make it more internally parallel or consistent.
- A short word or phrase is expanded into a longer word or phrase that was known from other (similar or parallel) "biblical" texts.
- A verse that the psalm's context or structure suggested was missing is added.
- A refrain, perhaps connected to new liturgical uses or types of performances of a composition, is added.
- A coda is added.
- A new frame is supplied.

Reasons for Supplementation: Supplementation as Correction

Much supplementation is correction of one type or another.[54] But correction is a highly subjective notion—what one person views as a correction, others may see as a disaster, destroying an original work. These "corrections" are of many types and extents—from supplementing single letters, to words, verses, repeated verses, refrains, codas, and new framing.

Such corrections are accomplished for a wide variety of reasons; the most prosaic involves making sure that the reader reads the text "correctly," as intended by the supplementer. (Of course, the supplementer making this judgment may make an error, and may miscorrect the text.) Larger supplements go beyond this reason by adding phrases or words and may involve making the composition suitable for a new occasion other than the one in which it was originally used. Thus, a psalm that

---

54. See Charles Augustus Briggs and Emilie Grace Briggs, *A Critical and Exegetical Commentary on the Book of Psalms*, 2 vols., ICC (London: T&T Clark, 2004), 1:lii: "*A very large proportion of the changes in the text of the Psalms was due to corrections of the scribes and glossators, who for various reasons endeavoured to improve the text to make it more intelligible and useful*" (italics in original). See also the very long list on lii–liv.

likely was originally recited by an individual—ארוממך אלוהי המלך—may be turned into a community psalm—ואנחנו נברך יה מעתה ועד עולם הללו יה. It may even be reworked throughout so that it is suitable for antiphonal recitation. As it was supplemented, one form of closure—an acrostic—is replaced by another—inclusion. It may be given a new setting, as implied by the final visible words in column 17 of 11QPs[a]. Thus, most broadly, supplementations are of two types: those that aim to correct a perceived deficiency and are conservative in nature (they try to preserve a text) and those that try to change the earlier text into something new.

Broader Implications for the Psalter

Psalm 145 is not unique in the manner in which its different versions reflect supplementation, and looking closely at this psalm suggests various areas that should be explored more extensively within the Psalter in relation to supplementation.

- Supplementation in which more full (plene) spelling is introduced to assure that a word is pronounced correctly.

My hope is that someone will look through the Psalter systematically to collect cases of this prosaic type of supplementation, where *matres lectionis* have been added incorrectly to the MT, resulting in improper readings.

- Supplementation in which abbreviations are filled in so that the reader will not fill them in incorrectly.

Although the likely presence of abbreviations has been long noted by scholars as far back as Kenicott and Eichorn, I was surprised to see three likely cases of this phenomenon in this relatively short psalm. I see no reason why Ps 145 should be unique in this respect, and I believe that it would be wise to build upon the work of Felix Perles and others to study this issue systematically in the Psalter.[55] Perhaps because of the extensive parallelism, some scribes may have used abbreviations more frequently in poetry such as psalms than in other books, with the assumption that the content and the verse structure would make it obvious how the abbreviation should be supplemented and read. (It is also possible that physical factors need to be considered: a scribe might have had a much smaller piece of parchment than his *Vorlage* and had to abbreviate so he could fit the entire composition.)

---

55. See the studies cited in Tov, *Textual Criticism*, 238; note esp. the example concerning Ps 3:8 in Felix Perles, *Analekten zur Textkritik des Alten Testaments* (Munich: Theodor Ackerman, 1895), 24.

- Supplementation in which a missing letter, changing the meaning, was added—this reflected the supplementer's desire to transmit a more correct text.

Here it is quite possible that the short, "erroneous" text could have been miscorrected, and this phenomenon deserves a more comprehensive study.

- Supplementation by adding a word, typically a particle, to disambiguate a phrase, to make sure that its syntax is properly understood.

To the best of my knowledge, this has never been looked at systematically, either by comparing the various versions of the same text (though it certainly will not always be visible in the versions), or in cases where such an unnecessary word seems to bring a stich out of balance. It is quite possible that such words were sometimes added incorrectly by a scribe, and their removal might lead to a different understanding of the syntax, and thus the meaning of a verse. Finally, it would be worthwhile to see what types of grammatical or other ambiguities such supplementation attempted to resolve. In other words, what situations were "deserving of" supplementation?

- Supplementation that is intended to harmonize a composition, in order to make it more internally parallel or consistent.

This phenomenon should serve as an important warning to scholars that internal structures of a psalm are not always the work of its original or early author(s) but may reflect late supplementation. This is not surprising; there is no reason to assume that the desire to create a more satisfying rhetorical structure died with the first composer. But this also means that arguing that a verse or phrase is integral to a composition because it fits well—whatever that might mean—is spurious.

- Supplementation that is accomplished by expanding a short word or phrase into a longer word or phrase that was known from other (similar or parallel) "biblical" texts.

These, too, have never, to the best of my knowledge, been collected. Here too metrical considerations and comparisons to the versions are helpful. Collecting these would aid in reaching earlier stages of the text and would also allow us to see better what texts and phrases were "influential" in the world of the supplementers, provoking supplements.

- Supplementation that is accomplished by adding a verse that the context or structure suggested was missing.

The case of the *nun* verse is especially significant since it shows that supplementers could try to recreate a verse that they felt was missing.

Fortunately, in the case of 11QPsª, the supplementer did a poor job. This is a good reminder that we should look carefully for other verses in Psalms that do not fit well in their context. We should not be bothered by the fact that removing them disturbs the literary context even more. After all, these verses that look secondary might very well be the work of a supplementer who encountered a textual lacuna and tried his best to fill it in.

- Supplementation that is accomplished by adding a refrain, perhaps connected to new liturgical uses or types of performances of a composition.

The example adduced above suggests that refrains may be secondary. This deserves more significant consideration in the study of Psalms, which typically views such refrains as part of the original composer's craft.[56] This has important bearing for interpretation, since scholars have emphasized, quite reasonably, that refrains create stanzas that need to be taken seriously by the interpreter.[57] But if refrains are secondary, then they may be, in certain cases, ignored by the interpreter or understood as a secondary, perhaps incorrect, attempt to organize the ideas in a Psalm.

In particular, I wonder if Ps 136 originally existed without the refrain כי לעולם חסדו, an opinion perhaps more popular a century ago than now,[58] but whose viability is supported by the addition of a refrain in 11QPsª. In the case of Ps 136, to the best of my knowledge, no textual evidence points to a version lacking this refrain—but it is certainly worth considering that it might be secondary, which would have important implications for the psalm's genre and interpretation. In the way that I used *ashrei* earlier as a postbiblical example to show a type of supplementation likely found in the biblical text, I would here point to the Passover Haggadah poem דיינו. Its name derives from the concluding word of each poetic line, דיינו, "enough," while each line begins with אלו, "if." One line reads: "If [אלו] He had brought us out of Egypt and not brought judgment upon them.... Enough [דיינו]!"[59] דיינו is immediately followed in the Haggadah by a version of the poem without the refrain, which is earlier than, and gave birth to, the דיינו version.[60] This may be seen by the fact that the second version is logical, while the refrain created in the דיינו version presents some problematic lines, such as "If He had split the sea for us and not brought us

---

56. No consideration for the possible secondary nature of refrains is found in the comprehensive study of Paul R. Raabe, *Psalm Structures: A Study of Psalms with Refrains*, JSOTSup 104 (Sheffield: JSOT Press, 1990).
57. Ibid.
58. See, e.g., Briggs and Briggs, *Book of Psalms*, 2:482.
59. Lawrence A. Hoffman and David Arnow, eds., *My People's Haggadah: Traditional Texts, Modern Commentaries*, 2 vols. (Woodstock, VT: Jewish Lights, 2008), 2:41.
60. See E. D. Goldschmidt, *The Passover Haggadah: Its Sources and History* [in Hebrew] (Jerusalem: Bialik Institute, 1960), 51.

through it on dry land ... Enough!"[61] — a line suggesting that God would have allowed Israel to be stranded in the Reed Sea forever! This example teaches us (1) that some refrains may be secondary; and (2) by removing refrains, the more original, better sense of the poetic composition may be restored. This does not mean that all refrains are secondary but does suggest that some might be.

- Supplementation accomplished by adding a coda.

As others have noted, it is quite unfortunate that the words following זואת לזכרון in 11QPs[a] are missing. זואת is a deictic particle, and it likely pointed to Ps 145 as a whole, suggesting somehow that it should be understood as a זכרון for something, which would have fundamentally reframed the psalm's understanding, which on the face of it has nothing to do with זכרון.

(• Supplementation accomplished by adding an introduction.)

Although this was not attested in the versions of Ps 145, it is well attested elsewhere. It has long been observed, for example, that the LXX and other versions have superscriptions that are lacking in the MT.[62] From the technical side, as noted above, supplementing at the beginning was easy, given that lines were typically skipped between psalms, as reflected in manuscripts of many types, from 11QPs[a] to Aleppo. This made it very easy for a supplementer to add material there. As is well known, such supplements could reframe how a psalm should be read either by connecting it to the life of David, imagined to be the psalm's author, or by connecting it to a festival. For example, the new introduction to Ps 92 (מזמור שיר ליום השבת) would cause the reader to interpret the psalm in relation to creation, while without that verse, its main theme is theodicy.[63] Thus, the supplemented version of Ps 145 found at Qumran is an important reminder that psalms with introductions and conclusions might be interpreted twice — once taking into account how the beginning or end affect interpretation, and once without this beginning or ending, which might be secondary.

- Supplementation accomplished by adding a new frame.

This phenomenon is the combination of the two noted above. It may also create a new structure for the psalm, such as an inclusio(n). This is

---

61. Hoffman and Arnow, *My People's Haggadah*, 2:41.

62. See now the comprehensive study of Abraham Josiah Chappell, "Approaching the Psalms: The Psalm Headings in the Early Versions" (PhD diss., University of California Los Angeles, 2015). A more limited, but useful comparison of the superscriptions in MT, LXX, and 11QPs[a] is in Flint, *Dead Sea Psalms Scrolls*, 118–34.

63. See my forthcoming commentary, and note the observations concerning later rabbinic reinterpretation of psalms for festival use in Sigmund Mowinckel, *Psalm Studies* (orig., Kristiania: Dybwad, 1921–1924), trans. Mark E. Biddle, 2 vols., HBS 2–3 (Atlanta: Society of Biblical Literature, 2014), 1:165–66.

a reminder that such structures may be secondary, and isolating them is not a conclusive argument that they were original. Later supplementers may have different, or even better, literary skills than the authors of the compositions that they are reworking.

Broader Implications for the Study of Psalms

Looking at the cases of supplementation that derive from a careful study of Ps 145 may have important implications for understanding Psalms more broadly. For example, the additions to the beginning and end of Ps 145 when it was turned into the *ashrei* prayer, as noted above, turned a psalm of the individual into a psalm of the community. This offers indirect, but nevertheless important, support to the hypothesis of Mowinckel and others that various psalms have been supplemented, changing them from psalms of the individual to psalms of the community.[64] This empirical study does not prove his contention but shows that it is reasonable, most especially in cases where the final verse in other ways does not fit well with the previous psalm.[65]

The evidence for supplementation noted above also offers important support for the *plausibility* of the hypothesis by H. G. M. Williamson that the "certainty of hearing motif" in petitions or laments of the individual is best explained by assuming that these psalms, in their current form, are really songs of thanksgiving recited after the person's petition has been heard by God.[66] Psalm 6 offers an excellent example of this[67]—it is possible to read vv. 2–9a as the petition. (Verse 1 is a musical superscription.) The more original psalm then ended with a monocolon in v. 9a, quite appropriate to the situation: סורו ממני כל פעלי און; elsewhere, monocola signal closure.[68] The psalm was then supplemented by adding what is now vv. 9b–11; I would translate the initial כי as "indeed":

---

64. Mowinckel, *Psalm Studies*, 1:165–72; see also, e.g., Briggs and Briggs, *Book of Psalms*, 1:xlix–l.

65. This is especially the case when the following supplement destroys closure; for some examples, see the literature on closure cited in n. 45 above.

66. H. G. M. Williamson, "Reading the Lament Psalms Backwards," in *A God So Near: Essays on Old Testament Theology in Honor of Patrick D. Miller*, ed. Brent A. Strawn and Nancy R. Bowen (Winona Lake, IN: Eisenbrauns, 2003), 3–15. For a different position and a summary of various explanations in the change of tone in these psalms, see Federico G. Villanueva, *The 'Uncertainty of a Hearing': A Study of the Sudden Change of Mood in the Psalms of Lament*, VTSup 121 (Leiden: Brill, 2008).

67. Villanueva, "'Uncertainty of a Hearing,'" 59–64.

68. See Wilfred G. E. Watson, *Classical Hebrew Poetry: A Guide to Its Techniques*, corrected ed. (Edinburgh: T&T Clark, 2005).

כי שמע יהוה קול בכיי
שמע יהוה תחנתי יהוה תפלתי יקח
יבשו ויבהלו מאד כל איבי ישבו יבשו רגע

Verse 11, with its use of ישבו fits well with the rest of the psalm,[69] but this is not evidence that the verse is original—as *ashrei* shows, a good supplementer can rework preexisting material in a rhetorically sensitive fashion.

Hope for the Future

I recognize that other scholars looking at a broader group of texts than Ps 145 will develop different or additional categories of supplementation and might offer different suggestions of how such categories might be organized into continua. My hope is that someone will look at the Psalter as a whole with these categories in mind, to discern which patterns are common and which are less so, and if supplementation of different types follows any discernible historical or other patterns. Such research will add to our understanding of the growth of the book of Psalms.

Finally, I wonder, in relation to the broader examples of supplementation discussed in this book: Does Psalms, as a poetic book, supplement differently from prose books, the focus of half of the other papers in this volume? Is liturgical poetry, like liturgy in general,[70] particularly open to supplementation? And are any types of supplementation that are especially obvious in poetry or the Psalter capable of offering compelling examples that scholars of other (prose) books might find helpful?

---

69. See, e.g., John Goldingay, *Psalms*, 3 vols., BCOTWP (Grand Rapids: Baker Academic, 2006), 1:141.

70. Excellent examples of supplementation in liturgy include the versions of the Nicene Creed recited in Christian liturgy and the versions of the אבינו מלכנו prayer in Judaism.

Textual Supplementation in Poetry: The Song of Hannah as a Test Case

REINHARD G. KRATZ
Universität Göttingen

1. Textual and Literary History in the Psalms

Since the discoveries of the Dead Sea Scrolls, we have external evidence for the phenomenon of textual supplementation in biblical and parabiblical texts of ancient Judaism. The two most important pieces of evidence are (a) the numerous manuscripts of biblical, parabiblical, and nonbiblical books; and (b) the manuscripts of what is known as "rewritten scripture." Both have confirmed and extended our knowledge of the textual-historical and compositional-historical processes to which ancient versions (esp. the LXX and the Samaritan Pentateuch) had already borne witness before the discovery of the Dead Sea Scrolls.

In scholarship this evidence is usually assigned to the field of textual criticism. Although the textbooks always emphasize the smooth transitions between textual history and literary history, in principle and in practice they maintain a firm distinction.[1] Other scholars see external evidence as proof of the virtual impossibility of literary-critical analysis of the biblical and parabiblical books.[2] In order to say anything at all about the origin of the Bible, however, a practice of reckoning with only two or three literary strata per book has become common. Scholars who have worked seriously with manuscripts can only shake their heads or laugh at this practice, the more so as a rejection of literary-critical analysis often goes hand in hand with a vivid imagination when reconstructing preliterary, oral traditions or historical scenarios of textual growth.

Translated by Ruth Ludwig-Welch (Göttingen).
1. Emanuel Tov, *Textual Criticism of the Hebrew Bible*, 3rd ed. (Minneapolis: Fortress, 2012).
2. David M. Carr, *The Formation of the Hebrew Bible: A New Reconstruction* (New York: Oxford University Press, 2011).

In contrast, I would like to take an approach that acquires criteria for literary-historical analysis from external evidence.[3] I believe that, while it is clear that there are limitations to an analysis based on internal criteria, and that we will miss many stages of the process of textual growth (which, by the way, is also the case with external evidence),[4] we have no reason to capitulate before the task. Rather, the complexity of the external evidence should be an incentive for us to look more closely and to identify as precisely as possible those phenomena in the text that are also attested by the external evidence und thus indicate possible textual growth.[5]

This is true, as we shall see, for poetic texts, and in particular for Psalms, as well as for all other—legal, narrative, and prophetic—texts of the Hebrew Bible. Here are just a few examples from the so-called Small Hallel, taken from the Psalms Scroll 11Q5 and the LXX.

In Ps 145, we find that a refrain has been added after each line of the acrostic (similar to Ps 136), which is not attested in the LXX. Furthermore, the missing *nun*-line in Hebrew was added, which is also witnessed in the LXX, as well as a signature, which unfortunately has not been completely preserved and is therefore somewhat unintelligible.[6]

---

3. See *Evidence of Editing: Growth and Change of Texts in the Hebrew Bible*, ed. Reinhard Müller, Juha Pakkala, and Bas Ter Haar Romeny, RBS 75 (Atlanta: Society of Biblical Literature, 2014). See also the following works by Reinhard G. Kratz: "Innerbiblische Exegese und Redaktionsgeschichte im Lichte empirischer Evidenz," in *Das Judentum im Zeitalter des Zweiten Tempels: Kleine Schriften I*, 2nd ed., FAT 42 (Tübingen: Mohr Siebeck 2013), 126–56; "Das Alte Testament und die Texte vom Toten Meer," ZAW 125 (2013): 198–213; "Rewriting Torah in the Hebrew Bible and the Dead Sea Scrolls," in *Wisdom and Torah: The Reception of 'Torah' in the Wisdom Literature of the Second Temple Period*, ed. Bernd U. Schipper and D. Andrew Teeter, JSJSup 163 (Leiden: Brill, 2013), 273–92; "Law and Narrative in Deuteronomy and the Temple Scroll," in *The Reception of Biblical War Legislation in Narrative Contexts: Proceedings of the EABS Research Group "Law and Narrative,"* ed. Christoph Berner and Harald Samuel, BZAW 460 (Berlin: de Gruyter, 2015), 109–22 ; "Bibelhandschrift oder Midrasch? Zum Verhältnis von Text- und Literargeschichte in den Samuelbüchern im Licht der Handschrift 4Q51 (4QSam^a)," in *The Books of Samuel: Stories – History – Reception History*, ed. Walter Dietrich in cooperation with Cynthia Edenburg and Philippe Hugo, BETL 274 (Leuven: Peeters, 2016), 153–80; "Reworked Pentateuch and Pentateuchal Theory," in *The Formation of the Pentateuch: Bridging the Academic Cultures of Europe, Israel, and North America*, ed. Jan C. Gertz et al., FAT 111 (Tübingen: Mohr Siebeck, 2016); "Nahash, King of the Ammonites, in the Deuteronomistic History," in *Insights into Editing in the Hebrew Bible and the Ancient Near East: What Does Documented Evidence Tell Us about the Transmission of Authoritative Texts?*, ed Reinhard Müller and Juha Pakkala, CBET 84 (Leuven: Peeters, 2017), 163–88; "Sources, Fragments, and Additions: Biblical Criticism and the Dead Sea Scrolls" (forthcoming).

4. Kratz, "Innerbiblische Exegese," 156.

5. Phenomena within a given text that indicate—with or without any external evidence in manuscripts or versions—a possible example of textual growth, I call in this essay "internal evidence." Both internal evidence and external evidence are not objective proofs but indications, which, of course, require a (subjective) interpretation in every single case.

6. See Reinhard G. Kratz, "Das Sch^ema' des Psalters: Die Botschaft vom Reich Gottes nach Psalm 145," in *Das Judentum im Zeitalter*, 190–205; Kratz, "'Blessed Be the Lord and

Psalm 145 (11Q5 XVI–XVII)

1 תהלה לדוד ארוממך אלוהי המלך ואברכה שמך לעולם ועד
   ברוך יהוה וברוך שמו לעולם ועד
2 בכל יום אברכך ואהללה שמך לעולם ועד
   ברוך יהוה וברוך שמו לעולם ועד

etc.

13 מלכותך מלכות כל עלמים וממשלתך בכל דור ודור
   ברוך יהוה וברוך שמו לעולם ועד
(נ) נאמן אלוהים בדבריו וחסיד בכול מעשיו
   ברוך יהוה וברוך שמו לעולם ועד
   πιστὸς κύριος ἐν τοῖς λόγοις αὐτοῦ καὶ ὅσιος ἐν πᾶσι τοῖς ἔργοις αὐτοῦ
14 סומך יהוה לכל הנפלים וזוקף לכל הכפופים
   ברוך יהוה וברוך שמו לעולם ועד

etc.

21 תהלת יהוה ידבר פי ויברך כל בשר שם קדשו לעולם ועד
   ברוך יהוה וברוך שמו לעולם ועד
   זאת לזכרון [--] ל[--] ל[--]ל[ל] ל[--] ל[--]

In Ps 146, a line is inserted between vv. 9 and 10 that is in part quoted verbatim from Ps 33:8, and to some extent recalls Ps 145:12.

Psalm 146 (11Q5 II, 1–5); cf. Ps 33:8 and 145:12

8 יהוה פקח עורים יהוה זקף כפופים יהוה אהב צדיקים
9 יהוה שמר את־גרים יתום ואלמנה יעודד ודרך רשעים יעות
   מיהוה כול הארץ ממנ[ו --] [--] בהודעו לכול מעשיו ברא] -- [ ] גבורותיו
10 ימלך יהוה לעולם אלהיך ציון לדר ודר הללו־יה

In Ps 148 in the LXX, we find a supplement to v. 5, taken, again, from Ps 33:9.

Psalm 148 (11Q5 II, 6–16; LXX)

5 יהללו את־שם יהוה כי הוא צוה ונבראו
   αἰνεσάτωσαν τὸ ὄνομα κυρίου ὅτι αὐτὸς εἶπεν καὶ ἐγενήθησαν αὐτὸς ἐνετείλατο
   καὶ ἐκτίσθησαν (cf. Ps 33:9, כי הוא אמר ויהי הוא־צוה ויעמד)
6 ויעמידם לעד לעולם חק־נתן ולא יעבור

In Ps 149, an additional line is inserted after v. 9, making a connection to Ps 148:14.

Blessed Be His Name Forever': Psalm 145 in the Hebrew Bible and in the Psalms Scroll 11Q5," in *Prayer and Poetry in the Dead Sea Scrolls and Related Literature: Essays in Honor of Eileen Schuller on the Occasion of Her 65th Birthday*, ed. Jeremy Penner, Ken M. Penner, and Cecilia Wassen, STDJ 98 (Leiden: Brill, 2012), 229–43 (German version in Kratz, *Das Judentum im Zeitalter*, 206–17). See further the contribution by Marc Z. Brettler in this volume.

Psalm 148:14 (11Q5 II, 6–16)

13 יהללו את־שם יהוה כי־נשגב שמו לבדו הודו על־ארץ ושמים
14 וירם קרן לעמו תהלה לכל־חסידיו לבני ישראל עם־קרבו הללו־יה

Psalm 149 (11Q5 XXVI, 1–3)

1 הללו יה שירו ליהוה שיר חדש תהלתו בקהל חסידים
...
9 לעשות בהם משפט כתוב הדר הוא לכל־חסידיו הללו־יה
(... הדר הוא לכול חסידיו) לבני ישראל עם קודשו הללו יה

This is interesting because Ps 149 in 11Q5 is disconnected from Ps 148 in the Small Hallel and relocated to a different place. The addition was most likely made before this rearrangement, when the two Psalms (148 and 149) followed each other, as in the MT. In this context, it is likely that Ps 148:14 is itself an addition, producing a connection to Ps 149:1. Thus, a transition is created from Ps 148, which clearly comes to an end in v. 13, to Ps 149, which addresses the righteous ones of Israel. The external evidence thus leads to the following genealogy: Ps 148:1–13 → 149:1–9 → 148:14 → 149:9+ (addition in 11Q5) → rearrangement in 11Q5.

In addition to such examples of textual supplementation, which can easily be multiplied, we must also consider other phenomena of editing in the psalms that are attested by the external evidence. This includes the rearrangement of the psalms in 11Q5 and also the addition of entire psalms, such as Ps 151 in the LXX (Syrian Psalm I), which is also witnessed in a different format and alongside other additional psalms in 11Q5. Finally, we encounter the patchwork composed of pieces from different psalms that have undergone textual supplementation during this process. Examples are Ps 136 in 11Q5, which was supplemented with verses from Ps 118 (the so-called *catena*), and Ps 100 and Ps 135 in the MT, which were composed of elements from other psalms and, at the same time, were supplemented by new material.[7] For all these phenomena, the external evidence provides us with criteria that we can use in a literary-critical analysis.

And so I will begin this essay with the external evidence and feel my way cautiously from there back to the literary history of the Psalms. At the same time, we should not be under any illusion that the external evidence is any less problematic than the results of an internal analysis. As a rule, external evidence is ambiguous and needs critical interpretation. Its explanation is no less hypothetical than literary-critical analysis. Scholars who want to give up literary-critical analysis because it produces too many

---

7. For the latter, see Reinhard G. Kratz, "Die Tora Davids: Psalm 1 und die doxologische Fünfteilung des Psalters," in *Das Judentum im Zeitalter*, 280–311, here 297 with n. 43, 308 with n. 79; and Kratz "Reste hebräischen Heidentums am Beispiel der Psalmen," in *Mythos und Geschichte: Kleine Schriften III*, FAT 102 (Tübingen: Mohr Siebeck, 2015), 156–89, esp. 178–79.

layers and too many conflicting hypotheses should also give up the study and explanation of external evidence. They should restrict themselves to paraphrasing the Bible or resort to (literary) historical speculation.

My focus will be the Song of Hannah in 1 Sam 2. My reason for choosing this text is that it is attested in several versions and documents a wide variety of textual-historical and literary-historical phenomena.

2. The Song of Hannah

The Song of Hannah in 1 Sam 2 is attested in three versions: the Masoretic Text (MT), the LXX (followed by Peshitta and Vetus Latina), and a fragmentary version in manuscript 4Q51 (4QSam^a). In what follows, I quote the text of all three versions verse by verse. The English translation is based on the NRSV for the Masoretic and Qumran texts, and the NETS for the LXX.

1 Samuel 2:1–10 (4Q51 IIa–d, 15–35)

[MT, Q, and LXX with selected variants according to Brooke-McLean, grouping according to DJD 17: G^B Egyptian recension (Bya$_2$); G^L Lucianic recension (b'boc$_2$e$_2$; V = Vetus Latina, Josephus); G^O Hexaplaric recension (Acx); S Peshitta]

1:28 וגם אנכי השאלתהו ליהוה כל־הימים אשר היה הוא שאול ליהוה וישתחו שם ליהוה
G^{L}SV ישתחוו שם ליהוה

Therefore I have lent him to the Lord; as long as 'he lives,' he is given to the Lord. And he (they) worshiped the Lord there.

[ ] וגם אנכי השאלתיהו ליה[ו]ה כול הימ[י]ם [אשר חי הוא שאול ליהוה]
ותעזב[הו שם ותשתח[ו] [ליהוה]

... as long as he lives, he is given to the Lord and she left him there and worshiped the Lord.

κἀγὼ κιχρῶ αὐτὸν τῷ κυρίῳ πάσας τὰς ἡμέρας, ἃς ζῇ αὐτός, χρῆσιν τῷ κυρίῳ
κυρίω] + και προσεκυνησεν (-σαν) εκει τω κυριω G^L

And I lend him to the Lord as long as he lives, a loan to the Lord.

2:1 ותתפלל חנה ותאמר
Hannah prayed and said
[ותאמר][ ][ ]

Καὶ εἶπεν
και προσηυξατο αννα (ותתפלל חנה ותאמר) G^{LA}
And she said

עלץ לבי ביהוה רמה קרני ביהוה רחב פי על־אויבי כי שמחתי בישועתך
[ ][עלץ לבי ביהוה] רמה קרני בי[הו]ה [רחב] [פי על אויבי שמחתי בישועתך]

My heart exults in the Lord; my strength is exalted in the Lord. My mouth derides my enemies, because I rejoice in your victory.

ἐστερεώθη ἡ καρδία μου ἐν κυρίῳ ὑψώθη κέρας μου ἐν θεῷ μου ἐπλατύνθη ἐπὶ ἐχθροὺς τὸ στόμα μου εὐφράνθην ἐν σωτηρίᾳ σου
<small>επι εχθρ. το στ. μου] το στ. μου επι εχθρ. μου G^O</small>
My heart was made firm in the Lord; my horn was exalted in my Lord; my mouth was made wide against enemies; I was glad in your deliverance,

2 אין־קדוש כיהוה כי אין בלתך ואין צור כאלהינו

There is no Holy One like the LORD, because there is no one besides you; and there is no Rock like our God.

[כ]יא אין קדוש כיה[וה] [ואין צדיק כאלוהינו ואין בלת]ך ואין צור כאלוהינו

Because there is no one holy like the LORD; and there is no one righteous like our God; and there is no one besides you; and there is no Rock like our God.
ὅτι οὐκ ἔστιν ἅγιος ὡς κύριος καὶ οὐκ ἔστιν δίκαιος ὡς ὁ θεὸς ἡμῶν οὐκ ἔστιν ἅγιος πλὴν σοῦ
<small>δικαιος– fin.] πλην σου και ουκ εστιν δικαιος ως ο θεος ημων G^O | ουκ εστιν] και ουκ εστιν G^L (ואין)</small>
Because there is none holy like the Lord, and there is none righteous like our God; there is none holy besides you.

3 אל־תרבו תדברו גבהה גבהה יצא עתק מפיכם כי אל דעות יהוה ולו[ולא] נתכנו עללות

Talk no more so very proudly, let not arrogance come from your mouth; for the LORD is a God of knowledge [pl.], and by him actions are weighed.

[אל תרבו תדברו גבהה אל יצא ע]תק מפיכם כי אל דעת [יהוה ואל תוכן עללותיו]

... because the LORD is a God of knowledge, and a God who balances his own actions.
μὴ καυχᾶσθε καὶ μὴ λαλεῖτε ὑψηλά μὴ ἐξελθάτω μεγαλορρημοσύνη ἐκ τοῦ στόματος ὑμῶν ὅτι θεὸς γνώσεων κύριος καὶ θεὸς ἑτοιμάζων ἐπιτηδεύματα αὐτοῦ
<small>υψηλα] + εις υπεροχην G^{LO} | γνωσεων] γνωσεως G^{BL} | αυτου] αυτων A</small>
Boast not, and speak not lofty things; let not big talking come forth from your mouth, because the Lord is a god of knowledge, and a god who balances his (their) own actions.

4 קשת גברים חתים ונכשלים אזרו חיל

The bow(s) of the mighty are broken, but the feeble gird on strength.

[קשת גבורי[ם חתה ונ[כ]שלים אז[רו] [חיל]

The bow of the mighty is broken...
τόξον δυνατῶν ἠσθένησεν καὶ ἀσθενοῦντες περιεζώσαντο δύναμιν
The bow of the mighty has become weak, and weak ones have girded themselves with might.

5 שבעים בלחם נשכרו ורעבים חדלו עד־עקרה ילדה שבעה ורבת בנים אמללה

[שבעים בלחם נשכרו ורעבים חד]ל[ו עד ע]קרה ילדה [שבעה ורבת בנים אמללה]

Those who were full have hired themselves out for bread, but those who were hungry are fat with spoil. The barren has borne seven, but she who has many children is forlorn.
πλήρεις ἄρτων ἠλαττώθησαν καὶ οἱ πεινῶντες παρῆκαν γῆν ὅτι στεῖρα ἔτεκεν ἑπτά καὶ ἡ πολλὴ ἐν τέκνοις ἠσθένησεν
Full of bread they suffered loss, and the hungry have forsaken the land, because a barren one has borne seven, and she who is rich in children became weak.

Textual Supplementation in Poetry 27

6 יהוה ממית ומחיה מוריד שאול ויעל
[יהוה ממית ומח]יה מוריד [שאול ויעל]

The Lord kills and brings to life; he brings down to Sheol and raises up.
κύριος θανατοῖ καὶ ζωογονεῖ κατάγει εἰς ᾅδου καὶ ἀνάγει
The Lord puts to death and brings to life; he brings down to Hades and brings up.

7 יהוה מוריש ומעשיר משפיל אף־מרומם
[יהוה מוריש ומעשיר משפיל] אף [מרומם]

The Lord makes poor and makes rich; he brings low, he also exalts.
κύριος πτωχίζει καὶ πλουτίζει ταπεινοῖ καὶ ἀνυψοῖ
The Lord makes poor and makes rich; he brings low, and he raises on high.

8a מקים מעפר דל מאשפת ירים אביון להושיב עם־נדיבים וכסא כבוד ינחלם
[מקים מעפר דל ומאשפות ירים אביון להושיב עם] נדיב]ים וכסא כבוד ינחלם

He raises up the poor from the dust; he lifts the needy from the ash heap, to make them sit with princes and inherit a seat of honor.
ἀνιστᾷ ἀπὸ γῆς πένητα καὶ ἀπὸ κοπρίας ἐγείρει πτωχὸν καθίσαι μετὰ δυναστῶν λαῶν καὶ θρόνον δόξης κατακληρονομῶν αὐτοῖς
  εἰς καθίσαι] + αυτον A | λαων] λαου G^{LO}
He raises up the needy from the ground and lifts the poor from the dunghill, to make them sit with the mighty of the peoples, even making them inherit a throne of glory.

8b כי ליהוה מצקי ארץ וישת עליהם תבל
[כי ליהוה מצוקי ארץ וישת] עליהם תב[ל]

For the pillars of the earth are the Lord's, and on them he has set the world.
LXX ——

9 רגלי חסידו [חסידיו] ישמר ורשעים בחשך ידמו כי־לא בכח יגבר־איש

He will guard the feet of his faithful ones, but the wicked shall be cut off in darkness; for not by might does one prevail.
[ ]ודרך ח[סידיו ישמור ורשעים בחשך ידמו] נתן נד[ר]ל[נוד]ר ויברך ש[נות צדיק כי לוא בכח יגבר איש]
He will guard the way of his faithful ones, but the wicked shall be cut off in darkness; he grants the vow to the one who takes vows, he blesses the years of the righteous, for not by might does one prevail.
διδοὺς εὐχὴν τῷ εὐχομένῳ καὶ εὐλόγησεν ἔτη δικαίου ὅτι οὐκ ἐν ἰσχύι δυνατὸς ἀνήρ
  δικαιου] δικαιων A
Granting the prayer to the one who prays, he has even blessed the years of the righteous, because not by strength is a man mighty.

10a יהוה יחתו מריבו [מריביו]

The Lord! His adversaries shall be shattered.

a¹ יהוה יחת מר[י]בו מי ק[דוש כיהוה]
a² [ ]ם [ ]ו°תם בשלמ[ ]° -- אל יתהלל חכם [ ]
a³ [בחכמתו]ואל ית[ה]ל[ל] הגבור בגבורתו ואל יתהלל עשיר]

a⁴ [בעשרו כי בזאת יתהלל המתהלל השכל וידע את יהוה]
a⁵ [ולעשו]ת מש[פט וצדקה בתוך הארץ]

The LORD shatters his adversary (adversaries). Who is holy like the LORD...
... when he repays (?) ... Let not the wise boast of his wisdom, and let not the strong boast of his strength, and let not the rich boast of his riches, but let the one who boasts boast about this: that he has the understanding and knows the LORD and to exercise justice and righteousness in the midst of the land.

κύριος ἀσθενῆ ποιήσει ἀντίδικον αὐτοῦ κύριος ἅγιος μὴ καυχάσθω ὁ φρόνιμος ἐν τῇ φρονήσει αὐτοῦ καὶ μὴ καυχάσθω ὁ δυνατὸς ἐν τῇ δυνάμει αὐτοῦ καὶ μὴ καυχάσθω ὁ πλούσιος ἐν τῷ πλούτῳ αὐτοῦ ἀλλ᾽ ἢ ἐν τούτῳ καυχάσθω ὁ καυχώμενος συνίειν καὶ γινώσκειν τὸν κύριον καὶ ποιεῖν κρίμα καὶ δικαιοσύνην ἐν μέσῳ τῆς γῆς

The Lord will make his adversary weak; the Lord is holy. Let not the clever boast in his cleverness, and let not let the mighty boast in his might, and let not let the wealthy boast in his wealth, but let him who boasts boast in this: to understand and know the Lord and to execute justice and righteousness in the midst of the land.

10ayb עלו [עליו] בשמים ירעם יהוה ידין אפסי־ארץ ויתן־עז למלכו וירם קרן משיחו

The Most High will thunder in heaven. The LORD will judge the ends of the earth; he will give strength to his king, and exalt the power (horn) of his anointed.

[עלה בשמים] וירעם [יהוה] ידין אפסי ארץ ויתן עז למלכנו וירם קרן] משיחו[ ]]

The LORD ascended to heaven and thundered ...

κύριος ἀνέβη εἰς οὐρανοὺς καὶ ἐβρόντησεν αὐτὸς κρινεῖ ἄκρα γῆς καὶ δίδωσιν ἰσχὺν τοῖς βασιλεῦσιν ἡμῶν καὶ ὑψώσει κέρας χριστοῦ αὐτοῦ

The Lord ascended to the heavens and thundered. He will judge earth's ends and gives strength to our kings and will exalt the horn of his anointed.

11 וילך אלקנה הרמתה על־ביתו והנער היה משרת את־יהוה את־פני עלי הכהן

Then Elkanah went home to Ramah, while the boy remained to minister to the LORD, in the presence of the priest Eli.

Καὶ κατέλιπον αὐτὸν ἐκεῖ ἐνώπιον κυρίου καὶ ἀπῆλθον εἰς Αρμαθαιμ, καὶ τὸ παιδάριον ἦν λειτουργῶν τῷ προσώπῳ κυρίου ἐνώπιον Ηλι τοῦ ἱερέως

και κατελιπον – απηλθον] και κατελιπεν αυτον – απηλθεν Gᴮ | και κατελιπον – κυριου] + προσεκυνησαν (-σεν) τω κυριω Gᴸ

And they left him there before the Lord and departed to Harmathaim, and the lad was ministering to the face of the Lord, before Eli the priest.

This first overview quickly reveals where the problems lie and where the three versions diverge most: in the transitions to and from the narrative in 1 Sam 1:28 and 2:11, and in vv. 1–3, 8b–10 of the psalm. In contrast, the tradition in the corpus of the psalm in vv. 4–8a is relatively stable. The evidence is interpreted differently by scholars.

In DJD 17, Frank Moore Cross and his students endeavor to explain the problems—as far as possible—using text-critical means. The editors usually assume technical errors in copying, reckon occasionally with "conflated readings," and only if it is unavoidable suggest textual supplementation in the course of the copying process.[8]

In contrast, Emanuel Tov emphasizes more the autonomy of the three versions and speaks of "different editions" in the MT, the LXX, and 4Q51.[9] He rightly includes the transitions to the narrative in 1 Sam 1–2 in the discussion of the textual problems, the importance of which for textual history and literary history had already been pointed out by Julius Wellhausen in his comparison of the MT and the LXX.[10]

Following Cross, Tov, and other scholars, Anneli Aejmelaeus notes that the version of 4Q51 in some readings is very close to the Hebrew *Vorlage* of the LXX and, like the LXX, often reflects the more original text.[11] This more original text was already conjectured in the earlier studies of Wellhausen and Samuel Rolls Driver, who had only the LXX as an aid.[12] The manuscript of 4Q51 has beautifully confirmed their conjectures. Aejmelaeus is, however, inclined to assume a much stronger, deliberate editing in 4Q51. Aejmelaeus attributes this work to the scroll's scribe, who evaluated the various manuscripts that he had at his disposal in order to produce a manuscript that was as complete as possible. She also assumes three different editions: an older one in the LXX, a corrected one in the MT, and an enhanced one in 4Q51.

In the following, I would like to examine the evidence to determine whether it allows further conclusions to be made about the literary history and a possible earlier (not *the* original but a more original) form of the psalm. To this end, I will discuss in turn the purely text-critical phenomena (orthographic variations, scribal errors, and variants), the major differences in the text (pluses and minuses), and, finally, the internal indications of textual supplementation and the relationship between external and internal evidence.

---

8. Frank M. Cross et al., eds., *Qumran Cave IV.XII: 1–2 Samuel*, DJD XVII (Oxford: Clarendon, 2005), 30–38 (hereafter DJD 17).

9. Emanuel Tov, "Different Editions of the Song of Hannah and of Its Narrative Framework," in *The Greek and Hebrew Bible: Collected Essays on the Septuagint*, VTSup 72 (Leiden: Brill, 1999) 433–55.

10. Julius Wellhausen, *Der Text der Bücher Samuelis* (Göttingen: Vandenhoeck & Ruprecht, 1871), 42.

11. Anneli Aejmelaeus, "Hannah's Psalm in 4QSamª," in *Archaeology of the Books of Samuel: The Entangling of the Textual and Literary History*, ed. Philippe Hugo and A. Schenker, VTSup 132 (Leiden: Brill, 2010), 23–37, esp. 36–37.

12. Wellhausen, *Der Text der Bücher Samuelis*; Samuel R. Driver, *Notes on the Hebrew Text and the Topography of the Books of Samuel: With an Introduction on Hebrew Palaeography*, 2nd ed. (Oxford: Clarendon, 1913).

3. Orthography, Scribal Errors, and Variants

A number of differences between the three versions of the Song of Hannah can be explained by text-critical means, beginning with orthography, such as the Qumranic כיא and the plene spelling in 4Q51 (1:28 כול; 2:2 כאלוהינו). Textual criticism also includes scribal errors and variants, in which textual history occasionally merges into literary or compositional history. For clarity, I will deal with both categories together, following the order of the verses in the Hebrew Bible.

1:28 כל־הימים אשר היה הוא שאול ליהוה is to be translated "all the days, which he was, he is given to the Lord." Since "tense and meaning are incongruous," Wellhausen had conjectured, with reference to the LXX, that the text should be אשר חי הוא הוא instead of אשר היה הוא.[13] 4Q51 is not preserved here; the restored text in brackets follows the LXX and the conjecture of Wellhausen. In my opinion, the doubling of הוא, as suggested by Wellhausen, does not seem to be necessary. The error can be readily explained by the confusion of ח and ה, incorrect word partitioning and a dittography involving ה.

2:1 פי על־אויבי כי שמחתי בישועתך, ἐπλατύνθη ἐπὶ ἐχθροὺς τὸ στόμα μου. The כי is out of place and not provided in the LXX. The word order in the LXX (apart from G^O) leads us to suppose that the MT also originally read פי, which was corrupted to כי, or perhaps was read as a final *mem* of אויבים (LXX) and was therefore added at the front,[14] or that two distinct readings were combined in the MT. Other scholars propose a prosaic supplement.[15] Also attractive is P. Kyle McCarter's assumption that in the LXX and 4Q51 the following ὅτι or כי is to be found in the *kaph* of בישועתך, one of two exceptional cases of direct address in the psalm, with the text originally reading: כי שמחתי בישועת "I rejoice in *my* vindication, For."[16]

2:1 ביהוה[2], ἐν θεῷ μου (באלהי). The LXX variant is usually preferred because of the variety of expression. A clear decision is not possible in such cases.

2:2 כי אין בלתך, οὐκ ἔστιν ἅγιος πλὴν σοῦ (without כי but with קדוש). This is more likely to be a variant than a scribal error.

2:2 ואין צור כאלהינו, καὶ οὐκ ἔστιν δίκαιος ὡς ὁ θεὸς ἡμῶν (כאלוהינו ואין צדיק). The rendering of צור with δίκαιος in the LXX is probably not a variant that is based on a different, independent Hebrew *Vorlage*.[17] It can either be traced

---

13. Wellhausen, *Der Text der Bücher Samuelis*, 42. The reading is also found in some Hebrew manuscripts (see BHS).
14. Thus Wellhausen, *Der Text der Bücher Samuelis Text*, 42–43.
15. P. Kyle McCarter, *I Samuel: A New Translation with Introduction, Notes, and Commentary*, AB 8 (Garden City, NY: Doubleday, 1980), 68.
16. Ibid.
17. DJD 17, 36; McCarter, *I Samuel*, 68–69.

back to a scribal error (caused by a slip of the pen changing צור into צדיק) or represents the translator's deliberate avoidance of the divine epithet.[18]

2:3 אל־תרבו תדברו גבהה גבהה, μὴ καυχᾶσθε καὶ μὴ λαλεῖτε ὑψηλά. Wellhausen objects to the repetition of the feminine גבהה, which occurs only once in some Hebrew manuscripts and, in the versions, is usually rendered by a simple plural. He understands the form to be masculine with ה-locale, part of a quotation of proud enemies: "Do not say repeatedly: up high, up high!"[19] This is an inventive solution. I think that it is in any case more appealing than McCarter's explanation; he reckons with a twofold dittography and a conflation of two variants in both the LXX and the MT, one "correct," the other "corrupt."[20]

2:3 יצא, μὴ ἐξελθάτω (אל יצא). McCarter prefers the reading of the LXX.[21] However, we could also be dealing with an additional clarification that the translator either found in the *Vorlage* or made himself. In one Hebrew manuscript the variant עשק before עתק is to be found (see *BHS*); it is probably an explanatory addition.

2:3 כי אל דעות יהוה, ὅτι θεὸς γνώσεων κύριος, יהוה [כי אל דעת. The defective spelling in 4Q51 can be read as singular as well as plural and was later disambiguated with a *mater lectionis* in the MT. The Greek tradition preserves both singular and plural readings.

2:3 ולא [ולו] נתכנו עללות, καὶ θεὸς ἑτοιμάζων ἐπιτηδεύματα αὐτοῦ (ואל תוכן עללותיו). Wellhausen believes that the reading of the MT (with the *qere*) is original, that of the LXX a simplification under the influence of Ezek 18:25, which explains the suffix in "his/their actions." McCarter believes the opposite.[22] The different readings are likely—whichever way they developed—to have been created by a scribal error, namely, by transposition of לא and אל.

2:4 קשת גברים חתים, τόξον δυνατῶν ἠσθένησεν, חתה ם[גבורים קשת]. The reading in the LXX and 4Q51 (adjective sing. fem.) is grammatically correct and is therefore usually preferred,[23] but it could also be a secondary correction. GKC (§146a) explains the plural with a construct connection, in which the predicate sometimes conforms not to the construct noun (*nomen regens*) but to the genitive. With reference to Mitchell Dahood, McCarter postulates a defectively written plural masculine *qāšōt*.[24] The MT has a similar problem in Jer 51:56.

2:5 נשכרו, ἠλαττώθησαν. The translation of שכר with ἐλαττοῦν is peculiar.

---

18. Tov, "Different Editions," 441; Aejmelaeus, "Hannah's Psalm," 28.
19. Wellhausen, *Der Text der Bücher Samuelis*, 43. Contra Karl Budde, *Die Bücher Samuel*, KHC 8 (Tübingen: Mohr Siebeck, 1902), 15.
20. McCarter, *I Samuel*, 69; see also DJD 17, 36.
21. McCarter, *I Samuel*, 69.
22. Wellhausen, *Der Text der Bücher Samuelis*, 43; McCarter, *I Samuel*, 69.
23. Aejmelaeus, "Hannah's Psalm," 24–25.
24. McCarter, *I Samuel*, 69.

Wellhausen suspects the reason to be a variant of the root ח-ס-ר but gives preference to the MT as the *lectio difficilior* and refers to the parallelism.²⁵

2:5 חדלו עד־עקרה is a *crux interpretum*. The NRSV translation "are fat with spoil" apparently reflects an understanding in which the root ח-ד-ל here means "to be fat" and עד "spoil" or "food."²⁶ This is an attractive solution to the problem. Also widespread is the assumption of letter loss and the reconstruction חֲדֵל עֲבֹד, "And they that were hungry, stop working."²⁷ Or can we read עַד, "that is still barren"? The reading of the LXX (παρῆκαν γῆν ὅτι) is not a variant but an attempt at interpretation: it adds an object and understands עד in terms of כי.²⁸ Most unlikely, in my opinion, is a dittography or conflation of חדל, once in the sense of "to forsake" and then as "world" (= חלד).²⁹ See Jer 15:9 on the formulation.

2:7 מוריש as the opposite of to "be rich" is unusual; a form of רוש, "being poor," would be closer. For this reason, Budde assumes a scribal error and suggests מריש (hiphil of רוש).³⁰

2:8 להושיב, καθίσαι, G^A and some other codices καθισαι αυτον, a Hebrew manuscript להושיבי (see *BHS*). The variant is also found in Ps 113:8, where 1 Sam 2:8 is cited fully and the MT reads the suffix of the first person, the LXX the suffix of the third person singular. I suspect that initially the suffix of the third person was added for clarification and then ו and י were confused. In any case the suffix of the firstt person is secondary; it relates the statement to the supplicant and removes its universality.

2:8 מאשפת, καὶ ἀπὸ κοπρίας. Since the two parallel cola are connected in vv. 4–6 by a copula, the copula may also be original here or based on harmonization.³¹ A final decision is not possible.

2:8 עם־נדיבים, μετὰ δυναστῶν λαῶν, G^LO μετα δυναστων λαου. The expansion of the expression is encountered also in Ps 113:8 (LXX 112:8): להושיבי עם־נדיבים עם נדיבי עמו (τοῦ καθίσαι αὐτὸν μετὰ ἀρχόντων μετὰ ἀρχόντων λαοῦ αὐτοῦ). The variant is probably secondary.

2:9 [חסידיו] חסידו, or ח]סידיו רגלי, or ודרך חסידו. The variant in 4Q51 is aligned with the text of Prov 2:8 (ישמר [חסידיו] חסידו ודרך) and is therefore secondary.

2:10 [מריביו] מריבו, יהוה יחתו מריבו, κύριος ἀσθενῆ ποιήσει ἀντίδικον αὐτοῦ, יהוה יחת מר[י]בו. The more difficult construction in the MT (*casus pendens*) requires the plural (*qere*; cf. NRSV). The following singular suffix in עלו [עליו], however, clashes with this. The variant in the LXX and 4Q51 has Yhwh as the subject and understands the object as a singular, like the *ketiv* of the MT.

---

25. Wellhausen, *Der Text der Bücher Samuelis*, 43.
26. Cf. McCarter, *I Samuel*, 72.
27. Driver, *Notes on the Hebrew Text*, 25.
28. Wellhausen, *Der Text der Bücher Samuelis Text*, 43.
29. McCarter, *I Samuel*, 69.
30. Budde, *Die Bücher Samuel*, 15.
31. The variant is found also in the Hebrew manuscripts (see *BHS*).

This variant is more in accordance with the continuation of the MT and is to be preferred.³²

2:10 עלה] עליו, κύριος ἀνέβη εἰς οὐρανοὺς καὶ ἐβρόντησεν, ירעם בשמים [עליו] עלו, וירעם [בשמים. The MT refers [עליו] עלו to the aforementioned opponents of Yhwh: "he thunders against him [them] in heaven"; the LXX starts with a new sentence and takes up the subject κύριος (יהוה) once more after the long insertion. Without the inserted text we have two variants (עלו [עליו] ... ירעם and עלה ... וירעם). The NRSV translation "The Most High" points in another direction, conjecturing an abbreviation or a slip of the pen for עליון to lie behind עלו.³³ Today we are more inclined to think of an old Ugaritic name for God עלי (*ēlî*), from which the variants in the versions have developed.³⁴ This is also a possibility, especially as the error can be easily explained by the frequent confusion of י and ו. But it seems to me that the reading in the LXX and 4Q51 (with the *Wiederaufnahme* of the subject, the finite verb, and the copula before וירעם) is more likely to be related to the insertion than to the name of God (see §4 below).

2:10 יהוה ידין, αὐτὸς κρινεῖ (הוא ידין). The LXX variant is probably related to the addition and other changes in v. 10 (see below). The personal pronoun is adequate following the resumption of the subject at the beginning of the sentence in v. 10b.

2:10 למלכו, τοῖς βασιλεῦσιν ἡμῶν. The LXX assumes not only a suffix in the plural ("our") but also י as *mater lectionis*. The variant collectivizes the psalm and is therefore probably secondary.

These are the orthographic variations, scribal errors, and variants, which can be easily multiplied by further intra-Greek variants. All this is in line with what we usually find in manuscripts. In themselves, errors in the text contribute little to the question of textual supplementation. All the same, rudiments of text editing can be detected here and there even in the errors (e.g., v. 10), whether it be that the revision of the text produces errors or variants, or that an error has led to further revision. The variants in particular show that the text remained in this processing flow for a long time and was being continually reworked. Although we can hardly place all this under the category of textual supplementation, the phenomenon does come quite close in some cases, especially if the scribe or translator turns into a producer of variants and additions.³⁵

Above all, we must not make the mistake of seeing scribal errors and variants merely as post-history and the offshoots of textual history.

---

32. McCarter, *I Samuel*, 70; Aejmelaeus, "Hannah's Psalm," 25.

33. See Budde, *Die Bücher Samuel*, 16, who assumes a vocalization error and changes the reading of יִרְעַם to יַרְעֵם (from the root רעם) according to Ps 2:9. The location "in the heavens" speaks more for "thunder."

34. McCarter, *I Samuel*, 70–71, 73.

35. See the contribution of Marc Z. Brettler in this volume.

As the external evidence from Elephantine (TAD A4.7–8) or from Qumran shows, errors and variants appear in the text with the correction of the first writing or with the first copy. They begin very early and run through the entire history of a text. To a certain extent, they accompany text creation, lie on different levels, and cannot always be neatly separated from the changes induced by the text's literary growth. The literary growth, however, is indicated mainly by the pluses and minuses of textual tradition.

4. Pluses and Minuses

Dealing with textual errors and variants has already confirmed our first impression that textual problems occur mainly at the outer edges of the psalm: at the transitions to and from the narrative (1:28; 2:11), and in vv. 2–3 and 8b–10. The tradition in the middle part in vv. 3–8a is, in contrast, relatively uniform. The same picture is reflected also by the pluses and minuses in the text. They occur in 1 Sam 1:28; 2:1–2 and massively in 2:8–10. This seems to me to be a first indication of the psalm's genesis. The distribution of the textual problems suggests the assumption that the (older) core of the psalm is to be sought in vv. 3–8a, while the verses at the edges were processed more vigorously and in some cases added later. We will examine this assumption in the following discussion.

The Narrative Framework (1 Sam 1:28 and 2:11)

Wellhausen pointed out that the Song of Hannah was inserted into the MT and the LXX in two different places: in the MT after a man's proskynesis (Elkanah) and before Elkanah's departure; in the LXX before Hannah hands over the boy to the priests and her departure. The relinquishing of the boy to the priests is missing in the MT, and the proskynesis is missing in the LXX (except G^L in 1:28 and 2:11). The two versions confirm Wellhausen's suggestion—which he had pointed out on the basis of 1 Samuel 1:24–28—that we are dealing with two different versions in the MT and the LXX: one version in which Hannah is the main actor and another version in which Hannah and Elkanah together are the actors.[36] The two versions, however, got mixed up: in 1 Sam 1:24–28a the MT represents the version with Hannah, the LXX the version with Hanna and Elkanah as active subjects; in 1:28b and 2:11, it is the other way around: the subject is Elkanah

---

36. Wellhausen, *Der Text der Bücher Samuelis*, 41–42. See Tov, "Different Editions," 434–41.

in the MT (according to some versions both parents in pl.), in the LXX it is
Hannah (in sing.) or according to some manuscripts, both parents (in pl.).

> MT (Elkanah or both parents)
> 1:28b וישתחו שם ליהוה (SV pl. ישתחוו שם ליהוה)
> 2:11 וילך אלקנה הרמתה על־ביתו והנער היה משרת את־יהוה על־פני עלי הכהן
> LXX (Hannah or both parents)
> 1:28b —
> (G^L + και προσεκυνησεν (-σαν) εκει τω κυριω)
> 2:11 G^B Καὶ κατέλιπεν αὐτὸν ἐκεῖ ἐνώπιον κυρίου καὶ ἀπῆλθεν εἰς Αρμαθαιμ
> καὶ τὸ παιδάριον ἦν λειτουργῶν τῷ προσώπῳ κυρίου ἐνώπιον Ηλι τοῦ ἱερέως
> (G^L Pl. κατελιπον; + προσεκυνησαν (-σεν) τω κυριω; απηλθον)

Manuscript 4Q51 confirms the version of the LXX in almost every respect,
both in the case of 1 Sam 1:24–28a, where the active subject is Elkanah
or both parents, and in 1:28b (or 2:11), where Hannah is the active subject. The Qumran manuscript has a slightly different text, however, and
inserts the Song of Hannah again at another location. It contains both the
relinquishing of the child (like the LXX but with a shorter text) and the
proskynesis (like the MT) and places the Song of Hannah—different from
the LXX but with the MT—*after* the handover and proskynesis and *before*
Hannah's departure. LXX 2:11 is therefore partially *before* the Song of Hannah, that is, at the position of 1:28b: [ליהוה] ותעזב[הו שם ותשתח[ו].

> 1:28/2:11 and the Song of Hannah 2:1–10
> MT: proskynesis (he = Elkanah) — Song of Hannah — departure
> (Elkanah)
> LXX: (G^L proskynesis in sing./pl.) — Song of Hannah — handover
> and departure (G^B sing. = Hannah, G^L handover, proskynesis and
> departure in pl.)
> 4Q51: handover and proskynesis (Hannah) — Song of Hannah —
> departure (Hannah)

While the evidence is not entirely straightforward, it is on the whole clear.
First, it proves that the Song of Hannah is not original here but was added
secondarily at two different places in the narrative context. Furthermore,
the evidence shows that the narrative was edited, presumably before the
insertion of the song. As a consequence, the evidence cannot be explained
primarily by text-critical (mechanical) means, but only by redaction-critical means.

Thus, the plus in the LXX and 4Q51 in 1 Sam 1:24–28a is clearly
proven to be a secondary textual supplementation ascribing a special role
to Elkanah in the occurrences previously dominated by Hannah; the MT

provides the older text here.[37] In the following (1:28b; 2:11), the LXX and 4Q51 seem to have preserved the older text in which Hannah plays the active role, while the MT reflects the influence of the revision that highlights Elkanah's role. The MT therefore presupposes the revision in 1 Sam 1:24–28b that is witnessed in the LXX and 4Q51. Of the three actions in 1:28b/2:11, the departure is in any case more likely to be original, which, before the insertion of the Song of Hannah, is preceded by the proskynesis (MT), only by the relinquishing (LXX), or by both (4Q51; G^L). The different variants were probably created by the song's insertion.[38] The versions were then subject to various efforts of alignment that put verbs into the plural and named both parents as active subjects.

Verse 1

We now come to the psalm itself, and vv. 1–2 and vv. 8–10 in particular. In all three versions the heading presupposes Hannah as the active subject. The LXX reads a simple "and she said" (Καὶ εἶπεν = ותאמר), which agrees with the fact that here, as well as in 4Q51, no change of subject has occurred and Hannah is the subject in 1:28. The MT is different. In this text, after the proskynesis in 1:28 with a male subject (Elkanah), Hannah is introduced as supplicant in 2:1, resorting to 1:26 ותאמר חנה ותתפלל (likewise G^L καὶ προσηύξατο αννα). The longer heading in the MT is thus secondary and based on textual supplementation.

Verse 2

In v. 2, we can observe the transition from a variant, possibly a scribal error, to textual supplementation. Among the textual witnesses that are available to us, we find the following variants:

MT אין־קדוש כיהוה כי אין בלתך ואין צור כאלהינו (כי?)
4Q51 [כ]יא אין קדוש כיה[וה] + x[כי אין/ואין (קדוש) בלת[ך ואין צור כאלהינו
LXX ὅτι οὐκ ἔστιν ἅγιος ὡς κύριος καὶ οὐκ ἔστιν δίκαιος ὡς ὁ θεὸς ἡμῶν οὐκ ἔστιν ἅγιος πλὴν σοῦ
G^L ὅτι οὐκ ἔστιν ἅγιος ὡς κύριος καὶ οὐκ ἔστιν δίκαιος ὡς ὁ θεὸς ἡμῶν καὶ οὐκ ἔστιν ἅγιος πλὴν σοῦ
G^O ὅτι οὐκ ἔστιν ἅγιος ὡς κύριος καὶ οὐκ ἔστιν πλὴν σοῦ καὶ οὐκ ἔστιν δίκαιος ὡς ὁ θεὸς ἡμῶν

---

37. See Kratz, "Bibelhandschrift oder Midrasch?," 161–62.
38. Before the insertion of the song, the sequence "relinquishing – Hannah's departure" could have been the original order. In the LXX the song was placed before these two actions. The MT presupposes the revision, which highlights Elkanah's role and therefore, with the insertion of the song, differentiates between the role of Hannah (song) and Elkanah (departure, 2:11). The previous relinquishing of the child was replaced by the proskynesis of Elkanah in 1:28b, which underlines Elkanah's role before Hannah takes the floor and is introduced as supplicant and speaker. 4Q51 combines both readings but retains Hannah as the subject throughout. All other variants can be understood as secondary alignments.

We can distinguish three components in these variants:

a (כי) אין־קדוש כיהוה
b אין־קדוש בלתך, b' אין בלתך
c ואין צור באלהינו, c' καὶ οὐκ ἔστιν δίκαιος ὡς ὁ θεὸς ἡμῶν (witnessed only in Greek, see under §3 above)

These three components are arranged differently: *abc* in the MT, *axbc* in 4Q51, *ac'b'* in the LXX and G^L, *abc'* in G^O.³⁹ There are also differences in the introductory כי and the copula ו. Common to all versions is that *a* is in the first position and most likely belongs to the core. Also relatively stable is the order *abc* if we disregard the variants *b'* and *c'*, and the addition of another element (*x*) in 4Q51. Only this order explains the additional element קדוש in *b'*, which is taken from the immediately preceding term *a* and was most probably added secondarily in the *Vorlage* of the LXX.⁴⁰ Based on this, the variants in the LXX and G^L would also be classified as secondary.⁴¹ If we then take into account that *b'* is not a Hebrew but merely a Greek variant, then G^O already assumes the translation and harmonizes this with the arrangement in the MT and is therefore probably secondary as well. Thus, component *c* and its position at the end in the MT and 4Q51 are also proved stable and, like *a*, could likewise belong to the core. Both 4Q51 and the secondary variants in the Greek tradition presuppose the core and the sequence *abc* in the MT.

The changes in the versions appear to have begun with the expansion of the second component *b*, which is witnessed in the LXX. They continue in 4Q51 in the unknown but, on the basis of the space, required textual supplementation of the MT. 4Q51 might already presuppose the supplementation of *b* in the order of MT but not the transposition to the last position in the LXX. If the *x* we are dealing with in 4Q51 is one of the components *a*–*c* (most likely *c*) we could explain this more easily by text-critical means as a contamination of two readings, or as a result of a deliberate comparison and combination of different textual traditions. If, however, we are dealing with a separate fourth variant *d* (even if it exists only in component *c'* in the Greek tradition) it would be preferable to assume textual supplementation over a mechanical explanation such as scribal error or text adjustment. The supplementation and subsequent positioning of *b* and the addition of another component could suggest

---

39. See Tov, "Different Editions," 441–42; Tov speaks of three "versions (editions)" but leaves the question open of how they originated. Aejmelaeus considers the possible alternatives of scribal error ("Hannah's Psalm," 27–31). See also DJD 17, 36 and 38; McCarter, *I Samuel*, 68–69.

40. Wellhausen, *Der Text der Bücher Samuelis*, 43.

41. A different explanation is provided by Aejmelaeus, who believes the order of the LXX to be original ("Hannah's Psalm," 30–31).

that all of *b* is secondary and that the original text contained only *a* and *c*:
(כי) אין־קדוש כיהוה ואין צור כאלהינו.

Verse 8
The next major plus, encountered in v. 8, is witnessed by both the MT and 4Q51 but is completely missing in the LXX.

כי ליהוה מצקי ארץ וישת עליהם תבל
[[כי ליהוה מצוקי ארץ וישת עליהם תב]ל

There is a broad consensus that this is textual supplementation. Verse 8b stands out both in style and content, and it would certainly be classified by most scholars as secondary, even without external evidence. The external evidence of the LXX only makes the decision easier.[42] The plus inserts a cosmic dimension into the psalm, pursuing a tendency to universalize.

Verse 9
The versions also differ in v. 9. Besides the variants in the MT and 4Q51 (see §3), the MT and the LXX each offer shorter texts, 4Q51 a longer text.

MT
a רגלי חסידו [חסידיו] ישמר ורשעים בחשך ידמו ...
b —
c כי־לא בכח יגבר־איש

4Q51
a ודרך ח[סידיו ישמור ורשעים בחשך ידמו]
b נתן נד[ר]ל[נוד]ר ויברך ש[נות צדיק
c כי לוא בכח יגבר איש]

LXX
a —
b διδοὺς εὐχὴν τῷ εὐχομένῳ καὶ εὐλόγησεν ἔτη δικαίου (G^A δικαιων)
c ὅτι οὐκ ἐν ἰσχύι δυνατὸς ἀνήρ

The external evidence suggests that element *c*, which is witnessed in both the MT and the LXX and probably in 4Q51 (on the basis of space), represents the older text, supplemented by element *a* in the MT and by ele-

---

42. Wellhausen, *Der Text der Bücher Samuelis*, 43: "Das letzte Glied überfüllt den Vers, liegt dem Zusammenhange nicht nahe und fehlt mit Recht in LXX." See Tov, "Different Editions," 442–44; Aejmelaeus, "Hannah's Psalm," 31; and perhaps also DJD 17, 38, where v. 8b is missing, although the evidence is not discussed anywhere. In contrast, McCarter believes the version of 4Q51 to be original and for vv. 8b–10a expects massive text loss in both the MT and the LXX: "4QSam^a shows that both MT and LXX have suffered losses of material here" (*I Samuel*, 69–70). The loss of v. 8b is not explained, and its omission in the LXX and the possibility of a plus are not even discussed.

ment *b* in the LXX or the *Vorlage* of the LXX. 4Q51 accordingly represents a secondary combination of the two additions *a* (with text variant according to Prov 2:8) and *b*.[43] This explanation clearly deserves preference over the view that 4Q51 represents the original text, with the text in the MT and the LXX understood to have been corrupted by haplography and "losses of material," though without proof or a reconstruction of the individual processes using the text.[44]

The pluses comment on the Song of Hannah and on its content concerning God's actions in different ways. Element *a*, that is, v. 9a MT, places the reversal of circumstances through God in the theological opposition between the "pious" and the "wicked." We can speak of a "piety revision" here. Those responsible for element *b*, that is, v. 9a LXX, would apparently like to include the narrative of Hannah in the hymn and therefore insert the idea of fulfillment of vows and the blessing of the righteous with old age.[45]

I assume, with Tov, that both pluses have entered independently into the text. Accordingly, the emergence of the verse can be reconstructed approximately as follows:

Originally v. 9b (element *c*) was connected directly to v. 8a.

8a מקים מעפר דל מאשפת ירים אביון להושיב עם־נדיבים וכסא כבוד ינחלם
9b כי לא בכח יגבר איש

Element *b*, the plus in the LXX, which in the Hebrew *Vorlage* requires a participle, connects perfectly from a grammatical perspective to the Hebrew text in v. 8a and does not yet seem to be aware of the pluses in the MT, vv. 8b, 9a.[46]

8a מקים מעפר דל מאשפת ירים אביון להושיב עם־נדיבים וכסא כבוד ינחלם
9a [נתן נדר]לנודר ויברך שנות צדיק
9b כי־לא בכח יגבר־איש

---

43. See Tov, "Different Editions," 444–48. Similarly Aejmelaeus, "Hannah's Psalm," 32–33, who, however, believes only the MT to be secondary compared to the LXX and hence holds the originality of element *b*.

44. See McCarter, *I Samuel*, 69–70; contra Tov, "Different Editions," 448 n. 44. DJD 17 seems to assume that only the last element *c*, which is common to all the witnesses, is secondary (37–38). Reasons are not given. See, however, Budde, *Die Bücher Samuel*, 16.

45. Wellhausen, *Der Text der Bücher Samuelis*, 44: "Es sieht aus, als ob dieser Text den Psalm der im Alter mit Kindern noch gesegneten Hanna als Danklied für die Erfüllung ihrer Bitte mundgerechter machen wollte. Denn worüber Gott hier nach dem Zusammenhänge des *Liedes* gepriesen wird, das ist sein Ueberschwänglichthun über alle Bitten, nicht sein διδόναι εὐχὴν τῷ εὐχομένῳ; sein Erheben des Verachteten auf den Fürstenstuhl, nicht sein εὐλογεῖν ἔτη δικαίου."

46. See Aejmelaeus, "Hannah's Psalm," 32.

8a ἀνιστᾷ ἀπὸ γῆς πένητα καὶ ἀπὸ κοπρίας ἐγείρει πτωχὸν καθίσαι μετὰ
   δυναστῶν λαῶν καὶ θρόνον δόξης κατακληρονομῶν αὐτοῖς
9 διδοὺς εὐχὴν τῷ εὐχομένῳ καὶ εὐλόγησεν ἔτη δικαίου ὅτι οὐκ ἐν ἰσχύι δυνατὸς
   ἀνήρ

The plus in v. 9a (MT) connects, for better or for worse, to the help for the poor in v. 8a, as well as to the universalistic plus in v. 8b, and is particularly formulated toward v. 9b: It is the wicked who set the power of man above the power of God.

8a מקים מעפר דל מאשפת ירים אביון להושיב עם־נדיבים וכסא כבוד ינחלם
8b כי ליהוה מצקי ארץ וישת עליהם תבל
9a רגלי חסידו [חסידיו] ישמר ורשעים בחשך ידמו
9b כי־לא בכח יגבר־איש

Both additions are included and combined in 4Q51. In this context, the plus in the LXX, which is focused on Hannah's story, also serves the opposition of the "pious/righteous" and the "wicked," to which the psalm and God's actions described in it are related secondarily. The intra-Greek variant in G^A makes this interpretation explicit by changing the singular "the righteous" to the plural.

If this reconstruction of textual supplementation in vv. 8–9 is reasonably accurate, we can then ask ourselves whether v. 9b, that is, the element c (כי־לא בכח יגבר־איש), witnessed in all versions, also represents a plus. The verse responds to the elevation of the poor, whom God helps, to great honor. It really almost goes without saying that this is not the work of man, and that a man cannot become great by his own power. It only needs to be said if it is intended to give the psalm a parenetic note (cf. Ps 33:16; Zech 4:6) or if something else follows that is devoted to the same topic (v. 10).

Verse 10
This brings us to v. 10 and the last place in the Song of Hannah where the versions diverge. Here the LXX provides a large plus missing from the MT.

10a יהוה יחתו מריבו [מריביו]
10a κύριος ἀσθενῆ ποιήσει ἀντίδικον αὐτοῦ
+ κύριος ἅγιος μὴ καυχάσθω ὁ φρόνιμος ἐν τῇ φρονήσει αὐτοῦ καὶ μὴ καυχάσθω
ὁ δυνατὸς ἐν τῇ δυνάμει αὐτοῦ καὶ μὴ καυχάσθω ὁ πλούσιος ἐν τῷ πλούτῳ αὐτοῦ
ἀλλ᾽ ἢ ἐν τούτῳ καυχάσθω ὁ καυχώμενος συνίειν καὶ γινώσκειν τὸν κύριον καὶ
ποιεῖν κρίμα καὶ δικαιοσύνην ἐν μέσῳ τῆς γῆς

10b עלו [עליו] בשמים ירעם יהוה אפסי־ארץ ויתן־עז למלכו וירם קרן משיחו

10b κύριος ἀνέβη εἰς οὐρανοὺς καὶ ἐβρόντησεν αὐτὸς κρινεῖ ἄκρα γῆς καὶ δίδωσιν ἰσχὺν τοῖς βασιλεῦσιν ἡμῶν καὶ ὑψώσει κέρας χριστοῦ αὐτοῦ

The plus is more or less identical to Jer 9:22–23, the difference being that in 1 Samuel humans should exercise righteousness and justice in the land, whereas in Jeremiah it is the Lord, who exercises mercy, justice, and righteousness. Jer 9:22–23 reads:

22 Τάδε λέγει κύριος Μὴ καυχάσθω ὁ σοφὸς ἐν τῇ σοφίᾳ αὐτοῦ καὶ μὴ καυχάσθω ὁ ἰσχυρὸς ἐν τῇ ἰσχύι αὐτοῦ καὶ μὴ καυχάσθω ὁ πλούσιος ἐν τῷ πλούτῳ αὐτοῦ 23 ἀλλ' ἢ ἐν τούτῳ καυχάσθω ὁ καυχώμενος συνίειν καὶ γινώσκειν ὅτι ἐγώ εἰμι κύριος ποιῶν ἔλεος καὶ κρίμα καὶ δικαιοσύνην ἐπὶ τῆς γῆς ὅτι ἐν τούτοις τὸ θέλημά μου λέγει κύριος

Since the reproduction is different, we can rule out the possibility that the translator took the plus from Jeremiah. Hence, we can assume an appropriate *Vorlage* in the book of Samuel. This Hebrew *Vorlage* seems to be witnessed in 4Q51, but only fragments have survived, which, incidentally, contain a slightly different text. At this point it is necessary to delve a little deeper into textual tradition and to deal with the paleographic evidence.[47] DJD 17 provides the following transcription of 4Q51 II, 29–35:

(29) 10a¹ יהוה יחת מר[י]בו מי ק[דוש כיהוה --]
(30) a² [--]•[ס]•תם בשלמ[ו] -- אל יתהלל חכם[
(31) a³ [בחכמתו]ואל ית[ה]ל[ל] הגבור בגבורתו ואל יתהלל עשיר]
(32) a⁴ [בעשרו כי בזאת יתהלל המתהלל השכל וידע את יהוה]
(33) a⁵ [ולעשו]ת מש[פט וצדקה בתוך הארץ]
(34) 10ayb [יהוה עלה בשמים] וירעם [יהוה ידין אפסי ארץ ויתן עז למלכנו וירם קרן]
(35) משיחו[ ]

The reading and conjecture in v. 10¹ (line 29) are daring but quite plausible in view of the beginning of the Greek plus: κύριος ἅγιος. The plus apparently refers back to v. 2: כיא אין קדוש כיהוה.

The reading]•תם בשלמ[in v. 10a² (line 30) is clear but has no counterpart in the MT or the LXX. If DJD 17 is correct and, in the LXX and 4Q51, we are dealing with the same plus, then it has been increased here by another line! What was read here can no longer be reconstructed.[48]

---

47. Relevant here are the photos of the Leon Levy Dead Sea Scrolls Digital Library B-480676 and -5 (pl. 998, frag. 5 = 4Q51 col. II, lines 26–31) and B-840684 and -5 (pl. 998, frag. 7 = 4Q51 col. II, lines 33–34).

48. See Andrew Fincke, *The Samuel Scroll from Qumran: 4QSamᵃ Restored and Compared to the Septuagint and 4QSamᶜ*, STDJ 43 (Leiden: Brill, 2001), 9, 34; he reads: השלמים בשלמותם.

The reading of v. 10a³ is extremely problematic. DJD 17 reads ‏ואל ית[ה]ל[ל, which would be consistent with the LXX and prove that we are dealing with the same plus. This reading, however, is frequently disputed. McCarter and Tov read here: ‏רגלי ח[סידיו ישמור; Andrew Fincke reads: ‏הגבור ב[חלי ו]‏.⁴⁹ In my opinion, the reading of Cross in DJD 17 still seems to be best, even if, try as I might, I cannot detect either the second ל or the head in line 30 that lies above; so, in fact, I read: ‏[ואל ית]הלל.

In contrast, in v. 10a⁵ (line 33) the fragments can be quite clearly correlated with the plus of the LXX: ποιεῖν κρίμα = ‏מש]פט[‏ולעשו]ת.⁵⁰ Before the *mem* of ‏משפט we can clearly see the foot of a *taw*, so that we must read here not the infinitive absolute (as do Tov and Fincke) but the infinitive construct. Accordingly, v. 10ayb witnesses a common text in the MT and the LXX.

So while the situation is not entirely clear, it is clear enough to support the assumption that the plus in the LXX is also witnessed by 4Q51—here, however, enriched by another plus. The correlation of the LXX and 4Q51 is suggested also by the plus being at the same location and by the same variant being found in the 4Q51 as in the LXX: ‏יהוה עלה בשמים [וירעם corresponds to κύριος ἀνέβη εἰς οὐρανοὺς καὶ ἐβρόντησεν; MT has here [עליו] עלו בשמים ירעם.

There is more or less consensus that we are dealing here with textual supplementation.⁵¹ The only exception is McCarter, who maintains that the long text in 4Q51 is original. Yet he can explain neither the earlier text nor the scribal errors: "So this seems to be a case where our usual preference for a shorter reading must be set aside. The scroll, fragmentary as it is, seems to be the only surviving witness to the primitive text."⁵² If nothing else, the variant in v. 10b (see §3 above) speaks for a plus. The variant is easily explained by the addition at this place. As a consequence of the plus the earlier ‏עלו [עליו] בשמים ירעם lost its link to the aforementioned adversaries (*ketiv*), so that the subject κύριος (‏יהוה) in v. 10a had to be resumed and repeated here. The preposition with suffix [עליו] עלו became the verb ‏עלה; the following ‏ירעם was provided with a copula: κύριος ἀνέβη εἰς οὐρανοὺς καὶ ἐβρόντησεν = ‏יהוה עלה בשמים וירעם; and, in the following, a personal pronoun sufficed (αὐτὸς κρινεῖ instead of ‏יהוה ידין).

It is unclear where the plus came from. Since the passage in the book of Jeremiah is also very likely to be secondary and the text is not com-

---

49. McCarter, *I Samuel*, 70; Tov, "Different Editions," 452; Fincke, *Samuel Scroll*, 9, 34. Eugene C. Ulrich also maintains that the surpluses in the LXX and 4Q51 do not have much in common (*The Qumran Text of Samuel and Josephus*, HSM 19 [Missoula, MT: Scholars Press, 1978], 49).

50. McCarter reads:]*ml*[(*I Samuel*, 70).

51. Wellhausen, *Der Text der Bücher Samuelis*, 44; Tov, "Different Editions," 448–52; Aejmelaeus, "Hannah's Psalm," 33–35.

52. McCarter, *I Samuel*, 70.

pletely identical, we might think of a sapiential tradition—one that was free-floating and was added independently to both places. Although this may well be the case, it is, of course, impossible to prove and indeed, in my opinion, also unlikely. The literary connections in the two versions are too close for an independent emergence. I believe that the plus in Jer 9 is primary, no matter where the formulations came from. While it is true that it fits into the context here just as badly as it does in 1 Sam 2,[53] still it is not the only plus of this kind in Jer 8–10. A point of contact here is the polemic against the "wise people" and the "wise" in Jer 8:7–9; there are particular connections to the following polemic against idols in Jer 10:1–16, which is also sapientially marked and stresses the contrast between God, the creator and ruler of the world, and idols, made by human hands.

Keyword associations ("god of knowledge," "heroes," "rich," in 1 Sam 2:3, 4, 7), the idea of pride in v. 3, the universalistic plus in v. 8b (cf. Jer 10:10–13), and, finally, the statement about the powerlessness of people in v. 9b[54] could have suggested to the scribe that he cite Jer 9:22–23 in 1 Sam 2. The differences are also explained better by the transfer from Jer 9. The change could be due to the context: whereas the version in Jer 9 focuses on the power of God, who is praised in contrast to the people and their "wise ones," as well as in contrast to idols and the peoples, 1 Sam 2 differentiates between the righteous (pious) ones and those who do wrong. That they rely on their own strength (v. 9) and boast about themselves (v. 10) applies only to the wicked. They are contrasted with the ideal of the pious, who "do righteousness and justice."[55] Therefore, it makes complete sense to insert the plus after v. 10a and before v. 10b, and not after v. 9b, because it does not apply to all the people but only to God's enemies.[56]

5. Reconstruction of the Literary and Textual History

To summarize the external evidence for the Song of Hannah, we have an earlier psalm that entered the narrative context of the story of Sam-

---

53. DJD 17, 37: "Presumably we are dealing with an anonymous piece of floating tradition. Its prosodic pattern differs from that of the body of Hannah's Song and, as well, from the surrounding material in Jeremiah 9."

54. See also the question of comparability in 1 Sam 2:2/Jer 10:6–7; כה in 1 Sam 2:9/Jer 1:12; תחת in 1 Sam 2:10/Jer 8:9; 10:2.

55. Tov ("Different Editions," 450 n. 49) refers to Isaac Seligmann (*Studies in Biblical Literature*, ed. A. Hurvitz et al. [Jerusalem: Magnes, 1992], 325–26), who believes that the version of 1 Sam 2 is original and that the Hebrew reading of Jer 9 is derived from it and secondary. When we consider the saying in the two versions as such, this makes sense. In my opinion, however, the context speaks more in favor of the direction of tradition as suggested above.

56. Tov finds the placement "inappropriate" and because of this considers a marginal note, which had been integrated incorrectly ("Different Editions," 199, 452). This is of course a possibility and cannot be excluded with absolute certainty.

uel in 1 Sam 2 secondarily and was enhanced by textual supplementation either beforehand, in the process, or—which is more likely—after its incorporation.

The basic text begins with a supplicant's call to praise God and the triumph over enemies and rescue (v. 1). The following praise comprises three sections, where the first and third sections form a frame around the middle, second section: (1) the juxtaposition of the incomparable God and the proud enemies (vv. 2–3); (2) a hymn to the God who humiliates the strong and brings honor to the weak (vv. 4–8a); (3) the conclusion, which makes reference to the supplicant's call to praise and the first section and juxtaposes God's dealings with his enemies and the ends of the earth, on the one hand, and with his king and anointed, on the other (vv. 9b, 10).

From the conclusion in v. 10 the text reveals itself to be a psalm about or maybe even of a king *(Königspsalm)*: it extols the victory of the Lord (Yhwh) over the supplicant's enemies and ends in an intercession for Yhwh's king and anointed one, who might be identical with the supplicant.[57] Comparing v. 1b with v. 10, it is clear that the supplicant's (king's) enemies are also God's enemies, although it is not clear in v. 10 whether it concerns the opponents of the aforementioned human being (the "man" in v. 9b) or the opponents of Yhwh.[58] This ambiguity was probably the reason for the additions, which underline the superiority, uniqueness, and holiness of God, on the one hand (vv. 2, 8b, 10), and, on the other hand, make a distinction between the pious and the wicked (vv. 9a, 10). A further plus appears to have emphasized the idea of retribution for the enemies' injustice (v. $10a^2$ in 4Q51). In light of these additions, any statements about the power of God and the salvation of the supplicant, or about the intervention of God for the weak, refer to the righteous and pious, and all statements about the enemies of the supplicant and of Yhwh refer to the wicked. The supplicant thus becomes a prayer leader for the righteous and pious ones.

The additions follow two complementary trends: they universalize and theologize the psalm. The additions identify the judge (v. 10) with the creator of the world (v. 8b); furthermore, they refer the conflict of the supplicant (maybe the king) with his enemies in vv. 1–3, 10 and the com-

---

57. If the supplicant (speaking in the first person singular) is the king, in v. 10 he speaks about himself or the intercession is spoken by someone else as a kind of response; cf. Ps 18:30–50, 51. The complex composition history of Ps 18 consisting of at least three different layers (vv. 4–20, thanksgiving hymn of an individual including a depiction of Yhwh's theophany; vv. 33–51, thanksgiving hymn of a king; vv. 21–32, theological reflections connecting the two thanksgiving hymns) is in many respects similar to the compositon of the Song of Hannah.

58. See Aejmelaeus, "Hannah's Psalm," 25.

plementary opposites, which in vv. 4–8a describe the sovereign acts of God, to the confrontation of two theologically qualified, clearly defined parties, the righteous and the wicked. In v. 9 a further intention was to align the psalm with the narrative context in which it entered secondarily. This has led to certain changes at the edges as well as in the narrative itself (1 Sam 1:28/2:1, 11).

Finally, the external evidence also suggests a further assumption, with which we leave the empirical level and turn to the field of internal indications for textual supplementation. As has already been mentioned several times, it is striking that the text-critical problems and the additions cluster in the framing passages in vv. 1–3, 8b–10, where the text varies greatly. In contrast, the central passage in vv. 4–8a is relatively stable. If we disregard the additions indicated by the external evidence and more closely consider the basic text that remains, it becomes clear that vv. 1–3 and 9b–10 also differ in formal and conceptual aspects from the body of the psalm in vv. 4–8a. While vv. 4–8a make general statements about God's actions to man, such as reversing the usual conditions, humiliating the strong and honoring the weak, killing and restoring life, and so on, the framing verses concern the fate of an individual—the king and anointed—and his enemies.

For this reason, I tend to believe that the basic text reconstructed so far on the basis of the external evidence also has a literary history that reaches further back. I see the core in God's statements in vv. 4–8a, an earlier piece of tradition that was related to the king and his enemies secondarily in vv. 1–3 and 9b–10. The starting point was probably the context in vv. 4 and 8b, which use political images that, in the earlier part of the psalm, are examples of the reversal of conditions and, in the framing passages, were related to the king and the actual political domain.

Whether the interpretation and supplementation of the traditional passage were made before or during the insertion into the narrative context of 1 Samuel is hard to say. I suspect the former, since the theme of the king does not fit that well into the context. A later chapter in Samuel–Kings would have been more suitable for this theme. But we cannot of course exclude the other alternative since Hannah, when all is said and done, does give birth to Samuel, the kingmaker. But I suspect that the evidence for the insertion of the psalm in the context was more likely to have been the statement in v. 5b, which best describes Hannah: עקרה ילדה (עד־) שבעה.

To conclude this section, I reproduce the different literary layers of the psalm according to the internal and external evidence in a relative chronological order (from the right to left):

46   *Psalms and Lyrical Literature*

External evidence   Internal Evidence

1:28b/2:1 ... וישתחו שם ליהוה ותתפלל חנה ותאמר
[ותעזב]הו שם ותשתח[ו] ליהוה ותאמר ...

1a עלץ לבי ביהוה רמה קרני ביהוה (/באלהי)
1b רחב פי על־אויבי (כי) שמחתי בישועת(ך)
2 (כי) אין־קדוש כיהוה ... ואין צור כאלהינו
[4Q51 + ?] כי אין (קדוש) בלתך
3a אל־תרבו תדברו גבהה גבהה (אל־) יצא עתק מפיכם
3b כי אל דעות (/דעת) יהוה ולא [ולו] נתכנו עללות (ואל תוכן עללותיו)
4 קשת גברים חתים (/חתה) ונכשלים אזרו חיל
5a שבעים בלחם נשכרו ורעבים חדלו (עד)
5b (עד־) עקרה ילדה שבעה ורבת בנים אמללה
6 יהוה ממית ומחיה מוריד שאול ויעל
7 יהוה מוריש ומעשיר משפיל אף־מרומם
8a מקים מעפר דל מאשפת ירים אביון
להושיב עם־נדיבים וכסא כבוד ינחלם
8b כי ליהוה מצקי ארץ וישת עליהם תבל
9a רגלי (/ודרך) חסידו [חסידיו] ישמר ורשעים
בחשך ידמו
נתן נד[ר ל](נוד]ר ויברך ש[נות צדיק ...

9b כי־לא בכח יגבר־איש
10a יהוה יחתו (/יחת) מריבו [מריביו]
a¹ מי ק[דוש כיהוה --]
a² [--]תם בשלמ[◦ -- אל יתהלל חכם]
a³ [בחכמתו]ואל ית[ה]ל[ל הגבור
בגבורתו ואל יתהלל עשיר]
a⁴ [בעשרו כי בזאת יתהלל המתהלל השכל]
וידע את יהוה
a⁵ [ולעשו]ת מש[פט וצדקה בתוך הארץ]

עלו [עליו] בשמים ירעם
10ayb יהוה ידין אפסי־ארץ ויתן־עז למלכו וירם קרן משיחו
[יהוה עלה בשמים] וירעם הוא/יהוה ידין ...

2:11 וילך אלקנה הרמתה על־ביתו ...
Καὶ κατέλιπον αὐτὸν ἐκεῖ ἐνώπιον κυρίου καὶ ἀπῆλθον εἰς Αρμαθαιμ ...

6. External and Internal Evidence

In this last section, I would like to address the question of what we learn from the external evidence for identifying textual supplementations in texts for which we have no or very little empirical evidence and must therefore depend entirely on internal evidence. A kind of test question here could be whether, in the Song of Hannah, we could come to the same conclusion without external evidence that we reached with our comparison of the versions.

The example of the Song of Hannah has taught us that we need to distinguish different types of changes in a text: orthographic variations, scribal errors, textual variants, pluses or minuses. Orthographic variations and scribal errors can be detected and identified without external evidence. For the textual variants we need the external evidence. Without this evidence we would have missed these changes. Yet at each step we must expect all these phenomena in any text right from the beginning. Examples of textual supplementation can also be found in the scribal errors and variations, albeit to a limited extent. Without external evidence we would only notice it when, as in 1 Sam 1:28 or 2:5, it has led to a disruption of the text or a recognizable error and we have the revised text before us. If, however, as in the case v. 10 (עלה ... וירעם and עלו [עליו] ... ירעם), the transitions of textual supplementation have been adjusted, we would probably not notice the variant or amendment. However, a trained eye would not miss the insertion itself, which is recognizable by the *Wiederaufnahme* of the subject.

The clearest traces of textual supplementation are undoubtedly the pluses and minuses in a text, for which there is empirical evidence. But even this evidence is far from clear. In each case, we must consider whether we are dealing with a loss of text or an extension. For (mechanical or deliberate) text loss in the Song of Hannah—contrary to the usual explanation in DJD 17 and McCarter's commentary—no sufficient evidence has been found. But this does not mean that this phenomenon did not occur. Text loss by homoioteleuton and the like, or by a deliberate omission, is documented in manuscripts and parallel versions (rewritings). But text loss must be clearly recognizable and must be able to be accounted for as such. Where this is not the case, we need to think of textual supplementation as being more likely.

Textual supplementation is indicated in particular when without the plus the text ends join each other smoothly or when the plus interrupts or disturbs the flow of a text, its syntax, or its train of thought. This is the case with our example in vv. 2 (כי אין בלתך), 8b, 9, and 10. If we only had the amended text and not a text without the plus, we would certainly have been able to find stylistic, poetic, narratological, or theological reasons for the originality of the interruption or disturbance of the text flow. The external evidence, however, proves that such interruptions or disturbances can just as well be based on text growth. An experienced and astute literary critic would have identified the text components in question as a plus even without the empirical evidence. Moreover, he or she would also have separated vv. 1–3 and 9–10 from the core of the psalm in vv. 4–8a.

Theoretically, mechanical text loss can also indicate textual supplementation, namely, when the plus has been inserted by the technique of *Wiederaufnahme* and has led to an *aberratio oculi* with the next scribe. Such a case would be conceivable for v. 10, if the short text in the MT offered the wording of the LXX and 4Q51: יהוה יחת מריבו יהוה עלה בשמים וירעם הוא/ יהוה ידין. Text loss, even if it can be detected by external evidence, does not automatically lead us to the original text, but only to the text that preceded the scribal error. There is no definite proof of which option, text loss or growth, applies, not even in cases where we know several versions. Like internal evidence, external evidence is ambiguous and needs interpretation. The generally accepted rule of textual and literary criticism applies here, namely, that preference should be given to the explanation that is the simplest and can most easily be accounted for.

External evidence is also revealing with regard to the quantity of possible layers. In the Song of Hannah, pluses and minuses have led us to at least three literary layers: the basic text, a series of supplementations, and the narrative context. Indeed, there are many more layers if we take into account the scribal errors and variants as well as the differentiation of the supplementations, which, as the evidence in 1 Sam 2:9 shows, do not all lie on one level. Furthermore, there are indications in the external evidence of a further differentiation in the basic text according to internal criteria. The current trend in scholarship to distinguish no more than two or three literary layers in a text thus proves to be false and inappropriate given the complexity of the texts. The extent to which we can determine all the layers is debatable. But the external evidence teaches us that we must assume more rather than fewer layers, even if—with or without external evidence—we miss many in the analysis.

Finally, this example has taught us that, with the manifold changes in the tradition, we are dealing with very different tendencies. We must not expect that textual supplementation always pursues special conceptual or theological interests. Often the scribes were simply concerned to deliver the best or most complete text, which is why they included variants or pluses from other manuscripts in their copy. The manuscript 4Q51 is a good example. Frequently encountered motives for changes are the clarification of the content, the emphasis of statements, and the smoothing or conciliation of contradictions. Occasionally, however, we also find that in textual supplementations importance is given to weighty substantive concerns of the scribe, as shown by the theologizing tendency of the additions in the Song of Hannah. Typical of textual supplementations are universalistic statements about God and the distinction between the pious and the wicked, which theologically and sociologically reinterpret the conflict of the supplicant with his enemies. Another pattern that we observe frequently is that supplementation is provoked by certain statements in a text and points them in a new direction or updates or deepens them.

For literary criticism, this means that differences in tendency should be taken very seriously as evidence of possible textual supplementation, even if there is no interruption or disturbance of the text. Furthermore, in view of the external evidence, we will also pay attention in the internal analysis to less spectacular phenomena, such as clarifications, repetition, harmonization or ulterior motives and must consider these as evidence of textual growth. Even if they do not disturb the text and in the opinion of some exegetes belong to the poetics or narratology style of ancient Hebrew literature, external evidence proves that such phenomena are often the result of textual supplementation. In order to contest disagreeable analyses and hold on to the originality of complex text structures, general methodological or stylistic arguments are not enough.

To demonstrate what an internal analysis of the Psalms looks like, based on the criteria of external evidence, I would like to touch on a few psalms dealt with in detail elsewhere.[59]

Psalm 29: (I) The voice of the weather god, Yhwh over the waters, in the woods, in the desert (vv. 3–9a); (II) Yhwh and the heavenly council (vv. 1–2, 3b, 9b); (III) The people of God (vv. 10–11); (IV) Superscription (v. 1).

Psalm 93: (I) Yhwh-Yam (vv. 3–4); (II) Yhwh-Malak (vv. 1, 5b); (III) Confession and Torah piety (vv. 2, 5a; cf. Ps 19:8; 90:2).

Psalm 97: (I) Theophany of the weather god (vv. 2, 3–5) and Yhwh's enthronement (vv. 1, 2b, 6a, 7b, 9); (II) Peoples and Zion (vv. 6b, 8); (III) Polemic against idolatry (v. 8); (IV) The righteous and the wicked (vv. 10–12).

Psalm 104: (I) Weather god (vv. 1a, 2b, 3–4, 10a, 13a, 14b, 15, 32–33); (II) Sun god (vv. 1b, 2a, 10b–12, 13b, 14a, 20–24a, 24c, 25a, 26a, 27-29a, 30–31, 34); (III) Creator god (vv. 5–9, 16–19, 24b, 25b, 26b, 29b); (IV) Sinners and wicked (v. 35).

Psalm 118: (I) Todah formula (vv. 14, 17–19, 21, 28) and expansions (vv. 15–16); (II) Collective festival hymn (vv. 1–4, 22–27, 29); (III) Trust in God and the righteous ones (vv. 6–13, 15b, 20).

For these examples, too, external evidence is available, albeit it is of a very different kind. The evidence is the religious historical analogies from Syria and Palestine, Mesopotamia and Egypt. These analogies represent the standards on which the literary-critical analysis of the Psalms must

---

59. See Reinhard G. Kratz, "Gottesräume: Ein Beitrag zur Frage des biblischen Weltbildes," in *Mythos und Geschichte*, 125–40; and, in the same volume, "Der Mythos vom Königtum Gottes in Kanaan und Israel," 141–55; and "Reste hebräischen Heidentums am Beispiel der Psalmen," 156–89.

be measured. The stages of Israelite-Judean religious history can be read in the Psalms in the interaction of religio-historical comparison and literary-critical analysis.[60]

In the oldest stratum of these texts, Yhwh appears in the role of the weather god Baal. Gradually the weather god assumes the traits of the king of the gods, El, the Egyptian sun god, and the Mesopotamian god of creation. Further textual supplementations give the psalms a typical biblical veneer. The dominant tendencies are the same in many respects as what we saw in the Song of Hannah. They can be summarized under the key words of *universalization, nationalization,* and *individualization* (or *theologization*) and include issues such as the rule over all nations, monotheism and polemics against idolatry, the relationship of Yhwh to his people (Israel, Zion), the distinction between the righteous and the wicked in God's people, and Torah piety. The literary technique of textual supplementation is the same as what we witness in the Song of Hannah, and the internal analysis of the Psalms evidences nothing that has not also been encountered in the external evidence.

---

60. See Hermann Spieckermann, *Heilsgegenwart: Eine Theologie der Psalmen*, FRLANT 148 (Göttingen: Vandenhoeck & Ruprecht, 1989); followed and developed by Kratz (see n. 59) and Reinhard Müller, *Jahwe als Wettergott: Studien zur althebräischen Kultlyrik anhand ausgewählter Psalmen*, BZAW 387 (Berlin: de Gruyter, 2008).

II

Narrative Texts of the Pentateuch

Genre Conventions and Their Implications for Composition History: A Case for Supplementation in Exodus 16

ANGELA ROSKOP ERISMAN
Hebrew Union College–Jewish Institute of Religion

Manuscript evidence contributes richly to discussions of composition history because it allows us to see where and how a text was changed from one version to the next. Marc Brettler's contribution to this volume highlights different types of change one can observe when comparing extant versions of Ps 145. He situates the changes along a continuum: those that correct impossible or unlikely readings, those that differentiate one possible reading from another, those that harmonize one part of a text with another, and those that transform a text.[1] This continuum gives us a sense of what types of change were possible, if not typical, and constitutes a guide for discussing composition history where we lack manuscript evidence. I choose the word "guide" carefully, because it would be a mistake to limit the possible types to those for which there is manuscript evidence. Examples that are consistent with the spirit of documented cases can, on the contrary, enrich the continuum.

The problem is how to ground strong arguments for composition history where we lack manuscript evidence. Arguments based on internal criteria have necessarily dominated modern critical study of the Pentateuch. Yet the warrants for dividing a text into sources or layers are often arbitrary, hidden behind expressions such as "smooth" (*What constitutes a smooth text?*) and "awkward" (*What makes it awkward?*), and one person's sign of composition history is often another person's literary device. Even where there is general consensus on where the fractures are in a text, as is the case for the manna–quail story in Exod 16, there is often disagreement about which model—documentary or supplementary—best explains them. Brettler offers hope when he points out that manuscript evidence

---

1. See Brettler, "Supplementation in Psalms," 13–19.

sometimes demonstrates textual development where we would have been able to detect it even without. We can strengthen arguments based on internal criteria by being less eager to prove a particular model and more focused on interpreting the text based on "expectations that emerge from the literature itself."[2] When we do, we may find ourselves looking at the text differently than before.

Genre should factor significantly in our discussions of composition history where we lack manuscript evidence. Once we recognize that a text uses a particular genre, our expectations are no longer arbitrary but are shaped by the conventions of that genre to the extent we know them. Where the text fulfills those expectations, we naturally see coherence; where it breaks them without purpose, we have good reason to suspect a fracture.[3] The itinerary genre certainly comes into play in a study of Exod 16, because the manna–quail narrative is framed by itinerary notices, and I will come back to this. My immediate concern is the complaint genre, since it shapes the bulk of the episode. Complaint episodes have a typical plot structure whose elements tend to occur in the same order: (a) a situation prompts complaint, (b) the Israelites complain, (c) Moses responds, (d) Yhwh responds, (e) Moses carries out some action that involves a miracle, and the episode concludes with (f) an etiology.[4] Looking at how Exod 16 uses genre will lead us to reevaluate where the fractures occur and understand its composition history anew.

When the Israelites arrive in the wilderness of Sin, they express a wish to have died in Egypt, where at least they would not have died hungry, and they accuse Moses and Aaron of bringing them out into the wilderness to starve them to death (Exod 16:2–3, elements [a] and [b] of the complaint genre). In response, Yhwh tells Moses that he is about to "rain down bread from heaven," instructs him what the Israelites are supposed to do with it, and identifies the situation as a test of obedience to תורתי, "my *tôrâ*" (Exod 16:4–5, element [d]). Two things have long struck commentators as problematic about vv. 4–5. First, they are not the response from Moses that our knowledge of the typical plot structure of complaint episodes leads us to expect (element [c]); that response comes only in vv. 6–9. Second, Yhwh responds again in vv. 11–12, this time in the expected place, following

---

2. David H. Aaron, *Etched in Stone: The Emergence of the Decalogue* (New York: T&T Clark, 2006), 191.

3. See Angela R. Roskop, *The Wilderness Itineraries: Genre, Geography, and the Growth of Torah*, HACL 3 (Winona Lake, IN: Eisenbrauns, 2011) for a discussion of how genre awareness is formed (ch. 2) and how our ability to recognize genre patterns influences how the itinerary notices in Exodus and Numbers might be read, with implications for composition history (chs. 3 and 5–6).

4. Aaron, *Etched in Stone*, 193; George W. Coats, *Rebellion in the Wilderness: The Murmuring Motif in the Wilderness Traditions of the Old Testament* (Nashville: Abingdon, 1968).

Moses's response.⁵ For these two reasons, there is general consensus that vv. 4–5 belong to a different source or layer than the surrounding verses.⁶ Problems such as these are typically identified as "contradictions,"⁷ but they are better characterized as violations of genre conventions. It matters what we call them. A contradiction is a problem we usually try to solve by applying one or another model of composition history. A violation of genre conventions generates a complex array of questions whose answers may not fit neatly in a particular model and may vary from one case to another: Is it deliberate? If it is, what literary or ideological purpose does it serve? If it is not, does it point to flawed composition, or is it a sign of editorial work? And if it is a sign of editorial work, what kind of editorial work is it: the patching together of independent sources by a compiler, wholesale revision, or glossing?

To assess the second problem—the fact that Yhwh responds twice—it helps to note some important differences between the two speeches. The heart of the second speech (vv. 11–12) is a message that Moses is to relate to the Israelites. It addresses them directly, in second person plural, and it responds to their complaint in v. 3 point by point:

Exod 16:3
בשבתנו על סיר הבשר
באכלנו לחם לשבע

Exod 16:12
בין הערבים תאכלו בשר
ובבקר תשבעו לחם

Their wish for בשר and לחם is picked up in the order they articulated it, like the dialogue technique of echoing someone's speech to show that you have been listening. The speech is otherwise concerned with establishing the authority of Moses to speak on behalf of Yhwh. It begins with a message just to Moses—שמעתי את תלונת בני ישראל—that echoes what Moses already told the Israelites in v. 9 and constitutes encouragement to him that he spoke correctly. Its position in the story is also significant:

---

5. E.g., Benno Jacob, *The Second Book of the Bible: Exodus*, trans. Walter Jacob (Hoboken, NJ: Ktav, 1992), 441; George W. Coats, *Exodus 1–18*, FOTL 2A (Grand Rapids: Eerdmans, 1999), 130; William H. C. Propp, *Exodus 1–18: A New Translation with Introduction and Commentary*, AB 2 (New York: Doubleday, 1999), 589.

6. For a sample documentary analysis, see Joel S. Baden, "The Original Place of the Priestly Manna Story in Exodus 16," *ZAW* 122 (2010): 491–504, here 492. For supplementary analyses, see Thomas B. Dozeman, *Exodus*, ECC (Grand Rapids: Eerdmans, 2009), 363, 374, 381–83; William Johnstone, *Chronicles and Exodus: An Analogy and Its Application*, JSOTSup 275 (Sheffield: Sheffield Academic, 1998), 250–51; Eberhard Ruprecht, "Stellung und Bedeutung der Erzählung vom Mannawunder (Ex 16) im Aufbau der Priesterschrift," *ZAW* 86 (1974): 257–307, here 279, 301–2; John Van Seters, *The Life of Moses: The Yahwist as Historian in Exodus–Numbers* (Louisville: Westminster John Knox, 1994), 186; Jan A. Wagenaar, "The Cessation of Manna: Editorial Frames for the Wilderness Wandering in Exodus 16,35 and Joshua 5,10–12," *ZAW* 112 (2000): 192–209, here 196–98.

7. Baden, "Original Place," 492.

It comes after the *kābôd* appears, so the Israelites witness it[8] and consequently have reason to trust what Moses later claims that Yhwh said. Yhwh's first speech (vv. 4–5), by contrast, comes before the appearance of the *kābôd*, talks about the Israelites in the third person, and is directed *only at Moses*. The divine speeches in vv. 4–5 and 11–12 are thus not alternatives (a "doublet") but complements, each of which functions differently in the story. Verses 11–12 reassure the Israelites that Yhwh heard them and will respond as well as establish Moses's authority to relate divine speech, while vv. 4–5 convey knowledge of what is about to unfold to which only Moses is privy. The presence of two divine speeches appears to be a purposeful violation of genre conventions.

This becomes even clearer when we understand the specific function of the first Yhwh speech in vv. 4–5, for which we must go beyond the complaint in our study of genre. Michael Fishbane wondered in passing whether Exod 16 might constitute a "possible instance" of ad hoc legal exegesis.[9] Simeon Chavel prefers to call this genre the *oracular novella* because this better accounts for the integration of legal and narrative features; he, too, notes that Exod 16 "probably constitutes one of the most integrated of Priestly episodes in terms of law and narrative," yet he does not follow up on Fishbane's suggestion.[10] The oracular novella involves framing a new legal ruling in a brief narrative fitted within the story line of the Pentateuch. The four well-known cases have a typical set of formal elements: (i) someone brings a problem to Moses; (ii) Yhwh is consulted to clarify the law; (iii) Yhwh gives a decision to Moses; and (iv) the new law is enacted. Each case involves an old law transformed into a new one that goes beyond what the immediate situation warrants and is presented as having the same authority as the old.[11] Exodus 16 diverges from the oracular novella genre enough to say that it is not a typical instance. But a text can be shaped by more than one genre, and this narrative does have enough marks of the oracular novella to suggest its influence alongside the complaint genre.

The problem (element [i]) to which Moses responds in Exod 16 is not the complaint itself but is generated by the arrival of meat and bread in vv. 13–14. While the quail clearly constitutes meat, the Israelites are naturally puzzled about how the stuff that looks like a layer of dew constitutes bread. The discrepancy prompts them to ask מן הוא, "What is it?" (v. 15). Moses helps

---

8. S. R. Driver, *The Book of Exodus in the Revised Version*, CBSC (Cambridge: Cambridge University Press, 1918), 178.
9. Michael Fishbane, *Biblical Interpretation in Ancient Israel* (Oxford: Clarendon, 1988), 106 n. 52, 133 n. 74.
10. Simeon Chavel, *Oracular Law and Priestly Historiography in the Torah*, FAT 2/71 (Tübingen: Mohr Siebeck, 2014), 19–20.
11. Fishbane, *Biblical Interpretation*, 102–4.

them make the connection, which any of them could have done based on the divine speech in vv. 11–12: because it came in the morning, it must be the promised bread. But he goes on to explain what they are to do with it, knowledge only he has, based on what Yhwh told him in vv. 4–5. Moses's instructions are prefaced by an introduction that identifies them as Yhwh's words—זה הדבר אשר צוה יהוה—but what follows in v. 16 is not a report of what Yhwh said.[12] It is an *elucidation*, particularly of the expression דבר יום ביומו (v. 4). First Moses adds ממנו to לקטו from v. 4: "gather *some of it*." In other words, דבר יום ביומו means not everything that is there. But how much is "some"? Moses gives three different answers to this question: איש לפי אכלו, עמר לגלגלת מספר נפשתיכם, and איש לאשר באהלו. The expression איש לפי אכלו occurs elsewhere only in the instructions for Passover (Exod 12:4), where preparation is done by household, and determining how much lamb each household needs means making sure there is enough for each person in the household. איש לאשר באהלו parallels the concern for the household as the unit of preparation (שה לבית, Exod 12:3), and מספר נפשתיכם parallels במכסת נפשת in Exod 12:4. The difference is that an exact measurement is given here in Exod 16:16: עמר לגלגלת. Moses is interpreting Yhwh's instruction in vv. 4–5 so it might be effectively applied, and his extended instructions carry the weight of the initial instruction from Yhwh by being framed as though they were part of it.

Moses continues to teach and interpret as the episode unfolds. In one case, he jumps in without prompting. After the Israelites gather and find that they indeed have איש לאשר באהלו, an *omer* apiece (vv. 17–18), Moses instructs them, אל יותר ממנו עד בקר (v. 19). This, too, is an elucidation of דבר יום ביומו rather than a report of Yhwh's speech. While the elucidation in v. 16 relates to how much food, this one relates to how the food should be managed: an implication of דבר יום ביומו is that one does not leave any until the next day. Then the Israelites come to Moses with another problem (element [i] of the oracular novella genre): on the sixth day, they find they have two *omers* of food and go to Moses with this new puzzling phenomenon (v. 22), just as they did with the puzzling dewy substance (v. 15). Because they were not privy to Yhwh's speech in vv. 4–5, they have no reason to think that the sixth day would be any different than the preceding five. Moses explains why they have double—שבתון שבת קדש ליהוה מחר—and tells them what to do with the surplus: preserve what you have gathered and save it as "a sacred obligation until morning" (v. 23). This teaching is extrapolated from Yhwh's statement in v. 5 that the Israelites will find double on the sixth day, yet it is introduced as הוא אשר דבר יהוה. What counts as תורתי, "my [Yhwh's] *tôrâ*" (v. 4) in this episode is not just the original instruction itself but also Moses's interpretation

---

12. See Lev 24:13; Num 9:9; 15:35; and 27:6 for similar formulae in the oracular novellae.

and extension of it. Oracular novellae often frame the new law and its extension not only with ויאמר יהוה אל משה לאמר or equivalent on the front end, but also with כאשר צוה יהוה את משה or equivalent on the back end (e.g., Num 27:6, 11). Notably, when Exod 16:24 narrates the execution of Moses's instruction, it states that the Israelites act not כאשר דבר יהוה but כאשר צוה משה, betraying the claim of equivalence between Moses's instruction and divine *tôrâ* itself.

A number of commentators have recognized that Moses's instructions throughout the episode are linked to Yhwh's instruction in vv. 4–5.[13] But the implications for composition history are often missed because a particular model of composition history is assumed. George W. Coats, for example, acknowledges that Moses's instruction in v. 23 is linked with Yhwh's instruction in vv. 4–5 and is interpretive in character, but he states that v. 23, which is P, "presupposes [a P] introduction similar to vss. 4–5," which would have been replaced with vv. 4–5, which are J, when the sources were combined.[14] The simpler interpretation—which does not require one to presume missing text—is that Yhwh's instruction in vv. 4–5 is part of the same composition as Moses's interpretations in vv. 16, 19, and 23.[15]

Recognizing the blend of oracular novella and complaint genres in this episode helps us understand why the narrative is structured this way: to characterize Moses as an authoritative priestly teacher and interpreter of *tôrâ*. A number of biblical texts indicate that priests were responsible for *tôrâ*, but Ezek 44:23–24 is perhaps most instructive: the duties outlined there involve ritual instruction, which is what Moses offers in Exod 16:16; it refers to תורתי and חקתי, similar to מצותי ותורתי in Exod 16:28; and it is concerned with the priest's responsibility to maintain the sanctity of the Sabbath(s), the cause to which all of Moses's teaching in Exod 16 is dedicated. Violations of what is typical of both genres in Exod 16 can be understood in this light. First, the author delayed Moses's response to the Israelites' complaint in order to make room for Yhwh to give his instruction before anything else happens. Second, although oracular novellae are fictionalized, they presumably involve real legal questions, or at least legal questions the scribes sought to resolve in theory; מן הוא is not a legal question at all but a prompt for Moses to teach the *tôrâ* Yhwh gave him. Finally, the scribe did not have Moses consult Yhwh for a new law, as one expects of an oracular novella, because he needed to put the legal innovation in the

---

13. E.g., Van Seters, *Life of Moses*, 184; Jacob, *Second Book*, 444–45; Umberto Cassuto, *A Commentary on the Book of Exodus*, trans. Israel Abrahams (Jerusalem: Magnes, 1967), 196–98; Coats, *Rebellion in the Wilderness*, 86–87; Chavel, *Oracular Law*, 19–20.

14. Coats, *Rebellion in the Wilderness*, 87; George W. Coats, *Moses: Heroic Man, Man of God*, JSOTSup 57 (Sheffield: JSOT Press, 1988), 119.

15. W. A. M. Beuken, "Exodus 16:5, 23: A Rule Regarding the Keeping of the Sabbath," *JSOT* 32 (1985): 3–14.

mouth of Moses, who in this story embodies the office of the priest, and to give the new teaching the authority of the existing *tôrâ* by ascribing it to Yhwh. These violations of genre convention in Exod 16:4–5 do not constitute fractures, or places where coherence breaks down and we detect signs of editorial activity; rather, they are the purposeful result of an effort to blend two genres in the service of a priestly literary goal.

The Israelites do not listen to Moses's instruction to avoid saving any food for the next day (v. 19), and their leftovers go rancid (v. 20). Moses then gives another instruction they fail to obey: do not go out to gather on the seventh day, because you will not find anything (vv. 25–26). This second failure prompts Yhwh to enter the scene with עד אנה מאנתם לשמר מצותי ותורתי (v. 28). As is the case for vv. 4–5, there is general consensus that v. 28 and some degree of surrounding material should be assigned to a source or compositional layer other than P. A significant issue contributing to this consensus is the third masculine singular pronoun on שמו in v. 31 (ויקראו בית ישראל את שמו מן), which is clearly meant to refer to the bread, or manna, not to the immediate referent in v. 30, יום השבעי. If v. 31 followed v. 25 (or 26), with its third masculine singular pronouns that refer to the manna, there would be no ambiguity about the referent of שמו.[16]

One of the most compelling reasons to see v. 28—and v. 4, where the test is introduced—as non-Priestly is the apparent Deuteronomistic character of the test, particularly the expressions מצותי ותורתי here in v. 28 and תורתי in v. 4. Whether they are understood as Deuteronomistic glosses on J, elements of a relatively late Yahwistic composition dependent on D, a pre-Priestly D composition, or a post-Priestly Deuteronomistic supplement, the two verses are linked to the same non-priestly fate.[17] But Deuteronomistic literature does not have a monopoly on *tôrâ*. It is common in priestly contexts as well: the instructions for various kinds of ritual in the Pentateuch are introduced with זאת תורת, while the instructions for

---

16. This is noted in both documentary and supplementary analyses. See, e.g., Baden, "Original Place," 492–93; Ludwig Schmidt, "Die Priesterschrift in Exodus 16," ZAW 119 (2007): 483–98, here 493; A. H. McNeile, *The Book of Exodus with Introduction and Notes*, WC (London: Methuen, 1908), xxii–xxiii.

17. For J, see, e.g., Driver, *Book of Exodus*, 144. For Deuteronomistic glosses on J, see, e.g., Martin Noth, *Exodus: A Commentary*, OTL (Philadelphia: Westminster, 1962), 130, 132, 136; Coats, *Rebellion in the Wilderness*, 83, 86–87; Coats, *Exodus 1–18*, 128. For elements of a relatively late Yahwistic composition dependent on D, see Van Seters, *Life of Moses*. For a pre-Priestly D composition, see Johnstone, *Chronicles and Exodus*. And for a post-Priestly Deuteronomistic supplement, see Ruprecht, "Stellung und Bedeutung," 273–74; Frank Crüsemann, *The Torah: Theology and Social History of Old Testament Law*, trans. Allan W. Mahnke (Edinburgh: T&T Clark, 1996), 299–300; Thomas C. Römer, "Israel's Sojourn in the Wilderness and the Construction of the Book of Numbers," in *Reflection and Refraction: Studies in Biblical Historiography in Honour of A Graeme Auld*, ed. Robert Rezetko, Timothy H. Lim, and W. Brian Aucker, VTSup 113 (Leiden: Brill, 2007), 419–33 (here 432–33); and Schmidt, "Die Priesterschrift," 493.

the temple in Ezek 43:11–12; 44:5 are also framed as חקים and תורות and the whole is referred to as זאת תורת הבית.[18] And we have now seen the critical role *tôrâ* plays in vv. 4–5 in the unfolding of a story with decidedly priestly goals. As David Frankel has already argued, the test in vv. 4 and 28 is priestly in character.[19]

Assigning v. 28 to a non-priestly source or compositional layer is also problematic in terms of plot and thematic development. First, עד אנה מאנתם לשמר מצותי ותורתי in v. 28 makes sense only in the wake of *repeated* failure. Verses 26–27, often understood as non-priestly (with v. 28) contain one failure, but the first is in vv. 19–20, often understood as Priestly. Yet the two failures together build up to עד אנה מאנתם לשמר מצותי ותורתי in v. 28 in a coherent plot development that should not be broken up. Second, עד אנה מאנתם לשמר מצותי ותורתי in v. 28 gives rise in v. 29 to the final extension of the initial divine instruction in vv. 4–5 that not only prohibits work on the seventh day but commands that people stay home, thus protecting the law and ensuring Sabbath observance, the legal innovation to which Moses's teaching has been building throughout the narrative. It is difficult to tell whether the text of v. 29 is spoken by Moses or Yhwh. Yhwh is clearly speaking in v. 28, but v. 29 shifts to speak about Yhwh in the third person. This sometimes happens in divine speeches,[20] but it also raises the possibility that the text has shifted to Moses as the speaker *deliberately without marking the shift*, a possibility that is consistent with the growing sense of identity between what Yhwh says and what Moses teaches as the episode has progressed.

The referent of the pronoun on שמו in v. 31 *is* a grammatical error, and this should not be overlooked. Taken in the context of these other concerns, however, it cannot bear the weight of an argument for dividing the text into sources or compositional layers. This grammatical misstep may be better understood as a flawed aspect of an otherwise largely coherent

---

18. David Frankel, *The Murmuring Stories of the Priestly School: A Retrieval of Ancient Sacerdotal Lore*, VTSup 89 (Leiden: Brill, 2002), 28. For ritual instructions introduced with זאת תורת, see Lev 6:2, 7, 18; 7:1, 7, 11; 11:46; 12:7; 13:59; 14:2, 32, 54, 57; 15:32; Num 5:29–30; 6:13, 31; 19:14, 21; 31:21. One wishes to be very careful here, because many occurrences of the expression הלך בתורת יהוה (as in Exod 16:4) occur in Deuteronomistic and post-Deuteronomistic contexts (see Moshe Weinfeld, *Deuteronomy and the Deuteronomic School* [Oxford: Clarendon, 1972; repr., Winona Lake, IN: Eisenbrauns, 1992], 334), and Norbert Lohfink understandably views Exod 16:4, 28 as most closely related to Ps 78, supporting the case for viewing these verses as post-Priestly Deuteronomistic supplements (*Theology of the Pentateuch: Themes of the Priestly Narrative and Deuteronomy*, trans. Linda M. Maloney [Minneapolis: Fortress, 1994], 89). But even Weinfeld notes that the expression "refers to general instruction and not to the specific 'Law'" in Exod 16:4, and he does not include this verse among the Deuteronomistic passages (334).

19. Frankel, *Murmuring Stories*, 81.

20. Baden, "Original Place," 494 n. 13; examples include Gen 18:17–23; 45:17–21; Exod 2:20–21; 8:16–20; 9:1–6, 13–20.

and well-crafted composition.[21] Although the syntax makes the referent *technically* problematic, the text makes sense only when the referent is understood as the bread, so the error does not impede understanding.

Signs of composition history in Exod 16 are thus not where they have typically been thought to be. We do, however, find fractures in the manna–quail narrative in the itinerary notices on its borders. Because itineraries are so stereotypical and formally consistent throughout a given text, they are easily recognizable, create strong coherence where genre conventions are fulfilled, and provide clear warrant for seeing a fracture in the text where those conventions are broken.[22] The itinerary notices that structure the wilderness narrative are often taken to be compositionally distinct simply because of their distinct genre. But scribes can combine genres, as we have seen, so this alone is insufficient, and other indications of fracture are required to see an itinerary notice as distinct from its accompanying episode. There are no signs of fracture between the itinerary notices that frame the manna–quail episode and the episode itself. But the itinerary notices are at odds with the water episodes that precede and follow. The fracture at the front of the manna–quail episode is evident when we compare the expressions for movement in the preceding Marah complaint episode—במדבר ימים שלשת וילכו (Exod 15:22), מרתה ויבאו (v. 23), and ויבאו אלימה (v. 27)—which *do not* contain the highly recognizable departure (נסע) and camping (חנה) notices characteristic of itinerary notices in the wilderness narrative, with the arrival in the wilderness of Sin in Exod 16:1, which *does*: ויסעו מאלים ויבאו כל עדת בני ישראל אל מדבר סין אשר בין אלים ובין סיני. Both express movement, but only one uses the itinerary genre to do so. The fracture at the end is evident in the following rock–water episode, this time in terms of geography rather than genre. The itinerary notice in Exod 17:1 takes the Israelites away from the wilderness of Sin to Rephidim, which conflicts with the setting of the rock–water episode otherwise at Horeb (the mountain of God) and Massah-Meribah.[23]

Now that we see these fractures, we must determine what kind of editorial work they suggest. Could we see the episode in Exod 16:2–36 as part of a Priestly source document and the itinerary notices as the work of a compiler? Joel Baden understands the compiler of the four source documents to have worked with a very light touch, concerned mainly to juggle the chronological outlines of each source into a combined narrative. This

---

21. For the possibility of flawed composition, see Aaron, *Etched in Stone*, 191; and Angela Roskop Erisman, "Literary Theory and Composition History of the Torah: The Sea Crossing (Exod 14:1–31) as a Test Case," in *Approaches to Literary Readings of Ancient Jewish Writings*, ed. Klaas Smelik and Karolien Vermeulen, SSN 62 (Leiden: Brill, 2014), 52–76 (here 70–71).

22. Roskop, *Wilderness Itineraries*, 50–82.

23. Roskop, *Wilderness Itineraries*, 176–84.

generated minor "factual" and "pattern" corrections, and placement of parallel stories at two different chronological points in the combined narrative generated small "derivative additions" but otherwise nothing more.[24] But the itinerary notices in Exod 16:1 and 17:1 are part of a wide-ranging priestly effort to reemplot the wilderness narrative as an annal and accomplish far more than juggling chronology; they profoundly transform the geography, ideology, and generic character of the wilderness narrative.[25] This is the very kind of "large-scale rewriting" Baden claims there is none of in the Pentateuch.[26] Given the absence of fracture between these two itinerary notices and the manna–quail episode that comes between them, the fact that the Exod 16:1 itinerary notice has the Israelites arrive in the wilderness of Sin just in time for Shabbat,[27] and the fact that the priestly goals of the manna–quail episode (relating to Shabbat observance and the role of the priest as teacher of *tôrâ*) complement the priestly goals of the annalistic reemplotment of the wilderness narrative (reconstruction of a temple-centered Israelite society after exile), it is best to see the entire manna–quail episode as part of this reemplotment, a supplement to the complaint episodes that precede and follow that is integrated with them using the itinerary genre.

Brettler, following the *OED*, defines a supplement as "something added to supply a deficiency."[28] A deficiency is not always an error that makes a text problematic to read but can also be the perception that a text does not accomplish what it otherwise might; this perception can be generated by a different vision for a text as much as by failure of a text to achieve the goals it initially sought. The wilderness narrative was already an effort to ground ideas about Israelite social structure and law (e.g., the judiciary in Exod 18) in a valorized past. But the idea that Yhwh dwells in a fixed location was no longer tenable for a people in exile, and the priestly authors saw an opportunity to ground their particular vision for restoration—and their role in it—by co-opting and revising that same text.[29] The annalistic reemplotment of the wilderness narrative, of which the manna–quail narrative in Exod 16 is an important part, is thus consistent with the spirit of examples on the more transformative end of Brettler's continuum, which illustrate the changes in genre that can come about as a text is adapted for a new use. Our study of Exod 16 also enriches the

---

24. Joel S. Baden, *J, E, and the Redaction of the Pentateuch*, FAT 68 (Tübingen: Mohr Siebeck, 2009), 255–86.

25. Roskop, *Wilderness Itineraries*, 144–74. For a list of itinerary notices that belong to the Priestly reemplotment, see 178.

26. Baden, *J, E, and the Redaction of the Pentateuch*, 263.

27. Roskop, *Wilderness Itineraries*, 165–67.

28. See Brettler, "Supplementation in Psalms," 5–6, 13.

29. For the pre-Priestly character of Exod 18 and the Priestly effort to recontextualize it, see Roskop, *Wilderness Itineraries*, 180–84.

Genre Conventions and Their Implications for Composition History 63

continuum as an example of ideological transformation that is as generically conservative as it is innovative: even as it introduces new elements of the itinerary and oracular novella genres, it also mimics the complaint genre in the Marah and rock–water episodes that immediately precede and follow, an effort to accommodate to the genre of the previously existing narrative.

A second place we find evidence of composition history in the manna–quail narrative is the response of Moses and Aaron to the Israelites' complaint in vv. 6–8, which virtually everyone acknowledges are riddled with problems. The phrase ונחנו מה occurs near the end of v. 8 as well as in v. 7, constituting a *Wiederaufnahme*, while vv. 6b–7a take the form of glosses on ערב and בקר, introduced by citation of a lemma followed by comment on that particular element.[30] Resumptive repetition can be a rhetorical device as well as mark interpolated material, and glosses can be written by the scribe who authored the text as well as by a later copyist. But other features are unquestionably problematic: v. 8 contains two dependent clauses (בשמע יהוה את and בתת יהוה לכם בערב בשר לאכל ולחם בבקר לשבע תלנתיכם אשר אתם מלינם עלינו) but nothing for them to be dependent upon. The syntactic problem concerning the referent of the third person masculine singular pronoun on שמו in v. 31 is easily navigable because out of two clear options only one makes sense. The syntactic problem here, however, makes the text virtually unreadable. Verses 6–8 also contain developmental problems. The cryptic references to evening and morning as well as meat and bread preempt Yhwh's announcement of the pending arrival of food in vv. 11–12 and compromise the effect of responding to the Israelites in a way that echoes their complaint. Verse 7 preempts the arrival of the *kābôd* in v. 10. And וידעתם כי יהוה הוציא אתכם מארץ מצרים in v. 6 mimics but also expands on the self-identification formula וידעתם כי אני יהוה אלהיכם in v. 12.

The fact that vv. 6–8 anticipate so much of what comes in vv. 9–12 has led many commentators to argue that they were an addition or that they once came after v. 12 but were transposed to their present position.[31] As Brevard Childs points out, however, a response from Moses typically follows the complaint, and this element (c) of the genre often involves transferring the complaint to Yhwh.[32] The rhetorical question ונחנו מה כי תלונו עלינו in Exod 16:7 does suggest that the complaint against Moses and Aaron is misdirected, while לא עלינו תלנתיכם כי על יהוה in v. 8 does identify the proper object as Yhwh. So there is good reason to see

---

30. For discussion of this form, see Fishbane, *Biblical Interpretation*, 266.
31. See a summary of the history of scholarship in Brevard S. Childs, *The Book of Exodus: A Critical, Theological Commentary*, OTL (Philadelphia: Westminster, 1974), 276–80; and Frankel, *Murmuring Stories*, 65–67.
32. Childs, *Book of Exodus*, 278, 280.

at least part of vv. 6–8 as belonging right where they are. Taken together, the problems outlined above suggest the following analysis of the base narrative and supplements:

Base narrative   Supplements
⁶ויאמר משה ואהרן אל כל בני ישראל

                                                                   עֶרֶב וידעתם כי יהוה הוציא אתכם
                                                                   מארץ מצרים ⁷וּבֹקֶר וראיתם את כבוד
                                                                   יהוה בשמעו את תלנתיכם על יהוה

ונחנו מה כי תלונו עלינו

                                                                   ⁸ויאמר משה בתת יהוה לכם בָּעֶרֶב בשר
                                                                   לאכל ולחם בַּבֹּקֶר לשבע בשמע יהוה את
                                                                   תלנתיכם אשר אתם מלינם עלינו וְנַחְנוּ מָה

לא עלינו תלנתיכם כי על יהוה

The floating dependent clauses in v. 8 are marked off by the *Wiederaufnahme* (ונחנו מה), and the ערב and בקר glosses in vv. 6–7 are formally distinct, leaving a base narrative that does what we expect this element of a complaint episode's plot structure to do based on our knowledge of the genre, yet without the syntactic and developmental problems that make these verses very difficult to read.

The Israelites' complaint involves accusing *Moses and Aaron* of taking them out of Egypt *to starve them to death* (v. 3). While the base narrative of vv. 6–8 transfers this complaint to Yhwh, it does not offer a counterargument. This is not necessarily a problem, because the counterargument is implicit as the narrative unfolds: it is *Yhwh* who brought them out of Egypt, *and he will sustain them* when food is not readily available (whether that is due to the sparse wilderness setting of the narrative or the implications of a law that prohibits work on Shabbat). But it is not difficult to see how the base narrative of vv. 6–8 might be perceived as insufficiently developed by a scribe who would have preferred to see the counterargument be immediate and explicit. The glosses on ערב and בקר in vv. 6b–7a repair exactly this perceived deficiency. The gloss on ערב counters the first part of the Israelites' complaint, making clear that it is Yhwh, not Moses and Aaron, who brought the Israelites out of Egypt by adapting the self-identification formula וידעתם כי אני יהוה אלהיכם from v. 12, where that point is not fully developed.[33] The gloss on בקר begins to address the second part of the Israelites' complaint by stating that Yhwh will respond to their complaint in person; only in vv. 12–13 does it become clear that Yhwh (in the form of the *kābôd*) is showing up in order to provide sustenance. These are not typical glosses because the lemmata are not explained; instead,

---

33. Coats argues that the self-identification formula in v. 12 is an effort to get at the idea that Yhwh "instigated and directed" the exodus (*Rebellion in the Wilderness*, 91–92), but that point is implicit in v. 12 and is made explicit only in v. 6.

the glosses supply the more fully developed ideas, while the lemmata, ערב and בקר, direct the reader to the next appearance of these terms in the narrative (vv. 12–13), where the counterargument will be completed. The scribe who (later?) added the floating dependent clauses in v. 8 perhaps had less confidence that readers could make the connection without help, because he added two further comments on ערב and בקר that explicitly link these ideas with the promise and delivery of meat and bread.[34] The glosses on ערב and בקר and the floating dependent clauses in v. 8 are akin to the clumsy repair of the missing *nun* verse in the Qumran version of Ps 145, insofar as they are efforts to correct perceived deficiencies—here thematic and structural rather than formal—that result in a problematic text.[35]

A third difficulty in the manna–quail narrative that *may* constitute a sign of composition history is the tension between bread and meat. The first Yhwh speech in vv. 4–5 contains no reference to meat, as God states that he will rain down לחם (v. 4), generating an expectation that the story will be about bread alone. This expectation is strengthened every time the plot focuses on manna, from the question that prompts the Israelites to go to Moses for instruction (v. 15), to the statement that it melts at the end of each day (v. 21), to the preservation of an *omer* of it for posterity (vv. 31–35). Some clauses, however, do refer to meat:

(v. 3) בשבתנו על סיר הבשר
(v. 12) בין הערבים תאכלו בשר
(v. 13) בערב ותעל השלו
(v. 20) וירם תולעים ויבאש
(v. 23) ואת אשר תבשלו בשלו
(v. 24) ולא הבאיש ורמה לא היתה בו

These references are usually accounted for as part of a Priestly source or layer that deals with both bread and meat and has been combined with the non-priestly bread-only version anchored in vv. 4–5.[36] But we have now

---

34. It is common to see the floating dependent clauses in v. 8 as further glosses on or variants of the two clauses in vv. 6–7 because they, too, contain ערב and בקר, but their function is not discussed; see, e.g., Noth, *Exodus*, 134; Coats, *Rebellion in the Wilderness*, 84; Ruprecht, "Stellung und Bedeutung," 280–81.

35. See Brettler, "Supplementation in Psalms," 10–11.

36. Documentary analyses include F. V. Winnett, *The Mosaic Tradition*, NMES (Toronto: University of Toronto Press, 1949), 128; Noth, *Exodus*, 131; Ronald E. Clements, *Exodus*, CBC (Cambridge: Cambridge University Press, 1972), 98; Childs, *Book of Exodus*, 275; Gnana Robinson, *The Origin and Development of the Old Testament Sabbath: A Comprehensive Exegetical Approach*, BBET 21 (Frankfurt am Main: Lang, 1988), 228; Baruch A. Levine, *Numbers 1–20: A New Translation with Introduction and Commentary*, AYB 4B (1993; repr., New Haven: Yale University Press, 2008), 337–38. For supplementary analyses, see, e.g., Johnstone, *Chronicles and Exodus*, 252–53; and Van Seters, *Life of Moses*, 189.

seen that vv. 4–5 are a central element of the Priestly narrative. Although we cannot isolate an entire version of the story that involves meat, it is possible that a Priestly bread-only story was supplemented with the clauses above to make it about both bread and meat; bracketing out these clauses, one is left with a coherent, well-developed bread-only narrative.

On the other hand, one could read both the bread and the meat as integral to the base Priestly narrative and see that each is brought to the forefront where it best illustrates the immediate goal. For example, the bread informs the question the Israelites ask Moses in v. 15 because it is unclear how manna constitutes "bread," while the meat better illustrates that failure to obey has consequences because it goes rancid when it is not preserved (vv. 20, 24). What makes this second option attractive is the fact that meat actually pervades the episode despite the expectation of a bread-only narrative generated by vv. 4–5: the meat is a point of contention along with the bread in the Israelites' complaint (v. 3); it is promised along with the bread in Yhwh's speech to the Israelites (v. 12); it appears along with the "bread" in the narration that follows (v. 13); and it is accounted for alongside the bread in Moses's instructions for how to preserve the food for consumption on the Sabbath (v. 23).[37] Still, one wonders why בשר would not be mentioned alongside לחם in v. 4. We are left, then, to navigate competing sets of expectations that emerge from the literature. If we focus on the pervasiveness of meat throughout the episode, we may be inclined to see the reference to bread alone in v. 4 as less significant and the references to meat as integral to the narrative.[38] If we focus on the reference to bread alone in v. 4, the tension between bread and meat becomes more dominant, and we may be more inclined to see the clauses pertaining to meat as a supplement. In a situation like this, it may not be possible to make a strong argument either for or against supplementation.

In other cases, supplementation may be done so well that no clear sign of it remains. Exod 16:35 contains two parallel sentences:

(v. 35a) ובני ישראל אכלו את המן ארבעים שנה עד באם אל ארץ נושבת

(v. 35b) את המן אכלו עד באם אל קצה ארץ כנען

Source critics have typically assigned one to P and one to J.[39] Since the second elaborates on the first, a more recent trend has been to see v. 35b

---

37. Cassuto, *Commentary on the Book of Exodus*, 190.

38. Ruprecht, for example, is not bothered by the mention of the quail only in passing once the episode gets under way and thinks it understandable for the manna to be described and not the quail, since quail is clearly meat, while manna is a rather strange "bread" ("Stellung und Bedeutung," 286, 298).

39. E.g., Coats, *Rebellion in the Wilderness*, 87 (b is J, a is P); and Coats, *Exodus 1–18*, 128, although Propp (*Exodus 1–18*, 590) resists dividing the verse into J and P because אכלו in v. 35b assumes a plural subject (בני ישראל), which is supplied only in v. 35a.

as a supplement to v. 35a specifying that ארץ כנען is what is meant by ארץ נושבת.⁴⁰ But the parallel syntax in Exod 16:35 could also have been created by the priestly author of the episode to convey that ארץ כנען, the destination to which the Israelites are headed, is an ארץ נושבת.⁴¹ *If* v. 35b is a supplement, it illustrates that supplementation can be done seamlessly, in contrast to supplements such as those in vv. 6–8 that aim to correct a perceived deficiency but end up creating a problematic text in the process. Of course, the problem with seamless editorial work is that it leaves us with no traces of its existence unless we are in a position to compare manuscripts. Here our ability to detect composition history based on internal criteria breaks down.

Examples such as the tension between meat and bread and the parallel statements about the land in Exod 16:35 should caution us not to be overconfident about our ability to understand the composition history of the Pentateuch. We will bump up against limits and may often need to calibrate our arguments, remaining content in some cases with laying out possibilities where strong conclusions cannot be drawn. In other cases, focusing attention on expectations that emerge from the literature—based on its use of genre and its development of plot, character, and theme—can help us see clearly where the narrative is coherent and where that coherence breaks down, even in the absence of manuscript evidence. And it just so happens that, at least in this case, an aesthetic approach to historical criticism supports a supplementary over a documentary model of textual growth.

---

40. See Wagenaar, "Cessation of Manna," 194, on the typical source attributions of the two parts of the verse.

41. See Num 21:1–3, where the Israelites enter it from the south. On Num 21:1–3 as part of the end of the Priestly annalistic emplotment of the wilderness narrative, see Roskop, *Wilderness Itineraries*, 193–203.

Joseph and the Egyptian Wife (Genesis 39): A Case of Double Supplementation

THOMAS RÖMER
Collège de France (UMR 7192) and Université de Lausanne

Since the beginnings of critical biblical scholarship, the Joseph narrative (Gen 37–50) has puzzled commentators. On the one hand, many scholars agree that we have here an impressive piece of narrative art and storytelling and that, contrary to the foregoing Abraham and Jacob narratives, it is impossible to reconstruct "kleinere Einheiten" (smaller units) which would have existed independently before redactors combined them into a longer, comprehensive novella. On the other hand, the Joseph story has often been considered as one of the best proofs of the validity of the Documentary Hypothesis because of the large number of possible "doublets":

In Gen 37, Joseph has two dreams that he reports to his brothers; he is brought to Egypt either by the Ishmaelites or by the Midianites; in Gen 40 he interprets two dreams (one of the chief cupbearer, one of the chief baker); in Gen 41 Pharaoh also has two dreams; in Gen 42–44 Joseph's brothers travel twice to Egypt in order to buy grain; Joseph twice hides something in his brothers' sacks. In addition, Reuben and Judah both intervene in Gen 37 to protect Joseph's life and later (Gen 42 and 43), to convince Jacob to let Benjamin descend with them to Egypt. The patriarch is mostly called Jacob, but sometimes Israel. All of these observations have been used in order to reconstruct two parallel Joseph narratives, a "J" version and an "E" version. Scholars advocating this approach must, however, confront two major problems: it is impossible to reconstruct these parallels in a comprehensive way, and the traditional criteria for the Documentary Hypothesis, the use of the tetragrammaton by the Yahwist and of אלהים or האלהים by the Elohist, do not work.

There is of course no consensus on how to reconstruct the original Joseph story, but most scholars would agree that chapters 38 and 46, as well as 48–49 do not belong to it.[1] In addition, it is evident that Gen

---

1. The case of Gen 38 is widely accepted. This chapter is a story about Judah, who, in contrast to his character in the Joseph narrative, is already a married man and in fact quite

50:24–25 is a late passage that combines a pentateuchal and a hexateuchal redaction. Verse 24 with the theme of the oath to the patriarchs provides, together with Deut 34:4, a frame for the Pentateuch. Verse 25 belongs to a hexateuchal redaction introducing the motif of Joseph's bones, which are buried in Josh 24:32.[2] The passage in which Joseph invents capitalism and transforms the Egyptians into slaves of Pharaoh (47:13–26) is also an addition.[3] This account does not fit well with the context of the Joseph narrative: It does not mention Joseph's brothers and contradicts Joseph's advice to Pharaoh as well as his actions in 41:25–56*.

If one accepts this material as secondary to the original narrative,[4] one can observe the following: the author or authors use almost exclusively אלהים or האלהים when speaking of the deity and, in contrast to Gen 12–36, never suggest a direct divine intervention. All comments about the deity's involvement appear on the lips of the protagonists (Joseph, Jacob, Pharaoh, the brothers). One can therefore understand the story in a totally "profane" way or accept the theological interpretations given by Joseph or other actors.

The only exception to these observations is the story of Joseph's encounter with the Egyptian woman who wants to have sex with him (Gen 39).[5] This story mentions the divine name Yhwh several times, and

---

old. The tribal blessings in Gen 49 are originally unrelated to the Joseph narrative (Jean-Daniel Macchi, *Israël et ses tribus selon Genèse 49*, OBO 171 [Fribourg: Presses universitaires; Göttingen: Vandenhoeck & Ruprecht, 1999], 235–43). Genesis 46 and 48 are insertions the aim of which is to strengthen the link with the foregoing patriarchal narratives and to prepare the ground for the exodus story (see Erhard Blum, *Die Komposition der Vätergeschichte*, WMANT 57 [Neukirchen-Vluyn: Neukirchener Verlag, 1984], 246–54).

2. See Donald B. Redford, *A Study of the Biblical Story of Joseph (Genesis 37–50)*, VTSup 20 (Leiden: Brill, 1970), 25; Blum, *Die Komposition der Vätergeschichte*, 255–57; Thomas Römer, *Israels Väter: Untersuchungen zur Väterthematik im Deuteronomium und in der deuteronomistischen Tradition*, OBO 99 (Freiburg: Universitätsverlag; Göttingen: Vandenhoeck & Ruprecht, 1990), 561–66; Thomas C. Römer and Marc Z. Brettler, "Deuteronomy 34 and the Case for a Persian Hexateuch," *JBL* 119 (2000): 401–19, here 410. The new introduction of the speech in v. 25 clearly shows that both verses do not belong to the same layer, *pace* Jan Christian Gertz, *Tradition und Redaktion in der Exoduserzählung. Untersuchungen zur Endredaktion des Pentateuch*, FRLANT 186 (Göttingen: Vandenhoeck & Ruprecht, 1999), 363–65.

3. Horst Seebass, *Geschichtliche Zeit und theonome Tradition in der Joseph-Erzählung* (Gütersloh: G. Mohn, 1978), 58–61; Peter Weimar, "Gen 47,13–26—ein irritierender Abschnitt im Rahmen der Josefsgeschichte," in *Auf dem Weg zur Endgestalt von Genesis bis II Regum: Festschrift für Hans-Christoph Schmitt zu seinem 65. Geburtstag*, ed. Martin Beck and Ulrike Schorn, BZAW 370 (Berlin: de Gruyter, 2006), 125–38.

4. We will not discuss the question whether there was a P account or a Priestly redaction of the Joseph narrative; on this question, see Thomas Römer, "The Joseph Story in the Book of Genesis: Pre-P or Post-P?," in *The Post-Priestly Pentateuch: New Perspectives on Its Redactional Development and Theological Profiles*, ed. F. Giuntoli and K. Schmid, FAT 101 (Tübingen: Mohr Siebeck, 2015), 185–201.

5. One cannot really say that she "seduces" Joseph, because she very directly commands him: "Sleep with me!"

the narrator explicitly states that Joseph's ascent in the house of "Potiphar,"[6] as well as in the house of the chief jailer, are the result of Yhwh's involvement. This leads to the question whether the narrative of chapter 39 belongs to a supplementation of the Joseph novella. In the following, I seek to demonstrate that, in fact, it is possible to detect in Gen 39 traces of two major stages of supplementation.[7]

Genesis 39 in Its Present Context

The story of Joseph's resistance to the sexual advances of his master's wife and her false accusations against him that result in his imprisonment (vv. 7–20) is framed by two passages that emphasize Joseph's ascent: first in the house of his master, who puts him in charge of his whole household (vv. 1–6), and later in the prison (vv. 21–23). All occurrences of the divine name Yhwh occur in these frames; the parallel between vv. 1–6 and vv. 21–23 is reinforced by the use of the root צלח in vv. 2, 3, and 23, as well as through the use of the substantive חן in v. 4 and v. 21 (Joseph finds favor in the sight of his Egyptian master and the chief jailer). In its present form, Gen 39 presents therefore a triptych of ascent, descent, and new ascent, anticipating in a way Joseph's destiny in Egypt.

Genesis 39, however, does not fit smoothly in its context. Following the false accusation of his master's wife, Joseph is thrown in jail, likely to await judgment.[8] Curiously, at the end of the story, Joseph, because of Yhwh's favor, finds so much favor in the sight of the chief jailer that the jailer gives Joseph everything under his authority ("in his hand") so that Joseph is rewarded with a position similar to that which he received in v. 4, where he is established "over his [= the Egyptian's] house" (על הבית).[9] Neither of these scenarios fits with the beginning of chapter 40. In this narrative, in which Joseph interprets the dreams of the chief cupbearer and the chief baker, he is neither a prisoner (which is suggested by 39:19–20)

---

6. We will return to the problem of Joseph's master's name.

7. I do not have as much faith as several of my colleagues in the possibilities of the *Literarkritik* to reconstruct precisely all the strata in the formation of a biblical text. Nevertheless, there are enough indicators in most texts to retrace the major steps or strata of supplementation.

8. The idea of prison as a place of punishment for a crime is not attested in Egypt before the Ptolemies. See Renate Müller-Wollermann, *Vergehen und Strafen: Zur Sanktionierung abweichenden Verhaltens im alten Ägypten*, PÄ 21 (Leiden: Brill, 2004), 217; and Joseph Vergote, *Joseph en Egypte: Genèse chap. 37–50 à la lumière des études égyptologiques récentes*, OBL 3 (Louvain: Publications universitaires/Instituut voor oriëntalisme, 1959), 37–40. For the situation in ancient Israel, see Reinhard Kratz, "Gefängnis," *NBL* 1:756–57.

9. For this title, see 1 Kgs 18:3; 2 Kgs 15:5; Isa 22:15; and the so-called Shebna Inscription.

nor the overseer of the jail (as suggested in 39:22–23). Joseph is, according to 40:4, a servant of the "chief of the guard," who charges him with the royal prisoners in order to be at their service (שרת). Curiously, the chief jailer bears here the same title as the Egyptian man who, according to 39:1, buys Joseph when he is brought to Egypt. For this reason, some commentators have argued that the "chief of the guard" (שר הטבחים) in chapter 40 should be the same person who buys Joseph and makes him the overseer of his house.[10] In a way this is true. In order to clarify the situation we need first of all to analyze the beginning of chapter 39.

The Name and the Titles of the "Egyptian" in Genesis 39:1

The introduction in 39:1 refers back to the end of chapter 37 (37:36), a verse that, together with 37:28, frames the scene about the brothers' presentation of Joseph's robe to Jacob:

> 37:28: Men, Midianite merchants, passed by. They drew Joseph up, lifting him out of the pit. They sold him to the Ishmaelites for twenty pieces of silver. And they took Joseph to Egypt.

> 37:36: The Medanites had sold him in Egypt to *Potiphar, "eunuch" of Pharaoh, the captain of the guard*.

> 39:1: Joseph had been taken down to Egypt. *Potiphar, "eunuch" of Pharaoh, the captain of the guard*, an Egyptian, bought him from the Ishmaelites who had brought him down there.

The relationship between the three verses is not easy to define. In the present context, 37:36 and 39:1 frame the story about Judah and Tamar in chapter 38, and 39:1 can be read as a *Wiederaufnahme* of 37:28 and 36 after the insertion of chapter 38. The mention of the Ishmaelites in 39:1 refers back to 37:28b, whereas the lexeme Medanites[11] takes up the mention of the Midianite merchants of 37:28a. The appearance of both groups in chapter 37 has been explained by the conflation of two parallel accounts (J/E).[12]

---

10. For instance, Jürgen Ebach, *Genesis 37–50*, HThKAT (Freiburg im Breisgau: Herder, 2007), 207–8; and Rüdiger Lux, *Josef: Der Auserwählte unter seinen Brüdern*, 2nd ed., Biblische Gestalten 1 (Leipzig: Evangelische Verlagsanstalt, 2014; 1st ed. 2001), 119.

11. The masoretic vocalization in 37:36 is strange. It is probably an attempt to identify Midianites and Ishmaelites as suggested already by Abraham Ibn Ezra. See the discussion in Ebach, *Genesis 37–50*, 110.

12. Genesis 37 has always been understood as a strong case for the validity of the Documentary Hypothesis. On this, see Baruch J. Schwartz, "How the Compiler of the Pentateuch

A better solution could be to understand the mention of the Midianites as a gloss intended to identify Ishmaelites and Midianites (cf. Judg 8:22–24, where both seem to have been identified).[13] If one considers 37:28aα as an insertion, one obtains a smooth story line according to which the brothers, following Judah's advice, sell Joseph to the Ishmaelites.[14] This is clearly the original scenario as presupposed in 45:4, where Joseph tells his brothers, "I am your brother, Joseph, whom you sold into Egypt." Genesis 37:36 presupposes the introduction of the gloss in 37:28 and may therefore be later than 39:1,[15] which speaks of the Ishmaelites. It is also possible, however, that both texts have been reworked simultaneously in regard to the characterization of Joseph's Egyptian master, who is described in exactly the same way in both verses.

The name Potiphar (פוטיפר). This name is clearly of Egyptian origin, meaning "he whom Re gives" (P3-di-p3-R') and is attested from the Saite to the Ptolemaic periods.[16] Curiously, Joseph's father-in-law, the priest of Heliopolis (Gen 41:45, 50; 46:20[17]) bears exactly the same name. The MT tries to differentiate in writing the priest's name as פּוֹטִי פֶרַע, but the LXX always uses the same transliteration Πετεφρης for both cases, an indication that both persons bear the same name. Manfred Görg has suggested, however, that the name in 37:36 and 39:1 should be related to another Egyptian personal name, P3-dj-p3-R'3, "He whom Pharaoh gives." Such a name would fit very well for an officer of the king, whereas P3-dj-p3-R', "He whom Re gives," would be much more appropriate for a priest of the sun god.[18] The problem with this theory is that such a reconstructed name is not attested in any Egyptian document. In Gen 39 the name Potiphar

---

Worked: The Composition of Genesis 37," in *The Book of Genesis: Composition, Reception, and Interpretation*, ed. Craig A. Evans, Joel N. Lohr, and David L. Petersen, VTSup 152, FIOTL 6 (Leiden: Brill, 2012), 263–78; and Horst Seebass, *Genesis III: Josephgeschichte (37,1–50,26)* (Neukirchen-Vluyn: Neukirchener Verlag, 2000), 24–27; see, however, his cautious remarks on 212.

13. For an overview of the different explanations, see Joel S. Baden, *The Composition of the Pentateuch: Renewing the Documentary Hypothesis*, ABRL (New Haven: Yale University Press, 2012), 4–12.

14. See, similarly, Franziska Ede, *Die Josefsgeschichte: Literarkritische und redaktionsgeschichtliche Untersuchungen zur Entstehung von Gen 37–50*, BZAW 485 (Berlin: de Gruyter, 2016), 38. There is, however, no need to postulate a "Midianiter Bearbeitung" (Ede, *Josefsgeschichte*, 48), since the Midianites are only mentioned in 37:28 and 36 (in another vocalization). In this case, 37:36 is later than 39:1 and presupposes the introduction of the gloss in 37:28.

15. See also Erhard Blum, "Zwischen Literarkritik und Stilkritik: Die diachrone Analyse der literarischen Verbindung von Genesis und Exodus—im Gespräch mit Ludwig Schmidt," *ZAW* 124 (2012): 492–515, here 500; and Ede, *Josefsgeschichte*, 43.

16. Redford, *Study of the Biblical Story*, 228.

17. This verse is a late insertion in a Priestly genealogy (P^s).

18. Manfred Görg, "Potifar und Potifera," *BN* 85 (1996): 8–10.

appears only in v. 1. In the whole narrative, Joseph's Egyptian master is mostly referred to as his "lord" (אדון),[19] also when he speaks of him to his wife. It seems quite clear, therefore, that originally, Joseph's owner had no name and that Potiphar in 39:1 (and 37:36) is a case of supplementation. A redactor was looking for a proper Egyptian name and took the one he found in chapter 41. Maybe he wanted also to suggest that Joseph had already stayed in the house of his future father-in-law.[20]

The "eunuch" of Pharaoh. The term סרס occurs in Gen 39 only in v. 1. It is used in 40:2 and 7 as a designation of the chief cupbearer and the chief baker. It is disputed whether the etymology of the word indicates castration.[21] In any case, for the cupbearer and the baker, the title more generally denotes the status of a high official whom the king trusts. A connotation "eunuch" has no function in Gen 40. One may suspect that the redactor in 39:1 took over the term from chapter 40 in order to suggest that Joseph's lord held the same hierarchical rank as the one held by the chief cupbearer and chief baker. But perhaps there was also some ironic intent: if Joseph's master were indeed a eunuch, one could of course easily understand that his wife was sexually frustrated.[22]

The captain of the guard. The expression שר הטבחים means literally "chief butcher," which would bring the bearer of this title close to the chief cupbearer and the chief baker. The same title, however, is used in 40:3 and 4 as a title for the overseer of the jail, so that a translation as "chief of the (royal) bodyguard" seems to be most appropriate.[23]. Since this title does not occur in the narrative of chapter 39, one could equally consider it an example of later supplementation of the beginning of the story and claim that the original story spoke only of an anonymous Egyptian without any

---

19. Twice as "the Egyptian" in vv. 2 and 5.
20. This would also make sense on a theological level. Joseph's father-in-law is an Egyptian priest. The Egyptian in Gen 39 is positively depicted and treats Joseph well because of Yhwh's intervention. The identification of the Egyptian with the priest Potiphar could then suggest that Yhwh also controls and influences the representative of Egyptian deities. The identification of the priest Potiphar with Joseph's master is quite common in the Jewish and Christian traditions. On this, see already Jub. 40:12 and T. Jos. 18; for more references, see Louis Ginzberg, *Bible Times and Characters from Joseph to the Exodus*, vol. 2 of *The Legends of the Jews* (1910; repr., Philadelphia: Jewish Publication Society of America, 1977), 43 with n. 100 in vol. 5:337.
21. See the discussion in Ebach, *Genesis 37–50*, 163–64.
22. See Gen. Rab. 86. See also Josy Eisenberg and Benno Gross, *Un Messie nommé Joseph*, A Bible Ouverte V (Paris: Albin Michel, 1983), 251–52.
23. Manfred Görg, "Die Amtstitel des Potifar," BN 53 (1990): 14–20, here 15–17. In 2 Kgs 25 and Jer 39–40 the expression רב הטבחים relates to the closest officer to the Babylonian king: "chief of the bodyguard."

qualification (see the term "Egyptian" in vv. 2 and 5) who bought Joseph.[24] If one considers, however, the fact that, according to Gen 40:3–4 and 41:12, the "chief of the guard" seems to be a known person and that in this story Joseph is not a common prisoner—in contrast to his status after the false accusation of the Egyptian wife—then one may conclude that the original form of Gen 39:1 was in fact the introduction of the story of the two dreams of the chief cupbearer and the chief baker in Gen 40*.

The Original Transition from Genesis 37 to the Story of Joseph's Dream Interpretation in Genesis 40

The original Joseph story continued after Joseph's descent into Egypt in chapter 37* with Joseph's interpretation of the dreams of Pharaoh's two high officials. Thus, the two dreams of Joseph in chapter 37 are immediately put in parallel or in contrast with the two dreams of the chief cupbearer and the chief baker in chapter 40. The first part of the original Joseph novella, before his ascent to the status of a vizier, would therefore be all about dreams: Joseph's dreams, the prisoners' dreams, and Pharaoh's dreams.[25] Since Joseph's function, according to 40:3, is to serve (שרת) the royal prisoners and the same root שרת is used in Gen 39:4a to describe his activity in his master's house, it is possible that 39:4a, along with 39:1*, belongs to the oldest version of the story.[26] Tentatively, we can reconstruct the transition between Gen 37 and 40 in the following way:

> 39:1* *Joseph had been taken down to Egypt. The captain of the guard, an Egyptian, bought him from the Ishmaelites who had brought him down there.* 39:4a *Joseph found favor in his sight and served him.* 40:1aα *Some time after this,* 40:2 *Pharaoh became angry with his two officers, the chief cupbearer and the chief baker,* 40:3a *and he put them under arrest in the house of the captain of the guard.* 40:4 *The captain of the guard charged Joseph with them, and he waited on them; they continued for some time in custody.*

---

24. Claus Westermann, *Genesis*, 3 vols., BKAT 1 (Neukirchen-Vluyn: Neukirchener Verlag, 1982), 3:57; Christoph Levin, *Der Jahwist*, FRLANT 157 (Göttingen: Vandenhoeck & Ruprecht, 1993), 278.
25. As Saul Olyan has pointed out to me (oral communication), this theme is quite appropriate for a court tale and has close parallels in the first part of the book of Daniel.
26. See similarly Ede, *Josefsgeschichte*, 103 and 111, who wants to assign the whole of v. 4 to the oldest narrative. Verse 4b, however, presents Joseph as *'al habbayît*, a title that denotes a very high position (the second in the house), which fits well with chapter 39 but not really with Joseph's role in chapter 40.

The reasons for this reconstruction[27] are the following: It is clear that 40:1aßb is a supplement introduced by a redactor who wanted to explain why the Pharaoh became angry with his officers by claiming that they both "sinned" against the king of Egypt. Note also that this verse omits the lexeme שר when speaking of the cupbearer and the baker.[28] Genesis 40:3b presents Joseph as "confined" (אסור) in the prison and belongs, therefore, to the same revision of chapter 40 that was made at the same time that chapter 39 was introduced as a supplement to the Joseph story.[29]

Before we consider the reasons that led to the insertion of the narrative about Joseph and the Egyptian wife, we have to address the question of whether the supplementation of Gen 39 occurred in one or more steps.

Genesis 39: A Case of a Twofold Supplementation

The story about Joseph's resistance to the sexual advances of the Egyptian woman in Gen 39:7–20 is a unified narrative. The repetitions—the wife twice attempts to have sex with Joseph and repeats her accusation first to the servants, then to her husband—are part of the style of the story and do not necessitate the assumption that the narrative underwent several revisions.[30] Such revisions have been suggested in particular by Christoph Levin, who speaks of a "Righteousness Edition,"[31] and by Franziska

---

27. For a similar reconstruction, see Hans-Christoph Schmitt, *Die nichtpriesterliche Josephsgeschichte: Ein Beitrag zur neuesten Pentateuchkritik*, BZAW 154 (Berlin: de Gruyter, 1980), 33.

28. The same holds true for 40:5, which probably belongs to the same revision of chapter 40 that occurred after the insertion of chapter 39*.

29. See similarly Norbert Kebekus, *Die Joseferzählung: Literarkritische und redaktionsgeschichtliche Untersuchungen zu Genesis 37–50*, Internationale Hochschulschriften (Münster: Waxmann, 1990), 48. The same revision may be found in 40:15, a verse that tries to transform Joseph into a prisoner (ibid., 49–50).

30. If one reads the text carefully, one realizes that these are not simple repetitions; on the contrary, the apparent redundancies introduce subtle changes. The first order the woman gives to Joseph, "sleep with me," shows that she considers herself hierarchically superior to Joseph. Joseph, however, counters by stating that he is the second in the house and introduces a "theological" argument characterizing adultery as a "great wickedness" (רעה) and a sin against אלהים (39:8–9). At the woman's second attempt, he runs away, an action that sets the stage for her double accusation. This accusation is also constructed in a very subtle way. The woman is not simply repeating herself but first attempts to create solidarity with the Egyptian servants against the Hebrew slave, and then accuses her husband, who brought a foreigner into the house to abuse her of doing wrong, thus leaving no other choice to the husband than to punish Joseph (see the discussion in Ebach, *Genesis 37–50*, 183–85). Redford's rhetorical question "must the author therefore be so unimaginatively repetitive?" (Redford, *Study of the Biblical Story*, 78) misses the point.

31. Christoph Levin, "Righteousness in the Joseph Story: Joseph Resists Seduction (Genesis 39)," in *The Pentateuch: International Perspectives on Current Research*, ed. Thomas B.

Ede, who postulates a "gesetzesorientierte Bearbeitung."[32] However, the only reference to law that we can find is to Deut 22:25, but there is no clear allusion to this text in Gen 40. Adultery is stigmatized in Egypt as well as in the ancient Levant and Mesopotamia, so it is not necessary to postulate a "legal revision." The expression "great wickedness" and the idea of sin against the deity do not refer to a specific law text in the Pentateuch; they recall much more the episode of Abimelech, who wants to sleep with Sarah in Gen 20:9[33] and the Egyptian tale of the two brothers, where similar expressions are used. The whole story in vv. 7–20 is about Joseph's "righteous" behavior; it is not necessary, therefore, to introduce a diachronic distinction based on this criterion.[34]

In contrast, the frequent mention of the tetragrammaton in the frame 39:1–6 and 21–23 may well indicate a later supplementation of the original story. First, v. 4 seems out of place after vv. 2–3, which describe how Joseph succeeds in the house of his master because of Yhwh's assistance. Similarly, v. 6 makes better sense when following v. 4 directly.[35] Therefore the original introduction to the story of Joseph resisting the Egyptian wife can be reconstructed as follows:

> 39:1* *Joseph had been taken down to Egypt. The captain of the guard, an Egyptian, bought him from the Ishmaelites who had brought him down there.* 39:4a *Joseph found favor in his sight and served him.* 39:4b He made him overseer of his house and put him in charge of all that he had. 39:6 He left all that he had in Joseph's charge; and, with him there, he had no concern for anything but the food that he ate. Now Joseph was handsome and good-looking.

The author of the original introduction to the story in Gen 39 took up the transitional remarks in 39:1 and 4a (in italics) and supplemented them in order to introduce the story he wanted to add. The original story of Joseph's encounter with the Egyptian wife ended in Gen 39:20: "Joseph's master took him and put him in the prison, the place where the king's

---

Dozeman, Konrad Schmid, and Baruch J. Schwartz, FAT 78 (Tübingen: Mohr Siebeck, 2011), 223–40.

32. Ede, *Josefsgeschichte*, 93–102; 105–6.
33. On these parallels, see also Ede, *Josefsgeschichte*, 94–97.
34. If one consults Levin's reconstruction of the righteousness edition ("Righteousness in the Joseph Story," 238–40), it appears that he considers only vv. 7, 12aαb, 16, 17aαb, and 20 as belonging to the older narrative that the Yahwist integrated into his work. This is a quite unimpassioned "story."
35. See also David M. Carr, *Reading the Fractures of Genesis* (Louisville: Westminster John Knox, 1996), 209–10; Peter Weimar, "'Jahwe aber ward mit Josef' (Gen 39,2): Eine Geschichte von programmatischer Bedeutung," in Weimar, *Studien zur Josefsgeschichte*, SBA 44 (Stuttgart: Katholisches Bibelwerk, 2008), 61–124, esp. 92–94.

prisoners were confined[36]; he remained there in prison." This verse was the followed by:

> 40:1aα Some time after this, 40:2 Pharaoh became angry with his two officers, the chief cupbearer and the chief baker, 40:3a and he imprisoned them in the house of the captain of the guard 40:3b in the prison where Joseph was confined.[37]

As a result of the integration of Gen 39, the reader now understands that Joseph's status in prison is no longer that of a servant but that of a prisoner. But through the integration of 39:4b, 6, 7–20, the audience is led to assume that the chief of the prison is not identical with the Egyptian "chief of the guard," in whose house Joseph stayed first. For that reason, the Yahwistic redactor in 39:21–23 also introduced a new title for the one responsible for the royal prisoners, שר בית הסהר, in order to emphasize the distinction between Joseph's master, whose wife assaulted him, and the chief jailer in whose house he resides in chapter 40.[38] The redactor of 39:21–23, who is probably identical with the redactor who inserted 39:2–3 and 5, refers back to these verses (cf. v. 21 and vv. 2, 4,[39] v. 22 and v. 4; v. 23 and v. 2 and v. 6) and emphasizes once again, contrary to the main story, Yhwh's presence and assistance.

Further Reasons to Consider Genesis 39 a Case of Supplementation

Genesis 39 displays some stylistic particularities in comparison with the other parts of the Joseph novella. The preposition כ followed by an infinitive occurs in the whole Joseph story seven times: five times in chapter 39 and only twice elsewhere (44:30–31).[40] Furthermore, 50 percent of all usages of ויהי are concentrated in chapter 39.[41] Finally, the preposition

---

36. The comment "the place where the king's prisoners were confined" is often considered a gloss or a later insert (so, e.g., Kebekus, *Die Joseferzählung*, 41–42). It makes perfect sense, however, as a means to integrate Gen 39* into its older context because it prepares the audience for the following story of the royal cupbearer and baker.

37. Genesis 40:3b was probably added either by the first supplementer, who inserted the story of Gen 39*, or by the Yahwistic redactor of vv. 2–3, 5, and 21–23.

38. The title שר בית הסהר occurs only three times in Gen 39:21, 22, 23, which indicates a strong intention to make clear that Joseph is now under the custody of someone else, and which is also another argument for the work of a redactor or "supplementer."

39. The redactor also takes up the older v. 4a and attributes to Yhwh's intervention the fact that Joseph finds favor in the sight of his master.

40. Redford, *Study of the Biblical Story*, 43. In other chapters, the construction appears with the preposition ב.

41. See the list in ibid., 53.

באשר ("because") occurs only in Gen 39:9 and 23;[42] in the other parts of the narrative the author uses כאשר (twelve times). It has often been observed that the story of Joseph's encounter with the Egyptian woman has no real conclusion, because the woman's lie remains undiscovered and unpunished, in contrast to the crime committed by Joseph's brothers. In the whole Joseph narrative, the episode in chapter 39 is never alluded to.[43]

The Aim of the Twofold Supplementation of the Joseph Story in Genesis 39

There can be little doubt that the author of Gen 39 found his inspiration in the Egyptian tale of the two brothers,[44] an idea about which most commentators agree. Of course the motif of the spurned wife is quite common and occurs in the legends of Bellerophon, Hippolytus, and others,[45] but the parallels between Gen 39 and the Egyptian tale, of which only one manuscript is extant,[46] are much closer.[47] Both contain the motif of the clothes (although used differently). In the Egyptian tale, the woman speaks to Bata, the younger brother, in a manner quite similar to that of the wife in Gen 39 and also tries to take hold of him: "She got up, took hold of him, and said to him: Come let us … sleep together." Bata delivers a speech similar to that of Joseph, characterizing the woman's proposal as "this great wrong that you said to me," and, as in Gen 39, the woman mis-

---

42. The other occurrences in the Hebrew Bible are in Qoh 7:2 and 8:4, an indication of a late form.

43. See Krzysztof Dariusz Lisewski, *Studien zu Motiven und Themen zur Josefsgeschichte der Genesis*, EHS.T 23/881 (Bern: Lang, 2008), 323. Even in 40:15, which may belong to a later revision (see above), Joseph explains the fact that he is in jail by the comment that he has been kidnapped from the land of the Hebrews and that he had done nothing for which they should have put him into the "pit" (*bôr*), an allusion to the pit in Gen 37: כי שמו אתי בבור.

44. For a translation, see Miriam Lichtheim, *The New Kingdom*, vol. 2 of *Ancient Egyptian Literature: A Book of Readings* (Berkeley: University of California Press, 1976), 203–11.

45. Redford, *Study of the Biblical Story*, 92.

46. The narrative is to be found in the D'Orbiney Papyrus, which is from the New Kingdom. But this is not an argument that the story of Gen 39 must be very old, since an allusion to Bata and his castration exists also in the Papyrus Jumilhac, which was written in the Ptolemaic period. See Jacques Vandier, *Le Papyrus Jumilhac* (Paris: Centre national de la recherche scientifique, 1962), 46–47, 105, 114–15. This shows that this tale was certainly known in the Persian and Hellenistic periods. I would like to thank my colleagues Bernd U. Schipper (Berlin) and Nicolas Grimal (Paris) for their help with this question.

47. See also Hans Jochen Boecker, "Überlegungen zur Erzählung von der Versuchung Josephs (Genesis 39)," in *Altes Testament: Forschung und Wirkung; Festschrift für Henning Graf Reventlow*, ed. Peter Mommer and Winfried Thiel (Frankfurt am Main: Lang, 1994), 3–13, here 8.

represents the events in the presence of her husband by taking up Bata's speech as if not he, but she, would have protested.

In contrast to Gen 39, the tale of the two brothers is a complicated and long mythological text that functions to legitimate Bata as Pharaoh. The author of Gen 39 has taken over only the first part of the tale, although it can be argued that the Joseph story is also about Joseph's ascent.[48] Contrary to Gen 39, the Egyptian Anpu, the elder brother, learns that his wife has cheated on him and kills her.

The author of Gen 39 has used this mythological story for several reasons. First of all, he transforms Joseph through this story into a model of loyalty and chastity. He presents Joseph as the ideal young lad who follows the exhortation of the first part of the book of Proverbs, which was composed at the beginning of the Hellenistic period, and which constantly warns against the "foreign" woman:

> Prov 7:13 *She seizes him* and kisses him, and with impudent face she says to him, ... 7:16 I have decked my couch with coverings, colored spreads of *Egyptian* linen; ... 7:18 Come, let us take our fill of love until morning; let us delight ourselves with love. 7:19 *For my husband is not at home*; he has gone on a long journey.... 7:21 With much seductive speech she persuades him; with her smooth talk she compels him.... 7:23 ... He is like a bird rushing into a snare, not knowing that it will cost him his life. 7:24 And now, my children, listen to me, and be attentive to the words of my mouth. 7:25 Do not let your hearts turn aside to her ways; do not stray into her paths. 7:26 For many are those she has laid low, and numerous are her victims. 7:27 Her house is the way to Sheol, going down to the chambers of death.

It is quite possible that the author of Gen 39 was familiar with this text.[49] In any case, in the light of this text Joseph appears as a model follow for the young male audience of the story to follow. Whereas the original Joseph story is about Joseph's integration into Egypt and his reconciliation with his brothers, the redactor who inserted Gen 39* introduced a new topic into the narrative, making his diaspora audience aware that life in the

---

48. Some scholars think that Gen 39* existed first as an independent oral (and written) tradition before it was inserted as a supplement (Redford, *Study of the Biblical Story*, 181–82; Schmitt, *Die nichtpriesterliche Josephsgeschichte*, 84–85). The fact that the story has no real ending shows, however, that the redactor conceived of it as a "prologue" to Gen 40.

49. The author may also allude to the story of 2 Sam 13, where Amnon rapes his half-sister Tamar. Both stories share several expressions and motifs (the beauty of the person who is sexually harassed, the use of force, the order "sleep with me," and the shouting). See Yair Zakovitch, "Through the Looking Glass: Reflections/Inversions of Genesis Stories in the Bible," *BibInt* 1 (1993): 139–52, here 149–51; Lisewski, *Studien zu Motiven*, 328–31.

diaspora can also have some dangers and that one must behave in an absolutely loyal way.

The second redactor, who inserted the Yahwistic frame, was eager to correct the lack of divine intervention in the Joseph story. By supplementing Gen 39 through the eightfold mention of the name of Israel's God, he emphasizes that, in contrast to the original Joseph novella, Yhwh was present in Egypt from the very beginning and not only protected Joseph but also blessed the Egyptians who were friendly to him. The Yahwistic supplementation was perhaps triggered by the integration of Gen 38 in its present context, another case of supplementation. In the latter chapter, the name Yhwh is used twice, and this may have inspired the redactor who framed the narrative in chapter 39. The juxtaposition of both stories also creates an opposition between Judah, who sleeps with his daughter-in-law playing a prostitute, and Joseph, who resists the Egyptian woman.

Summing Up

The story of Joseph's encounter with the Egyptian woman can be understood as a case of twofold supplementation. The original Joseph narrative told that Joseph was bought by an Egyptian official, the "captain of the guard" who was in charge of royal prisoners. This Egyptian official employed Joseph to serve the royal prisoners who were waiting for judgment (Gen 39:1*, 4a; 40:1*, 2–3a; etc.). A redactor inserted the story about Joseph's harassment by the Egyptian woman (vv. 7–20) and her false accusation. Through this supplement, Joseph's sojourn in prison is now to be understood as a punitive confinement. In addition, the identity of the "captain of the guard" is split up: Joseph's buyer is now to be distinguished from the chief jailer. After the insertion of chapter 38, a second redactor inserted a Yahwistic frame in 39:2–3, 5 and 21–23, introducing a major theological modification to the original Joseph story, in which only אלהים or האלהים was used, and the narrator never made any comment about divine intervention. He now emphasizes that this אלהים is Yhwh and that he is present in Egypt. This double supplementation shows that those who transmitted the writings that later will become part of the Hebrew Bible felt the need to rework the older texts they were in charge of. Supplementation, in the case of Gen 39, is a literary phenomenon. The first supplementation aimed to transform Joseph into a model of loyalty and a figure of identification for young people living in the diaspora. The aim of second stage of supplementation was to give a clear theological interpretation through the affirmation that Joseph was always under the protection of Yhwh, the God of Israel, who is never mentioned in the first editions of the Joseph story.

Appendix 1

Reconstruction of the Different Layers

39:1 Joseph had been taken down to Egypt. Potiphar, an officer of Pharaoh, *the captain of the guard, an Egyptian, bought him from the Ishmaelites who had brought him down there.*

<u>39:2 Yhwh was with Joseph, and he became a successful man; he was in the house of his Egyptian master. 39:3 His master saw that Yhwh was with him and that Yhwh caused all that he did to prosper in his hands.</u> 39:4a *Joseph found favor in his* [Egyptian master's] *sight and waited on him.* 39:4b He made him overseer of his house and put him in charge of all that he had. 39:<u>5: From the time that he made him overseer of his house and over all that he had, Yhwh blessed the Egyptian's house for Joseph's sake; the blessing of the Lord was on all that he had, in house and field.</u> 39:6: He left all that he had in Joseph's charge; and, with him there, he had no concern for anything but the food that he ate.

Now Joseph was handsome and good-looking. 39:7 And after a time his master's wife cast her eyes on Joseph and said, "Lie with me." 39:8 But he refused and said to his master's wife, "Look, with me here, my master has no concern about anything in the house, and he has put everything that he has in my hand. 39:9 He is not greater in this house than I am, nor has he kept back anything from me except yourself, because you are his wife. How then could I do this great wickedness, and sin against God?" 39:10 And although she spoke to Joseph day after day, he would not consent to lie beside her or to be with her. 39:11 One day, however, when he went into the house to do his work, and while no one else was in the house, 39:12 she seized his garment, saying, "Lie with me!" But he left his garment in her hand and fled and ran outside. 39:13 When she saw that he had left his garment in her hand and had fled outside, 39:14 she called out to the members of her household and said to them, "See, my husband has brought among us a Hebrew to insult us! He came in to me to lie with me, and I cried out with a loud voice; 39:15 and when he heard me raise my voice and cry out, he left his garment beside me, and fled outside." 39:16 Then she kept his garment by her until his master came home, 39:17 and she told him the same story, saying, "The Hebrew servant, whom you have brought among us, came in to me to insult me; 39:18 but as soon as I raised my voice and cried out, he left his garment beside me, and fled outside." 39:19 When his master heard the words that his wife spoke to him, saying, "This is the way your servant treated me," he became enraged. 39:20 And Joseph's master took him and put him into the prison, the place where the king's prisoners were confined; he remained there in prison.

39:21 Yhwh was with Joseph and showed him loyalty; he gave him favor in the sight of the chief jailer. 39:22 The chief jailer committed to Joseph's care all the prisoners who were in the prison, and whatever was done there, he was the one who did it. 39:23 The chief jailer paid no heed to anything that was in Joseph's care, because the Lord was with him; and whatever he did, Yhwh made it prosper.

40:1aα *Some time after this,* 40:<u>1aβb the cupbearer of the king of Egypt and his baker offended their lord the king of Egypt</u> 40:2 *Pharaoh became angry with his two officers, the chief cupbearer and the chief baker,* 40:3a *and he imprisoned them in the house of the captain of the guard,* 40:3b in the prison where Joseph was confined. 40:4 *The captain of the guard charged Joseph with them, and he waited on them; and they continued for some time in custody.* 40:5 *One night they both dreamed—each his own dream, and each dream with its own meaning—*<u>the cupbearer and the baker of the king of Egypt, who were confined in the prison.</u>

Italics: the original narrative
Roman type: the first supplementation
<u>Underlined text: the second supplementation</u>
<small>Small characters: other additions</small>

III

Deuteronomistic Historical Narrative

Outbidding the Fall of Jerusalem: Redactional Supplementation in 2 Kings 24

KONRAD SCHMID
Universität Zürich

However one determines its extent and redactional layers, the so-called Deuteronomistic History's redactional supplementation is a well-known phenomenon that belongs to the very origins of the Deuteronomistic hypothesis in the history of scholarship.[1] In contrast to the hypothetical authors of the pentateuchal sources, the Deuteronomist has usually been conceived as a redactor—or, alternatively, the Deuteronomists have usually been conceived as multiple redactors—collecting and reinterpreting preexisting literary material by means of redactional expansions. Such expansions are found mainly in speeches and prayers of the protagonists in the Former Prophets. To be sure, Martin Noth preferred to describe the "Deuteronomist" as one "author"[2] in order to stress the conceptual

---

1. See Thomas Römer, *The So-Called Deuteronomistic History: A Sociological, Historical and Literary Introduction* (London: T&T Clark, 2005); see also the surveys of scholarship by Thomas Römer and Albert de Pury, "L'historiographie deutéronomiste (HD): Histoire de la recherche et enjeux du débat," in *Israël construit son histoire: L'historiographie deutéronomiste à la lumière des recherches récentes*, ed. Albert de Pury, Thomas Römer, and Jean-Daniel Macchi, MdB 34 (Geneva: Labor et Fides, 1996), 9–120; Timo Veijola, "Martin Noths 'Überlieferungsgeschichtliche Studien' und die Theologie des Alten Testaments," in Veijola, *Moses Erben: Studien zum Dekalog, zum Deuteronomismus und zum Schriftgelehrtentum*, , BWANT 149 (Stuttgart: Kohlhammer, 2000), 11–28; Walter Dietrich, "Martin Noth und die Zukunft des deuteronomistischen Geschichtswerkes," in Dietrich, *Von David zu den Deuteronomisten: Studien zu den Geschichtsüberlieferungen des Alten Testaments*, BWANT 156; Stuttgart: Kohlhammer, 2002), 181–98; Udo Rüterswörden, ed., *Martin Noth—aus der Sicht der heutigen Forschung*, BThSt 58 (Neukirchen-Vluyn: Neukirchener Verlag, 2004). For the book of Kings, see Michael Avioz, "The Book of Kings in Recent Research (Part I)," *CuRBR* 4 (2005): 11–55, here 14–16; Baruch Halpern and André Lemaire, "The Composition of Kings," in *The Books of Kings. Sources, Composition, Historiography and Reception*, ed. André Lemaire and Baruch Halpern, VTSup 129 (Leiden: Brill, 2010), 123–53. See also the contributions in Steven L. McKenzie and M. Patrick Graham, eds., *The History of Israel's Traditions: The Heritage of Martin Noth*, JSOTSup 182 (Sheffield: Sheffield Academic, 1994).

2. See Martin Noth, *Überlieferungsgeschichtliche Studien*, SKG.G 18.2 (Stuttgart: Kohlhammer, 1943), 105.

unity of his work, but Noth was in fact able to distinguish clearly between pre-Deuteronomistic tradition and Deuteronomistic supplementation in Deuteronomy–Kings. After Noth, only a minority of scholars (e.g., John Van Seters, Steven McKenzie, and Erhard Blum[3]) has upheld the notion of a single "Deuteronomist" author or redactor. But ever since the observations of Gerhard von Rad, Hans Walter Wolff, Rudolf Smend, Helga Weippert, Frank Moore Cross and his students, Norbert Lohfink, Gottfried Vanoni, André Lemaire, Iain Provan, Mark A. O'Brien, Ansgar Moenikes, Erik Eynikel, Reinhard Kratz, Marvin Sweeney, Thomas Römer, Erik Aurelius, Jacob Wright, and others,[4] it has become obvious that whatever

---

3. John Van Seters, "Histories and Historians of the Ancient Near East: The Israelites," *Or* 50 (1981): 137–85; Van Seters, *In Search of History: Historiography in the Ancient World and the Origins of Biblical History* (New Haven: Yale University Press, 1983); Steven L. McKenzie, *The Trouble with Kings: The Composition of the Book of Kings in the Deuteronomistic History*, VTSup 42 (Leiden: Brill, 1991); Erhard Blum, *Studien zur Kompositionen des Pentateuch*, BZAW 189 (Berlin: de Gruyter, 1990), 109 n. 35; cf. Blum, "Historiographie oder Dichtung? Zur Eigenart alttestamentlicher Geschichtsüberlieferung," in *Grundfragen der historischen Exegese: Methodologische, philologische und hermeneutische Beiträge zum Alten Testament*, ed. Wolfgang Oswald and Kristin Weingart, FAT 95 (Tübingen: Mohr Siebeck, 1995), 31–54.

4. Gerhard von Rad, "Die deuteronomistische Geschichtstheologie in den Königsbüchern" (1947), in *Gesammelte Studien zum Alten Testament*, ed. Rudolf Smend, TB 8 (Munich: Kaiser, 1958), 2:189–204; earlier than Noth, see, e.g., Wilhelm Rudolph, *Der "Elohist" von Exodus bis Josua*, BZAW 68 (Berlin: Töpelmann, 1938), 240–44; Hans Walter Wolff, "Das Kerygma des deuteronomistischen Geschichtswerks," *ZAW* 73 (1961): 171–86 (reprinted in *Gesammelte Studien zum Alten Testament*, TB 22 [Munich: Kaiser, 1964], 308–24); Rudolf Smend, "Das Gesetz und die Völker," in *Probleme biblischer Theologie: Gerhard von Rad zum 70. Geburtstag*, ed. Hans Walter Wolff (Munich: Kaiser, 1971), 494–509 (reprinted in Smend, *Die Mitte des Alten Testaments: Gesammelte Studien 1*, BEvTh 99 [Gütersloh: Gütersloher Verlagshaus, 1986], 124–37); Smend, *Die Entstehung des Alten Testaments*, 4th ed., ThW 1 (Stuttgart: Kohlhammer, 1989), 111–25, esp. 113; Helga Weippert, "Die 'deuteronomistischen' Beurteilungen der Könige von Israel und Juda und das Problem der Redaktion der Königsbücher," *Bib* 53 (1972): 301–39; Frank Moore Cross, "The Themes of the Book of Kings and the Structure of the Deuteronomistic History," in idem, *Canaanite Myth and Hebrew Epic: Essays in the History of the Religion of Israel* (Cambridge, MA: Harvard University Press, 1973), 274–89; Richard D. Nelson, *The Double Redaction of the Deuteronomistic History*, JSOTSup 18 (Sheffield: Sheffield Academic, 1981); Baruch Halpern and David S. Vanderhooft, "The Editions of Kings in the 7th–6th Centuries B.C.E.," *HUCA* 62 (1991): 179–244; Gary N. Knoppers, *Two Nations under God: The Deuteronomistic History of Solomon and the Dual Monarchies*, 2 vols., HSM 52, 53 (Cambridge, MA: Harvard University Press, 1993, 1994), 1:51–52; Norbert Lohfink, "Kerygmata des Deuteronomistischen Geschichtswerks," in *Die Botschaft und die Boten: Festschrift für Hans Walter Wolff zum 70. Geburtstag*, ed. Jörg Jeremias and Lothar Perlitt (Neukirchen-Vluyn: Neukirchener Verlag, 1981), 87–100; Gottfried Vanoni, "Beobachtungen zur deuteronomistischen Terminologie in 2Kön 23,25–25,30," in *Das Deuteronomium: Entstehung, Gestalt und Botschaft*, ed. Norbert Lohfink, BETL 73 (Leuven: Peeters, 1985), 357–62; André Lemaire, "Vers l'histoire de la rédaction des livres des Rois," *ZAW* 98 (1986): 221–36; idem, "Toward a Redactional History of the Book of Kings," in *Reconsidering Israel and Judah: Recent Studies on the Deuteronomistic History*, ed. Gary N. Knoppers and J. Gordon McConville, SBTS 8 (Winona Lake, IN: Eisenbrauns, 2000), 446–61; Iain W. Provan, *Hezekiah and the Book of Kings*, BZAW 172 (Berlin: de Gruyter, 1988); Mark A. O'Brien, *The Deuteronomistic History Hypothesis: A Reas-*

Noth identified as "Deuteronomistic" in the Former Prophets stems from more than one hand. In what follows, I discuss a test case from 2 Kgs 24–25 where processes of layered textual supplementation seem obvious to me. The focus will be on 24:13–14 and 24:3–4.[5] This case study, however, is to a certain extent exceptional, since the supplementation is, as I will demonstrate, not "Deuteronomistic"—whether in a narrow or broad sense of the term[6]—but something else.

1. The Conquest of Jerusalem in 587 BCE according to 2 Kings 25

Jerusalem was conquered twice by the Babylonians, first in 597 and then in 587 BCE.[7] The Bible covers these events in 2 Kgs 24 and 25. For reasons that will become clear later on, I begin with the account of the *second* conquest in chapter 25, which includes the city and temple's destruction by fire in 587 BCE. The basic historicity of this event cannot be doubted.[8] Although we have no extrabiblical reference to this event and the

---

sessment, OBO 92 (Fribourg: Éditions universitaires; Göttingen: Vandenhoeck & Ruprecht, 1992); Ansgar Moenikes, "Zur Redaktionsgeschichte des sogenannten Deuteronomistischen Geschichtswerks," ZAW 104 (1992): 333–48; Erik Eynikel, *The Reform of King Josiah and the Composition of the Deuteronomistic History*, OTS 33 (Leiden: Brill, 1996); Reinhard G. Kratz, *Die Komposition der erzählenden Bücher des Alten Testaments: Grundwissen der Bibelkritik*, UTB 2157 (Göttingen: Vandenhoeck & Ruprecht, 2000; Eng. trans. *The Composition of the Narrative Books of the Old Testament*, trans. John Bowden [London: T&T Clark, 2005]); Marvin A. Sweeney, *King Josiah of Judah: The Lost Messiah of Israel* (Minneapolis: Fortress, 2001); Thomas Römer, "Une seule maison pour le Dieu unique? La centralisation du culte dans le Deutéronome et dans l'historiographie deutéronomiste," in *Quelle maison pour Dieu?*, ed. Camille Focant, LD (Paris: Cerf, 2003), 49–80; Römer, *So-Called Deuteronomistic History*; Erik Aurelius, *Zukunft jenseits des Gerichts: Eine redaktionsgeschichtliche Studie zum Enneateuch*, BZAW 319 (Berlin: de Gruyter, 2003); Jacob L. Wright, *David, King of Israel, and Caleb in Biblical Memory* (Cambridge: Cambridge University Press, 2014).

5. The specific profile of 2 Kgs 24:13–14 was noticed early on. See Bernhard Stade, "Wie hoch belief sich die Zahl der unter Nebucadnezar nach Babylon deportirten Juden?" ZAW 4 (1884): 271–75. A detailed discussion can be found in Marc Brettler, "2 Kings 24:13–14 as History," CBQ 53 (1991): 541–52.

6. For a discussion, see the essays in Linda S. Schearing and Steven L. McKenzie, eds., *Those Elusive Deuteronomists: The Phenomenon of Pan-Deuteronomism*, JSOTSup 268 (Sheffield: Sheffield Academic, 1999); Christophe Nihan, "'Deutéronomiste' et 'deutéronomisme': Quelques remarques de Méthode en lien avec le débat actuel," in *Congress Volume: Helsinki 2010*, ed. Martti Nissinen, VTSup148 (Leiden: Brill, 2012), 409–42.

7. See Christian Frevel, *Geschichte Israels* (Stuttgart: Kohlhammer, 2015), 270–77.

8. See Rainer Albertz, "Die Zerstörung des Jerusalemer Tempels 587 v. Chr.: Historische Einordnung und religionspolitische Bedeutung," in *Zerstörungen des Jerusalemer Tempels: Geschehen – Wahrnehmung – Bewältigung*, ed. Johannes Hahn, WUNT 147 (Tübingen: Mohr Siebeck, 2002), 23–39; in the same volume, see also Walter Mayer, "Die Zerstörung

archaeology of the temple in Jerusalem is inaccessible,[9] the event is so well attested and reflected in various biblical texts that we can safely infer its basic historicity from these texts.[10]

The biblical text that reports these events in 2 Kgs 25 has a prelude in 24:18–20 and includes all of chapter 25 except for the last four verses about King Jehoiachin's parole in Babylon. 2 Kings 24:18 starts with the description of Zedekiah's reign, which lasted for eleven years. The preceding verse makes clear that Zedekiah was not a sovereign king but a puppet of Babylon's king who had appointed Zedekiah as king and even renamed him from "Mattaniah" to "Zedekiah." This renaming is a clear sign of suzerainty.[11] Verses 19–20 add a negative theological evaluation of Zedekiah, but they offer only an implicit connection between the "evil doing" (ויעש הרע) of Zedekiah and the "anger of Yhwh" (אף יהוה)[12] that follows.[13] The text establishes no explicit causal link between them, but v. 20b eventually mentions a mundane explanation for the catastrophe: Zedekiah "rebelled" against the king of Babylon (וימרד צדקיהו במלך בבל), which, in historical terms, means that he stopped paying tribute.

Second Kings 25:1–2 then jumps ahead to the ninth year of Zedekiah and describes the two-year siege of Jerusalem by Nebuchadnezzar. The date in 25:3 has to be restored according to the information in the parallel account of Jer 52:6 בחדש הרביעי בתשעה לחדש, "on the ninth day of the

---

des Jerusalemer Tempels 587 v. Chr. im Kontext der Praxis von Heiligtumszerstörungen im antiken Vorderen Orient," 1–22.

9. See Israel Finkelstein, Ido Koch, and Oded Lipschits, "The Mound on the Mount: A Possible Solution to the Problem with Jerusalem," *JHebS* 11 (2011), https://ejournals.library.ualberta.ca/index.php/jhs/article/view/11527.

10. See the seminal methodological principles of Ernst Troeltsch, "Über historische und dogmatische Methode in der Theologie" (1898), in Troeltsch, *Zur religiösen Lage, Religionsphilosophie und Ethik: Gesammelte Schriften* (Tübingen: Mohr, 1913), 2:728–53 (English translation available at http://faculty.tcu.edu/grant/hhit/). Troeltsch claimed that three methodological steps are required for historically assessing biblical texts: "critique," "analogy," and "correlation." There are some Neo-Babylonian sources pertaining to the end of the kingdom of Judah, but unfortunately they do not cover the catastrophe of 587 BCE: The so-called Neo-Babylonian Chronicles 2–5 report the military actions of the Babylonian kings up to the year 594/593 including the conquest of Jerusalem in 597.

11. On naming as an element of domination, see Annette Schellenberg, *Der Mensch, das Bild Gottes? Zum Gedanken einer Sonderstellung des Menschen im Alten Testament und in weiteren altorientalischen Quellen*, ATANT 101 (Zurich: Theologischer Verlag, 2011), 304–5.

12. On this notion, see Reinhard Kratz, "Chemosh's Wrath and Yahweh's No: Ideas of Divine Wrath in Moab and Israel," in *Divine Wrath and Divine Mercy in the World of Antiquity*, ed. Reinhard Kratz and Hermann Spieckermann, FAT 2/33 (Tübingen: Mohr Siebeck, 2008), 92–121.

13. See Konrad Schmid, "Die Geschichte im Credo: Genealogie und Theologie des Geschichtsbezugs alttestamentlichen Glaubens," in *Freiheit im Bekenntnis: Das Glaubensbekenntnis der Kirche in theologischer Perspektive*, ed. Pierre Bühler, Emidio Campi, and Hans Jürgen Luibl (Zurich: Pano, 2000), 129–49.

fourth month." After a breach in the city wall, the king and his soldiers flee the city,[14] but they are eventually captured. Zedekiah is brought to Nebuchadnezzar's headquarters in Ribla in northern Syria, where he is blinded and his sons are slaughtered. Afterward, Zedekiah is deported to Babylon. Eventually, Nebuchadnezzar's high officer Nebuzaradan orders the destruction of the temple, the palace, and all the great houses (25:9). In addition, the city walls are broken down (25:10). Except for some poor farmers, the city's population is deported to Babylon (25:12). The pillars and vessels of the temple are also brought to Babylon, which is described in detail (25:13–17). The priests are brought to Riblah and killed (25:18–21). 2 Kings 25:22–26 recounts the episode about Gedaliah and his murder, whereas 25:27–30 deals with the last days of King Jehoiachin's exile, even mentioning that he was allowed to dine at the table of the king of Babylon.

When one considers 2 Kgs 25, it is apparent that the chapter offers no explicit theological interpretation of the events it narrates.[15] It is noteworthy that the tetragrammaton Yhwh occurs only three times in chapter 25, each time in the expression "house of Yhwh" (בית־יהוה, vv. 9, 13, 16), denoting the temple in Jerusalem. But the text is silent about possible acts of God surrounding the destruction of Jerusalem. The chapter reports only what the Babylonians are doing but does not mention divine agency. It is up to the reader to add a theological dimension to the events. In particular, the long passage about the looting of the temple seems implicitly to stress that this event is of special importance: God's own temple is deprived of its vessels and is thus no longer able to operate as a cult place.

For the following discussion pertaining to 2 Kgs 24, note that, according to 25:11, the events of 587 BCE *empty the land*:

ואת יתר העם הנשארים בעיר	And the rest of the people who were left in the city
ואת־הנפלים	and the deserters
אשר נפלו על־המלך בבל	who had defected to the king of Babylon,
ואת יתר ההמון	all the rest of the population,
הגלה נבוזראדן רב־טבחים:	Nebuzaradan the captain of the guard carried into exile.

---

14. Christoph Levin doubts the historicity of this event: "The fact that this account of events is fictitious can be deduced from the extremely precise topographical information: 'by the way of the gate between the two walls, by the king's garden,' 'in the direction of the Arabah,' 'in the plains of Jericho.' The original Annals were not interested in details of this kind. The very way in which the writer suggests historical exactness betrays that this exactness did not exist" ("The Empty Land in Kings," in *The Concept of Exile in Ancient Israel and Its Historical Contexts*, ed. Ehud Ben Zvi and Christoph Levin, BZAW 404 [Berlin: de Gruyter, 2010], 61–89, here 74).

15. See Konrad Schmid, *Is There Theology in the Hebrew Bible?*, trans. Peter Altmann, Critical Studies in the Hebrew Bible 7 (Winona Lake, IN: Eisenbrauns, 2015).

Only the few poor farmers remain (25:12):

ומדלת הארץ השאיר	But some of the poorest people of the land
רב־טבחים	the captain of the guard left
לכרמים וליגבים:	to be vinedressers and tillers of the soil.

Furthermore, it is important to note that *the temple treasuries were brought to Babylon in 587 BCE,* according to 2 Kgs 25:13–17:

ואת־עמודי הנחשת	The bronze pillars
אשר בית־יהוה	that were in the house of Yhwh,
ואת־המכנות ואת־ים הנחשת	as well as the stands and the bronze sea
אשר בבית־יהוה	that were in the house of Yhwh,
שברו כשדים	the Chaldeans broke in pieces,
וישאו את־נחשתם בבלה:	and carried their bronze to Babylon.
ואת־הסירת ואת־היעים	They took away the pots, the shovels,
ואת־המזמרות ואת־הכפות	the snuffers, the dishes for incense,
ואת כל־כלי הנחשת	and all the bronze vessels
אשר ישרתו־בם לקחו:	used in the temple service,
ואת־המחתות ואת־המזרקות	as well as the fire pans and the basins.
אשר זהב זהב	What was made of gold
ואשר־כסף כסף	and what was made of silver,
לקח רב־טבחים:	the captain of the guard took it away.
העמודים שנים הים האחד	As for the two pillars, the one sea,
והמכנות	and the stands,
אשר־עשה שלמה לבית יהוה	which Solomon had made for the house of Yhwh,
לא־היה משקל	the bronze of all these vessels
לנחשת כל־הכלים האלה:	was beyond weighing.
שמנה עשרה אמה קומת	The height of the one pillar
העמוד האחד	was eighteen cubits,
וכתרת עליו נחשת	and on it was a bronze capital;
וקומת הכתרת שלש אמה	the height of the capital was three cubits;
ושבכה ורמנים על־הכתרת סביב	latticework and pomegranates were on the capital all around.
הכל נחשת	All was of bronze,
וכאלה לעמוד השני	The second pillar had the same,
על־השבכה:	with the latticework.

2. The Perspective of 2 Kings 24

Upon moving from 2 Kgs 25 to the preceding chapter, which depicts the events of Jerusalem's first conquest ten years prior in 597 BCE,[16] there are some astonishing observations to be made. First, according to 24:14, already in 597, *all* of Jerusalem went into exile:

והגלה את־כל־ירושלם	He carried away all Jerusalem,
ואת־כל־השרים	all the officials,
ואת כל־גבורי החיל	all the warriors,
עשרה אלפים גולה	ten thousand deportees,
וכל־החרש והמסגר	all the armorers and the smiths;
לא נשאר זולת דלת עם־הארץ:	no one remained, except the poorest people of the land

It is difficult to understand how 2 Kgs 25:11 can report a similar deportation ten years later if nearly everyone had already been deported in 597 according to 24:14. Who could have been carried away from Jerusalem after 597 BCE if one takes 24:14 at face value?

Second, the precious vessels of the temple that 25:13–17 says were taken to Babylon after 587 BCE had already been carried off ten years earlier, according to 24:13:

ויוצא משם	He carried off
את־כל־אוצרות	all the treasures
בית יהוה	of the house of Yhwh,
ואוצרות בית המלך	and the treasures of the king's house;
ויקצץ את־כל־כלי הזהב	he cut in pieces all the vessels of gold,
אשר עשה שלמה מלך־ישראל	which Solomon, king of Israel, had made
בהיכל יהוה	in the temple of Yhwh,
כאשר דבר יהוה:	all this as Yhwh had foretold.

The remark about Yhwh's foretelling may refer to 2 Kgs 20:17, but it may also have no specific scriptural reference in mind.[17] At least in terms of the narrative logic, the possibility that in 597 only a part, and in 587 the remainder, of the temple vessels were taken is not feasible, since 2 Kgs 24:13 itself clearly states that "all the treasures of the house of Yhwh"

---

16. Martin Noth, "Die Einnahme von Jerusalem im Jahre 597 v. Chr.," in Noth, *Archäologische, exegetische und topographische Untersuchungen zur Geschichte Israels* vol. 1 of *Aufsätze zur biblischen Landes- und Altertumskunde*, ed. Hans Walter Wolff(Neukirchen-Vluyn: Neukirchener Verlag, 1971), 111–32.

17. See Ernst Würthwein, *Die Bücher der Könige*, 2 vols. ATD 11 (Göttingen: Vandenhoeck & Ruprecht, 1984), 2:473.

(את־כל־אוצרות בית יהוה) were taken. We have a clear contradiction here, reflecting two competing views about when the temple vessels were carried away from the Jerusalem temple: 24:13 holds that it happened in 597 BCE, whereas 25:13–17 dates the event a decade later.

At this point, we can highlight two peculiarities. First, the depictions of the conquests of Jerusalem in 597 BCE and 587 BCE in 2 Kgs 24 and 2 Kgs 25 each contain an account of how the population and the temple vessels were brought to Babylon. Second, there are obviously other aims reflected in the accounts of 2 Kgs 24 and 25; more is involved than just depicting historical realities.

Thus, the following questions arise: What is the motivation behind the literary production of these contradictions? Why is the carrying away of the population and temple vessels connected with two events that are ten years apart?

3. Redactional Reworking and Theological Interpretation in 2 Kings 24

A first step in dealing with these questions is to ask to what extent 2 Kgs 24 reflects historical realities and to identify the chapter's ideological overlay. For the events described in chapter 24 there are both biblical and extrabiblical accounts available. Of course, the difference between biblical and extrabiblical sources is not that the former are ideological and the latter are trustworthy, as some "minimalist" scholars tend to assume. Both sources are in need of critical evaluation, and the information in one needs to be balanced against what we find in the other.[18]

The Neo-Babylonian Chronicle 5 reports:[19]

> He [sc. the king of Akkad, i.e., Nebuchadnezzar] encamped against the city of Judah [*ina* [*muḫḫi*] *āl Ia-a-ḫu-du;* sc. Jerusalem] and on the second day of the month Adar he captured the city (and) seized [*ik-ta-šad*] (its) king. A king of his own choice he appointed [*ip-te-qid*] in the city (and) taking the vast tribute he brought it into Babylon.

---

18. See, e.g., Bob Becking, "No More Grapes from the Vineyard? A Plea for a Historical Critical Approach in the Study of the Old Testament," in *Congress Volume: Oslo 1998*, ed. A. Lemaire and M. Sæbø, VTSup 80 (Leiden: Brill, 2000), 123–41; Steven W. Holloway, "Expansion of the Historical Context of the Hebrew Bible/Old Testament," in *From Modernism to Post-Modernism (the Nineteenth and Twentieth Centuries)*, part 1, *The Nineteenth Century—a Century of Modernism and Historicism*, ed. Magne Sæbø, vol. 3 of *Hebrew Bible / Old Testament: The History of Its Interpretation* (Göttingen: Vandenhoeck & Ruprecht, 2013), 90–118.

19. A. Kirk Grayson, *Assyrian and Babylonian Chronicles* (1970; repr., Winona Lake, IN: Eisenbrauns, 2000), 102.

This account can be compared to those of other military campaigns of Nebuchadnezzar in the same chronicle. "Seizing" a king is also reported with reference to the conquest of Ashkelon in 604 BCE, but "appointing" a new king is mentioned only here. The deportation of Jehoiachin is not mentioned, but it should be taken for granted, since Jehoiachin shows up in Babylonian texts that presuppose his sojourn in Babylon.[20] Taking a "vast" tribute is the most common element in the Neo-Babylonian Chronicles. Apparently, economic benefit was one of the important aims of such campaigns.[21]

We may, therefore, infer that 2 Kgs 24 provides correct historical information on the siege and capture of Jerusalem, which only the Neo-Babylonian Chronicle dates exactly. (2 Kings 24:10 only states: בעת ההיא, "at that time," referring back to 24:8.) Also reliable is the seizing of King Jehoiachin and his replacement by Mattaniah/Zedekiah. And finally, from common Neo-Babylonian military practice, and from the mention in the Neo-Babylonian Chronicle 5 and 2 Kgs 24, we can infer that "vast tribute" had been carried from Jerusalem to Babylon. However, this tribute arguably did not include "all" treasures from the temple, since a text such as Jer 27:19–21, which presupposes a setting between 597 and 587 BCE, refers three times to "vessels" remaining in the temple and palace.[22]

Regarding a possible deportation in 597 BCE, there is no information available from the Neo-Babylonian Chronicle 5. As mentioned, the deportation of King Jehoiachin is to be considered a historical fact, given the later references to him from Babylon.[23] But regarding a possible deportation of the population in 597 BCE, we have to examine critically the text of 2 Kgs 24. The relevant passage is in vv. 12–16:

ויצא יהויכין מלך־יהודה	King Jehoiachin of Judah went out
על־מלך בבל	to the king of Babylon,
הוא ואמו	he himself, his mother,
ועבדיו ושריו וסריסיו	his servants, his officers, and his palace officials.
ויקח אתו מלך בבל	The king of Babylon took him
בשנת שמנה למלכו:	in the eighth year of his reign.

---

20. See Manfred Weippert, *Historisches Textbuch zum Alten Testament*, GAT 10 (Göttingen: Vandenhoeck & Ruprecht, 2010), 425–30; Bob Becking, "Does Exile Equal Suffering? A Fresh Look at Psalm 137," in *Exile and Suffering: A Selection of Papers Read at the 50th Anniversary Meeting of the Old Testament Society of South Africa OTWSA/OTSSA, Pretoria August 2007*, ed. B. Becking and D. Human, OtSt 50 (Leiden: Brill, 2008), 183–202, here 186; see also Marvin Sweeney, *I & II Kings: A Commentary*, OTL (Louisville: Westminster John Knox, 2007), 459 n. 4.

21. See Angelika Berlejung, "The Assyrians in the West: Assyrianization, Colonialism, Indifference, or Development Policy?," in *Congress Volume: Helsinki 2010*, 21–60.

22. Oded Lipschits, *The Fall and Rise of Jerusalem: Judah under Babylonian Rule* (Winona Lake, IN: Eisenbrauns, 2005), 301 n. 122.

23. See n. 20.

ויוצא משם את־כל־אוצרות	He carried off all the treasures
בית יהוה	of the house of Yhwh,
ואוצרות בית המלך	and the treasures of the king's house;
ויקצץ את־כל־כלי הזהב	he cut in pieces all the vessels of gold,
אשר עשה שלמה מלך־ישראל	which Solomon, king of Israel, had made
בהיכל יהוה	in the temple of Yhwh,
כאשר דבר יהוה:	all this as Yhwh had foretold.
והגלה את־כל־ירושלם	He carried away all Jerusalem,
ואת־כל־השרים	all the officials,
ואת כל־גבורי החיל	all the warriors,
עשרה אלפים גולה	ten thousand deportees,
וכל־החרש והמסגר	all the armorers and the smiths;
לא נשאר זולת דלת עם־הארץ:	no one remained, except the poorest people of the land.
ויגל את־יהויכין בבלה	He carried away Jehoiachin to Babylon;
ואת־אם המלך ואת־נשי המלך	the king's mother, the king's wives,
ואת־סריסיו ואת אולי הארץ	his officials, and the elite of the land,
הוליך גולה מירושלם בבלה:	he took into captivity from Jerusalem to Babylon.
ואת כל־אנשי החיל	And all the warriors,
שבעת אלפים	seven thousand,
והחרש והמסגר אלף	the armorers and the smiths, one thousand,
הכל גבורים עשי מלחמה	all of them strong and fit for war,
ויביאם מלך־בבל גולה בבלה:	the king of Babylon brought them captive to Babylon.

This passage betrays clear signs of literary disunity and redactional reworking. After reporting the seizing of King Jehoiachin (v. 12), it mentions the carrying away of the temple's and palace's treasures (v. 13) and the deportation of "all Jerusalem," "all the officials, all the warriors, ten thousand deportees, all the armorers and the smiths," adding that only the poor remained in the land (v. 14). Then the deportation of the king is reported, which included his household and the land's elite (v. 15). Finally, we are again told that "all the warriors" were carried away to Babylon, but now they number seven thousand along with one thousand "artisans and smiths" (v. 16).

Verse 15 is the least suspicious verse, containing as it does historically accurate information (as already discussed). But v. 14 and v. 16 present conflicting views. It seems that v. 14 takes up v. 16, which is plausibly placed after v. 15, which mentions the king and his entourage, and expands and generalizes the information contained therein: ten thousand captives were deported to Babylon, not eight thousand, and it was "all Jerusalem" that was carried away.

Therefore, one may assume that vv. 15–16 belong to the basic layer of chapter 24, mentioning information that is probably historically accurate—namely, the deportation of the king, his officials, and those responsible for Judah's military industry. But there can be no conclusion other than to identify the general descriptions about carrying away "all the treasures" and "all Jerusalem" in vv. 13–14 as additions.[24] These verses are the result of a secondary expansion that attempts to portray Jerusalem as already emptied in 597 BCE, a claim in conflict with the following verses as well as with other biblical texts that presuppose a significant population in Jerusalem after 597 BCE (e.g., Jer 27–29 or 37–44). In addition, one might also point to the literary continuity between v. 12 and v. 15, once vv. 13–14 are identified as an addition.[25] But why are 2 Kgs 24:13–14 interested in portraying a total deportation after the events of 597 BCE?[26] What kind of theological interest is connected with this position?

4. The "Golah-Oriented" Character of 2 Kings 24:13–14

To address these questions, we must first recognize that the main body of theological interpretation at the end of the books of Kings is provided in 2 Kgs 24 instead of 2 Kgs 25.[27] The somewhat less decisive events in 597 BCE seemed to have been given more interpretive weight than those of 587 BCE.

---

24. See Stade, "Wie hoch belief sich die Zahl"; Brettler, "2 Kings 24:13–14"; Kratz, *Die Komposition der erzählenden Bücher*, 173, 193.

25. See Lipschits, *Fall and Rise of Jerusalem*; Levin, "Empty Land," 67.

26. Regarding the deportations recounted in 2 Kgs 25:11–12, newer research has suggested that the Babylonians indeed carried away a significant portion of the population. On this, see Lipschits, *Fall and Rise of Jerusalem*, 300 n. 16, 149–54; Lipschits, "Demographic Changes in Judah between the Seventh and the Fifth Centuries B.C.E.," in *Judah and the Judeans in the Neo-Babylonian period*, ed. Oded Lipschits and Joseph Blenkinsopp (Winona Lake, IN: Eisenbrauns, 2003), 323–76; Lipschits, "The Rural Settlement in Judah in the Sixth century B.C.E.: A Rejoinder," *PEQ* 136 (2004): 99–107; see also Israel Finkelstein, "The Territorial Extent and Demography of Yehud/Judea in the Persian and Early Hellenistic Periods," *RB* 117 (2010): 39–54; cf. the discussion in Ehud Ben Zvi, "Total Exile, Empty Land and the General Intellectual Discourse in Yehud," in Ben Zvi and Levin, *Concept of Exile*, 155–68. Traditional scholarship in the twentieth century believed that the biblical reports about the numbers of deportees were highly exaggerated and preferred to trust in the kind of information that can be found in Jer 52:28–30. But the text of Jer 52:28–30 is not very trustworthy, since these verses are absent from the LXX.

27. See, among many others, Christopher R. Seitz, *Zion's Final Destiny: The Development of the Book of Isaiah; A Reassessment of Isaiah 36–39* (Minneapolis: Fortress, 1991); see also the discussion in Jakob Wöhrle, "Die Rehabilitierung Jojachins: Zur Entstehung und Intention von 2 Kön 24,17–25,30," in *Berührungspunkte: Studien zur Sozial- und Religionsgeschichte Israels und seiner Umwelt: Festschrift für Rainer Albertz zu seinem 65. Geburtstag*, ed. Ingo Kottsieper, Rüdiger Schmitt, and Jakob Wöhrle, AOAT 350 (Münster: Ugarit-Verlag, 2008), 213–38.

The most explicit interpretive passage is to be found at the beginning of chapter, in vv. 2–4.[28] This passage interrupts the narrative flow between v. 1 and v. 5 and stands out because of its specific theological profile. Verses 3–4 in particular are closely linked to what we identified in vv. 13–14 as an addition in chapter 24. Verses 3–4 read as follows:

אך על־פי יהוה היתה ביהודה	Surely this came upon Judah at the command of Yhwh,
הסיר מעל פניו	to remove them out of his sight,
בחטאת מנשה	for the sins of Manasseh,
ככל אשר עשה:	for all that he had committed,
וגם דם־הנקי אשר שפך	and also for the innocent blood that he had shed;
וימלא את־ירושלם דם נקי	for he filled Jerusalem with innocent blood,
ולא־אבה יהוה לסלח:	and Yhwh was not willing to pardon.

To begin, it is necessary to determine the meaning of the clause "this came upon Judah." Does it only refer back to the sending of the different bands in the days of Jehoiakim (v. 2)? Such is not likely the case, since the end of v. 2b explicitly holds that "he sent them against Judah *to destroy it*" (וישלחם ביהודה להאבידו). Verse 2b is thus an elliptical formulation that already anticipates the decisive events narrated later on in chapters 24–25. In addition, v. 3 states explicitly להסיר מעל פניו, "to remove [them] out of his sight." This verse points forward to the total deportation of "all" Jerusalem mentioned in v. 14.

The most astonishing interpretive device in 24:3–4 is the prominent and exclusive blaming of Manasseh for what happens to Jerusalem and Judah according to 24:13–14: "for the sins of Manasseh, for all that he had committed, and also for the innocent blood that he had shed; for he filled

---

28. There is a text-critical issue at the beginning of v. 2, since Yhwh is named in the Hebrew text as the explicit subject of the sending of Babylonian troops against Judah (וישלח יהוה בו), whereas the Greek text provides no explicit subject, but refers back to Nebuchadnezzar as the subject in v. 1 (καὶ ἀπέστειλεν αὐτῷ). Würthwein thinks the Greek version is original, so that "Yhwh" as subject would have intruded from the statement in v. 2b: "according to the word of Yhwh that he spoke by his servants the prophets." This is possibly, but not necessarily, a reference back to 2 Kgs 20:17. See Würthwein, *Die Bücher der Könige*, 2: 473. The reason, according to Würthwein, is that nowhere else in the basic layer of the Deuteronomistic History ("DtrG": see the discussion in Römer, *So-Called Deuteronomistic History*; Gary N. Knoppers, "Theories of the Redaction(s) of Kings," in Lemaire and Halpern, *Book of Kings*, 69–88) does Yhwh intervene so directly in the course of historical events (Würthwein, *Die Bücher der Könige*, 2: 468 n. 2). But later on we will see that 2 Kgs 24:2–4 is not really "Deuteronomistic" in its theology, which raises the question of whether the text stems from a Deuteronomistic hand. Furthermore, the wording of v. 2b (להאבידו) is a strong argument against Würthwein's suggestion that 24:1–2 originally had "Nebuchadnezzar" as the subject instead of "Yhwh." With reference to Judah, אבד (*hiphil* "to destroy") always has God as its subject (Deut 28:53, 61; Jer 1:10; 18:7; 31:28).

Jerusalem with innocent blood, and Yhwh was not willing to pardon." This statement is very much at odds what we know from elsewhere in the books of Kings: the kings—at least the "bad" ones—or the people are seen as responsible, not simply a single king as in 24:3–4.[29] Obviously, 24:3–4 provides a peculiar perspective on the catastrophe of Jerusalem (according to chapter 24) and the theological rationale behind it. Manasseh is the villain who is responsible for all the evil that came upon Judah and Jerusalem. But why Manasseh?

In order to approach this question, a look at the Manasseh passage in 2 Kgs 21:1–10 is necessary, which, besides the summary in 2 Kgs 23:26, is the only text in Deuteronomy–Kings that holds such a view (cf. Jer 15:4). 2 Kings 21 is unique not only in how it blames Manasseh alone but also in how it evaluates him in other respects:

First, 2 Kgs 21:3 mentions that Manasseh rebuilt the high places that Hezekiah had destroyed previously. No king apart from Manasseh "*re*built" high places, which seems here to be seen as an extraordinary cultic crime.

Second, worshiping all the host of heaven is said only of Manasseh (2 Kgs 21:5). 2 Kings 17:16 mentions such worship in the northern kingdom of Israel, but Manasseh is the only king from either Israel or Judah to fail in this way.

Third, in v. 6, his practices of soothsaying, augury, and dealing with the dead are also unique.

Fourth, it is quite often said that kings of the northern kingdom "provoked" (בעס *hiphil*)[30] Yhwh (Jeroboam: 1 Kgs 14:9; 15:30; Baasha: 1 Kgs 16:7; Omri: 1 Kgs 16:26; Ahab: 1 Kgs 16:33; Ahaziah: 1 Kgs 22:54; Israel's kings in general: 2 Kgs 23:19; the people of Israel: 1 Kgs 16:2, 13; 2 Kgs 17:11, 17). But Manasseh is the only king of *Judah* who is said to have "provoked" Yhwh (2 Kgs 21:6).

Fifth, the reproach against Manasseh for having "caused Israel to sin" (חטא *hiphil*, 2 Kgs 21:11, 16) is also unique for a Judean king. It is very common for Jeroboam (1 Kgs 14:16; 15:26, 30, 34; 16:2, 19, 26; 22:53; 2 Kgs 3:3; 10:29, 31; 13:2, 11; 14:24; 15:9, 18, 24, 28; 17:21; 23:15), as well as for a few other kings of the northern kingdom (Baasha and Elah: 1 Kgs 16:13; Ahab: 1 Kgs 21:22).

Taken together, two main motives can be identified in the Manasseh passage in 2 Kgs 21. First, Manasseh is guilty of especially serious sacrilege and offenses, and, second, some of these iniquities are portrayed as

---

29. For a historical reconstruction of the time of Manasseh, see Ernst Axel Knauf, "The Glorious Days of Manasseh," in *Good Kings and Bad Kings*, ed. Lester L. Grabbe, LHBOTS 393 (London: T&T Clark, 2005), 164–88; and, in the same volume, Francesca Stavrakopoulou, "The Blackballing of Manasseh," 248–63.

30. See F. Stolz, "בעס," *THAT* 1:838–42, here 840–41.

the misdeeds of northern kings. In other words, the "sins of Manasseh" (2 Kgs 21:17; 24:3) responsible for Judah's fall seem to parallel the "sin of Jeroboam" that ultimately caused the northern kingdom's downfall. But why does 2 Kgs 21 together with 2 Kgs 23:26 and 24:3–4 develop this peculiar perspective? It is at odds with the mainstream theology of the books of Kings, which condemns the bad kings (all those from the northern kingdom and about half from the southern kingdom) and the people, while refraining from singling out an individual as responsible for the fall of Jerusalem.

The key to answering this question lies in the specific theological profile of 2 Kgs 24. The most important interpretive passage is 24:13–14, two verses that almost certainly are a later addition to the chapter, as we have seen. The secondary nature of these verses is obvious for two reasons already mentioned: First, they contradict the following chapter by saying that ten years before 587 BCE (in 597 BCE), "all" treasures of the temple and "all" Jerusalem were carried away, leaving nothing to be taken during the events narrated in chapter 25. Second, v. 15 smoothly links up with v. 12. There must be a specific reason why this addition in vv. 13–14 so obviously twists the historical reality. *Apparently, these verses strive to date the decisive elements of Jerusalem and Judah's catastrophe to 597 BCE, effectively minimizing the significance of 587 BCE.*

Why is this so? The answer can be deduced from the historical information included in v. 15, which belongs to the older stratum in 2 Kgs 24:

> He carried away Jehoiachin to Babylon; the king's mother, the king's wives, his officials, and the elite of the land, he took into captivity from Jerusalem to Babylon. And all the warriors, seven thousand, the armorers and the smiths, one thousand, all of them strong and fit for war, the king of Babylon brought them captive to Babylon.

In this 597 deportation of the king and his entourage, including the elite of the land, lies the main root of the conflict between those who were exiled in Babylon and returned to the land in the wake of Cyrus's edict and those who remained in Judah during the exile. The conflict is documented in several passages from postexilic texts in the Hebrew Bible.[31]

Karl-Friedrich Pohlmann has pointed out what he calls the "gola-orientierte Redaktion" ("*golah*-oriented redaction") in the books of Jeremiah and Ezekiel, by which he means a redaction maintaining and expressing the political and theological interests of those exiled to Babylon

---

31. See the texts discussed in Dalit Rom-Shiloni, *Exclusive Inclusivity: Identity Conflicts between the Exiles and the People Who Remained (6th–5th Centuries BCE)*, LHBOTS 543 (New York: T&T Clark, 2013).

in 597 BCE with King Jehoiachin.[32] Perhaps the best sample text to illustrate this redaction is in Jer 24.[33]

Jeremiah 24 includes a vision dated after the events of 597 BCE. The vision presents two baskets of figs—one basket with good figs, the other one with bad figs. The good figs represent the group around King Jehoiachin that was deported to Babylon in 597 BCE; the bad figs stand for those who remained in the land. The good figs will have a future, but the bad ones will not. Instead, they will be dispersed and disappear.

It is obvious that Jer 24 makes a sharp distinction within the people of Israel: the legitimate part of the people is the first *golah* deported under Jehoiachin. The promise they get is the following (Jer 24:6–7):

ושמתי עיני עליהם לטובה	And I will set my eyes upon them for good,
והשבתים על־הארץ הזאת	and I will bring them back to this land.
ובניתים ולא אהרס	And I will build them up, and not tear them down;
ונטעתים ולא אתוש:	I will plant them, and not pluck them up.
ונתתי להם לב	I will give them a heart
לדעת אתי כי אני יהוה	to know that I am Yhwh;
והיו־לי לעם	and they shall be my people
ואנכי אהיה להם לאלהים	and I will be their God,
כי־ישבו אלי בכל־לבם:	for they shall return to me with their whole heart.

This program is crystal clear, but it certainly does not stem from the historical prophet Jeremiah. In Jer 27–28, as well as in chapters 32 and 37–38, we can see how Jeremiah thought about the situation between 597 and 587 BCE. By no means was he of the opinion that the legitimate part of Israel had been carried away to Babylon, with those remaining in the land doomed to perish. Rather, he held that it was necessary to place one's neck under the yoke of the king of Babylon, because this was the only way to have a chance at survival.

Jeremiah 24 with its perspective of judgment for the Zedekiah generation argues differently: there is no possibility at all for survival after 597 BCE. In fact, according to this position, the land was emptied during the exile. It is obvious that this perspective reflects the interests of the exiled

---

32. Karl-Friedrich Pohlmann, *Studien zum Jeremiabuch*, FRLANT 118 (Göttingen: Vandenhoeck & Ruprecht, 1978).

33. See Konrad Schmid, *Buchgestalten des Jeremiabuches: Untersuchungen zur Redaktions- und Rezeptionsgeschichte von Jer 30–33 im Kontext des Buches*, WMANT 72 (Neukirchen-Vluyn: Neukirchener Verlag, 1996), 253–69; differently Hermann-Josef Stipp, "Jeremia 24: Geschichtsbild und historischer Ort," in Stipp, *Studien zum Jeremiabuch: Text und Redaktion*, FAT 96 (Tübingen: Mohr Siebeck, 2015), 349–79.

community that originated through the 597 BCE deportation. This community wanted to evoke the impression that they are the only legitimate representatives of monarchic Judah after the downfall of Jerusalem.

The same theological program attested in Jer 24 can be found in the book of Ezekiel.[34] Already the dating system in Ezekiel, which is aligned with the reign of Jehoiachin (Ezek 1:2; 8:1; 20:2; 26:1; 29:1, 17; 30:20; 31:1; 32:1, 17; 33:21; 40:1), shows that the Ezekiel tradition is closely linked with the community of the deportees from 597 to which Ezekiel himself belonged. In addition, the book of Ezekiel concurs with the position of Jer 24 that there is no possibility for a future life in the land for those who remained there after 597 BCE (see Ezek 12:19; 14:21–23; 15:8; and 33:21–29).

Given the archeological evidence from the exilic period, it can be maintained that the population of the land was indeed significantly diminished in that time, but the land was by no means empty. In other words, this perspective is historically inaccurate, driven by ideology and probably presupposing some historical distance from the events it describes, as Pohlmann has pointed out.

If one is acquainted with the clear-cut program in Jer 24 and some other texts in Jeremiah (e.g., 29:16–20) and in Ezekiel, it becomes obvious that 2 Kgs 24:2–4 and 13–14 belong to the same ideological movement. They may even have been written by the same hand.[35] 2 Kings 24 has been reinterpreted in order to adapt the end of the book of Kings to the theological program of the *golah*-oriented redaction. The decisive event at the end of the monarchy was the deportation of King Jehoiachin and his entourage in 597 BCE, not the destruction of the temple in 587 BCE and the abduction of King Zedekiah to Riblah.

All of this explains why 2 Kgs 24 is so loaded in theological terms. But the question remains open as to why chapter 25 seems so unpretentious in theological terms. Why is there hardly any explicit interpretive perspective on the theological significance of these events? This is especially noteworthy, since several texts from the period of Jerusalem's fall and the Babylonian exile, such as Lam 1:7–8 or Jer 13:20–22, develop strong interpretations regarding the events of 587 BCE.

---

34. See Karl-Friedrich Pohlmann, *Das Buch des Propheten Hesekiel*, 2 vols., ATD 22 (Göttingen: Vandenhoeck & Ruprecht, 1996, 2001). See also Michael Konkel, "Die Gola von 597 und die Priester: Zu einem Buch von Thilo Alexander Rudnig," *ZABR* 8 (2002): 357–83.

35. See in more detail Konrad Schmid, "Manasse und der Untergang Judas: 'Golaorientierte' Theologie in den Königsbüchern?," *Bib* 78 (1997): 87–99. Brettler considers whether 2 Kgs 24:13–14 might have been originally written for the context of 2 Kgs 25 and then been moved to 2 Kgs 24 ("2 Kings 24:13–14," 550). But the specific profile of 24:13–14 speaks rather for a redactional expansion in chapter 24.

This makes the question even more urgent. Why is there so little explicit theology in 2 Kgs 25?[36] Several possible answers come to mind:

First, if 2 Kgs 25 is chronologically close to the events depicted in the chapter, it may be that not much theological interpretation had been developed at that time and was therefore unavailable to the author. This explanation, however, is not very likely given, for example, the specific shape of the evaluation formula of the last four kings of Judah.[37] In addition, the examples from Lamentations and Jeremiah suggest that historical distance is not necessarily needed for taking an interpretive stance.

Second, if Frank Moore Cross's theory of the composition of the Deuteronomistic History is correct in some of its basic tenets, especially regarding a first edition from the time of Josiah's reform ending in 2 Kgs 23,[38] then the assignment of the main interpretive elements to 2 Kgs 17, after the fall of Samaria and the wicked northern kingdom, and to the evaluations of the kings of Israel and Judah, is reasonable, and there was not yet the place and the need to add a major interpretive perspective within 2 Kgs 25. This was added only in a second edition of the Deuteronomistic History.

Third, it needs to be kept in mind that 2 Kgs 25 and the book of Kings were probably never transmitted and read alone.[39] There was also the prophetic tradition, including at least Isaiah, Jeremiah, Hosea, Amos, Micah, and maybe others (at the time of 2 Kgs 25's first composition), and these prophetic writings were probably already interpreted in some way. Both the extant prophetic writings and Kings looked back at the possible reasons for the catastrophe and, at least to some extent, looked forward into the future. So the main theological interpretation was provided by the prophetic, not the narrative, books of the Hebrew Bible. These two collections were meant to be read and interpreted together.

---

36. See n. 15 for the category "theology" in that respect.
37. See Vanoni, "Beobachtungen zur deuteronomistischen Terminologie," 357–62.
38. See n. 10. Wellhausen was sympathetic with this view. See Julius Wellhausen, *Die Composition des Hexateuchs und der historischen Bücher des Alten Testaments*, 3rd ed. (Berlin: Reimer, 1899), 294–98; and Konrad Schmid, "Hatte Wellhausen recht? Das Problem der literarhistorischen Anfänge des Deuteronomismus in den Königebüchern," in *Die deuteronomistischen Geschichtswerke: Redaktions- und religionsgeschichtliche Perspektiven zur Deuteronomismusdiskussion in Tora und Vorderen Propheten*, ed. Markus Witte et al., BZAW 365 (Berlin: de Gruyter, 2006), 23–47.
39. See Ernst Axel Knauf, "Kings among the Prophets," in *The Production of Prophecy: Constructing Prophecy and Prophets in Yehud*, ed. Diana V. Edelman and Ehud Ben Zvi (London: Equinox, 2009), 131–49.

The Evolution of the Gideon Narrative

JACOB L. WRIGHT
Emory University

The introduction to the Gideon account in the book of Judges portrays Yhwh sending a prophet to the nation to remind them that he brought them up from Egyptian bondage, drove out their enemies from the promised land, and therefore expects their undivided loyalty (6:7–10). Julius Wellhausen claimed in his *Prolegomena* (1878) that these five verses were added to the narrative "in its final redaction," and many commentators throughout the twentieth century came to similar conclusions.[1] As Frank Moore Cross and other scholars studied Qumran manuscripts related to Judges (4QJudg[a]), they found precisely this passage to be missing, with the narrative running seamlessly from the preceding passage to the one that follows it.[2]

The external evidence from Qumran is not the focus of this paper. But, aside from offering us a firsthand material glimpse of textual growth, it raises a basic question: What other portions of the Gideon account might also represent supplements? My contribution to this volume addresses this question as well as some of the difficulties that narrative texts in general present for diachronic analysis. My aim is to demonstrate that, although one cannot always confidently reconstruct the first editions of biblical narratives, it is still possible to isolate supplements to them.

---

1. Julius Wellhausen, *Prolegomena to the History of Israel*, Scholars Press Reprints and Translations (1878; repr., Atlanta: Scholars Press, 1994), 234. George Foot Moore ascribed the passage to E; see *A Critical and Exegetical Commentary on Judges*, ICC (New York: Scribner's Sons, 1903; first published 1895), 181.
2. Robert G. Boling wrote his Anchor Bible commentary on Judges before the publication of the Qumran evidence (*Judges: Introduction, Translation, and Commentary*, AB 6A [Garden City, NY: Doubleday, 1975], 40), yet he cites at length what he learned about it from Frank Moore Cross.

Two Approaches: *A posteriori* versus *a priori*

When reconstructing the composition history of a narrative text, we have a choice between two diachronic approaches. The first is the process of elimination: we subtract parts of the story that, with the help of various criteria, we can determine to be supplements. To return to the example of Judg 6:7–10, this passage severs the connection between 6:6b and 6:11, runs counter to an established narrative pattern in Judges, employs different expressions, and introduces new ideas.[3] The external evidence found at Qumran confirms that such criteria are not unreasonable or hypercritical (as they are often deemed to be) and that the passage is indeed a late supplement. When employing this *a posteriori* approach, we first eliminate the questionable parts; what remains should correspond, more or less, to the original text. The problem with this approach is that it rarely produces a smooth story line.

The alternative is to adopt an *a priori* approach. The latter proceeds by identifying those parts of the story that its other parts presuppose. With these presupposed parts as the point of departure, we attempt to retrace the older story line from beginning to end. While the *a priori* option may be the ideal method for reconstructing texts, it is not always practicable. The problem is that authors/editors may have incorporated and recast older materials. Consequently, the earliest versions of their narrative often will not conform to our expectations for a smooth story line. Further complicating the *a priori* approach is the possibility that early generations of readers/redactors sought to harmonize the text by supplementing it with new lines. In sum, a smooth story line may be the product of multiple hands.

Reinhard Kratz's astute analysis of the Gideon narrative illustrates the tensions between these two approaches.[4] Kratz isolates the framework of a narrative that corresponds, in a stripped-down version, to the form that we find in the MT: 6:11a, 19, 21, 24; 7:1b–8b, 13–15a, 16–21, 22b; 8:4, 10–12, 18–21ba. Gideon is introduced with his father's name and his place of origin; an angel approaches him; he builds an altar for Yhwh; he marches to battle against the Midianites; his men fight "for Yhwh and Gideon"; they triumph with the help of a cunning scheme; and, in the end, Gideon takes revenge on two Midianite kings named Zebah and Zalmunna. Kratz

---

3. To quote Richard D. Nelson on this point: "Judg. 6:7–10 is isolated from its context. While vv. 2–6 and 11–24 are connected together by the movement from crisis to salvation, they neither prepare for nor follow up on 7–10. Literary seams are visible at both ends. V. 7a picks up and repeats 6b, while after v. 10 the expected announcement of judgment does not occur and the oracle breaks off abruptly. In fact, the subject of foreign gods from 7–10 does not come up again until 6:25–32. Judg. 6:7–10 could drop out and not be missed" (*The Double Redaction of the Deuteronomistic History*, JSOTSup 18 [Sheffield: JSOT Press, 1981], 47).

4. Reinhard G. Kratz, *The Composition of the Narrative Books of the Old Testament*, trans. John Bowden (London: T&T Clark, 2005; German original 2000), 203–4.

shows how the remaining episodes presuppose themes from Judges and other parts of the Enneateuch. His guiding assumption, one that he shares with many others who have written on Judges, is that the first version of the Gideon account was not conceived for the narrative of the book.

Kratz's analysis is insightful at many points, but it also has its shortcomings. The most obvious one is evident in the episode in which Gideon captures, and later slays, Zebah and Zalmunna (8:4–21). The episode appears to be an alternative to the battle reported in the preceding chapter. The narrator tells how these kings and their armies were in Karkor, and how Gideon went up "by the caravan route east of Nobah and Jogbehah" (8:11), routed their armies, captured the kings, and then executed them. Not only does this episode not presuppose the earlier battle in chapter 7; it also alludes to events (e.g., the execution of Gideon's brothers) that chapter 7 does not report. How, then, are we to explain the inclusion of this strange episode? Perhaps we must reckon, as Wellhausen did many years ago, with the authors' use of older materials. But can we isolate these sources along with possible later supplements? If so, can we still reconstruct a coherent story line that provided the infrastructure for generations of early readers to compose these supplements? And finally, was this story line originally created for the narrative of Judges?[5]

Analysis of the Gideon Account: Judges 6:1–8:35

What follows is a section-by-section analysis of the narrative. The discussion treats the kinds of considerations and criteria that inform both the *a priori* and *a posteriori* approaches. In this first stage, however, the weight will fall on the latter approach. After subtracting what we can determine to be supplements, I will briefly synthesize the results and postulate how the narrative achieved its present form. It will become apparent that this kind of analysis promises a substantial payoff for the interpretation of biblical narratives in their canonical forms.

The Introduction: 6:1–10

The account is prefaced with an unusually lengthy introduction, which resembles the prologue to the Jephthah account in chapter 10. I already noted that the passage in vv. 7–10 likely forms a supplement and

---

5. For recent research on the Gideon account and a sensitive treatment of the diachronic issues, see Kelly Murphy, "Mapping Gideon: An Exploration of Judges 6–8" (PhD diss., Emory University, 2011).

that it is missing from a Qumran manuscript. The statement in v. 6b that the Israelites cried out to Yhwh would have originally continued with the introduction to Gideon in v. 11. Yhwh responded to the nation's appeal by sending his angel to commission Gideon, an interpretation supported by comparison with other accounts in Judges. The composition of vv. 7–10, however, declares that Yhwh responded by sending an unnamed prophet. His (first) choice was not Gideon![6]

With respect to the preceding lines, all that is required for the introduction is vv. 1–2a and v. 6b. Limited to these lines, the introduction would correspond closely to the beginnings of the Ehud (3:12–15a) and Deborah (4:1–3) accounts.[7] The intervening parts in vv. 2b–6a augment the introduction by painting a broader and more vivid backdrop to the ensuing war. The Midianites joined forces with others to destroy Israel's grain harvest and livestock. They would swarm in droves thick as locusts and lay waste to the land. Their unceasing aggression destroyed Israel's economy, forcing the impoverished Israelites to seek refuge in the mountains, caves, and strongholds. These new lines paint the enemy—and the divine punishment—in the most drastic terms.

Encounter with an Angel: 6:11–24

After the conventional introduction in 6:1–2a, 6b, the account of Gideon's activities begins with his encountering an angel of Yhwh. The scene is depicted at length (vv. 11–24) and contains clues that more than one author had a hand in its composition. The analysis is complicated by the rough transition between v. 11 and v. 12a, with its repetitive statement that "the angel of Yhwh appeared to him." One option is to read the first line (v. 11) in direct connection with vv. 19, 21–24. According to this reading strategy, Gideon would not have known that the visitor was a divine messenger. After the introductory section with background details (6:1–10), we meet the hero performing an activity that illustrates the conditions of fear that plagued his existence: instead of roaming about with his troops, he is back home threshing wheat. He performs his duties in a winepress to conceal the harvest from the Midianites. (This simple statement presupposes the description of these antagonists in vv. 1–2a and 6b, but it contradicts the details provided in vv. 2b–6a.[8]) As he is toiling away, he

---

6. Alternatively, the intention may have been to create a parallel between the prophet Deborah and Barak and this unnamed prophet and Gideon. But, in contrast to the Othniel and Ehud narratives in chapter 3, Yhwh does not "raise up a savior" in the Gideon account.

7. The introduction to the Deborah account was likely expanded with several glosses: vv. 1b and perhaps vv. 2b and (part of) 3b as well.

8. Verses 2b–6a, which describe the ecocidal destruction of the land, do not work well

notices a stranger sitting beneath the prominent oak tree that belonged to his father in Ophrah. Without delay, he shows the visitor generous hospitality, preparing a meal and placing it on a rock before him.[9] When the visitor touches the food with the tip of his rod, fire springs up from the rock and consumes it. Only after the visitor vanishes from sight does Gideon realize that he was an angel. To commemorate the encounter, he builds an altar, which "to this day stands at Ophrah of the Abiezrites" (v. 24).

This reading, which emphasizes the etiological function of the passage, poses a problem: it fails to portray the angel commissioning Gideon, so we do not know what prompted him to mobilize an offensive against the Midianites. Perhaps we are to understand that the visitation left him feeling emboldened and inspired, so that soon thereafter he mounted an attack on the Midianite camp. Conversely, the lines in vv. 13–18 confuse the story by presenting Gideon as if he already knew that the visitor was a divine messenger. This may not be the case with the conversation in vv. 12–15, but it is certainly so in vv. 16–18.

It is possible that vv. 12–16 evolved from a simple statement in vv. 12 and 14: "Yhwh is with you, O mighty warrior! … Go in this strength of yours and deliver Israel from the hand of Midian." This charge reflects an awareness, in keeping with the oldest legends (see below), that Gideon was a skilled warrior, rather than a chicken-livered farmer who required many assurances before undertaking a military action. In contrast, the immediately following lines diminish Gideon's martial prowess by placing an objection on his lips: "But sir, how can I deliver Israel? My clan is the weakest in Manasseh, and I am the least in my father's house" (v. 15). Gideon's objection belongs to the same compositional layer as that in which he repeatedly needs to put Yhwh to the test before taking up arms. The reader of the final edition should know that the hero is not an experienced and self-confident fighter. He is instead a timorous farmer who only gradually musters confidence and triumphs only with Yhwh's direct intervention.

In the verse that precedes the divine commission (6:13), Gideon remonstrates with the angel about divine justice in the face of affliction.

---

as background information on Gideon's activity. He is hiding grain from an enemy that pillaged and plundered, rather than from one who *"destroyed* the produce of the land" and who launched their onslaught during the *planting* season. Moreover, v. 11 and the remainder of the account present Gideon residing in a city, whereas vv. 2b–6a report that the Israelites were hiding in mountains, caves, and strongholds. This observation, that v. 11 presupposes vv. 1–2a and 6b, has important consequences for any attempt, such as that of Kratz, to isolate an account that is independent of the narrative framework in Judges.

9. The attention to grain in the description of the threshing, the unleavened cakes served to the angel, and later the barley cakes in the Midianite's dream (7:13) should be interpreted in light of the way the book of Judges highlights distinctive features of the nation's various regions and clans.

And when he does, he speaks the biblical language of protest. In keeping with Deuteronomy's pedagogical injunctions to parents, these words suggest that the members of Gideon's clan had often heard from their ancestors about the exodus and about Yhwh's other "mighty deeds." The overlap between these lines and the scene with the prophet (6:7–10) is obvious, and it seems likely that the authors of that scene had Gideon's protestations in view.

The Destruction of the Baal Altar: 6:25–32

Gideon and the other members of his clan may have been well versed in Yhwh's "mighty deeds" (v. 13), yet they had failed to behave in accordance with their concomitant obligation of undivided allegiance to him (v. 10). Such is the message of what seems to be a supplement in 6:25–32. The episode depicts Gideon, along with ten of his servants, obeying Yhwh's instructions to tear down his father's Baal-altar along with the Asherah that stood beside it. The iconoclastic act demanded courage (v. 27). But, in contrast to the angst that characterizes Gideon's personality in other episodes, this time he fears his father's house and the townspeople, who seek to execute him for his impiety. Surprisingly, his father defends him from the mob and turns out to be a more radical reformer and Yhwh-polemicist than his son: "Will you [the leaders of Ophrah] contend for Baal? Or will you defend his cause? If he is a god, let him contend for himself, because his altar has been pulled down" (v. 31).

The scene follows hard on the heels of Gideon's first act of building an altar, the one at Ophrah called "Yhwh Shalom." Why, then, would someone have drafted this supplement if it creates such a conspicuous doublet (compare 6:24 to 6:26, 28)? The author's most obvious motivation was to explain how Gideon came to be called "Jerubbaal," the name of Abimelech's father in Judg 9.[10] But the supplement does more than that: it presents Gideon as an early champion of the radical (and often violent) "Yhwh-alone" reforms.[11] The supplement suggests that fidelity to Yhwh and a program of (aggressive) cultic reforms are the prerequisites for successful military campaigns and a secure society; conversely, worship of foreign gods precipitates foreign aggression.

---

10. As is widely acknowledged, Jerubbaal must have been originally a separate figure from Gideon. As the father of Abimelech, his identification with Gideon is likely the work of the authors of Judges.

11. These reforms are promoted at greater length in the Deuteronomistic accounts of Elijah, Elisha, and Josiah, as well as in Chronicles and many of the prophetic writings.

The Cisjordanian Campaign: 6:33–7:22

The most complex portion of the account begins with the muster of troops in 6:33–35 and ends with the battle report in 7:19–22. The scenes with the fleece (6:36–40) and the dream (7:10–15) are easy to identify as supplements. They likely belong to a broader redactional effort to show how Gideon required all kinds of assurances and reassurances, through tests and signs, that Yhwh would indeed grant him a victory.[12]

With respect to the muster of troops, the overlap between 7:1b and 7:8b demarcates the intervening lines (vv. 2–8a), which explain why Gideon fought with only three hundred troops. The section in 7:2–8a must be viewed against the backdrop of the large-scale muster of troops in 6:35 and the subsequent battle accounts, in which Gideon commands a much smaller force and must call upon neighboring tribes to assist in the pursuit of the enemy (7:23–25). This section features the most creative editorial work, redefining the character and composition of Gideon's army. I discuss this larger purpose later in this essay.

To explain the formation of this complex section, we can begin by subtracting the lines that are most obviously secondary. The first one is 6:33. It tells how the Midianites joined forces with two other populations (the Amalekites and the "Children of the East"). Together, they crossed the Jordan and set up camp in the Jezreel Valley. These other populations are mentioned only in what seem to be secondary strata (6:3; 7:12; and 8:10). Their appearance transforms Gideon's campaign into a confrontation with legions of eastern armies. This redactional move to augment the enemy ranks can be seen elsewhere in Judges, such as in the narrative of the Moabites joining forces with the Ammonites and Amalekites in 3:13. The aim seems to have been to depict the deep solidarity of Israel's tribes in relation to the ad hoc coalitions of neighboring forces.

The following verse, 6:34, juxtaposes this prodigious force with the modest numbers that answer Gideon's call. Originally, the recruits consisted of the Abiezrites, Gideon's own clan.[13] The levies that follow — first, his larger tribe of Manasseh (v. 35a) and, later, the northern tribes of Asher, Zebulun, and Naphtali (v. 35b) — are likely supplemental. After v. 35 inflates the size of Gideon's army far beyond the small force that he initially mobilized, 7:2–8a tells how he mustered out most of the thirty-two thousand men who had volunteered for service, keeping only

---

12. Notice that the scene with the fleece in 6:36–40 refers to Elohim rather than to Yhwh. (The other places where Elohim appears are 6:20 and 8:1–3.) Similarly, the scene with the dream in 7:10–15 refers to Israel more explicitly than other parts of the account.

13. The Abiezrites were probably not the poorest or smallest clan in Manasseh; to the contrary, they appear first in two tribal lists (Num 26:31; Josh 17:2) and are attested in the Samaria ostraca.

three hundred for his campaign. (Once again, I discuss this portion later in the paper.)

What remains after this subtraction process is 6:34; 7:1, 8b, 9, 16–22. The lines in 7:1 and 8b are doublets, and 7:1 (without ירבעל הוא) seems to be older. The problem with Yhwh's orders in 7:9 is that 7:1 already reports that Gideon and his troops (notice that their number is unspecified) arose early in the night. Since their objective must have been to attack the Midianite camp, the orders are superfluous. The editorial intention seems to have been to depict Gideon and his men behaving in strict accordance with divine instructions.

As for the lengthy battle report in 7:16–19, scholars have long observed its inconsistencies and repetitions. Minimally, it needs to have comprised solely vv. 15, 17b, 18, 21, and 22abβ (without "when they blew their three hundred trumpets"). This reconstruction, however, is not without problems. For example, the subject of v. 19 refers to the hundred that accompanied Gideon. Is this a round figure referring to Gideon's unit, similar to his three hundred, Saul's six hundred, and David's four hundred?[14] Or does it presuppose the actions of forming an army of three hundred described in 7:2–8a and vv. 16–18? While the doublet in 7:1 and 8b suggests strongly that the oldest versions of the account did not report these actions, it is difficult to reconstruct a battle report that does not presuppose Gideon's three hundred.[15] Such is not the case with the battle report in chapter 8, and the evidence there has direct implications for our assessment of this problematic section.

Ephraim's Capture of the Two Midianite Captains: 7:23–8:3

Chapter 7 concludes with a report about the neighboring tribes who eventually participated in the war with the Midianites. The first statement,

---

14. Gideon divides his corps into *three* large "companies," ראשים, and he leads one hundred (7:16–20; compare the tripartite division in 9:43 as well as in 1 Sam 11:11; 13:2, 17; 2 Sam 18:2). Here the number hundred corresponds to conventional military units: tens, fifties, hundreds, and thousands (see, e.g., Exod 18:21, 25; Num 31:14, 48; Deut 1:15; 1 Sam 22:7; 29:2 et passim). These units could be much smaller than the respective number by which they were known. For example, the Roman *centuria* consisted of either sixty or eighty men. It is even possible that one version of the account knew only of one hundred soldiers (see the formulation of 7:19). The number three hundred represents a conventional military unit in Sparta, Boeotia, and Athens. Texts from the ancient Near East refer to three hundred as a general number for the size of an army (Carchemish, according to Sargon's annals; Ugarit PRU IV 17.59; Mari 6 28 = LAPO 17 573). Yet after the addition of 7:1b–8a, three hundred must be understood as an exact "number," מספר (7:6).

15. One could resort, by necessity, to the *ultima ratio* in redaction criticism and postulate that the subject of 7:19 has been reworded from an original "Gideon and the men who were with him" (see 7:1).

isolated in its present context (v. 23), is revealing: it presupposes that Gideon's force consisted solely of the Abiezrite clan. To expand participation in the war effort, this statement affirms that Israelite men from Naphtali, Asher, and the remainder of Manasseh faithfully answered the call to arms and pursued the Midianites. The statement is closely tied to the preceding description of Gideon mustering all of Manasseh, along with Asher, Zebulun, and Naphtali (6:35). If 7:23 is secondary, we could better understand why later only Gideon and his three hundred are in pursuit of the enemy (8:4).

The following section (7:24–25) tells how Gideon sent messengers throughout the hill country of Ephraim, petitioning the Ephraimites to "go down against the Midianites and seize from them the waters as far as Beth-barah, and also the Jordan." There they managed to capture and kill the two Midianite captains, Oreb and Zeev. The author of this paragraph likely had in view Gideon's dispatch of the two Midianite kings (Zebah and Zalmunna).[16]

In the continuation of this section, 8:1–3, the Ephraimites rebuke Gideon for failing to call upon them when fighting the Midianites. Their anger makes little sense after Gideon's invitation in 7:24–25. Could the latter have been secondarily prefaced to 8:1–3? If so, it would explain why 8:3a has the appearance of a harmonizing gloss. Whatever the case may be, these sections echo the later exchange between the Ephraimites and Jephthah in 12:1–3, rendering it likely that they emerged as part of a broader compositional theme spanning the book of Judges.[17]

Polemics against Two Transjordanian Towns: 8:5–9, 14–17

Gideon's passage to the eastern side of the Jordan is described in 8:4. This verse presupposes a stage of composition in which the campaign against Midian commenced in the Cisjordan. Its second half appears to have been reworked so that it now functions as a lead-in to the episode with two famous towns of the Transjordan.

Just as Gideon had solicited military assistance from the neighboring tribes, he now entreats the towns of Succoth and Penuel to provide succor

---

16. The paragraph concludes with the Ephraimites bringing the captains' heads "to Gideon on the other side of the Jordan." The location is a problem: Not until 8:4 does Gideon cross to the eastern side of the Jordan, and since the Ephraimites are Cisjordanians, the "other side" must refer to the eastern bank. Was the Gideon story, then, originally situated in the Transjordan? If so, we could explain why so much of the account relates to the Transjordan and why the name of Gideon's clan (Abiezrite) is linked to Gilead.

17. Compare also Ehud's petition to the Ephraimites in 3:27–29, and see my "War Commemoration and the Interpretation of Judges 5:15b–17," *VT* 61 (2011): 505–21, esp. 512–13. Perhaps 8:1–3 intends to present Gideon as a foil to Jephthah in 12:1–3.

for his exhausted troops who were pursuing the two Midianite kings. Surprisingly, both places refuse to provision his men, and their refusal stands in stark contrast to the exceptional hospitality that the Abiezrite hero showed the unknown visitor in the first episodes of his account. (Hospitality is a theme of many biblical narratives.) These towns on the eastern frontier had dodged their duties to the nation during wartime, and, just as promised, Gideon inflicts retribution on them.

With relative ease, we can isolate and separate this episode from the account of Gideon's battles in the Transjordan; minimally, it includes 8:5–9 and 14–17. I do not have space here to consider what would have prompted someone to amplify the narrative with this episode. It suffices to point out that it illustrates superbly how the biblical authors used war stories as the framework to honor or deprecate disputed members of the nation.[18] That the episode is indeed an interpolation can be seen from the tight connections that emerge between the surrounding verses, as well as from the way it presupposes Gideon's pursuit of Zebah and Zalmunna. The latter episode is not introduced properly until 8:10–12.

While the passage related to Succoth and Penuel is likely supplemental, it may not always have featured both towns. Did a later hand augment it to include the second town, Penuel (8:8–9 and 17)? If so, the author presents Gideon treating it more harshly than Succoth: he executes its male inhabitants.[19] In these actions, he anticipates (his son) Abimelech's callous behavior, as portrayed in the following chapter.

The Capture and Execution of the Two Midianite Kings: 8:10–13, 18–21

I noted in the discussion of 6:33–7:2 that the analysis of the two passages in 8:10–13, 18–21 bears directly on our evaluation of the Cisjordanian campaign. In the transmitted form of Gideon's story, these paragraphs are to be understood as depicting a second battle. Although this one was fought in the Transjordan, it too was fought when the enemy was off guard. This time, however, Gideon managed to capture the two Midianite kings.

The two passages pose many problems. A line in 8:10 refers to the earlier Cisjordanian conflict ("all who were left of all the army of the peo-

---

18. In *David, King of Israel, and Caleb in Biblical Memory* (New York: Cambridge University Press, 2014), I explore the relationship between war commemoration and the composition of biblical literature.

19. While there would have been a good reason to add specifically Penuel to Succoth (both towns are commemorated in the Jacob narratives), the choice to polemicize against *two* Transjordanian towns was perhaps prompted by an interest in creating parity with the *two* captains and the *two* kings.

ple of the East..."), but it is likely a gloss. To be sure, these paragraphs do know about a battle in the Cisjordan; but, when they refer to it, they only cause more problems. They present Gideon accusing the Midianite kings of having killed his brothers at Tabor. Chapter 7 mentions neither the battle at Tabor nor (the execution of) Gideon's brothers. Moreover, we would expect the two kings to have been (briefly) introduced already in chapters 6 and 7. Yet, up until now, we had no clue that the Midianites were even governed by kings.

These passages also present a very different image of Gideon. They stand in stark contrast to the rest of Gideon's story, which deflates his self-sufficiency and portrays him needing divine reassurance at each step along the way. These passages also introduce Gideon's firstborn son Jether as well as his brothers who, like Gideon, resemble "sons of kings."[20] Finally, it is telling that the account has solely Gideon as its subject (even when implying that his men accompanied him) and shows no interest in either the size or identity of his army.

If these two paragraphs allude to episodes that are missing from our version of the story, then the authors of the first versions of the Gideon account probably had access to older (written) legends of his exploits and drew selectively from them when drafting a story of his life. The image of him portrayed in this new, expanded version of his story is very different from the one reflected in the postulated legends. The death of his brothers at Tabor would have been portrayed in the postulated older legends. Is its omission from Judges part of a more general disinclination in the Bible to commemorate the death of native soldiers?[21]

Gideon's Ephod and Royal Aspirations: 8:22–27

The final episode portrays Gideon in an unflattering light. This is the first time in the narrative that the Israelites come together as one body (איש ישראל). What unites them, however, is not their eagerness to contribute to Gideon's war effort; rather, it is their desire to make Gideon and his descendants their rulers: "Reign over us, you and your son and the son of your son" (8:22). Gideon is here being invited to establish a monarchy, and the unexpected use of the term "reign/rule" (משל) draws an explicit link to Abimelech's words in the first lines of the following chapter: "Which is better for you: that all seventy sons of Jerubbaal *reign* over you or that one

---

20. The very next scene (8:22–27) responds to the implications of this scene by telling how Gideon refused to rule over Israel even while he exploited royal emblems in his quest for power.
21. Throughout the Hebrew Bible, battlefield deaths are not heroic and are often explicitly portrayed as punishment for wrongdoing; see my "Making a Name for Oneself: Martial Valor, Heroic Death, and Procreation in the Hebrew Bible," *JSOT* 36 (2011): 131–62.

man *reigns* over you?" (9:2). The nation's offer of kingship is presented as a reward for Gideon's feat of "saving" them from "the hand of Midian." The formulation of their offer conspicuously (and likely consciously) omits what is underscored throughout the final form of the account, namely, that Yhwh deserves credit for saving Israel and that Gideon was reluctant to fight all along.

This entire episode is likely a late supplement. Notice how the following statement ("Midian was subdued before the Israelites," 8:28) is out of place after vv. 22–27 yet flows smoothly after the execution of the Midianite kings in vv. 18–21. Although supplementary, the episode may have evolved over time. Perhaps it originally concluded with Gideon's repudiation of the offer and declaration that "Yhwh will reign over you!" (v. 23). If so, it would have presented Gideon in a favorable light and dissociated him from his sons' actions (9:2). However, the continuation (vv. 24–27) tells how Gideon immediately thereafter decided to collect payment for his efforts. Adding to his misconduct, the passage reports that he built an ephod with the seventeen hundred shekels of gold he amassed. (The account here is reminiscent of the story of Aaron and the golden calf.[22]) Some of the wealth is said to have once belonged to the Midianite kings and their camels, and Gideon displays the object in his hometown: "There all Israel prostituted themselves with it, and it became a snare to Gideon and his household" (8:27).

In casting aspersions on the hero's achievements and depicting his flirtation with kingship, these verses serve as a segue to the subsequent account of Abimelech's violent and short-lived reign. At this point in Judges, the narrative begins to spiral downward. Prior to Gideon's story, we witnessed how Deborah's unmitigated devotion to the nation and its God compete with Barak's thirst for honor. Beginning with Gideon, the male leaders who follow Deborah and Barak seek opportunities for self-aggrandizement and set their sights on royal power.

Life after Gideon: 8:28–35

The summary statement in 8:28 represents, in the final form of Judges, the natural continuation of the story of Midianites' defeat. This line, along with vv. 32–34, contains the kinds of details and conventional phraseology found in the conclusions to the other accounts in the book. We are told that it was only after Gideon's death that the nation relapsed and "prostituted themselves" with the Baals. This statement is discordant with the ephod

---

22. See Uwe Becker, *Richterzeit und Königtum: Redaktionsgeschichtliche Studien zum Richterbuch*, BZAW 192 (Berlin: de Gruyter, 1990), 181.

episode in vv. 24–27 and probably antedates those verses. Inserted within the conventional framework is a passage (vv. 29–31) that tells about Gideon's descendants and thereby provides the background to the Abimelech account. In reporting that Gideon had seventy sons, many wives, and a concubine in Shechem (Abimelech's mother), the paragraph echoes the censure of Gideon's quest to make a name for himself.[23]

Fear as the Unifying Theme

What unifies the extensively expanded form of Gideon's story is the motif of fear. The enemy is depicted as nervous and panicky (7:11b–15, 21–22; 8:12 [החריד]).[24] Gideon too must discharge more than two-thirds of the Israelite troops because of their trepidation (7:2–3: מי ירא וחרד). Most important, Gideon himself is presented as apprehensive and anxious. From the very beginning, he harbors doubts about his success (6:13–15) and requires various forms of oracular assurances before commencing his campaign (6:17–24 and 36–40).[25]

By portraying Gideon as unsure of success, the scribes responsible for these supplements significantly altered his heroic identity. A relatively early line identifies Gideon as a "valorous warrior" (גבור החיל) who is commissioned to use his military might against the Midianites (6:12, 14). The many supplements that we isolated deconstruct this memory, painting him as one who lacks any semblance of self-confidence. Thus, a line that was added to this scene presents him protesting: "With what can I save [אושיע] Israel? My clan is surely the poorest in Manasseh, and I am the least in my family!" (6:15). In a series of other scenes depicting Gideon's need for signs of divine favor, the scribes worked to attribute the impending victory to the divine presence that accompanies Gideon, rather than

---

23. In what appears to have been an early compositional stage of the book, the authors of Judges appended the story of Abimelech directly to the Gideon account. They identified Gideon as Abimelech's father by adding Jerubbaal to the name of the former (see 6:25–32 and 9:1). The account itself is likely relatively old (cf., e.g., v. 28 with Gen 34). Originally, it seems to have told the story of Abimelech's reign in Shechem without the degree of excoriation contained in the transmitted version. For the authors of Judges, however, this account represented rich material with which they could add details to their narrative of nonkingly leaders who save their communities from their collective enemies by mobilizing an army consisting of the people of Israel.

24. Notice the use of the same root in the place where Gideon's troops are mustered: עין חרד (7:1).

25. The story makes repeated reference to Gideon's home in Ophrah, to his father's wealth and status, and to his clan's name (6:11, 24–32, 34; 8:18–19, 27, 32). These details convey an image of Gideon as a local leader who owes his authority not solely to charisma but also to social rank.

his own martial prowess. Beginning as a fearless commander who leads a band of skilled warriors, he has, thanks to these supplements, become a chicken-hearted farmer who gradually musters the courage to leave his threshing duties and lead a group of citizen soldiers into battle.

The earliest legends appear to have told about a professional fighter and his own army. But the authors of Judges have created from these legends a new story of Gideon's life that tells how the Israelites volunteered in droves to partake in a collective war effort. The older legends have nothing to say about Gideon's troops; we are simply told that "Gideon went up ... and attacked the army" (8:11–12). Similar to small corps of soldiers led by Abimelech, Jephthah, and David, he would likely have commanded his own private army. They answered to him and fought his battles. In contrast, the new story of his life drafted by the authors of Judges presents him sounding the shofar to mobilize a *volunteer* militia (6:34). Thus, just as the authors of Judges transformed Gideon's character, they transformed the identity of his small army—from professional warriors to citizen soldiers.

The army's profile evolves in later strata so that it comes to include a multitude of Israelites from the surrounding tribes. Gideon sends messengers first throughout all Manasseh and then to Asher, Zebulun, and Napthali (6:35), with thirty-two thousand able-bodied denizens of this region rallying to the war effort (7:3).

The criterion for reducing the army to three hundred is a peculiar one. All those who lap water with their tongues are allowed to stay, while the others who use their hands are sent home.[26] Anyone who grew up reading cowboy-and-Indian stories knows that water holes are dangerous places. By lowering his mouth to the water, a warrior cannot maintain his guard. Similarly, when drinking at rivers and water holes, animals are on high alert; they must constantly lift their heads to look about. Accordingly, the three hundred men represent the least timorous of the ten thousand men. Yet they are also the most foolish and inexperienced, and so the victory is even more astounding.

In their foolish behavior, boldly dipping their heads down to water like dogs, these three hundred also demonstrate that they are the *most fearless* of the ten thousand. The method adopted to discharge the first two-thirds to ten thousand is even more explicitly related to a division of the lionhearted from the timorous. Gideon is commanded to proclaim to the troops, "Whoever is fearful and trembling, let him return home 'as a bird flies from the Gilead hills'" (7:2).[27]

---

26. As most commentators agree, the text is corrupt in vv. 5–6.

27. The language here is strikingly similar to Deut 20:8. The final words in "scare quotes" seem to have been an adage about temerity. It is noteworthy that the adage links

After the numbers are diminished to three hundred, the reader should understand the triumph over the Midianites by a very small nonprofessional militia as divine deliverance rather than a matter of numerical superiority: "The force with you is too large for me [Yhwh] to deliver the Midianites into their hands. Israel might claim for itself the glory due to me, concluding, 'My own hand has brought me this salvation'" (7:2). Although we can appreciate its intention, this explanation in 7:2 does not quite work.

First, with a cohort of three hundred fearless warriors, one can inflict a lot of damage on large armies.[28] Yet, if the numbers had remained at thirty-two thousand, or even at ten thousand (7:2), the feat would still have been remarkable: The Midianite forces were as "thick as locusts and their camels as numerous as the sands of the seashore" (6:5; 7:12), and, according to 8:10, the Midianites had 135,000 troops. Moreover, ten thousand is the number of men who fight on the side of Barak and Deborah when, in the immediately preceding episode, Israel manages to conquer a massive Canaanite force.

Second, the reader naturally concludes that Gideon's success was due to his *own* ingenious ploy. The deity only commands him to decrease the size of his army; it is Gideon who then comes up with cunning tactics. With three hundred men surrounding the camp, blowing horns, yelling, and smashing clay vessels in the dark of the night, it is no wonder that mayhem breaks out. Originally, the Midianites take to flight (7:16–21, 22b). But even if they had already begun to kill each other in the camp, this would not have been a miraculous act, as v. 22 intends for it to be understood. Such mass confusion and self-destruction are precisely the effects intended by tactics of night fighting and sonic warfare.

That the authors of Judges have Gideon go through such great trouble when mobilizing his army for battle—starting with three hundred, then mustering a vast volunteer army, and then downsizing it again to the original number of three hundred—was not, therefore, to show how his victory was a miracle. Instead, their editorial aim was to transform his army from a brigade of his own warriors into a representative cross-section of the population from neighboring tribes, who voluntarily participate in keeping with their national solidarity as the people of Israel. By portraying a general call-up of Manasseh and the others, the authors of Judges have thoroughly reconfigured the nature of Gideon's three hundred. This corps

---

fearfulness to Gilead: the Transjordan is also where the maligned Penuel and Succoth are located.

28. A case in point is the Battle of Thermopylae. In the Bible, lethal bands of professional warriors range in size from three hundred to six hundred. For units of three hundred in Sparta, Boeotia, and Athens, see Hans van Wees, *Greek Warfare: Myths and Realities* (London: Duckworth, 2004), 59.

does not exist prior to Gideon's recruitment of Israel's tribes. Rather than representing this warlord's own band of troops, the three hundred consist entirely of the nonprofessional militia of citizen soldiers who volunteered their service. They represent just a small fraction of the thirty-two thousand members of Israel who rally to Gideon from the surrounding tribes after the spirit of Yhwh envelops him (6:34).[29]

The broad participation of Israel's tribes in local battles is a major theme in the book of Judges. The story, however, requires only a small force since it portrays Gideon devising clever tactics of night fighting and sonic warfare in his effort to provoke the much larger enemy camp to panic and disband (7:16–21, 22b; compare the surprise tactic in 8:11). The authors could easily have depicted broader Israelite participation by portraying some other form of wartime contributions. The first is found in 8:4–9, 13–16, which reports that the inhabitants of Succoth and Penuel *refused* to feed the famished three hundred as they pursued the Midianite kings.[30] In another passage, we are told that *after* the battle, "the *men of Israel* from Naphtali, Asher, and all Manasseh" were called out to pursue the retreating enemy (7:23; and later also the Ephraimites, 7:24 and 8:3a).

In order to make the feat even more spectacular, it is likely that the same authors responsible for the redaction also increased the size of Midianite forces: According to an older passage, Gideon fights against a force of fifteen thousand (8:10a*), which is already a daunting force. But a later gloss explains this number as those who *remained* from the 135,000 who answered Gideon's call to arms.

The Gideon story intersects with the fundamental concerns of the biblical authors to reimagine Israel as a nation-in-arms that fights its wars

---

29. Gideon's corps has its own battle cry: "[A Sword] for Yhwh and for Gideon" (7:18, 20). Such war cries or anthems are known for many armies in history: *alala* for the Hellenes, *nobiscum deus* for late Roman and Byzantine armies, *Allahu akbar* for early Muslim armies, *Dieu et mon droit* for medieval English kings, to name just a few. Psychologically, the battle cry not only instills fear in the enemy but also rouses the courage of one's own troops. If the themes of fear and courage run through the final form of the Gideon account, it makes sense that the account highlights the battle cry. According to this battle cry, the troops fight both for Yhwh and for Gideon, Yhwh's representative. As such, these troops may be compared to David's army of four hundred (or six hundred) fighters, who are repeatedly designated "David's men." Seen from this perspective, Gideon's corps starkly differs from clan-based armies, which emphasize the equality of their men and whose war cries often consist simply of their own tribal name (such as the Ambrones at the Battle of Aquae Sextiae; see Plutarch, *Marius* 10.5–6).

30. These passages, which depict either enthusiastic volunteerism or a reticence to contribute, seem to constitute supplements to the narrative. The fact that the entire host is already long gone (7:22b) and that later only Gideon and his men are in pursuit of the enemy (8:1–21) shows that earlier versions of the account did not know about the post-battle assistance from Israel's tribes (7:23–25). Moreover, the account of the punishment of Succoth and Penuel also appears to have been secondarily spliced into an older narrative (8:10*, 11–12, 18–21, 25b–27a).

collectively, in direct relationship with Israel's national deity rather than in service to warlords and kings. For example, the Deuteronomic Code imagines Israel as people-in-arms with a volunteer army and temporally appointed generals in the place conventionally occupied by kings (see the war laws in chap. 20). This form of military organization is tightly linked to this code's concern with fear. For a nonprofessional militia, morale boosting through pre-battle arts of persuasion—whether they be oracles or rhetoric—was even more indispensable than for battle-tried professionals or soldiers who serve for pay. Deuteronomy foregrounds the pre-battle speeches themselves, as they present the vision for a just society that the people can build in the land they conquer.

Conclusions

In our analysis, the account of Gideon's life has fallen apart into a series of supplements. Their relationship to one another and the order of their priority are difficult to establish. Some presuppose the editorial framework and other texts in Judges. Yet some were penned specifically for the Gideon account and are almost impossible to situate in a compositional history. The more important questions are: What holds these supplements together? Is there some form of narrative substratum that connects them? And, assuming that this substratum must have once existed, can we still lay bare its original contours?

The older legends of Gideon's life present him as a royal warrior (8:18–21), but the story of his life found in the book of Judges presents him as a fearful farmer. Deuteronomy's laws of war proscribe fear among the national militia since Yhwh *accompanies* them and directly *saves* them (see 20:1, 4), while Gideon sends twenty-two thousand Israelite troops home because they were fearful and trembling (7:2–3). In keeping with one of the political agendas of Deuteronomy, the book of Judges sets forth an alternative to the monarchic model of heroes becoming kings after "saving" the nation.[31]

In reworking inherited material and supplementing the work of their predecessors, the authors of Judges devoted a significant amount of space to the prehistory of Gideon's success. On the one hand, their work shows how the valiant warrior, before venturing into battle, required multiple verifications that Yhwh would *accompany* him and *save* Israel by his hand. By presenting him harboring fears and doubts, the account divests his

---

31. See my article "Military Valor and Kingship: A Book-Oriented Approach to the Study of a Major War Theme," in *Writing and Reading War: Rhetoric, Gender, and Ethics in Biblical and Modern Contexts*, ed. Brad E. Kelle and Frank Ritchel Ames, SymS 42 (Atlanta: Society of Biblical Literature, 2008), 33–56.

name of the glory that a warrior-king required to rule. On the other hand, they transformed his personal band of warriors into a group of inexperienced citizen soldiers volunteering to fight Israel's common enemies under his leadership. The creative work of these authors made it possible to integrate Gideon into a narrative of the nation's past that illustrates and develops Deuteronomy's political vision.

IV

Prophetic Anthologies

"Biblicist Additions" or the Emergence of Scripture in the Growth of the Prophets

ANJA KLEIN
University of Edinburgh

Walther Zimmerli and the Updating of "Biblical" Tradition

In his major 1969 commentary on the book of Ezekiel (Eng. trans. 1979), Walther Zimmerli was the first to describe the phenomenon of literary supplementation and its significance for the literary growth of the Prophets. In his work, he coined the term *Fortschreibung* (literary continuation) to describe the successive elaboration of oracles and the reworking of existing units in light of subsequent events.[1] He also referred to "'biblicist' additions" in these processes of "updating of traditions,"[2] when texts from other later biblical books influenced the literary continuation of prophetic oracles in Ezekiel. The literary phenomenon that Zimmerli described as "biblicist additions" has been labeled by later scholars as "biblical interpretation" (Michael Fishbane)[3] and "inner-biblical exegesis/*Schriftauslegung*" (Reinhard G. Kratz, Konrad Schmid, Jan Christian Gertz)[4], acknowledging the fact that biblical interpretation starts within

---

1. Walther Zimmerli, *Ezechiel*, 2 vols., BKAT 13 (Neukirchen-Vluyn: Neukirchener Verlag, 1969), 1:106*–7* (Eng. trans.: *Ezekiel: A Commentary on the Book of the Prophet Ezekiel*, trans. Ronald E. Clements, Hermeneia [Philadelphia: Fortress, 1979, 1983], 1:69).
2. Zimmerli, *Ezekiel*, 1:69, 70.
3. Michael Fishbane, *Biblical Interpretation in Ancient Israel* (Oxford: Clarendon, 1985).
4. Reinhard G. Kratz, "Innerbiblische Exegese und Redaktionsgeschichte im Lichte empirischer Evidenz," in Kratz, *Das Judentum im Zeitalter des Zweiten Tempels*, FAT 42 (Tübingen: Mohr Siebeck, 2004), 126–56; Konrad Schmid, "Innerbiblische Schriftauslegung: Aspekte der Forschungsgeschichte," in *Schriftauslegung in der Schrift: Festschrift für Odil Hannes Steck zu seinem 65. Geburtstag*, ed. Reinhard G. Kratz, Thomas Krüger, and Konrad Schmid, BZAW 300 (Berlin: de Gruyter, 2000), 1–22; see further Konrad Schmid, *Schriftgelehrte Traditionsliteratur: Fallstudien zur innerbiblischen Schriftauslegung im Alten Testament*, FAT 77 (Tübingen:

the development of the biblical scriptures themselves. In particular, Odil Hannes Steck described the redaction history of the prophetic books in terms of a history of biblical interpretation.[5]

In this contribution, I want to draw on existing hermeneutical and exegetical studies and analyze the phenomenon of inner-biblical exegesis, focusing on three examples from the Major Prophets. I will demonstrate that there is a shift in the way inner-biblical exegesis contributes to the literary growth of the prophetic books: in the early stages of literary development, prophetic images and topics are taken up and reinterpreted; as the process continues, literary references increase; in late literary layers, exegesis comes close to quotations of earlier prophecies.[6] This phenomenon bears witness to a growing interest in distinguishing between exegesis and its "inner-biblical" *Vorlage*, indicating an understanding of scripture that was increasingly perceived as authoritative.[7]

For the purpose of discussion, I have chosen three examples from the Major Prophets that demonstrate in different ways how the dynamic exegetical process of literary supplementation is indicative of an emerging idea of scripture. The first is Ezek 38–39, the chapters about Gog from Magog, which are a classic example of Zimmerli's phenomenon of *Fortschreibung*. Here, the depiction of the enigmatic Gog draws first on foe imagery of other oracles, before the advent of the enemy is formally identified with earlier prophecies (38:17). In the book of Isaiah, however, I want to take a conceptual approach, tracing the idea of salvation in terms of a new exodus through the literary development of the book. Again, while the earliest prophecies engage with exodus metaphors, the latest supplementation in Isa 11:16 marks the events of new salvation as an explicit repetition of the first biblical exodus from Egypt. Finally, in Jeremiah, the focus is on the prophecy of the limitation of the exile to seventy years, which undergoes an exegesis in several books before the author of Dan 9:2 refers back by name to the scriptural prophecy of Jeremiah. These three examples will shed light on the various forms of literary supplementation in the Prophets and will demonstrate the significance of this phenomenon for the formation of the Hebrew Bible.

Mohr Siebeck, 2011), and Jan C. Gertz, "Schriftauslegung in alttestamentlicher Perspektive," in *Schriftauslegung*, ed. Friederike Nüssel, ThTh 8 (Tübingen: Mohr Siebeck, 2014), 9–41.

5. Odil Hannes Steck, *Die Prophetenbücher und ihr theologisches Zeugnis: Wege der Nachfrage und Fährten zur Antwort* (Tübingen: Mohr Siebeck, 1996); Odil Hannes Steck, *Gott in der Zeit entdecken: Die Prophetenbücher des Alten Testaments als Vorbild für Theologie und Kirche*, BThSt 42 (Neukirchen-Vluyn: Neukirchener Verlag, 2001).

6. I have already described this phenomenon for the book of Ezekiel (Anja Klein, "Prophecy Continued: Reflections on Innerbiblical Exegesis in the Book of Ezekiel," *VT* 60 [2010]: 571–82).

7. Ibid., 581.

Literary Supplementation in the Three Major Prophets

The Invasion of Gog from Magog in Ezekiel 38–39

During the last two decades of research on the book of Ezekiel, there has been renewed interest in the Gog chapters, Ezek 38–39.[8] This is due especially to the recognition of the Greek Papyrus 967 (Pap. 967), which attests to a differing placement of chapters 38–39 in the third part of the book of Ezekiel—sparking new discussion about how these chapters emerged. Among the scholars who assume a history of literary growth, there is increasing consensus that Pap. 967 represents an earlier edition of the book, preceding the Proto-Masoretic Text.[9] On this understanding, the Gog materials once followed directly on the oracle about the sanctification of God's holy name in 36:16–22 (23abα) and have to be understood as its continuation.[10] Yet opinions differ in reference to whether these chapters originated outside the book and were inserted as a whole (William A. Tooman, Christoph Rösel, Michael Konkel)[11] or if they developed from a

---

8. Since 2001, we have seen the publication of four monographs dealing with the Gog chapters: Sverre Bøe, *Gog and Magog: Ezekiel 38–39 as Pre-Text for Revelation 19:17–21 and 20:7–10*, WUNT 2/135 (Tübingen: Mohr Siebeck, 2011); Paul E. Fitzpatrick, *The Disarmament of God: Ezekiel 38–39 in Its Mythic Context*, CBQMS 37 (Washington, DC: Catholic Biblical Association of America, 2004); William A. Tooman, *Gog of Magog: Reuse of Scripture and Compositional Technique in Ezekiel 38–39*, FAT 2/52 (Tübingen: Mohr Siebeck, 2011); Christoph Rösel, *JHWHs Sieg über Gog aus Magog: Ez 38–39 im Masoretischen Text und in der Septuaginta*, WMANT 132 (Neukirchen-Vluyn: Neukirchener Verlag, 2012). See also the overview by Michael Konkel, "Ezek. 38–39 in Current Research: Questions and Perspectives," in *Ezekiel: Current Debates and Future Directions*, ed. William A. Tooman and Penelope Barter, FAT 112 (Tübingen: Mohr Siebeck, 2017), 199–209; my own analysis of Ezek 38–39 in Anja Klein, *Schriftauslegung im Ezechielbuch: Redaktionsgeschichtliche Untersuchungen zu Ez 34–39*, BZAW 381 (Berlin: de Gruyter, 2008), 111–67; and Bernd Biberger, *Endgültiges Heil innerhalb von Geschichte und Gegenwart: Zukunftskonzeptionen in Ez 38–39, Joel 1–4 und Sach 12–14*, BBB 161 (Göttingen: Vandenhoeck & Ruprecht, 2010).

9. Johan Lust, "Ezekiel 36–40 in the Oldest Greek Manuscript," *CBQ* 43 (1981): 517–33; Peter Schwagmeier, "Untersuchungen zu Textgeschichte und Entstehung des Ezechielbuches in masoretischer und griechischer Überlieferung" (PhD diss., University of Zürich, 2004); Karl-Friedrich Pohlmann, *Das Buch des Propheten Hesekiel (Ezechiel)*, 2 vols., ATD 22, with a contribution by Thilo A. Rudnig (Göttingen: Vandenhoeck & Ruprecht, 1996, 2001), esp. 2:524–26; see also Ingrid E. Lilly, *Two Books of Ezekiel: Papyrus 967 and the Masoretic Text as Variant Literary Editions*, VTSup 150 (Leiden: Brill, 2012).

10. Klein, *Schriftauslegung im Ezechielbuch*, 71–72. On the later addition of 36:23abα, see ibid., 143, referring back to the studies by Christoph Levin, *Die Verheißung des neuen Bundes in ihrem theologiegeschichtlichen Zusammenhang ausgelegt*, FRLANT 137 (Göttingen: Vandenhoeck & Ruprecht, 1985); and Stefan Ohnesorge, *Jahwe gestaltet sein Volk neu: Zur Sicht der Zukunft Israels nach Ez 11,14–21; 20,1–44; 36,16–38; 37,1–14.15–28*, FB 64 (Würzburg: Echter, 1991), 288–89.

11. See Tooman, *Gog of Magog*, 72–84; Rösel, *JHWHs Sieg*, 349–65; similarly, Konkel, "Ezek. 38–39," 199–209.

literary core within the book (Anja Klein, Bernd Biberger).[12]. There is further debate surrounding whether the Gog materials were inserted into a previous literary context 36:16–23abα; 39:23–29*, or if the prophetic word in 39:23–29 belongs to the Gog chapters themselves.[13] For the purpose of this paper, however, it suffices to say that the Gog materials have been inserted directly following the oracle in 36:16–23abα*. This text addresses the problem that the exile and diaspora of the people of Israel had defiled Yhwh's holy name, because their dispersion was interpreted by the nations as proof of Yhwh's lack of power (36:20). As a consequence, Yhwh announces that he will take action for the sake of his holy name (36:22). Against this literary background, the insertion of the Gog materials suggests that the shattering of Gog provides a—secondary—account about how Yhwh will prove his sovereignty toward the foreign nations.[14]

Let us now look at the Gog materials themselves to determine how the texts draw on other "biblical" texts. It is often noted that the two chapters are dominated by the bipartite division into chapters 38 and 39, both of which start from a prophecy against the enigmatic Gog announcing his downfall (38:1–9; 39:1–5). I find it difficult to ignore the double nature of this prophecy, which is usually indicative of literary supplementation.[15] Furthermore, the clustering of speech formulas in Ezek 38–39, several changes of addressees, and a number of shifts in content point to a history of literary growth.[16] On this assumption, a core can only be reconstructed with one of the prophetic words directed at Gog, either 38:1–9 or 39:1–5, as all the other units in the chapters prove to be dependent on these two

---

12. See Klein, *Schriftauslegung im Ezechielbuch*, 111–40; Biberger, *Endgültiges Heil*, 93–112.

13. An original connection between Ezek 36:16–23abα* and 39:23–29* has been advocated first by Pohlmann, *Das Buch des Propheten Hesekiel*, 485–87, 514–18; see also Klein, *Schriftauslegung im Ezechielbuch*, 140–69. Differently, Tooman (*Gog of Magog*, 77–83, 188–95), Biberger (*Endgültiges Heil*, 87–88, 102–3), and Konkel ("Ezek. 38–39," 204–7) have recently argued against this connection and consider 39:23–29* to be part of the Gog materials.

14. Klein, *Schriftauslegung im Ezechielbuch*, 125–27, 370; see further Biberger, *Endgültiges Heil*, 95–98, 104–6, 125–26, who, however, sees the basic oracle of the Gog chapters in 39:1–5, 7 as an *original* continuation of Ezek 36:26–23abα, classifying 39:23–29 as a later supplementation of the Gog chapters (102–3).

15. See, however, Tooman, *Gog of Magog*, 115, who attributes to the Gog chapters a character "unlike any other text within the HB. *It is a pastiche, an extreme example of a conflate text*" (italics in original).

16. Klein, *Schriftauslegung im Ezechielbuch*, 115. In general, scholarship since Zimmerli has tended to assume a history of literary growth (see Zimmerli, *Ezekiel*, 2:296–302; further, Frank-Lothar Hossfeld, *Untersuchungen zu Komposition und Theologie des Ezechielbuches*, FB 20 [Würzburg: Echter, 1977], 402–509; Leslie C. Allen, *Ezekiel 20–48*, WBC 29 [Dallas: Word, 1990], 202–4; Pohlmann, *Das Buch des Propheten Hesekiel*, 509–11; and Klein, *Schriftauslegung im Ezechielbuch*, 112–27). Yet recently an increasing number of studies suggesting literary unity or working from this assumption have appeared (see Rösel, *JHWHs Sieg*, 349–51; Tooman, *Gog of Magog*, 114–16, and Konkel, "Ezek. 38–39," 207–8).

oracles.[17] Between the two, the oracle in 39:1–5 turns out to be the shorter and more coherent version of Gog's defeat, which—contrary to 38:1–9—provides information about the outcome of Gog's campaign. It can thus be assumed that the oracle in 39:1–5 forms the literary core of the Gog chapters, in which Yhwh asks the prophet to announce judgment against Gog, who shall fall on the mountains of Israel (39:4: על־הרי ישראל תפול אתה).[18] It is especially this location—characteristic of the salvation prophecies in the book of Ezekiel (cf. 6:3, 13; 19:9; 33:28; 34:13–14; 35:12; 36:1, 4, 8; 37:22; 38:8; 39:2, 4, 17)—that constitutes an argument for the origin of the Gog materials within the book.[19] In their literary beginnings, the Gog prophecies represent the literary continuation of the oracle in 36:16–23abα, actualizing the discussion about how Yhwh can sanctify his name in the eyes of the foreign nations.

In the past, attempts to identify Gog with a historic enemy of Israel have proved to be rather fruitless.[20] When it comes to the textual evidence, the Hebrew name Gog (גּוֹג) occurs only in Ezek 38–39 in the MT, yet there are a number of parallels in the LXX, among which Num 24:7 and Amos 7:1 are possible texts of origin.[21] Numbers 24:7 is a prophecy from the Balaam cycle, which in its MT version announces the coming of a king, who will be higher than Agag (וירם מאגג מלכו). Yet a great number of the versions testify instead to the exaltation of the kingdom of Gog (cf. LXX: ὑψωθήσεται ἢ Γωγ βασιλεία).[22] It has been suggested that the author of the Gog materials "derived his villain from the Balaam Oracles."[23] The textual

---

17. Klein, *Schriftauslegung im Ezechielbuch*, 119. Similarly, Konkel, in his review of scholarship, limits the options to Ezek 39:1–5 (and 39:25–29) ("Ezek. 38–39," 207).

18. On the literary analysis, see Klein, *Schriftauslegung im Ezechielbuch*, 121. Most exegetes who assume literary growth suggest that some part of Ezek 39* represents the original core; see Zimmerli, *Ezekiel*, 2:298–99 (38:1–9*; 39:1–5, 17–20); Hossfeld, *Untersuchungen zu Komposition*, 431–44, 462–67 (38:1–3a; 39:1b–5); and Biberger, *Endgültiges Heil*, 95–98 (39:1–5, 7).

19. Klein, *Schriftauslegung im Ezechielbuch*, 125–27, 329–36, 370. Differently, Tooman notes the dependence on vocabulary from Ezekiel as a characteristic of the Gog chapters as a whole (*Gog of Magog*, 85–116), which for him is no argument against an origin outside the book.

20. On this discussion, see Margaret S. Odell, "'Are You He of Whom I Spoke by My Servants the Prophets?': Ezekiel 38–39 and the Problem of History in the Neobabylonian Context" (PhD diss., University of Pittsburgh, 1988), esp. 1–42.

21. See Bøe (*Gog and Magog*, 50–75) and Tooman (*Gog of Magog*, 139–43), both of whom discuss the LXX parallels in detail.

22. On this variant reading, see the Samaritan Pentateuch, the LXX, Theodotion, and the Vetus Latina.

23. Tooman, *Gog of Magog*, 142. Previously, the identification of Gog in Ezek 38–39 with the Balaam prophecy was argued for by Gillis Gerleman, "Hesekielbokens Gog," *SEÅ* 12 (1947): 148–62, here 161; Ernst Sellin, *Der alttestamentliche Prophetismus: Drei Studien* (Leipzig: Deichert, 1912), 154; see further George Buchanan Gray, *A Critical and Exegetical Commentary on Numbers*, ICC (Edinburgh: T&T Clark, 1903), 366, who comes to the conclusion that the

evidence, however, indicates that the MT represents the *lectio difficilior*, while the variant of the versions can be understood as a secondary simplification of the text—identifying the exemplary foe in Num 24:7 with the by-then-well-known enemy from the book of Ezekiel.[24] The second significant reference is the Greek text of Amos 7:1, which attests to an invasion in the form of a locust plague under the leadership of a locust king named Gog (βροῦχος εἷς Γωγ ὁ βασιλεύς). Yet again, this variant can be explained easily as a later clarification of the difficult MT reading "mowing" (גֵּזִי), which is difficult to interpret.[25] Finally, any postulated dependence of the MT of Ezek 38–39 on the Greek translation of either Num 24:7 and/or Amos 7:1 works only under the assumption that we deal with a late unified composition in Ezek 38–39—an assumption that is not supported by our textual analysis. In summary, to my mind, the name of the enemy in the Gog oracles cannot be explained with reference to the Greek text in Num 24:7 and/or Amos 7:1, but these oracles are clearly part of the reception history of Ezek 38–39.[26]

Even if the origin of his name cannot be determined, the portrayal of the enigmatic enemy in Ezek 38–39 provides some evidence to suggest his identity. First, characteristics of the nations in the oracles against foreign nations in Ezek 25–32 are attributed to him.[27] The prediction that Gog will fall on the open fields (39:5: על־פני השדה תפול) has one parallel only in the threat against the Pharaoh of Egypt (29:5: על־פני השדה תפול), which is strong evidence to suggest a literary dependence here. Furthermore, both enemies are told that their weapons will be dropped from their hands: a sword in the case of Pharaoh (30:22: והפלתי את־החרב מידו) and arrows with regard to Gog (39:3: והציץ מיד ימינך אפיל). Finally, Gog shares an inglorious

---

"reading Gog (...) cannot be seriously considered, unless, indeed, the poem be regarded as a late Messianic composition, in which case the allusion to Gog would be suitable enough."

24. The major Numbers commentaries retain the reading of the MT (מֵאֲגַג); see Martin Noth, *Das vierte Buch Mose: Numeri*, ATD 7 (Göttingen: Vandenhoeck & Ruprecht, 1966), 150; Philip J. Budd, *Numbers*, WBC 5 (Waco, TX: Word, 1984), 252; Ludwig Schmidt, *Das vierte Buch Mose: Numeri 10,11–36,16*, ATD 7.2 (Göttingen: Vandenhoeck & Ruprecht, 2004), 121; see, however, n. 23 for exceptions.

25. On the preference for the MT, see Hans Walter Wolff, *Dodekapropheton 2: Joel und Amos*, BKAT 14.2 (Neukirchen-Vluyn: Neukirchener Verlag, 1969), 337; the MT reading further underlies the translations by Francis I. Andersen and David Noel Freedman, *Amos: A New Translation with Introduction and Commentary*, AB 24A (New York: Doubleday, 1989), 739, and Shalom M. Paul, *Amos: A Commentary on the Book of Amos*, Hermeneia (Minneapolis: Fortress, 1991), 226.

26. On this assumption, see already Bøe, *Gog and Magog*, 311 ("To find relevance for the text [Num 24:7] Gog was a figure ready at hand"); and similarly Rösel, *JHWHs Sieg*, 220, 311, who explains the LXX readings as part of the reception history ("*Wirkungsgeschichte*") of Ezek 38–39.

27. On these parallels, see Klein, *Schriftauslegung im Ezechielbuch*, 128–29; Tooman, *Gog of Magog*, 108–9.

fate with Pharaoh: Both are left to be devoured by the wild animals, even though the animal species differ slightly in the two accounts (29:5: לחית לעיט צפור כל־כנף וחית השדה נתתיך לאכלה); 39:4: הארץ ולעוף השמים נתתיך לאכלה).[28]

Second, Gog in the original oracle (Ezek 39:1–5) displays some characteristics of an enemy threatening Israel from the north that appears in the prophecies of both Jeremiah and Isaiah. With regard to Jeremiah, the connections between Gog and the foe from the north have long been recognized.[29] Here, the prophecy in Ezek 39:5 comes close to Jer 6:22–23, since in both texts a foe is announced that advances (Ezek 39:2: והבאותך / Jer 6:22: בא) from the north (Ezek 39:2: מירכתי צפון / Jer 6:22: מארץ צפון), armed with a bow (Ezek 39:3: קשתך / Jer 6:23: קשת).[30] Yet a decisive difference can be observed: while in Jer 6:23 the threat is directed at the daughter Zion, the events in Ezek 39:2 take place on the mountains of Israel. A closer match with the location in Ezekiel can be found in Isa 14:4b–21, a taunt song that, according to the superscription, refers to the king of Babylon (14:4a: על־מלך בבל). The song itself describes the pending fall of an unnamed enemy who planned to elevate himself by taking his seat on the mountain of assembly in the north (14:13: בהר־מועד בירכתי צפון).[31] It can be assumed that the song was previously connected with the threat of Assyria, the downfall of which is prophesied in the literary context in Isa 14:25, locating the downfall of Assyria on Yhwh's mountains (על־הרי אבוסנו). Assessing these literary links, it becomes obvious that Gog in Ezek 38–39 is from his beginnings designed as a persona that combines

---

28. Similarly, Rösel observes in Ezek 39:4 a "relation to the Egypt-words" ("in V 4 erkennbare Beziehung zu den Ägypten-Worten") (*JHWHs Sieg*, 250).

29. See, e.g., Gustav Hölscher, *Hesekiel: Der Dichter und das Buch; Eine literarkritische Untersuchung*, BZAW 39 (Gießen: Töpelmann, 1924), 180–83; Zimmerli, *Ezekiel*, 2:299–300; Hanns-Martin Lutz, *Jahwe, Jerusalem und die Völker: Zur Vorgeschichte von Sach 12,1–8 und 14,1–5*, WMANT 27 (Neukirchen-Vluyn: Neukirchener Verlag, 1968), 125–30; Allen, *Ezekiel 20–48*, 204; Klein, *Schriftauslegung im Ezechielbuch*, 132–40. While Tooman acknowledges the links to Jeremiah, he finds the links to Isaiah 14 stronger (*Gog of Magog*, 175–76); see below.

30. Klein, *Schriftauslegung im Ezechielbuch*, 134. Tooman has good arguments to prefer the links to Isaiah above those to Jeremiah (see n. 29 above) (*Gog of Magog*, 175–76); his assessment, however, first of all proceeds from the assumption of literary unity in Ezek 38–39, and, second, his judgment that the links via קשת and בוא are "too common to be used as evidence" (176) does not register that Jer 6:22–23 and Ezek 39:1–5 are the only two texts in the Hebrew Bible in which the three words קשת, בוא and צפון appear together within two verses.

31. Even though the parallel in Isa 14:13—contrary to Jer 6:22—represents an exact match with Ezek 39:2 (see also Ezek 38:6, 15), Isa 14:13 does not explicitly give the direction from which the threat advances against Israel but specifies the place where the enemy desires to dwell (בירכתי צפון). In this respect, Ezek 39:2 seems to be closer to the Jeremiah reference, which is neglected by Tooman, *Gog of Magog*, 176, who dismisses the locution מארץ צפון in Jer 6:22 as an "inexact parallel," giving preference to Isa 14:13 (and the oracle 14:4b–21 as a whole) as *Vorlage* (see also nn. 29 and 30 above).

characteristics from several other prophetic texts, presented as a mysterious enemy at the end of time.[32]

During subsequent literary stages of the development of Ezek 38–39, the existing connections both to the oracles against foreign nations in the book itself and to the foe oracles in Jeremiah and Isaiah are strengthened further. First, the oracle in 38:1–9 is inserted preceding the prophetic announcement in 39:1–5. With the word reception formula in 38:1, the supplemented Gog prophecy is now shaped as an independent oracle and marked off from its context.[33] The supplementation in 38:1–9 repeats the pending threat by Gog describing it now on a larger scale by providing a range of information about the enemy and his army. As to the links with the oracles against the foreign nations, the description of the foe in Ezek 38:1–9 recalls the portrayal of the Assyrians and Babylonians in Ezek 25–32.[34] Regarding the foe from the north, the oracle in 38:1–9 confirms the origin of the foe from the far north (38:6: ירכתי צפון).

There is some evidence to suggest that the further literary development took place in parallel steps, so that the basic oracles in Ezek 38 and 39 share a time line of supplementation.[35] In this process, the two continuations in Ezek 38:17 and 39:8 are of special interest as they are evidence for a changed understanding of scripture. First, the supplementation in 39:8 is clearly recognizable as a single-verse continuation, since it is separated from its context by the recognition formula in the preceding verse 39:7 and the divine asseveration formula at its own end.[36] The short prophecy supplements the notion that the events prophesied will surely arrive and identifies them with the day of which Yhwh had spoken earlier (39:8: הנה באה ונהיתה נאם אדני יהוה הוא היום אשר דברתי). The announcement of coming events in the first part is a common topic in the Prophets, and the wording of Ezek 38:9 has an exact parallel in Ezek 21:12,[37] where the phrase refers to the coming judgment. Yet the prophecy in 39:8 stands out as it further identifies the coming events with the fulfillment of an earlier prophecy

---

32. See Tooman, *Gog of Magog*, 140: "A character designed by assimilating information from several texts about a mysterious eschatological enemy of Israel."

33. Klein, *Schriftauslegung im Ezechielbuch*, 122–23.

34. Ibid., 129; and Tooman, *Gog of Magog*, 102–4. In this supplementation, it is especially the description of the enemies as being "magnificently dressed" (לבשי מכלול) that occurs in Ezek 23:12 and 38:4 only and links the Gog oracles to the prophecies in Ezek 25–32.

35. Klein, *Schriftauslegung im Ezechielbuch*, 123–27.

36. See Klein, who further refers to the shift in content (*Schriftauslegung im Ezechielbuch*, 118): while the previous context in 38:6–7 is concerned with the holiness of the divine name, the following oracle 39:9–10 deals with the problem of how to dispose of the enemy's remains. Hossfeld similarly notes the closing formula in 39:8 (*Untersuchungen zu Komposition*, 423–24), but he classifies the verse as part of an oracle in 39:8–10.

37. Tooman, *Gog of Magog*, 265; for parallels in the Prophets announcing the coming of the day he refers to Isa 13:9; 39:6; Jer 7:32; 9:24; 16:14; 19:6; 23:5, 7; 30:3; 31:27, 31, 38; 33:14; 48:12; 49:2; 51:47, 52; Ezek 7:10; Amos 4:2; 8:11; 9:13; Zech 14:1; Mal 3:19.

"Biblicist Additions"   133

about a specific day, which recalls the idea of the day of Yhwh.³⁸ Even though it remains unclear if 39:8 refers to a specific text, the back-reference attests to an understanding that the Gog prophecies actualize a preceding announcement.

Second, this understanding is even more pronounced in the continuation 38:17, where Yhwh addresses Gog and explicitly relates his invasion to former prophecies: "You are³⁹ the one of whom I spoke in former days through my servants, the prophets of Israel" (אתה־הוא אשר־דברתי בימים קדמונים ביד עבדי נביאי ישראל). The prophecy is clearly marked off from its preceding context by the message reception formula at its beginning, while the following oracle 38:18–23 is delineated as something new by the elaborate back reference at the beginning of v. 18.⁴⁰ Furthermore, the masoretes understood this verse as disconnected from its context, and they bracketed it with *setumot*.⁴¹ The direct address of the invader in 38:17 stands out from the rest of the oracles, which are concerned with the interaction between Yhwh and the prophet. Evidently, the significance of this verse hinges on the understanding of the dating "in former days" (בימים קדמונים) and the identification of the group "my servants, the prophets of Israel" (עבדי נביאי ישראל). As to the date, the formulation does not have an exact parallel in the Hebrew Bible, but in relation to time, the adjective קדמני occurs three more times (1 Sam 24:14; Isa 43:18; Mal 3:4). In all of these cases, the term refers to a time period "that is long past from the point of view of the speaker."⁴² In Ezek 37:18, this time period is further specified as the time of Yhwh's servants, the prophets of Israel (עבדי נביאי ישראל), which combines the notion of the prophets as the servants of Yhwh with a specific Israel reference that is unique in the book.⁴³ The concept of

---

38. Klein, *Schriftauslegung im Ezechielbuch*, 138; and Tooman, *Gog of Magog*, 265.
39. The translation follows the reading of the versions (LXX: σὺ εἶ), while the MT attests an additional *he interrogativum* at the beginning (האתה־הוא), which, however, similarly aims at a positive identification (see Rösel, *JHWHs Sieg*, 216; also Tooman, *Gog of Magog*, 262). The MT reading could be explained by a dittographic repetition of the preceding he (יהוה האתה הוא), as proposed by Zimmerli, *Ezekiel*, 2:288; Allen, *Ezekiel 20–48*, 218; Klein, *Schriftauslegung im Ezechielbuch*, 138. Yet the LXX reading differs further in adding the address by name (τῷ Γωγ) in the speech introduction, so that the LXX seems to attest in general to a variant reading that establishes a more obvious connection between Gog and the former prophecies; see Rösel who concludes, "Inhaltlich scheint LXX von einer offensichtlicheren Verbindung zwischen Gog und den Worten der Propheten auszugehen, während MT durch die Frageform offener formuliert ist" (*JHWHs Sieg*, 74–76, 216–17, here 74–75).
40. Klein, *Schriftauslegung im Ezechielbuch*, 116–17; Rösel, *JHWHs Sieg*, 216.
41. See also Tooman, *Gog of Magog*, 136, 262.
42. Tooman, *Gog of Magog*, 263. Similarly, Rösel points to the time distance between the former days and the Gog events: "Die in 38,17 anschließend genannten 'früheren Tage' stehen im Gegensatz zum 'Ende der Tage' in v. 16, in denen das Gog-Geschehen stattfinden wird" (*JHWHs Sieg*, 217).
43. Zimmerli, *Ezekiel*, 2:312.

134   Prophetic Anthologies

the prophets as servants of Yhwh occurs especially in Deuteronomistic literature and with variations in the prophetic books.⁴⁴ An overview of these occurrences shows that the designation of the prophets as עבד in the narrative books indicates that the prophets of Israel are mouthpieces of Yhwh, who pass on his message dutifully and act on his command. Yet, especially in Jeremiah, it is a recurring motif that the people do not listen to Yhwh's servants the prophets.⁴⁵ The use of the term in Ezek 38:17 is closer to the occurrences in the narrative books, as it emphasizes the notion that a previous prophecy has been fulfilled.⁴⁶ Considering the inner-biblical links in the Gog materials, it seems likely that the insertion of Ezek 38:17 has to be understood as a later inner-biblical interpretation that comes close to a quotation by relating the prophecies about Gog to earlier prophetic *texts*, pointing to the books of Jeremiah and Isaiah.⁴⁷ This later insertion thus attests to an understanding of scripture as authoritative, which can be quoted and commented on.⁴⁸ In the actualization of earlier prophecies from Jeremiah and Isaiah, the invading threat from the north is merged with foe imagery in the book of Ezekiel and presented as the advance of an eschatological enemy, who, however, will be shattered by Yhwh on the mountains of Israel.

The New Exodus in Isaiah

While the analysis of the Gog materials has shown how an understanding of scripture emerged during the literary continuation of a core oracle, my second example in the book of Isaiah attests to the productive development of a theological motif throughout a book. It is widely accepted that the idea of a new or second exodus is a core part of the prophetic message in the book of Isaiah, especially in its second part Isa

---

44. See Daniel I. Block, *The Book of Ezekiel*, 2 vols., NICOT (Grand Rapids: Eerdmans, 1998), 2:453; Tooman, *Gog of Magog*, 264.
45. See 2 Kgs 9:7; 17:13, 23; 21:10; 24:2; Jer 7:25; 25:4; 26:5; 29:19; 35:15; 44:4; Amos 3:7; Ezra 9:11; Zech 1:6; Dan 9:6, 10.
46. Rösel, *JHWHs Sieg*, 218.
47. On the actualization of former prophecies in Ezek 38:17, see already Hölscher, *Hesekiel*, 182–83; and further Zimmerli, *Ezekiel*, 2:312; Rösel, *JHWHs Sieg*, 221; and Biberger, *Endgültiges Heil*, 61. The literary character of the interpretation is emphasized by Fishbane, *Biblical Interpretation*, 514; Allen, *Ezekiel 20–48*, 206; Klein, *Schriftauslegung im Ezechielbuch*, 138; and Tooman, *Gog of Magog*, 26. Even though Block (*Book of Ezekiel*, 2:453–56) and Paul Joyce (*Ezekiel: A Commentary*, LHBOTS 482 [New York/London: T&T Clark, 2007], 215) take note of the referential character of Ezek 38:17, they argue for a different understanding: "This verse is not about unfulfilled prophecy, but about earlier prophecies illegitimately appropriated" (Joyce, *Ezekiel*, 215, with reference to Block).
48. Klein, *Schriftauslegung im Ezechielbuch*, 138.

40–55(66).[49] These chapters have been analyzed thoroughly elsewhere,[50] and, for the present purpose, I want to focus on how the manner and technique of interpretation change through the literary development of the book.

The history of the new or second exodus in the book of Isaiah begins with the salvation oracle in 43:16–21. This prophecy is usually counted among the oldest oracles of the book,[51] even though its idea of time differs from the time conception in the other oracles of the original collection, which suggests a slightly later dating.[52] In its first part in 43:16–17, the ora-

---

49. The first scholar to observe this idea was Alfred Zillessen, "Der alte und der neue Exodus: Eine Studie zur israelitischen Prophetie, speziell zu Jesaja 40ff," AR 6 (1903): 289–304, here 290. Further studies on the topic include Walther Zimmerli, "Der 'neue Exodus' in der Verkündigung der beiden großen Exilspropheten," in Zimmerli, *Gottes Offenbarung: Gesammelte Aufsätze zum Alten Testament*, TB 19 (Munich: Kaiser, 1963), 192–204; Joseph Blenkinsopp, "Scope and Depth of the Exodus Tradition in Deutero-Isaiah 40–55," *Conc(D)* 2 (1966): 22–26; Dieter Baltzer, *Ezechiel und Deuterojesaja: Berührungen in der Heilserwartung der beiden großen Heilspropheten*, BZAW 121 (Berlin: de Gruyter, 1971), 12–26; Michael Fishbane, "The 'Exodus' Motif/The Paradigm of Historical Renewal," in Fishbane, *Text and Texture: Close Readings of Selected Biblical Texts* (New York: Schocken, 1979), 133–40; Klaus Kiesow, *Exodustexte im Jesajabuch: Literarkritische und Motivgeschichtliche Analysen*, OBO 24 (Göttingen: Vandenhoeck & Ruprecht, 1979); William H. Propp, *Water in the Wilderness: A Biblical Motif and Its Mythological Background*, HSM 40 (Atlanta: Scholars Press, 1987), 99–106; Hans Barstad, *A Way in the Wilderness: The 'Second Exodus' in the Message of Second Isaiah*, JSSMS 12 (Manchester: University of Manchester, 1989); Lena-Sofia Tiemeyer, *For the Comfort of Zion: The Geographical and Theological Location of Isaiah 40–55*, VTSup 139 (Leiden: Brill, 2011), 155–203; Øystein Lund, *Way Metaphors and Way Topics in Isaiah 40–55*, FAT 2/28 (Tübingen: Mohr Siebeck, 2007).

In a previous publication I investigated whether the motif of the second exodus belongs to the original prophecies in Isa 40–55; see Anja Klein, "'Zieht heraus aus Babel': Beobachtungen zum Zweiten Exodus im Deuterojesajabuch," ZTK 112 (2015): 279–99. Finally, Saul M. Olyan reviews the exodus texts in Second Isaiah with the specific question how "an individual creative voice might be recovered" ("The Search for the Elusive Self in Texts of the Hebrew Bible," in *Religion and the Self in Antiquity*, ed. David Brakke, Michael L. Satlow, and Steven Weitzman [Bloomington: Indiana University Press, 2005], 40–50, here 44).

50. The literary development of Second Isaiah has been the object of extensive research, from which has emerged a general consensus about whether a text belongs to older or younger layers of the book. On this, see Hans-Jürgen Hermisson, "Einheit und Komplexität Deuterojesajas: Probleme der Redaktionsgeschichte von Jes 40–55," in *The Book of Isaiah/Le Livre d'Isaïe: Les oracles et leurs relectures; Unité et complexité de l'ouvrage*, ed. Jacques Vermeylen, BETL 81 (Leuven: Leuven University Press, 1989), 287–312; Reinhard G. Kratz, *Kyros im Deuterojesaja-Buch: Eine redaktionsgeschichtliche Untersuchung zu Entstehung und Theologie von Jes 40–55*, FAT 1 (Tübingen: Mohr Siebeck, 1991); and Jürgen van Oorschot, *Von Babel zum Zion: Eine literarkritische und redaktionsgeschichtliche Untersuchung*, BZAW 206 (Berlin: de Gruyter, 1993).

51. Both van Oorschot (*Von Babel zum Zion*, 69–74) and Kratz, *Kyros im Deuterojesaja-Buch*, 148–57) count this oracle among the texts belonging to their respective "original collection" of prophetic words.

52. Thus Klein, "Zieht heraus," 95–288.

cle comprises an extended messenger formula praising Yhwh as the one who sets a way in the sea and a path in the mighty waters (43:16: הנותן בים דרך ובמים עזים נתיבה). Yhwh is praised further for bringing out chariot and horse, which, however, subsequently meet with a rather bitter end, lying quenched and extinguished (43:17: המוציא רכב־וסוס חיל ועזוז יחדו ישכבו בל־יקומו דעכו כפשתה כבו). The second part in 43:18–21 starts with two negative exhortations, in which the addressees are called upon neither to remember the former things nor to consider things of old (43:18). Rather, their attention is drawn to the new thing that Yhwh will do now (43:19: הנני עשה חדשה עתה), which includes guiding his people on a route in the wilderness and provision of water in the desert (43:19–20). Consequently, the whole oracle ends in 43:21 with the praise of the people that Yhwh had formed for himself (עם־זו יצרתי לי תהלתי יספרו).

In this oracle, it is water metaphors that connect the prophecy to the exodus events, and the images can be understood only if the biblical narratives are known. On this understanding, the way in the sea recalls the trek of the Israelites through the divided waters of the Reed Sea (Isa 43:16; cf. Exod 14), while the pairing of way and path points to a spiritualization of the exodus.[53] The oracle exhibits two lexical links to the exodus account: First, the mention of chariot and horse in 43:17 (רכב־וסוס) can be understood as a reference to the Egyptian army (Exod 14:9, 23; 15:1, 19, 21).[54] Consequently, the description of their fate in terms of being extinguished and quenched like a wick serves as a euphemism for their end in the returning waters of the Red Sea. Second, the final characterization of the people in Isa 41:21 as the people that Yhwh had formed for himself (עם־זו יצרתי לי) recalls the description of the people in the Song of the Sea (Exod 15:13: עם־זו גאלת; 15:16: עם־זו קנית).[55] The different choice of verb in Isa 43:21 can be explained with a book-internal reference to the divine oracle in 43:1–4 that in the literary pre-context employs the root יצר to refer to the creation of Jacob-Israel as the creation of Yhwh's own people (43:1: ויצרך ישראל).[56]

---

53. The pairing has a background in wisdom literature; see further Kiesow, *Exodustexte im Jesajabuch*, 77 ("Realsymbole"); Barstad, *Way in the Wilderness*, 97 ("poetical metaphors"); Tiemeyer, *For the Comfort of Zion*, 182–84' and in detail Lund, *Way Metaphors*, 181–97.

54. It needs to be said, though, that the mentions of horse and rider in both Exod 14 and 15 are most likely post-Priestly additions (see Christoph Berner, *Die Exoduserzählung: Das literarische Werden einer Ursprungslegende Israels*, FAT 73 [Tübingen: Mohr Siebeck, 2010], 376–77, 403; and, with regard to Exod 15, Anja Klein, *Geschichte und Gebet: Die Rezeption der biblischen Geschichte in den Psalmen des Alten Testaments*, FAT 94 [Tübingen: Mohr Siebeck, 2014], 39); this is further argument that the oracle Isa 43:16–21 does not belong to the original collection of prophecies in the prophetic book.

55. On these references, see Olyan, "Search for the Elusive Self," 43; Ulrich Berges, *Jesaja 40–(66)*, 2 vols., HThKAT (Freiburg im Breisgau: Herder, 2008), 1:306.

56. The oracle in 43:1–4 is generally assumed to be part of the original prophecies; see

Even if there is a good case for exodus language and imagery in Isa 43:16–21, there remains the question whether the oracle suggests a second or new exodus. The answer to this question lies in the hermeneutical distinction between the things of old and the new thing that structures the oracle.[57] While the former things are identified with Yhwh's guidance of his people through the Reed Sea and the destruction of the Egyptian enemy, the new salvation comprises guidance in the wilderness and the provision with water. The water now serves to sustain the people of Yhwh instead of killing their enemies. As to the exegetical technique, the author of the oracle in Isa 43:16–21 draws on images and words that recall the first exodus, against which the new salvation appears as a second or new exodus. He engages both Exod 14 and 15, even though the exegesis relies on association rather than on a specific textual *Vorlage*. Furthermore, the exodus is not in focus as a narrative event but constitutes the relationship between Yhwh and his people, whom he formed for himself (Isa 43:21). In drawing on the understanding of the exodus as a founding event in Exod 15, the oracle concurs with existing prophecies in the book (Isa 43:1: ‏כה־‎ ‏אמר יהוה בראך יעקב ויצרך ישראל‎).

The motif of water sustenance in the desert reappears in our second example, the two-part oracle in Isa 48:20–21, where, however, the textual links are more numerous. This prophetic word is usually considered to represent the closing of the original oracles in the book.[58] While its first part in 48:20 calls the exiles, in a sequence of five imperatives, to flee from Babylon/Chaldea (‏צאו מבבל ברחו מכשדים‎), the second part narrates the fate of a group that was led by Yhwh through the wilderness and was sustained with water from the rocks (48:21). The change in addressees together with the shift in topic suggests literary growth, classifying 48:21 as a later continuation of the call to leave Babylon in 48:20.[59] Yet it is this later continuation that shapes the preceding call to flee from Babylon into a call for a second exodus by establishing links to the first exodus from Egypt.[60] While the splitting of the rocks (‏ויבקע־צור‎) in Isa 48:21 recalls the dividing of the waters in Exod 14:16, 21 (‏בקע‎),[61] the trek through the desert

---

Kratz, *Kyros im Jesajabuch*, 148–74, 217; further van Oorschot, *Von Babel zum Zion*, 59–62 (with respect to 43:1–3a).

57. See on this Klein, "Zieht heraus," 291–92. See further the discussion in Lund, *Way Metaphors*, 181–97.

58. Kratz, *Kyros im Jesajabuch*, 216.

59. Klein, "Zieht heraus," 287. In general, scholarship argues for literary unity here, see, e.g., van Oorschot, *Von Babel zum Zion*, 159–67; and Kratz, *Kyros im Jesajabuch*, 148–51.

60. On the exodus imagery in Isa 48:21 see Lund, *Way Metaphors*, 224–26; Berges, *Jesaja 40–(66)*, 1:548–49; Tiemeyer, *For the Comfort of Zion*, 185–86.

61. An even closer parallel to the formulation in Isa 48:21 exists in the narration of the exodus events in Ps 78:15 (‏יבקע צרים במדבר‎), which, however, seems to be dependent on the oracle in Isa 48; see Klein, *Geschichte und Gebet*, 114, 116.

(Isa 48:21: בחרבות) recalls the drainage of the Reed Sea before Israel can pass through (Exod 14:21: וישם את־הים לחרבה). Furthermore, these reminiscences of the sea miracle in Exod 14 merge with the literary memory of the water miracles in the wilderness (Exod 15; 17; Num 20). Similar to Isa 43:16–21, the specific use of terms and images of the first exodus in order to describe the new salvation relates the two events in terms of first/old and second/new. The idea that the second exodus leads through dry land, where the water serves to sustain the people, connects the two oracles even more closely.

The water imagery also shapes the exegesis of the exodus in 43:1–7, an oracle that originally comprised a divine announcement of protection in 43:1–4. As already mentioned, in these verses Yhwh lays claim to his people, since he is the one who created and delivered them (43:1). From this claim results the affirmation that he will be with his people when they pass through both the waters (כי־תעבר במים) and the fire (43:2). The formulation עבר מים has a loose parallel in Exod 15:16 (עד־יעבר), but this is the only piece of evidence recalling the exodus events.[62] Yet things change with the later continuation in 43:5–7,[63] the author of which applies the original promise of protection to the gathering of the diaspora from all over the world (43:5: הביאי בני מרחוק; 43:6: ממזרח אביא זרעך וממערב אקבצך; ובנותי מקצה הארץ). Here, a redactor who is clearly familiar with the idea of a second exodus interprets the water imagery in 43:1–4 as a reference to the exodus events, supplementing the promise of gathering and return. His continuation, however, takes the idea of a second exodus a step further by extending the salvation to include the worldwide diaspora.

While these first examples mainly demonstrate the use of metaphors and imagery connected with the first exodus, in a second group of texts the concept is developed further with increasing literary links to the exodus narratives. Our first example is the oracle in 51:9–11, which belongs to the so-called Zion-continuations (*Zion-Fortschreibungen*)[64] in the book. Here, the original call to Yhwh's arm to awaken in 51:9–10a[65] praises the might

---

62. In contrast, the parallelism of the threats of water and fire is evidence that common hazardous situations, which are not related specifically to the exodus, are in focus. See Tiemeyer, *For the Comfort of Zion*, 182; Barstad, *Way in the Wilderness*, 90; Lund, *Way Metaphors*, 167–77; and Klein, "Zieht heraus," 287–88.

63. Both the literary *Wiederaufnahme* of the call not to fear in 43:5 (cf. 43:1) and the shift to the diaspora in 43:5–7 speak for a literary continuation. On this, see Kratz, *Kyros im Jesajabuch*, 48; Klein, "Zieht heraus," 285; similarly van Oorschot opts for an original oracle in 43:1–3a (*Von Babel zum Zion*, 9–62).

64. On the term and analysis, see Odil H. Steck, "Beobachtungen zu den Zion-Texten in Jesaja 51–54: Ein redaktionsgeschichtlicher Versuch," in Steck, *Gottesknecht und Zion: Gesammelte Aufsätze zu Deuterojesaja*, FAT 4 (Tübingen: Mohr Siebeck, 1992), 96–125; and Kratz, *Kyros im Jesajabuch*, 216–17. Differently, Hermisson delineates a collection of Zion texts that he counts among the original oracles of the book ("Einheit und Komplexität," 303–4).

65. Karl Elliger (*Deuterojesaja in seinem Verhältnis zu Tritojesaja*, BWANT 63 [Stuttgart:

of the divine arm that is victorious over the water powers—a clear allusion to the idea of Yhwh as chaos fighter. Similar to the interpretation of the water imagery of 43:1–4 in the later continuation 43:5–7, a later redactor in 51:10b–11 draws on the water imagery of 51:9–10a and relates it to the exodus. In this supplementation, the preceding drainage of the waters (51:10a: המחרבת ים) serves as a precondition to allow the redeemed ones to pass through (51:10b: לעבר גאולים) on their way back to Zion (51:10b–11). A number of lexical links with the exodus poetry in Exod 15 demonstrate the dependence of Isa 51:10b–11 on the Exodus materials (עבר, Isa 51:10b, cf. Exod 15:16; גאל, Isa 51:10b, cf. Exod 15:13). Both in the literary growth of Exod 15[66] and in Isa 51:9–11, the literary supplementation attests to an exegetical development in which the idea of Yhwh as chaos fighter is augmented with characteristics of the god that acts in biblical history on behalf of his people.

The second example, in Isa 52:11–12, demonstrates further how literary links to key passages contribute to a "scripturalization" of salvation prophecies in the book. This oracle represents a continuation of the book's epilogue (52:7–10), in which the prophet calls the people to depart "from there," referring to Babylon (52:11: צאו משם). Its second part in 52:12 illustrates the circumstances of this departure, which are described as neither hasty nor in flight (52:12: כי לא בחפזון תצאו ובמנוסה לא תלכון). In biblical history, the Israelites have departed in haste only once, namely, when they hurriedly ate the last Passover before leaving Egypt, following the divine instruction: "You shall eat it hurriedly" (Exod 12:11: ואכלתם אתו בחפזון); the command finds a literary echo in the Passover legislation in Deut 16:3: "because you went out of the land of Egypt in great haste" (כי בחפזון יצאת מארץ מצרים).[67] The second adverb in Isa 52:12, however, which describes the circumstances as "not in a flight" (ובמנוסה), has a different literary background. The only other occurrence of the term מנוסה can be found in the covenant curses in Lev 26:36. Here, it refers to the living conditions of Israel in the diaspora, where life is characterized by being on a constant run from the sword (מנסת־חרב). By way of inner-biblical exegesis, the author of Isa 52:12 describes the organized departure from Babylon against a double negative foil: Not only is it painted in rosy colors com-

---

Kohlhammer, 1933], 202–3) and Kiesow (*Exodustexte im Jesajabuch*, 93–94) questioned the literary affiliation of 51:12, before Odil H. Steck ("Zions Tröstung: Beobachtungen und Fragen zu Jesaja 51,1–11," in Steck, *Gottesknecht und Zion*, 73–91, here 77–79) furnished proof that 51:10b–11 as a whole has to be seen as a later continuation; see also Kratz, *Kyros im Jesajabuch*, 82; and Klein, "Zieht heraus," 282.

66. See on this Klein, *Geschichte und Gebet*, 15–78.

67. On the references to Exod 12:11 (and Deut 16:3), see already Bernhard Duhm, *Das Buch Jesaja*, 5th ed., HK 3.1 (Göttingen: Vandenhoeck & Ruprecht, 1968; original 1892), 393; further Kiesow, *Exodustexte im Jesajabuch*, 118; Fishbane, *Biblical Interpretation*, 134; Tiemeyer, *For the Comfort of Zion*, 197–98; and Olyan, "Search for the Elusive Self," 43.

pared with the first exodus from Egypt, but, because of the reference to Lev 26, it also promises a change for the better for the diaspora. In this exegetical relationship, the interpretation in Isa 52:11–12 is indicative of an emerging distance between *traditum* and *traditio*, by which the second exodus is depicted as a more orderly departure, thus surpassing the first biblical exodus from Egypt.[68] Furthermore, the reference to the fate of the diaspora in Lev 26 marks the return from exile as a paradigm that applies also to the worldwide diaspora.

The hermeneutical differentiation between *traditum* and *traditio* can be traced further in two texts that belong to later literary layers of the book of Isaiah. The first example, Isa 63:11–14, is part of the prayer of the servants of God in Isa 63–64, which at one point represented the closure of the book.[69] In this prayer, the group of speakers remember Yhwh's salvific deeds in biblical history, among which the exodus remembrance takes pride of place. The exodus is clearly depicted as an event from the biblical past, connected with the figure of Moses (63:11: ויזכר ימי־עולם משה עמו), and a number of lexical links are further proof that the prayer refers back to the exodus events in their literary form (Isa 63:12: מוליך לימין משה זרוע; cf. Exod 15:16; Isa 63:12: בוקע מים; cf. Exod 14:16, 21; Isa 63:13: מוליכם בתהמות; cf. Exod 15:5, 8). It is especially the idea that Yhwh made himself a name (Isa 63:12: לעשות לו שם עולם; cf. 63:14; see Exod 15:3: יהוה שמו) that serves as hermeneutical key for the present concern, as the rescue of the people in the events of the exodus is used as a paradigm of salvation for the present. By referring to Yhwh's reputation, the speakers hope to provoke him to intervene again on their behalf and save them from their present distress.[70] This time, however, it is not a second exodus that is in view; rather, the people hope for restitution of land, city, and sanctuary alike.

Our final example is the redactional passage in Isa 11:11–16 that prepares for the salvation prophecies in the second part of the book.[71] Here, the prophet announces that Yhwh will ban the tongue of the Sea of Egypt (11:15: והחרים יהוה את לשון ים־מצרים) so that one can cross with sandals (והדריך בנעלים); there will be a passage for his people "as there was for Israel on the day when they came up from Egypt" (11:16: כאשר היתה לישראל ביום עלתו מארץ מצרים). In this comparison, the particle כאשר clearly marks the way back from exile as a repetition of the first exodus and thus as

---

68. Olyan, "Search for the Elusive Self," 44; and, Klein, "Zieht heraus," 284.

69. On the redactional closure, see Odil H. Steck, "Zu jüngsten Untersuchungen von Jes 56,1–8; 63,7–66,2," in Steck, *Studien zu Tritojesaja*, BZAW 203 (Berlin: de Gruyter, 1991), 229–65, here 242; see further the study by Johannes Goldenstein, *Das Gebet der Gottesknechte: Jesaja 63,7–64,11 im Jesajabuch*, WMANT 92 (Neukirchen-Vluyn: Neukirchener Verlag, 2001).

70. Klein, "Zieht heraus," 297.

71. On this function, see Odil H. Steck, *Bereitete Heimkehr: Jesaja 35 als redaktionelle Brücke zwischen dem Ersten und Zweiten Jesaja*, SBS 121 (Stuttgart: Katholisches Bibelwerk, 1985), 62–63.

a second one, indicating a clear distance between both events.[72] Furthermore, the specific footwear of the Israelites, "sandals" (נעלים), represents a decisive link to the description of the last Passover in Egypt, when the Israelites were commanded to take the meal at the ready, with sandals on their feet (Exod 12:11: נעליכם ברגליכם).[73] As the sandals are now equally the footgear of choice in Isa 11, the new salvation literally walks in the shoes of the first exodus. The oracle in 11:11–16 can thus be seen as the endpoint of the literary-historical development that anchors firmly the notion of the second exodus in the book and that—due to its redactional placing as a hinge text—predetermines a line of interpretation for the salvation prophecies to follow in chapters 40–66. The oracle represents further the endpoint in hermeneutical perspective, as the exegesis distinguishes clearly between the future salvation and past events that serve as point of reference.[74] We are dealing here with a clear distinction between the first exodus from Egypt and the second exodus in Isaiah. In summary, the exegesis of the new exodus in the prophecies of Deutero-Isaiah demonstrates how the manner and technique of exegesis have changed through the literary growth of the book. While the earliest texts about the new exodus draw on metaphors and motifs, textual links increase in the subsequent literary layers. Finally, the latest interpretations are indicative of a clear distinction between *traditio* and *traditum*, correlating the exodus from Egypt and the exodus from exile as two distinct events of salvation.

The Seventy-Year Motif in Jeremiah

Our final example of interest is the seventy-year motif in the book of Jeremiah (Jer 25:11–13; 29:10), the beginnings of which, however, lie in the prophecies of Zechariah (Zech 1:12, 7–8), while its further exegesis extends to 2 Chr 36:21–22, Ezra 1:1 and Dan 9 (9:2, 24–27).[75] As to the relationship

---

72. On the exegesis of the first biblical exodus in Isa 11:11–16, see Hans Wildberger, *Jesaja*, 3 vols., BKAT 10 (Neukirchen-Vluyn: Neukirchener Verlag, 1972), 1:474; John D. W. Watts, *Isaiah 34–66*, WBC 24 (Nashville: Thomas Nelson, 1978; rev. ed., 2005), 217; further H. G. M. Williamson, *The Book Called Isaiah: Deutero-Isaiah's Role in Composition and Redaction* (Oxford: Clarendon, 1994), 125–27; and Klein, "Zieht heraus," 298.

73. Even though the lemma נעל occurs quite often in the Hebrew Bible, it is used in an exodus/Egypt context only in Exod 12:11; Deut 29:4, and Isa 11:15, which makes the link significant and suggests a conscious allusion on the part of the author in Isa 11.

74. Klein, "Zieht heraus," 298.

75. The exegesis of Jeremiah's seventy years does not end in the later biblical books but continues in further literature from the Second Temple period; see Christoph Berner, *Jahre, Jahrwochen und Jubiläen: Heptadische Geschichtskonzeptionen im Antiken Judentum*, BZAW 363 (Berlin: de Gruyter, 2006), 100–515. Of special interest is the Qumran Jeremiah Apocryphon, the author of which undertakes a further heptadic adjustment by transferring the prolonged time span of seventy-year weeks from Dan 9 into a jubilean periodization of history (4Q387

between these texts, in 1991 Kratz proposed a literary development that has found support in further research.[76] His model will thus be used as a working hypothesis in what follows, while my focus is on the manner and techniques of biblical interpretation as the texts develop.

According to Kratz's model, the idea of the seventy years has its beginnings in the vision of Zech 1:12, where the angel asks Yhwh how long he will withhold mercy even though seventy years have passed (שבעים שנה). Yhwh answers with the promise of restitution provisions (1:13–17), which culminate in the assurance that the temple will be built again (1:16). Zechariah 7–8 draws on this prophecy by connecting the time span with a period of fasting and by promising the dawning of salvation for the rest of the people (8:11–13).[77] The origin of the seventy-years figure has been discussed without any consensus having been reached. While the references to ancient Near Eastern parallels remain a possible option,[78] the easiest explanation can be found in the historic realities, as seventy years roughly corresponds to the time between the destruction of the First Temple (586 BCE), and the Second Temple's dedication (519 BCE) and completion (516 BCE).[79] Apparently, the seventy-year period has later come to be understood as a figure of exile, which is obvious in our next example, the prophecy in Jer 29:10.

---

2 II, 3–4: שנים יבלי עשרה); see Eibert Tigchelaar, "Jeremiah's Scriptures in the Dead Sea Scrolls and the Growth of a Tradition," in *Jeremiah's Scriptures: Production, Reception, Interaction, and Transformation*, ed. Hindy Najman and Konrad Schmid, JSJSup 173 (Leiden: Brill, 2016), 289–306; and, in the same volume, Anja Klein, "New Material or Traditions Expanded? A Response to Eibert Tigchelaar," 319–26.

76. Reinhard G. Kratz, *Translation imperii: Untersuchungen zu den aramäischen Danielerzählungen und ihrem theologiegeschichtlichen Umfeld*, WMANT 63 (Neukirchen-Vluyn: Neukirchener Verlag, 1991), 261–67. His model has been adopted by Berner, *Jahre, Jahrwochen*, 78–84. While the dependence of Dan 9 on the texts from the book of Jeremiah is *communis opinio*, scholarship differs especially in the assessment of the texts from Zechariah, which are usually considered to succeed the Jeremianic texts; see, e.g., Louis F. Hartman and Alexander A. Di Lella, *The Book of Daniel: A New Translation with Notes and Commentary on Chapters 1–9*, AB 23 (Garden City, NY: Doubleday, 1978), 246–47; Hartmut Bluhm, "Daniel 9 und die chronistische Geschichtsdarstellung," *TGl* 72 (1982): 450–60, here 451; Leslie C. Allen, *Jeremiah: A Commentary*, OTL (Louisville: Westminster John Knox, 2008), 287; or Carol A. Newsom with Brannan W. Breed, *Daniel: A Commentary*, OTL (Louisville: Westminster John Knox, 2014), 299–300; differently, however, Julius Wellhausen, *Die Kleinen Propheten: Übersetzt und erklärt*, 4th ed. (Berlin: de Gruyter, 1963), 179; Bernhard Duhm, *Das Buch Jeremia*, KHC 11 (Tübingen: Mohr Siebeck, 1903), 202.

77. Kratz, *Translatio imperii*, 261.

78. As a possible candidate, studies refer to the Esarhaddon inscription Ep 10:2b–9a/10:19–20 (on the edition, see Rykle Borger, *Die Inschriften Asarhaddons Königs von Assyrien*, AfOB 9 [Graz: Im Selbstverlage des Herausgebers, 1956], 15), which refers to the god Marduk shortening a previous seventy-year period of depopulation in Babylon to eleven years. One might assume that the figure denotes a fixed time period connected to the destruction of cities and temples (thus Kratz, *Translatio imperii*, 261).

79. Berner, *Jahre, Jahrwochen*, 81.

In the book of Jeremiah, chapter 29 contains the letter (29:1: ואלה דברי הספר) that the prophet sent to the exiled community in Babylon. Yhwh announces in writing that he will return them when Babylon's seventy years are completed (29:10: כי לפי מלאת לבבל שבעים שנה, cf. 29:14), thus fulfilling his earlier promise (דברי הטוב). Since the prophecy in Zech 8 provides for the rescue of the remnant (cf. 8:13: כן אושיע אתכם), it is possible to understand the term דברי הטוב in Jer 29:10 as a reference to this earlier prophecy, which is now interpreted as a promise of gathering and return. The exegetical trail is more obvious when it comes to the oracle in Jer 25:11–12, which presupposes Jer 29:10,[80] drawing on the idea that the seventy years denotes a time period for Babylon. After the fulfillment of this time (25:12: והיה כמלאות שבעים שנה) judgment will be implemented that leaves the land of the Chaldeans an everlasting waste (לשממות עולם). Thus, Jeremiah continues the discussion about the seventy years that started in Zechariah but focuses on the time period particularly with regard to its importance for the duration of the exile and the consequences for Babylon, while the promise of the rebuilding of the temple is not taken up.

It is not the judgment on Babylon but the interest in the duration of exile that the later interpretation in 2 Chr 36:21–22 continues. Drawing further on the concept of the empty land in Lev 26:31–35[81] and thus introducing a heptadic time frame, its author interprets the seventy-year period from Jeremiah as a time in which the land receives compensation for its Sabbaths (2 Chr 36:21: למלאות שבעים שנה), while the Persian king Cyrus is named as the one who will end the seventy years for Babylon (36:22). For the present question, however, it is noteworthy that the text emphasizes twice the accordance of its message with the words of the prophet Jeremiah. Whereas previously the focus was on the fulfillment of the time period of seventy years (Jer 29:10: מלאת לבבל שבעים שנה; Jer 25:12: כמלאות שבעים שנה), the text in 2 Chr 36:21–22 focuses on the fulfillment of the divine word *as authorized by Jeremiah* (36:21 למלאות דבר־יהוה בפי ירמיהו; 36:22: לכלות דבר־יהוה בפי ירמיהו). This chronistic note has a counterpart in the anterior chronistic frame in Ezra 1:1–4, which in its beginning parallels the reference to Jeremiah (Ezra 1:1: לכלות דבר־יהוה מפי ירמיה). Apparently, the prophets of Israel—or at least the figure of Jeremiah—were already ascribed a certain authority to which the authors of 2 Chr 36:21–22 and Ezra 1:1–4 referred in order to stress the significance of the events narrated.

---

80. Thus already Charles F. Whitley, "The Term Seventy Years Captivity," *VT* 4 (1954): 60–72, here 68; further Kratz, *Translatio imperii*, 261–62; and accordingly Berner, *Jahre, Jahrwochen*, 79.

81. Fishbane, *Biblical Interpretation*, 481–82; Raymond B. Dillard, *2 Chronicles*, WBC 15 (Waco, TX: Word, 1987), 301; Sara Japhet, *I & II Chronicles: A Commentary*, OTL (London: SCM, 1993), 1075–76; John J. Collins, *Daniel: A Commentary on the Book of Daniel*, Hermeneia (Minneapolis: Fortress, 1993), 352; Ralph W. Klein, *2 Chronicles: A Commentary*, Hermeneia (Minneapolis: Fortress, 2012), 544–45.

Finally, the interpretation in Dan 9 represents the biblical endpoint of the hermeneutical development, while at the same time it breaks with the preceding chronology in terms of years.[82] In Dan 9:2, we find the prophet pondering the books (בינתי בספרים) with regard to the number of the seventy years that Yhwh had spoken to the prophet Jeremiah (דבר־יהוה אל־ ירמיה הנביא למלאות). The prophet's scripture study, however, is not sufficient; Daniel needs the help of the *angelus interpres* Gabriel (9:20–23), who deciphers the numerical figure on the prophet's behalf. According to his interpretation of the seventy-year oracle (9:24–26), the Jeremianic seventy years have to be understood in terms of seventy weeks of seven years each (Dan 9:24: שבעים שבעים),[83] thus indicating an elongation of the period in question (490 years).[84] Furthermore, the number no longer denotes a period for Babylon, but it refers now to the time that is assigned for the ruins of Jerusalem (9:2: לחרבות ירושלם), meaning a time for the people and the holy city to bring their transgressions to an end and atone for them (9:24). Even though the interpretation in Dan 9 refers to the prophet Jeremiah by name (9:2), the lexical links provide sufficient evidence that the entire development of the seventy-year motif is in the literary background—this is evidenced already by the use of the plural "books" in Dan 9:2 (בספרים).[85] The seventy-year number in previous written prophecies is not simply redetermined, but the pondering of the prophet and the subsequent revelatory recalculation attest to a process of actualization that distinguishes clearly between *traditum* and *traditio*. In comparison with the chronistic evidence in 2 Chr 36:21–22 and Ezra 1:1–4, the author of Dan 9 equally refers to Jeremiah by name, but the additional mention of the scriptures (9:2: ספרים) establishes a *literary* reference. There has been some discussion about what entity the term ספרים refers to, but it can be safely assumed that the author of Daniel had access to Torah and Neviim, which were already well established (with parts of the Ketuvim) at his time.[86]

---

82. On the chronological reinterpretation in Dan 9, see Fishbane, *Biblical Interpretation*, 485–89; Odil H. Steck, "Weltgeschehen und Gottesvolk im Buche Daniel," in Steck, *Wahrnehmungen Gottes im Alten Testament: Gesammelte Studien*, TB 70 (Munich: Kaiser, 1982), 277–81; Bluhm, "Dan 9," 454–55; Kratz, *Translatio imperii*, 39, 263–67; and in detail Berner, *Jahre, Jahrwochen*, 19–99, 501.

83. A possible key to this interpretation is the doubling of the consonants for "seventy" (שבעים), which add up to "seventy weeks"; see Berner, *Jahre, Jahrwochen*, 47; and Newsom, *Daniel*, 299. On the interpretation in 9:24–27 see further Hartman and DiLella, *Daniel*, 249–50.

84. Kratz, *Translatio imperii*, 265–66.

85. Berner, *Jahre, Jahrwochen*, 75; on the wider literary background in Dan 9, see further Kratz, *Translatio imperii*, 39, while Newsom (*Daniel*, 290) deems it less likely that "Daniel is doing 'intertextual' interpretation, comparing Jeremiah's prophecies with passages from Leviticus."

86. Both Torah and Neviim are referred to in the prologue of Sirach (132 BCE). On the reference in Dan 9:2 pointing to Jeremiah as part of the—later scriptural—books of the Prophets, see Collins, *Daniel*, 348; Berner, *Jahre, Jahrwochen*, 43.

Therefore, the exegesis in Dan 9 is unique insofar as it not only draws on previous prophecies but also actualizes explicitly its *Vorlagen* and quotes these as authoritative "scripture." Hence, Dan 9 can rightly be seen as a precursor for the exegetical literature in Qumran (pesharim, midrashim), where we encounter the same hermeneutics with the difference that the interpretation in Qumran forms its own literary genre with specific form elements.[87]

The Emergence of Scripture in the Prophets

This contribution has focused on the phenomenon of literary supplementation in its specific form as inner-biblical exegesis. Therein, the diachronic differentiation of the texts has mostly been presupposed in order to demonstrate the technique and hermeneutics of the dynamic exegetical process. I started from the observation that there are a small number of oracles in the three Major Prophets of the Hebrew Bible that draw on other prophetic texts signifying a clear distance between *traditio* and *traditum*. By investigating their literary origins, it can be demonstrated that each of these texts represents the literary endpoint of a productive process of interpretation. First, the literary development of the Gog chapters in Ezek 38–39 is a classic example of the literary continuation (*Fortschreibung*) of a core oracle that deals with the threat of an enigmatic enemy, whose advance in later literary layers is identified explicitly with prophecies from other prophetic books (Ezek 38:17; cf. 39:8). Second, in the case of the new exodus, the literary development of this concept of salvation throughout the book of Isaiah witnesses to a borrowing from the first biblical exodus, which in the latest literary supplementations is related explicitly to the new act of salvation (Isa 11:16). Finally, the interpretation of the seventy-year prophecy in the prophetic literature shows how the oracle came to be connected with the figure of Jeremiah and is finally ascribed authority by making it the object of scriptural studies (Dan 9:2). Our three examples thus demonstrate a development in technique and hermeneutics of literary supplementation that culminates in the emergence of scripture as an authoritative variable that can be quoted and interpreted.

---

87. Berner, *Jahre, Jahrwochen*, 44. The closeness to the Qumran pesharim is noted also by Hartman and DiLella, *Daniel*, 247.

Fire and Worms: Isaiah 66:24 in the Context of Isaiah 66 and the Book of Isaiah

SAUL M. OLYAN
Brown University

They shall go forth and they shall look upon [‏וראו ב‎] the corpses of the persons [men?] who have transgressed against me [‏הפשעים בי‎]: For [‏כי‎] their worm [‏תולעתם‎] shall not die, and their fire shall not be extinguished. They shall be a horror [‏דראון‎] for all flesh.[1]

As has often been noted, Isa 66:24 exercised a considerable influence on the formulation of images of hell and final judgment in later biblical and postbiblical literature. Understood by early interpreters to speak of dead transgressors suffering unendingly from worms and fire and elicit-

---

I am particularly grateful to Marc Brettler and Reinhard Kratz for their helpful suggestions during the discussion of this paper at the symposium (10 May 2016). Any errors of fact or judgment, however, remain my responsibility alone.

1. Some scholars understand the idiom ‏ראה ב‎ in Isa 66:24 to mean "to gloat over," as in Obad 1:12; Pss 22:18; 112:8, a behavior characteristic of enemies (e.g., Joseph Blenkinsopp, *Isaiah 56–66. A New Translation with Introduction and Commentary*, AB 19B [New York: Doubleday, 2003], 317). The idiom also has a variety of other meanings, as is commonly noted (e.g., "to look at with anger" or "concern," as in Exod 2:11). BDB understands ‏וראו ב‎ in Isa 66:24 to mean to look upon with "abhorrence" and lists no other examples for this rendering. It is apparent that the precise nuance of the idiom in Isa 66:24 is unclear, particularly given that the identity of the witnesses who look upon the corpses is uncertain (on their identity, see my argument ahead). Thus, I render ‏וראו ב‎ as "they shall look upon" without reference to any particular emotion. Although the idiom ‏פשע ב‎ is legitimately translated "rebel against" in some contexts, I prefer to render it "transgress against" in Isa 66:24, given that the evidence suggests that the transgressors may well be a mix of Judeans and non-Judeans according to the author (see my argument ahead) and "rebel against" implies an assumed treaty relationship that "transgress against" does not (see, e.g., 2 Kgs 1:1; 3:5, 7; Isa 1:2; Jer 2:8, 29; Hos 7:13). The word ‏כי‎ in this passage, which I have translated "for," likely has the sense of "because": They shall look upon the corpses precisely because they are a sight to behold, given that their worm and fire are everlasting. For this understanding, see, e.g., LXX ὁ γὰρ σκώληξ αὐτῶν οὐ τελευτήσει, and Abraham Even-Shoshan, ed., *A New Concordance of the Bible* [in Hebrew] (Jerusalem: Kiryat Sepher, 2000), 529, 531.

ing a horrified response from witnesses, evidence of the influence of Isa 66:24 may be detected in the work of late first-millennium BCE exegetes such as the translator of Ben Sira into Greek (Sir 7:17) and the author of Judith (16:17), as well as early first-millennium CE writers such as Pseudo-Philo (LAB 63:4–5) and the author of Mark (9:43, 48, the latter quoting Isa 66:24 explicitly). It is also likely that Isa 66:24 was a primary source for the writer of Dan 12:2. While manuscripts A and C of Hebrew Ben Sira state that the "hope of humans is maggots," the Greek translator, working at the end of the second century BCE and influenced by Isa 66:24, says that "the punishment of the impious is fire and worms."[2] Judith 16:17 refers to the "day of judgment" when Yhwh will send fire and worms into the flesh of foreign enemies of Judeans who shall "weep forever." Pseudo-Philo envisions the future punishment of Doeg, the murderer of the priests of Nob, to consist of dwelling forever in unquenchable fire with a fiery worm boring into his tongue. And Mark 9:48 refers to Gehenna as a place "where their worm does not die and the fire is not extinguished." Daniel 12:2 may also reflect the influence of Isa 66:24, although the imagery of everlasting fire and worms is missing from this text. Instead, it is the "horror" (דראון) associated with the corpses of the dead transgressors in v. 24 that may well be reworked in the mention in Dan 12:2 of the "eternal horror" (דראון עולם) to which some who sleep in the dust will awake.[3] One could easily write a paper on the variety of ways in which the imagery of Isa 66:24 was interpreted and elaborated by later Jewish and Christian authors at work generating descriptions of hell and final judgment. My purpose here, however, is different. I will focus mainly on Isa 66:24 in the context of what is now Isaiah 66 and also comment on the verse in the larger setting of the

---

2. Sir 7:17: ... ὅτι ἐκδίκησις ἀσεβοῦς πῦρ καὶ σκώληξ. Hebrew ms A reads תקות אנוש רמה; ms C reads תקות אנוש לרמה. For the Hebrew manuscript evidence, see Pancratius C. Beentjes, *The Book of Ben Sira in Hebrew: A Text Edition of All Extant Hebrew Manuscripts and a Synopsis of All Parallel Hebrew Ben Sira Texts*, VTSup 68 (Atlanta: Society of Biblical Literature, 2006), 30, 97.

3. Given that the word דראון occurs only in these two passages and nowhere else, this seems a likely scenario to me. (See, similarly, Michael Fishbane, *Biblical Interpretation in Ancient Israel* [Oxford: Clarendon, 1985], 493, who goes further and characterizes דראון in Dan 12:2 as a "citation" of Isa 66:24. Many scholars note the two occurrences of דראון. See, e.g., Peter Höffken, *Das Buch Jesaja*, 2 vols., NSKAT 18 [Stuttgart: Katholisches Bibelwerk, 1998], 2:254; Reinhard G. Kratz, "Die Komposition des Hebräischen Jesjabuches," in *Transmission and Interpretation of the Book of Isaiah in the Context of Intra- and Interreligious Debates*, ed. Florian Wilk and Peter Gemeinhardt, BETL 280 [Leuven: Peeters, 2016], 16.) Furthermore, it may be that the author of Dan 12:2 has also taken the notion of everlasting punishment from the worm and fire imagery of Isa 66:24. The occurrence of דראון only in Isa 66:24 and Dan 12:2 is widely noted by scholars (e.g., John J. Collins, *Daniel: A Commentary on the Book of Daniel*, Hermeneia [Minneapolis: Fortress, 1993], 393), and Jeffrey M. Leonard has made a cogent case that "shared language that is rare or distinctive" constitutes compelling evidence for textual dependency ("Identifying Inner-Biblical Allusions: Psalm 78 as a Test Case," *JBL* 127 [2008]: 241–65, here 251–52). I thank Marc Brettler for providing the Leonard reference.

Fire and Worms 149

book of Isaiah. I will be asking what literary and ideological purposes this final verse of both chapter 66 and the book of Isaiah serves and on what earlier material in both the chapter and the larger book it depends.

It is a commonplace to note that Isa 66:24 is a relatively late addition to chapter 66 and the book of Isaiah, but commentators have often not bothered to tease out in detail its relationship to earlier material in both the chapter and the book.[4] Verse 24 brings to an end a diverse collection of supplementary materials that follows what was apparently the original end of the unit Isa 56–66 in 66:12-14.[5] Verses 13–14 speak of a favored Judean plurality (referred to as "you") who will be comforted by Yhwh and "will be comforted in Jerusalem,"[6] who will "see," whose heart will rejoice and who will otherwise prosper, while Yhwh's enemies will endure his rage.[7] What this favored plurality will "see" is not made clear in these verses although the identity of the plurality is likely those who are said in v. 10 to love and mourn for Jerusalem and who are commanded in that verse to rejoice with Jerusalem and exult in her. The focus on comforting mourners in vv. 13–14 likely alludes to Yhwh's command

---

4. Reasons why verse 24 is assumed by most commentators to be a late or even the latest accretion to the chapter and book include its function as "excipit to the book as a whole" in the words of Blenkinsopp, *Isaiah 56–66*, 316.

5. For the idea that verses 15–24 constitute a "delimited unit" with verses 10–14 as the unit preceding, see Leon J. Liebreich, "The Compilation of the Book of Isaiah," *JQR* 47 (1956): 114–38, here 138, brought to my attention by Kratz, "Die Komposition des Hebräischen Jesajabuches," 12–13 and n. 2. Blenkinsopp identifies vv. 12–14 as the original conclusion to chapters 56–66 (*Isaiah 56–66*, 307, 308, 311). On 311 he discusses what he calls the "successive appendices or addenda" at the end of the chapter and book, theorizing a possible order in which each item was added. W. A. M. Beuken sees vv. 15–24 as a final unit after vv. 7–14, with vv. 15–21 serving originally as an end to the unit Isa 40–55 + 56–66 and vv. 22–24 bringing the book of Isaiah to an end. (Verses 7–14 represent the ending of chapters 56–66 for Beuken.) (Beuken, "Isaiah Chapters LXV–LXVI: Trito-Isaiah and the Closure of the Book of Isaiah," in *Congress Volume: Leuven 1989*, ed. J. A. Emerton, VTSup 43 [Leiden: Brill, 1991], 204–21, esp. 207–8 and n. 5, and 221.) Although I agree with Beuken's demarcation of vv. 15–24 as the final larger unit of the book, I am not convinced by his understanding of the different functions of vv. 15–21 and 22–24. Kratz, for his part, sees vv. 15–24 as the final unit of the book with vv. 4–14 preceding ("Die Komposition des Hebräischen Jesjabuches," 21–22). Finally, note that a minority of commentators do not view the chapter as composite (e.g., Benjamin D. Sommer, *A Prophet Reads Scripture: Allusion in Isaiah 40–66* [Stanford, CA: Stanford University Press, 1998], 246 n. 26). It is worth mentioning that ancient manuscript evidence can be construed to support a break between vv. 14 and 15 (e.g., 1QIsa^a begins a new unit at v. 15; see the photograph in *Scrolls from Qumrân Cave 1*, photographs by John C. Trevor [Jerusalem: Albright Institute and Shrine of the Book, 1974], 61).

6. That is to say, the comforting "will be experienced in Jerusalem," as Blenkinsopp puts it (*Isaiah 56–66*, 307).

7. The third person masculine singular perfect verbal form זעם in the final colon of v. 14 is often emended to זעמו, likely on the grounds of parallelism (e.g., *BHS* n; *HALOT*, s.v. "זעם"; Blenkinsopp, *Isaiah 56–66*, 304 n. k; Brevard S. Childs, *Isaiah: A Commentary*, OTL [Louisville: Westminster John Knox, 2001], 530).

of Isa 40:1 that his people be comforted.[8] Yet in 66:13–14, it is the favored Judean plurality who are to be comforted rather than Yhwh's people as a whole, and the comforting is accomplished by Yhwh himself, in contrast to 40:1, in which agents—evidently divine—are commanded by Yhwh to "comfort, comfort my people."[9] In both Isa 40:1 and 66:13–14, comforting signals an end to the mourning following upon the catastrophe of 587 and therefore a new beginning for those whom Yhwh supports (Yhwh's people in 40:1; the favored Judean plurality in 66:13–14). By foregrounding Yhwh's acts of comforting, 66:13–14 establishes an important link to 40:1 and the work of Second Isaiah.

The supplementary materials following vv. 13–14 can be divided as follows: First, poetic materials in vv. 15–16, which speak of Yhwh's wrathful, fiery theophany and his judgment of "all flesh": Yhwh will "come in fire"; "his rebuke will be in flames of fire"; he will "judge" "all flesh" with fire; "and the slain of Yhwh [חללי יהוה] will be many" as a result.[10] The favored Judean plurality of vv. 13–14 makes no appearance in vv. 15–16, which focus on punishment of transgressors. These verses are themselves apparently supplemented by v. 17, which seems to function to identify the offenders who are to be punished by Yhwh and who will come to an end: "They who sanctify themselves and purify themselves for (?) the gardens ... who eat pig's flesh, despicable things and the mouse."[11] Following vv. 15–16 + 17 comes a second major supplementary unit, vv. 18–21. Cast in prose narrative, Yhwh speaks in the first person of his imminent, transformative acts: All nations and tongues "shall come and see my glory" and "all of your brethren" (כל אחיכם) shall be brought back to Jerusalem, Yhwh's "holy mountain," from all the nations by these alien pilgrims. After vv. 18–21 comes a third supplementary unit, vv. 22–23, with a positive focus not unlike vv. 18–21: "'For just as the new heavens and the new earth which I am about to create shall stand before me,' oracle of Yhwh,

---

8. Noted by Liebreich, "Compilation of the Book of Isaiah," *JQR* 46 (1956): 259–77, here 276 (brought to my attention by Kratz, "Die Komposition des Hebräischen Jesjabuches," 12–13 and n. 2); Childs, *Isaiah*, 541, 543; and Emmanuel Uchenna Dim, *The Eschatological Implications of Isa. 65 and 66 as the Conclusion of the Book of Isaiah*, BdH 3 (Bern: Lang, 2005), 272, among many others.

9. On the divine identity of the comforters of Isa 40:1, see Frank Moore Cross Jr., "The Council of Yahweh in Second Isaiah," *JNES* 12 (1953): 274–77, here 276, who is followed by a variety of more recent commentators, among them Christopher R. Seitz, "The Divine Council: Temporal Transition and New Prophecy in the Book of Isaiah," *JBL* 109 (1990): 229–47, here 231–32, 235–36, 243; Childs, *Isaiah*, 295–300; and Benjamin D. Sommer, *The Bodies of God and the World of Ancient Israel* (New York: Cambridge University Press, 2009), 166 and n. 93.

10. 1QIsa^a reads "his slain" (חלליו) rather than "the slain of Yhwh." LXX reads "Many shall be slain by the Lord" (ὑπὸ κυρίου), likely reflecting a *Vorlage* not unlike the MT.

11. Similarly, Blenkinsopp, *Isaiah 56–66*, 311. As others have noticed, v. 17 alludes to and builds on 65:3–4.

'so shall your progeny and your name endure'" (כן יעמד זרעכם ושמכם).[12] The passage concludes with Yhwh stating that perennially, "all flesh shall come to bow down before me." The chapter and book end with v. 24, which, like vv. 15–16 + 17, focuses on punishment rather than reward.

Of the varied material in vv. 15–23, v. 24 is most closely related to vv. 15–16, evidently building on its rhetoric and thought. The fire that characterizes Yhwh's theophany, his judgment of "all flesh," and his acts of punishment (e.g., his rebuke) in vv. 15–16 makes its appearance also in v. 24, where it is described innovatively as unceasing and is associated specifically with the corpses of those who are said to have transgressed against Yhwh (הפשעים).[13] The "slain of Yhwh" (חללי יהוה), who are said to be "many" and apparently die as a result of Yhwh's judgment according to v. 16, are mentioned in that verse in passing. Nothing is said there regarding their fate, for example, that they remain unburied or become food for predatory beasts and birds, typical biblical curses (e.g., Deut 28:26). In v. 24, the slain evidently make their appearance once again as "the persons [men?] who have transgressed against me" (הפשעים), but the focus in v. 24 is on their corpses and *their* particular fate rather than their great number: "Their worm shall not die, and their fire shall not be extinguished." Verse 24 makes it clear that those whom Yhwh slays are indeed transgressors, something only implicit in v. 16. It also informs us of the fate of the remains of the slain, something apparently of no interest to the writer of v. 16.[14] And their fate is something unique. Not the typical "food for the birds and beasts" that we find in curses, it is perhaps a worse fate, as it will never end. Finally, "all flesh," who are judged by Yhwh in v. 16 and many of whom die as a result, are mentioned also in v. 24 but function less prominently there, as implied witnesses to the horror described—and perhaps as direct witnesses as well (see ahead)— rather than as a target of Yhwh's wrath as in v. 16. This reshaping of the role of "all flesh" likely reflects the influence of v. 23, where "all flesh" are cast positively as

---

12. Alluding to 65:17, which itself alludes to 43:18!
13. Notice that in v. 24, it is the corpses of the transgressors that are eternally subject to worm and fire, not the transgressors themselves in an afterlife context. This will shift in later interpretations of the passage, as many others have noted. Blenkinsopp observes the fire "parallel" between vv. 15–16 and v. 24 (*Isaiah 56–66*, 311), as does Beuken, who speaks of the fire theme in v. 24 establishing "a good link with the beginning of the passage (vss 15–16)" ("Isaiah Chapters LXV–LXVI," 216). Beuken asserts that v. 24 itself suggests "the concept of Gehenna" (ibid.). If by this he means the idea of a hell-like afterlife in which transgressors suffer torments, the evidence does not support him. Jan Leunis Koole, in contrast, notes correctly that, in v. 24, it is the corpses themselves that are afflicted perpetually with fire and worms (*Isaiah*, 3 vols., HCOT [Kampen: Kok Pharos, 1997], 3:530). See, similarly, NJPS n. ad loc.
14. That dependent texts often address ambiguities or contradictions in the passages on which they build is noted by Leonard, who provides several examples from Ps 78 and pentateuchal texts to which it can be linked ("Identifying Inner-Biblical Allusions," 263–64).

pilgrims who come—presumably to Jerusalem—to worship Yhwh.[15] But of course this assumes that v. 23 precedes v. 24 as an accretion. (I'll have more to say about this ahead.)

The writer of v. 24 draws not only from vv. 15–16 and possibly v. 23 but likely from other passages in both chapter 66 and the larger book of Isaiah. As mentioned, v. 14 states that "you shall see [וראיתם] and your heart shall rejoice," although the text is not clear about what the favored Judean plurality "shall see." Verse 24 may be intended to address this ambiguity: "They shall go forth and they shall look upon" (וראו ב־) may refer to the same favored plurality of vv. 13-14—it is not clear to whom "they" refers in v. 24—and, furthermore, v. 24 states what it is that they look upon: the corpses of the dead transgressors. In v. 13, this plurality is said to be in Jerusalem, so it is likely that it is from Jerusalem that "they shall go forth" to view the corpses if they are indeed the witnesses.[16] If this reading is correct, the writer of v. 24 continues to clarify ambiguities present in earlier verses of the chapter. Just as v. 24 makes clear the identity of those who are slain by Yhwh in v. 16 as well as the fate of their remains, v. 24 also elucidates what it is that the favored Judeans of v. 14 "see." The mention of Yhwh's anger at his "enemies" in the last colon of v. 14 might also have contributed to the development of the punishment scenario in v. 24, as it is paired with a reference to Yhwh's saving acts for his servants in the third colon of v. 14, a theme elaborated in vv. 18–21, 22–23, though neither the vocabulary of reward nor that of punishment in the third and forth cola of v. 14 is reproduced or alluded to in vv. 18–21, 22–23, or 24.

An alternative interpretation of the identity of those who go forth and look upon the corpses in v. 24 is also possible. According to this reading, it is "all flesh" of v. 23 who come to worship Yhwh who are the witnesses in v. 24.[17] In favor of this interpretation, "all flesh" are mentioned as implied witnesses at the end of v. 24—the transgressors "shall be a horror to all flesh"—so it is certainly possible that "all flesh" are also the direct witnesses at the beginning of the verse: "all flesh" shall go forth and look upon the corpses, which shall be a horror to "all flesh." From where do they go forth? Presumably from Jerusalem, where v. 23 locates "all flesh" by implication.[18] "All flesh" "together" witness Yhwh's saving acts as well

---

15. Some speak of a division of "all flesh" in chapter 66 into transgressors and those faithful to Yhwh at the point that Yhwh judges "all flesh" and punishes the transgressors beginning in v. 16 (e.g., Kratz, "Komposition des Hebräischen Jesjabuches," 25).

16. I thank Marc Brettler for drawing my attention to the location of those who "shall go forth" (oral communication, 10 May 2016).

17. For this interpretation, see, e.g., John N. Oswalt, *The Book of Isaiah, Chapters 40–66*, NICOT (Grand Rapids: Eerdmans, 1998), 692; Blenkinsopp, *Isaiah 56–66*, 311; Dim, *Eschatological Implications*, 196. This understanding of the identity of the witnesses is not uncommon.

18. This location was suggested to me by Marc Brettler (oral communication, 10 May 2016).

as his glory according to 40:5. In 49:26, "all flesh" "will know" that Yhwh is Israel's deliverer and redeemer and Israel's oppressors will be severely punished, presumably in the sight of "all flesh," although the role of "all flesh" as witnesses to this punishment is at best only implied according to 49:26.[19] If "all flesh" are indeed the direct witnesses to the fate of the transgressors in Isa 66:24, the verse may be elaborating on the trope of "all flesh" as direct witnesses to Yhwh's decisive acts in Isa 40–55, with particular attention to their role of witnessing divine punishment.

Each of these interpretations has its potential weaknesses, however. "All flesh" in v. 23 governs a singular verb (יבוא), while two plural verbs occur in v. 24 (ויצאו וראו ב־). Although this change of verb is not decisive—we find something similar in 1 Kgs 18:39—it is nonetheless possible that the writer responsible for v. 24 had a subject other than "all flesh" in mind, and the change of verb to the plural *might* suggest this.[20] The favored Judeans of vv. 13–14 constitute a plurality whose actions are described by plural verbs and suffixes (e.g., "I shall comfort you," "You shall be comforted," "you shall see"), and what appears to be the same favored plurality of Judeans is promised an enduring lineage and name in v. 22 ("your seed," "your name"). In contrast to vv. 13–14 and 22, however, in which the favored Judean plurality is referred to using second person plural verb forms and suffixes, the verbs in v. 24 are in the third person plural, making for an awkward transition if the favored Judean plurality is indeed also the subject of the verbs in v. 24. Thus, neither understanding of the identity of the plurality of v. 24 who shall go forth and shall look upon the corpses is without at least some difficulty, and, at the same time, each interpretation has its appealing aspects. I consider each of these alternatives plausible.

The mention of the transgressors (הפשעים) in v. 24 may establish a connection with the beginning of the book of Isaiah, for in 1:28 the same word is used of those who have transgressed. Along with "sinners" (חטאים), "transgressors" (פשעים) will be shattered (*ישברו), while "those who have abandoned Yhwh" (עזבי יהוה) will come to an end.[21] In 66:24, the

---

19. The punishment of the enemies in Isa 49:26 is extreme: They will be made to eat their own flesh and become drunk on their own blood.

20. 1 Kgs 18:39 reads: ... וירא כל העם ויפלו על פניהם ויאמרו. Isa 66:23-24, for its part, reads: יבוא כל בשר ... ויצאו וראו בפגרי האנשים. Jouön cites 1 Kgs 18:39 in his discussion of collective subjects that govern both singular and plural verbs: "On peut mettre un premier verbe, surtout s'il précède le nom, au singulier, et le second verbe, qui suit le nom, au pluriel" (*Grammaire de l'hébreu biblique* [Rome: Institut biblique pontifical, 1923], §150e).

21. Reconstructing the *niphal* third person masculine plural prefixed verbal form ישברו (*yiššāberû*), "they will be shattered," on the basis of LXX συντριβήσονται, in place of the MT's impossible ושבר. The verb συντρίβειν is commonly used to translate Hebrew שבר (*qal, niphal, piel*). On this, see HRCS 2:1321–22. Scribal confusion of initial *waw* and *yod* likely contributed to the genesis of the MT's form ושבר. For further discussion of the text-critical issues of the verse, see Otto Kaiser, *Das Buch des Propheten Jesaja, Kapitel 1–12*, 5th ed., ATD 17 (Göttingen:

destruction of the transgressors is described in detail in a way that it is not in 1:28. The word פשעים is rare in the book of Isaiah, occurring, apart from 1:28 and 66:24, only in 46:8 and 53:12—and the focus of these other passages is not the punishment of the transgressors, as it is in 1:28 and 66:24.[22] Thus, like many other commentators, I think it likely that 66:24 alludes to 1:28 in its mention of the fate of transgressors (פשעים), establishing a link between the book's first and last chapters.[23] In addition, I argue that we learn from 66:24 the exact nature of the destruction of the transgressors of 1:28: death and the unending affliction of their corpses with fire and worms. Who are the transgressors of v. 24? Although their identity is not entirely clear, it seems likely that the author of the verse was thinking at least in part of Judeans, given that the transgressors of 1:28 stand—with the sinners—in parallel with those who are said to have abandoned Yhwh, and all of these persons are contrasted with the ransomed of Zion mentioned in 1:27. This suggests that Judeans—good and bad—are the concern of the author of 1:27–28 rather than non-Judeans. In contrast, the writer responsible for 66:24 likely also included non-Judeans as well among the transgressors, given that v. 24 builds on v. 16, and in v. 16 "all flesh" are the target of Yhwh's wrath, with many dying as a result. Thus, I think it likely that the transgressors of v. 24 are a mix of Judeans and others.[24]

Vandenhoeck & Ruprecht, 1981), 53 n. 11; and Hans Wildberger, *Jesaja*, 3 vols., BKAT 10 (Neukirchen-Vluyn: Neukirchener Verlag, 1980), 1:56.

22. Liebreich argues unconvincingly for a link between ובפשעיכם (50:1) and הפשעים in 66:24.

23. A not uncommon viewpoint, as Blenkinsopp notes. He suggests that the parallel with 1:28, along with another in 1:31 (less convincing in my view), reveals "the intention of presenting the book as a unified composition" (*Isaiah 56–66*, 316). See similarly Childs, *Isaiah*, 546; Sommer, *Prophet Reads Scripture*, 258; and Beuken, "Isaiah Chapters LXV–LXVI," 220-21, among others. This idea goes back at least to Liebreich, who argued that a relationship may be discerned between chapter 1 and chapter 66 as exemplified, for example, by 1:10 and 66:5, 1:28 and 66:24, and 1:31 and 66:24. In his words, "the position of chap. 66 at the end of the Book presupposes the unmistakable intention and fixed determination to make the Book end in the same vein with which it begins" ("Compilation of the Book of Isaiah," 276–77; quotation from 276). As mentioned above, I am not wholly convinced of a relationship between 1:31 (ואין מכבה) and 66:24 (לא תכבה), as these are not at all the same expressions and their subjects differ. Other scholars have proposed additional parallels between chapters 1 and 66 (e.g., Konrad Schmid, *Schriftgelehrte Traditionsliteratur: Fallstudien zur innerbiblischen Schriftauslegung im Alten Testament*, FAT 77 [Tübingen: Mohr Siebeck, 2011], 201, on 1:2 and 66:24, among other examples).

24. Koole also thinks that the transgressors are a combination of Judeans and non-Judeans (*Isaiah*, 3:529). Contrast Beuken, who believes that the transgressors are Judeans specifically ("Isaiah Chapters LXV–LXVI," 217). Debate about the identity of the transgressors goes back to antiquity, as John W. Olley shows ("'No Peace' in a Book of Consolation: A Framework for the Book of Isaiah?" *VT* 49 [1999]: 351–370, here 352).

Finally, there is the undying worm of v. 24. This image may represent an elaboration of the underworld and grave description in Isa 14:11, which mentions the worm (תולעה) as the dead king of Babylon's "covering," along with the maggot (רמה) as his bed. But in Isa 66:24 the worm consuming the corpses of the transgressors will never die, just as their fire will never be extinguished.[25] The origin of the idea that the corpses are afflicted unendingly is not entirely clear, although it is possible that 66:22–23, the two verses immediately preceding v. 24, have contributed to the shaping of this notion, given that these verses describe enduring states and practices, although with a positive focus: the new heaven and new earth that Yhwh creates will stand before him; the progeny and name of the favored Judean plurality will likewise endure; the pilgrimage of "all flesh" to worship Yhwh will continue from new moon to new moon and from Sabbath to Sabbath. In contrast, the author of v. 24 offers a vision of enduring punishment for transgressors with their corpses unburied and afflicted by undying worms and inextinguishable fire.[26] If I am correct that vv. 22–23 are the source of the idea that the corpses of the transgressors are afflicted perpetually and also that v. 23 contributed to the reshaping of the role of "all flesh" in v. 24 (as mentioned earlier), then v. 24 must postdate the addition of vv. 22–23.[27]

---

25. It is worth noting that תולעת underlies תולעתם, an alternative to תולעה of Isa 14:11. This could be construed to suggest that 66:24 does not depend on 14:11.

26. Oswalt sees a parallel between perpetual worship in v. 23 and enduring punishment in v. 24, although he does not note the similar parallel between v. 24 and v. 22, nor does he argue that v. 23 is the source of the idea for the author of v. 24 (*Book of Isaiah, Chapters 40–66*, 692–93 n. 88). See, similarly, Claus Westermann, *Das Buch Jesaja: Kapitel 40–66*, ATD 19 (Göttingen: Vandenhoeck & Ruprecht, 1966), 339, on the parallel between the eternal service of God in v. 23 and the everlasting judgment in v. 24. Blenkinsopp notes that "the permanence of posterity and name in 22–23 is matched by permanent punishment in v. 24," but he does not suggest that vv. 22–23 are the source for v. 24's idea of enduring punishment (*Isaiah 56–66*, 315).

27. 1QIsaᵃ seems to regard vv. 22–24 as a unit, suggesting perhaps that at least some ancient interpreters thought these verses came from the same hand. Some modern interpreters have also understood vv. 22–24 to constitute a unit of sorts (e.g., Höffken, *Das Buch Jesaja*, 253; Dim, *Eschatological Implications*, 191–98). Both v. 23 and v. 24 use the idiom "all flesh" and "all flesh" may also be the direct witnesses of the punishment of the transgressors in v. 24, as I have argued, allowing for a smooth transition between v. 23 and v. 24. Yet, although I believe that v. 24 is dependent on vv. 22–23 for its positive casting of "all flesh" and for the enduring nature of its punishments, I am not convinced that v. 24 was composed by the author of vv. 22–23. The unending punishments of v. 24 are described using a very different set of idioms from that used to speak of the enduring states and practices of vv. 22–23. Contrast "shall not die/be extinguished," both negated prefixed verb forms, with "shall stand (before me)" (expressed once with a non-negated prefixed verbal form and once with a plural participle) and "from new moon to new moon and from Sabbath to Sabbath," both nonverbal expressions of an enduring state. Furthermore, if the witnesses to the punishment of the transgressors in v. 24 are not "all flesh" but rather the favored Judean plurality,

I have argued that Isa 66:24 appears to depend on 66:15–16, 22–23; 1:28; and possibly also 66:14 and 14:11. It functions (1) to bring the reader's attention back to the punishment of transgressors, the focus of vv. 15–16 + 17 but not a theme of vv. 18–21 or 22–23, which bring the positive into relief; (2) to address a variety of ambiguities in earlier verses in the chapter (vv. 15–16; possibly v. 14) and the book (1:28); (3) to cast the punishment of the transgressors as perpetual, not unlike the positive enduring states and practices of vv. 22–23; and (4) to forge connections with earlier passages in the chapter (vv. 15–16, 22–23; possibly also v. 14) and elsewhere in the book of Isaiah (1:28; possibly also 14:11). Thus, the supplementary activity that can be identified in v. 24 is diverse in its functions; these range from changing the final focus of chapter and book to clarifying ambiguities in earlier verses to generating symmetry in vv. 15–23 with regard to punishment and reward to creating obvious links to material that precedes. Supplementation in v. 24 is accomplished most frequently by means of the exact reproduction or slight modification of distinct words or idioms found in earlier passages in a new context (e.g., אש, כל בשר, הפשעים; possibly ־ב ראו), thereby generating new meanings. Such supplementary activity is not unlike that found in previous verses of chapter 66, earlier in the book of Isaiah, and elsewhere in the Hebrew Bible, although what appear to be the particular priorities of the author of v. 24—to address the ambiguities of earlier material and to establish literary connections with earlier parts of the chapter and book—are certainly worthy of note, and the latter is much discussed with respect to the formation of the book of Isaiah as a whole.

Although most commentators see v. 24 as the final accretion to the chapter and the book, it is possible that the verse preceded the addition of vv. 18–21, given that v. 24 does not seem to engage their content in any obvious way.[28] According to this reconstruction, those who added vv. 18–21 may have inserted them between vv. 22–23, 24 and vv. 15–16 or 15–16 + 17 in order to bring a more positive focus to the end of the

---

a possibility I have raised, there would be no smooth transition between v. 23 and v. 24. And the mention of the favored Judean plurality of v. 22 in the second person ("your seed and your name") would be in tension with the mention of that plurality in the third person in v. 24 ("they shall go forth and they shall look upon …").

28. Unless one were to argue that the nations and tongues who come and see Yhwh's glory (ובאו וראו את כבודי) in v. 18 and report on it in v. 19 to others who have not seen it are the same persons who will come forth and look upon the corpses in v. 24. Nations and tongues seeing Yhwh's glory in 66:18 sounds a lot like "all flesh" doing the same in 40:5, and vv. 18 and 19 may well have been intended to allude to 40:5, establishing a link between the passages (Beuken, "Isaiah Chapters LXV—LXVI," 209, 210; Dim, *Eschatological Implications*, 273). The evidence suggesting a relationship between 66:24 and 66:18, 19 is less convincing, given that the only potential link is וראו in each verse (cf. "they shall look upon the corpses" and "they shall see my glory"). The "nations and tongues" of v. 18 make no appearance in v. 24, which utilizes the idiom "all flesh," not unlike vv. 16 and 23.

chapter and the book, more positive than vv. 22–23 alone could provide, although the chapter and book would nonetheless end with an emphasis on punishment rather than reward. It is certainly possible that vv. 18–21 were added by a different hand than vv. 22–23, given their differing styles (prose vs. poetry); in terms of content, it seems as if vv. 18–21 may well be intended to elaborate on vv. 22–23 and to clarify ambiguities in those verses, explaining, for example, that it is to Jerusalem that all nations will come to worship Yhwh and it is Yhwh himself who will bring them there.[29] Furthermore, both vv. 18–21 and 22–23 share a positive vision of the future for favored Judeans.

Whether v. 24 was the last accretion or preceded the addition of vv. 18–21, in its final form the supplementary section of chapter 66 is fairly balanced between reward for the righteous and punishment for transgressors, changing focus now and again: compare vv. 15–16 + 17 and 24, where the punitive is brought into relief, to vv. 18–21, 22–23, where reward for the favored is emphasized. This appears to be the result of multiple accretions over a period of time preceding the second century BCE (the composition of Dan 12:2; the translation of Ben Sira into Greek), reflecting perhaps a struggle to determine on what note the chapter and book will end.

---

29. The LXX also makes explicit that Jerusalem is the locus of worship in v. 23, as noted by Kratz ("Too Many Hands? Isaiah 65–66 and the Reading of the Book of Isaiah," unpublished manuscript, 4). This is not unlike what I am proposing for v. 20.

V

Legal Texts

Making a Case: The Repurposing of "Israelite Legal Fictions" as Post-Deuteronomic Law

SARA J. MILSTEIN
University of British Columbia

Amid the miscellany of cultic rules and ethical precepts in Deut 21–25 are a handful of casuistic laws that appear to have once operated as a set: Deuteronomy 21:15–17, the case of the man with two wives, one loved, the other hated; 21:18–21, the case of the rebellious son; 22:13–21, the case(s) of the slandered bride; 22:22, the case of the adulterers caught in flagrante delicto; 22:23–29, the triad of assault cases; 24:1–4, the case of the two-time divorcée; and 25:5–10, the case of the widow and the reluctant *levir* (brother-in-law). Parallels among these texts have prompted some to suggest that they once belonged to an independent, pre-Deuteronomic collection of "family law" or "women's law," perhaps something akin to Middle Assyrian Laws Tablet A.[1] I would like to offer an alternative explanation

---

I am grateful to Saul Olyan and Jacob Wright for including me in such a stimulating and organized symposium. My revision of the paper benefitted greatly from the questions and challenges that were proffered by the participants in that setting. Many thanks are due to Bruce Wells, Reinhard Kratz, and Daniel Fleming for their insightful comments and suggestions regarding this paper. I finally wish to acknowledge my research assistants at the University of British Columbia, Jova Chan and Carolina Franzen, for their dedicated and enthusiastic assistance.

1. Alexander Rofé suggests that Tablet A serves as an apt analogy to this "reconstructed [biblical] tractate," a collection that includes the texts cited above along with Exod 22:15–16, the seduction of the unengaged virgin; and Exod 21:22–25, the injury of a pregnant woman during a fight (*Deuteronomy: Issues and Interpretation*, OTS [London: T&T Clark, 2002], 172). The parallel between the overarching Deuteronomic program and Tablet A of the Middle Assyrian Laws has been most strongly drawn by Eckart Otto, who sees both as evidence of legal reforms: "Wie die MAG.A hat auch die protodtn Familienrechtsammlung Züge eines Reformprogramms, das im Familienrecht das Privatstrafrecht zugunsten des öffentlichen Strafrechts einschränkt und die Rechte der Frau stärkt." For Otto, the "Familienrechtsammlung" includes Deut 21:15–21aα; 22:13–21a, 22a, 23, 24a, 25, 27, 28–29; 24:1–4a; and 25:5–10 (*Das Deuteronomium: Politische Theologie und Rechtsreform in Juda und Assyrien*, BZAW

161

for the origins of this legal cluster, one with a potentially closer cuneiform model with respect to style and function. I suggest that a portion of these texts originated as a set of legal exercises that were copied in pedagogical contexts, or what I call "Israelite legal fictions" (henceforth, ILFs; see appendix).[2] This argument proceeds from a set of similarities between the ILFs and a handful of Sumerian legal exercises that were utilized in scribal education and may have some relation to the Old Babylonian (OB) law collections. I then propose that the ILFs underwent development beyond the pedagogical sphere, in that they were reimagined as "law" and put to new use in an extant form of Deuteronomy.[3] The incorporation of the ILFs into this work was facilitated by three interrelated forms of supplementation: (a) an "introduction" in Deut 17:2–7 that was designed to anticipate the ILFs; (b) a set of related additions to the ILFs, including the invention of several secondary scenarios (22:20–21, 22:22, 22:23–24, and 22:28–29); and (c) the composition of a completely new ILF—the "case of the rebellious son" (21:18–21)—a text that draws equally on the content of the ILFs and the terminology of 17:2–7. Together, these varied forms of supplementation demonstrate scribal efforts to put the standard conventions of Near Eastern law collections to entirely different ends.

I. The Origins of the Cuneiform Law Collections

Before addressing the repurposing of the ILFs as "law," it is first necessary to provide some background on the nature of the Near Eastern law collections. It has long been observed that the initial characterization of these collections as "codes" was misleading.[4] None of the hundreds

---

284 [Berlin: de Gruyter, 1999], 217), that is, roughly the list above. Along with the usual set, Carolyn Pressler includes the law pertaining to the captive bride in Deut 21:10–14 (*The View of Women Found in the Deuteronomic Family Laws*, BZAW 216 [Berlin: de Gruyter, 1993], 4, 9–10).

2. A "legal fiction" is "an assumption that something occurred or that someone or something exists which is not the case, but that is made in the law to enable a court to equitably resolve a matter before it" (*West's Encyclopedia of American Law*, 2nd ed., s.v. "legal fiction," http://legal-dictionary.thefreedictionary.com/legal+fiction). My use of the term reflects a play on the idiom but without the attendant connotations. I use it in this context to convey both the legal nature of these texts and their fictitious origins.

3. This particular conclusion is in agreement with Eckart Otto, who locates the pre-Deuteronomistic Deut 12–26 in "scholarly-judicial traditions of scribal education" ("Aspects of Legal Reforms and Reformulations in Ancient Cuneiform and Israelite Law," in *Theory and Method in Biblical and Cuneiform Law: Revision, Interpolation, and Development*, ed. Bernard M. Levinson, JSOTSup 181 [Sheffield: Sheffield Academic, 1994; repr. Sheffield Phoenix, 2006], 160).

4. This mislabeling originated with the imposing monument of the Laws of Hammurabi that was discovered at Susa (modern-day Shush, Iran) and is now housed at the Louvre

of contemporaneous Old Babylonian trial records makes reference to the Laws of Hammurabi (LH), thus casting doubt on its nature as a normative document. Jean Bottéro further observed that the so-called "Code of Hammurabi" was hardly comprehensive, in that major swaths of law were altogether neglected.[5] Eventually a general consensus emerged that the "laws" in LH (and other collections, for that matter) were not prescriptive but instead descriptive. That is, they largely originated in actual events that were stripped of their particulars and generalized into law; these were then supplemented by hypothetical variations of the event(s) at hand.[6] While this idea is persuasive, the specifics of this process have yet to be fully determined. Bottéro provides only one concrete example:

Museum in Paris. Vincent Scheil was the first to publish an edition of the "Code" and dubbed it as such, undoubtedly linking it to the Napoleonic Code (*La loi de Hammourabi [vers 2000 av. J.-C.]* [Paris: Ernest Leroux, 1904]). For critique, see esp. Fritz R. Kraus, "Ein zentrales Problem des altmesopotamischen Rechtes: Was ist der Codex Hammu-rabi?" *Genava* NS 8 (1960): 283–96. As Kraus points out, the epilogue of the Laws of Hammurabi itself refers to the preceding content as "just decisions" (*dīnāt mīšārim*). He suggests that the recognition of the collection "als Werk der altbabylonischen wissenschaftlichen Literatur" puts it in a new light (289). This latter line of thought is developed further by Jean Bottéro, "The 'Code' of Hammurabi," in *Mesopotamia: Writing, Reasoning, and the Gods*, trans. Zainab Bahrani and Marc Van De Mieroop (Chicago: University of Chicago Press, 1992), 156–84, esp. 169–77.

5. Ibid., 161. A case in point is the first precept of LH: while it stipulates a penalty for someone who accuses a person of murder without proof, the laws make no mention of the protocol regarding accusation of homicide *with* proof, let alone of the penalty for homicide itself.

6. For a helpful overview of the nature of the law collections, see Raymond Westbrook, "Biblical and Cuneiform Codes," in *Law from the Tigris to the Tiber: The Writings of Raymond Westbrook*, ed. Bruce Wells and F. Rachel Magdalene, 2 vols. (Winona Lake, IN: Eisenbrauns, 2009), 1:3–20. For Westbrook, these collections were not merely scientific treatises, as Kraus and Bottéro would have it, but rather reference works that were consulted by judges for difficult cases (10). Sophie Démare-Lafont takes the epilogue of LH to mean that a person who was living abroad and felt "wronged" by his local judicial system would have had the right to demand the application of LH and appeal his case before a Babylonian court ("Law Collections and Legal Documents," in *Handbook of Ancient Mesopotamia*, ed. Gonzalo Rubio [Berlin: de Gruyter, forthcoming]). She suggests further that this might have applied especially to soldiers and merchants who were living far from Babylon but nonetheless would have had the right to live by their native laws. For a nuanced treatment of the terms *law* and *law codes* informed by the field of law, see also Démare-Lafont, "Ancient Near Eastern Laws: Continuity and Pluralism," in Levinson, *Theory and Method in Biblical and Cuneiform Law*, 91–118. For a different view, however, see Hans Neumann, who suggests that courts would not necessarily have referred to known law: "Nicht selten ist in der Literatur die Rechtsnatur des Codex Hammurapi bestritten worden, zumal es im überlieferten Urkundenmaterial keinen eindeutigen Hinweis darauf gibt, dass man sich—entsprechend der Aufforderung im Epilog der Gesetzessammlung—beim Abschluss von Rechtsgeschäften oder bei der Durchführung von Prozessen ausdrücklich auf die Rechtsbestimmungen des Hammurapi berief. Jedoch ist bei der Anwendung bekannter und gewohnheitsrechtlich entstandener Regelungen die Berufung auf gesetzliche Bestimmungen nicht unbedingt notwendig gewesen. Zudem zeigt eine Reihe von Texten, dass im täglichen Rechtsverkehr durchaus im Sinne der Vorschriften des Codex Hammurapi verfahren wurde" ("Recht im antiken Mesopotamien," in *Die Rechts-*

an Old Babylonian letter written to two officials by Hammurabi that bears striking resemblance to LH 32.[7] While it is possible, if not likely, that other letters served as direct sources for LH, this avenue has yet to be explored fully, in part because Hammurabi's palace has not been excavated. Another potential set of sources for LH is that of the trial records produced during the Old Babylonian period. The available records typically include a brief reference to the dispute at hand, the plaintiff's claim in direct speech, brief mention of evidence/testimony or lack thereof, the judges' verdict, the names and seals of witnesses to the trial, and the date. Once again, however, no Old Babylonian trial records have been linked with actual laws, and the lack of access to Hammurabi's palace archives does not help in this regard.[8]

Intriguingly, however, there are a handful of Sumerian texts that *do* appear to have links to precepts in the Old Babylonian collections. Like the Old Babylonian trial records, these texts cover disputes between two named parties, including a case of homicide, two cases of adultery, the rape of a slave-girl, a dispute over office, and an inheritance dispute. Unlike the trial records, however, they feature no witnesses, seals, or dates. These texts are largely available only in single copies, though one text, the "Nippur Homicide Trial," exists in multiple copies, including one *Sammeltafel* (a compilation tablet) that featured three such "trials" in sequence.[9] Most of these texts refer either to the "assembly of Nippur" or simply to the "assembly," and at least two close with the statement that "the case was

---

kulturen der Antike: Vom Alten Orient bis zum Römischen Reich, ed. Ulrich Manthe [Munich: Beck, 2003], 55–122, here 88).

7. Bottéro, *Mesopotamia*, 167.

8. One possibility is that certain Ur III Sumerian "verdicts" served as fodder for the laws. These verdicts (known as "ditilla texts") were collected and found together, already indicating a level of redaction. Bertrand Lafont points to the parallels between #5 and LH 148; #6 and LH 131; #7 and Laws of Ur-Namma 9; and #24 and LH 238 ("Les textes judiciaires sumériens," in *Rendre la justice en Mésopotamie: Archives judiciaires du Proche-Orient ancien, IIIe–Ier millénaires avant J.-C]*, ed. Francis Joannès [Saint-Denis: Presses Universitaires de Vincennes, 2000], 34–67). Lafont does not suggest that such texts served as sources for the laws, but rather he notes that certain situations are evoked in the records several centuries before they appear in parallel form in the law collections. See also Démare-Lafont, who discusses how a letter that was sent by Samsu-iluna to the judges of Sippar documents the production of a law from a particular situation. The letter details two problems involving the *nadītu* priestesses; Samsu-iluna then provides an answer that essentially changes Hammurabian law and carries normative weight ("Ancient Near Eastern Laws," 97–100).

9. The classic edition of the Nippur Homicide Trial is that of Thorkild Jacobsen, "An Ancient Mesopotamian Trial for Homicide," in *Toward the Image of Tammuz and Other Essays on Mesopotamian History and Culture*, ed. William Moran, HSS 21 (Cambridge: Harvard University Press, 2014), 193–214; more recently, see the translation and discussion by Martha T. Roth, "Gender and Law: A Case Study from Ancient Mesopotamia," in *Gender and Law in the Hebrew Bible and the Ancient Near East*, ed. Bernard M. Levinson, Tikva Frymer-Kensky, and Victor H. Matthews, JSOTSup 262 (Sheffield: Sheffield Academic, 1998), 173–84.

accepted for trial at the assembly of Nippur," which suggests a general association of these texts with Nippur, the southern Babylonian city that accounts for over 80 percent of all known Sumerian literary texts and that appears to have been a center for scribal education.[10]

Two of these Sumerian texts are especially "literary" in nature. The sixty or so lines of the Nippur Homicide Trial are mainly composed of a debate within the assembly about whether the wife of the victim was in cahoots with the manslayers and should be executed alongside them. The other is a brief adultery case (henceforth, Adultery A) that involves the cuckolded husband tying his wife and her lover to the bed of deceit and carrying the bed to the "assembly of Nippur" as evidence in the trial.[11] Like a narrative, this text features three crimes in succession ("In the first place, she did X; in the second place, she did Y; in the third place, she did Z"), with the final offense—adultery—serving as the dramatic climax. It is worth adding that the two share the unusual detail of "covering X with a cloth," a parallel that seems to suggest a literary relationship.[12] A second adultery case from Ur (henceforth, Adultery B) bears a striking resemblance to Adultery A.[13] William Hallo suggested that these texts, along

---

10. For an excellent analysis of the excavations at House F at Nippur, see Eleanor Robson, "The Tablet House: A Scribal School in Old Babylonian Nippur," *RA* 95 (2001): 39–66. Robson remarks that the large number of literary tablets that were discovered at Nippur and at House F in particular has contributed enormously to the general picture of Sumerian literature but also has possibly skewed our understanding of what is normative for this corpus (52). On evidence for Nippur's role as a "place of decisions," both human and divine, see Stephen Lieberman, "Nippur: City of Decisions," in *Nippur at the Centennial: Papers Read at the 35e Rencontre Assyriologique Internationale, Philadelphia, 1988*, ed. Maria deJong Ellis, Occasional Publications of the Samuel Noah Kramer Fund 14 (Philadelphia: S. N. Kramer Fund, Babylonian Section, University Museum, 1992), 127–36.

11. When the text was first published, Jan van Dijk purported that it involved a husband who was caught in a homosexual act by his wife ("Textes divers du Musée de Bagdad III," *Sumer* 15 [1959]: 5–14). Samuel Greengus later demonstrated that this reading was in error and that the text instead involved a man catching his wife in the act with her lover ("A Textbook Case of Adultery," *HUCA* 40 [1969]: 33–44; esp. 33–35). While Greengus acknowledges the literary quality of the "evidence" (and notes its parallels to the tale of Aphrodite and Ares told in the Odyssey), he suggests that this detail "may very well be only a literary embellishment of an actual case, a dramatic infusion of storytelling into a legal report. We need not, however, doubt the essential historicity of the trial and the penalties" (44 n. 34). This stance is reflective of a consensus at that time that the model cases were more or less rooted in actual trials.

12. In the Nippur Homicide Trial, the narrator reports that the woman "did not open her mouth; she covered it with a cloth" (line 14). Likewise, in Adultery A, the guilty woman makes an opening in an oil jar and "covered it up with a cloth" (lines 9–10). While in Adultery A, the act of concealment is literal and nonredundant, in the Nippur Homicide Trial, the act is redundant and must be taken as idiomatic, as Roth suggests ("Gender and Law," 176). Though either direction of dependence is possible, I am inclined to say that the literal usage of the phrase represents the earlier of the two.

13. For the second adultery text, see Raymond Westbrook, *Old Babylonian Marriage Law*,

with several others, were best characterized as "a literary collection of legal decisions by the kings of Isin" or, as Martha Roth later dubbed them, "model court cases."[14] Most agree that these texts were rooted in actual records and would have been copied by scribes as an aid in the composition of trial records.[15] In this context, Hallo drew comparisons with the pedagogical practice of copying model contracts.[16] A closer comparison may be the genre of literary letters, a set of Sumerian texts that were likewise copied at an advanced stage in Old Babylonian scribal education and includes both literary features and actual historical figures.[17] While it is possible that one or more of these "model cases" is rooted in an actual record, the literary nature of both the Nippur Homicide Trial and Adultery A suggests that at least these two—if not the others—were composed from scratch for educational use.[18] Indeed, Alexandra Kleinerman reaches

---

AfO 23 (Horn, Austria: Berger, 1988), 133. Both adultery texts involve the husband catching his wife in the act with her lover and approaching the authorities (in Adultery B, the king; in Adultery A, the assembly). Both texts then state that the king/assembly, because the two lovers were caught in a tryst, issued the verdict that follows.

14. William H. Hallo, "The Slandered Bride," in *Studies Presented to A. Leo Oppenheim, June 7, 1964* (Chicago: Oriental Institute of the University of Chicago, 1964), 95–105; Hallo subsequently adopted Roth's designation, noting that the texts can be thought of along the lines of model contracts ("A Model Court Case Concerning Inheritance," in *Riches Hidden in Secret Places: Ancient Near Eastern Studies in Memory of Thorkild Jacobsen*, ed. Tzvi Abusch [Winona Lake, IN: Eisenbrauns, 2002], 142–43).

15. See, e.g., Martha T. Roth, "The Slave and the Scoundrel: CBS 10467, A Sumerian Morality Tale," *JAOS* 103 (1983): 275–82, here 282.

16. On the genre of model contracts, see Walter Bodine, *How Mesopotamian Scribes Learned to Write Legal Documents: A Study of the Sumerian Model Contracts in the Babylonian Collection at Yale University* (Lewiston, NY: Mellen, 2014); and Gabriella Spada, "Two Old Babylonian Model Contracts," *Cuneiform Digital Library Journal* 2 (2014): 1–13. Model contracts cover sample business transactions and were copied alongside proverbs at the last stage in the elementary phase of the curriculum. In addition to teaching students Sumerian grammar, they were likely used to help scribes write functional contracts, as Bodine notes (178). Spada observes that the model contracts are marked by an absence of witnesses and a date, though some indicate this omission in generic terms at the end (2). They were also found in compilation tablets, as is the case for the aforementioned *Sammeltafel* of "model cases."

17. On the creative and entertaining aspects of the Sumerian literary letters, see Alexandra Kleinerman, *Education in Early 2nd Millennium BC Babylonia: The Sumerian Epistolary Miscellany*, CM 42 (Leiden: Brill, 2011) 103–6. Kleinerman's study focuses on what she calls "the Sumerian Epistolary Miscellany," one of three sets of literary letters that were studied at Old Babylonian scribal schools in Nippur. She remarks on the "Nippur centrism" of the collection, which is illustrated by the inclusion of well-known historical figures from Nippur (53). For a broader overview of the epistolary genre, see also Fabienne Huber Vulliet, "Letters as Correspondence, Letters as Literature," in *The Oxford Handbook of Cuneiform Culture*, ed. Karen Radner and Eleanor Robson (Oxford: Oxford University Press, 2011), 486–507.

18. Bodine notes that the presence of "unusual features" in a contract signals the possibility that it derived from a pedagogical context, though he registers some reservations in this regard (*How Mesopotamian Scribes Learned to Write Legal Documents*, 164). On this point, see also Jacob Klein and Tonia M. Sharlach, who point to "fanciful or dramatic details"

a similar conclusion regarding a set of literary letters that was copied at Nippur, despite its inclusion of real personages from Nippur.[19] I thus suggest that these texts represent didactic, entertaining exercises that were inspired by the genre of trial records and possibly learned by selected scribes at an advanced stage in the curriculum. In order to highlight the fictional quality of these texts, I instead propose that they be called "Sumerian Legal Fictions" (SLFs).

What is perhaps most useful for our purposes is that almost all of the SLFs have parallels with "laws" in the Mesopotamian collections. As noted by Thorkild Jacobsen, the Nippur Homicide Trial seems to correspond to LH 153, a law that stipulates that if a woman has her husband killed on account of another man—precisely the hypothetical scenario posited by the "majority" of the assembly—she should be put to death.[20] Adultery A, as noted by Samuel Greengus, shares features with LH 141–143, in that both feature wives committing the three crimes of appropriating goods, squandering household possessions, and being wayward.[21] Adultery B bears strong resemblance to LH 129.[22] The rape of a slave girl, finally, corresponds to the Laws of Eshnunna 31, as suggested by J. J. Finkelstein.[23]

The question is how to explain these parallels. A simple comparison based on dates of copies is potentially misleading, for the SLFs could have earlier origins, whether oral or written.[24] Three possible explana-

---

that mark some model contracts ("A Collection of Model Court Cases from Old Babylonian Nippur [CBS 11324]," ZA 97 [2007]: 1–25, here 2, 4). In this light, it is worth adding that execution—the verdict in the Nippur Homicide Trial—is rare in actual trial records. In the Neo-Assyrian material published by Remko Jas, execution appears only once, and only if the murderer does not hand over a woman as substitute for blood money (no. 42 in Neo Assyrian Judicial Procedures, SAAS 5 [Helsinki: Neo-Assyrian Text Corpus Project, 1996]). Similarly, only one of the trials in Dominique Charpin's chapter on Old Babylonian trial records features execution, and even then it is only referenced by the plaintiff, not stated by the judge as a "verdict" (no. 48 in "Lettres et procès paleo-babyloniens," in Joannès, Rendre la justice en Mésopotamie, 69–111). The general paucity of execution verdicts in the records makes sense; it seems that if a judge prescribed execution, there would have been no need to document such a punishment in writing.

19. Kleinerman, Education in Early 2nd Millennium BC Babylonia, 55.

20. At the conclusion of the "debate," the majority states (as per Jacobsen's translation), "A woman who does not respect her husband may have given information to his enemy; he could have killed her husband. That her husband was killed, he (the enemy) may (then) let her hear." The woman is in turn executed along with the three murderers. It is noteworthy that the assembly already "generalizes" the trial into a scenario with wider applicability.

21. Greengus, "Textbook Case," 37–38.

22. In this text, the husband is said to have caught his wife "in the lap" of her lover; the king then puts both the woman and her lover to the stake (Westbrook, Old Babylonian Marriage Law, 133).

23. J. J. Finkelstein, "Sex Offenses in Sumerian Laws," JAOS 86 (1966): 355–72, here 360.

24. While the older consensus was that the Sumerian "cases" were used as fodder for laws, this cannot be assumed based on dates of tablets, for most of the actual copies are either contemporaneous with the law collections or later than them, save for one copy of the

tions emerge. The first is that the links are merely coincidental and simply reflect the fact that similar types of situations were imagined and written down in different literary contexts. Given that both the SLFs and the law collections were copied in pedagogical contexts, however, and given the fact that certain parallels are quite close, it seems that we are dealing with some sort of relationship. A second possibility is that the SLFs reflect advanced-level "scribal play" with known law: master scribes took up extant laws and created fictional cases from them that in turn could be copied by advanced scribes. This option would best suit the dates of the actual copies that are available in comparison with the dates of the Laws of Eshnunna and the Laws of Hammurabi. Third, the SLFs (in some form, whether oral or written) could have served as sources for precepts in the law collections.[25] This option is supported by the notion that the phenomenon of building collections by recasting specific events in generalized terms, along with the production of secondary scenarios, appears to account for the production of other Mesopotamian genres, such as medical and omen literature. Without further evidence, I am inclined to leave both the second and third options on the table. What is most important to emphasize at this stage is that the SLFs and the laws appear to exhibit some links and may derive from the same context. In a different but related way, the same appears to apply to the biblical laws in question.

II. Implications for the Development of Deuteronomy

Awareness of the SLFs—both as an extant genre and as material tied to the law collections—arguably has heuristic value for the study of Deu-

---

Nippur Homicide Trial that was dated by Jacobsen to the early years of Rim-Sin of Larsa, or approximately 1800s BCE ("Ancient Mesopotamian Trial for Homicide," 196). The other four duplicates are later copies, dating to the time of Samsu-iluna and later. Adultery B is undated. Adultery A dates to the early Old Babylonian period. Regarding the rape of the slave girl, Finkelstein states that the name of the deputy indicates that it cannot be earlier than Isin-Larsa period. On internal grounds, Hallo dated the entire group of model cases to the early Isin period (twentieth century BCE) ("Model Court Case Concerning Inheritance," 141–54). Regarding Hallo's inheritance case, a seal inscription referencing one of the parties dates to 1867 BCE, though this need not mean that the text *itself* dates to the same period. In fact, most of the postulated dates for these texts are based perhaps tenuously on names, not archaeological find-spots, and so the possibility remains that we are dealing with a corpus that is largely contemporaneous with LH rather than prior to it.

25. On this direction of dependence, Greengus states, "The literary legal decisions appear to be records of such real cases from which general principles of adjudication could have been extracted" ("Textbook Case," 43). More recently, however, he expresses doubt regarding our ability to determine which of the two genres might have preceded the other (personal communication).

teronomy.[26] First, it is noteworthy that the biblical laws under discussion amount to roughly the same number as the SLFs and cover a similar range of conflicts (adultery, rape, and inheritance disputes). They are thus much closer in quantity to the SLFs than to Tablet A of the Middle Assyrian Laws, with its fifty-six precepts, or to the sixty plus precepts pertaining to marriage and family law in Laws of Hammurabi. Second, the biblical texts share a number of features that appear to be pre-Deuteronomic.[27] For one, they all launch with כי איש/לאיש/אנשים/אחים X ("If a man/men/brothers . . .").[28] Second, not only do they involve women, but they pertain largely to issues of marriage and its dissolution. All of them feature triangular situations: disputes concerning one man and two women (Deut 21:15–17) or two men (alleged or not) and one woman (22:13–21; 22:23–29; 24:1–4; 25:5–10). Three refer to a "hated" woman (21:15–17; 22:13–21; 24:1–4), a term apparently associated with unjustified legal action.[29] Two feature

---

26. In his short but insightful discussion of Deut 22:13–21, Clemens Locher mentions the SLF regarding the rape of the slave girl, noting that both texts include direct speech and a threefold repetition of the case. He suggests that a text of this type was the source of the Deuteronomic text. On this basis, he challenges the widespread notion that the *Motivsatz* in Deut 22:19 is secondary, given the inclusion of a motive clause in the Sumerian text ("Deuteronomium 22, 13–21: Vom Prozessprotokoll zum kasuistischen Gesetz," in *Das Deuteronomium: Entstehung, Gestalt und Botschaft*, ed. Norbert Lohfink, BETL 68 [Leuven: Leuven University Press, 1985], 298–303, here 303). In this particular case, however, the "motive clause" in Deut 22:19 turns the family dispute into a crime concerning Israel; on these grounds, I deem it secondary. For further discussion on the relationship between Deut 22:13–21 and the aforementioned SLF, see also Locher, *Die Ehre einer Frau in Israel: Exegetische und rechtsvergleichende Studien zu Deuteronomium 22,13–21*, OBO 70 (Freiburg, Schweiz: Universitätsverlag; Göttingen: Vandenhoeck & Ruprecht, 1986), 93–101. Locher suggests that the slave text represents a type of trial record ("Prozessprotokoll") that formally would have been the same as the *Vorlage* of Deut 22:13–21 (*Die Ehre einer Frau in Israel*, 107).

27. On the overlapping features of these texts, see Pressler, *View of Women*, 4–5; and Jan Christian Gertz, *Die Gerichtsorganisation Israels im deuteronomischen Gesetz*, FRLANT 165 [Göttingen: Vandenhoeck & Ruprecht, 1994], 175–76. Gertz points out that the structural similarities of at least Deut 21:18–21; 22:13–21; and 25:5–10 suggest the hand of the same redactor.

28. Given the association of the particle כי with legal protases, it is possible that the specific formulation of these phrases is not pre-Deuteronomic. Bernard Levinson and Molly Zahn note that the term is employed in the Covenant Code strictly as a marker for new legal paragraphs, while Deuteronomy also employs it for subordinate clauses ("Revelation Regained: The Hermeneutics of כי and אם in the Temple Scroll," *DSD* 9 [2002]: 295–346, here 318). At the same time, as they also point out, the term כי and its Sumerian, Akkadian, and Hittite cognates are regularly employed in collections that cover a range of genres (law, omens, incantations, medical literature) (301).

29. As Bruce Wells points out, in marriage contracts from Mesopotamia and Syria, the term *hate* is used in cases of divorce where the spouse is not at fault; this causes the divorcing spouse to relinquish his/her rights (largely his) to money and property, usually in the form of the woman's dowry ("Is It Law or Religion? Legal Motivations in Deuteronomic and Neo-Babylonian Texts," in *Law and Religion in the Eastern Mediterranean: From Antiquity to Islam*, ed. Anselm C. Hagedorn and Reinhard G. Kratz [Oxford: Oxford University Press, 2013], 287–310, here 302 n. 49). He points out further that the term can also be used to signal

adjudication by the "elders" at the gate (22:13–21; 25:5–10).[30] Two feature claims delivered in direct speech by the plaintiff and the defendant (22:13-21; 25:5-10). Several then overlap in even more specific ways. Both the first case of the slandered bride and the final scenario in the rape triad issue a verdict of eternal marriage ("he cannot send her out all of his days"; Deut 22:19, 29; cf. 24:1–2). Both the first case of the slandered bride and that of the widow and *levir* prescribe a threefold punishment of humiliation.[31] Two pertain to inheritance disputes (21:15–17; 25:5–10). Two deal with the denigration of a "name" in Israel (22:13–21; 25:5–10). As Bruce Wells points out, these texts (and others) deal with "boundary problems," that is, legal issues that arise outside of the norm.[32] Other details link the texts even more closely, though because these appear to be later ties, I will reserve discussion of them for section III. The bulk of these texts do not derive from laws in the Book of the Covenant, so we must account for their origins and form by different means.

Alexander Rofé, who identifies these texts as rooted in a "women's law" collection, states that Deut 22:13–19 and 25:5–10 in particular "almost read like transcripts of trials later rewritten as laws."[33] Without access to actual Israelite trial records, it is difficult to evaluate such a statement. It is worth noting, however, that Mesopotamian trial records from all periods and regions are marked by an opacity that is true neither of the SLFs nor of the cuneiform law collections.[34] These records were clearly not written as

---

a demotion in the woman's status, as is the case for the "hated woman" in Deut 21:15–17. See also Wells's extended and nuanced discussion in "The Hated Wife in Deuteronomic Law," *VT* 60 (2010): 131–46, here 140–45.

30. It is possible, however, that the inclusion of the elders represents a secondary feature designed to imbue these cases with the illusion of an "early" judicial system at work in Israel. For extensive discussion of the "elder-laws" in Deuteronomy, see Timothy M. Willis, *The Elders of the City: A Study of the Elder-Laws in Deuteronomy*, SBLMS 55 (Atlanta: Society of Biblical Literature, 2001). Willis challenges the assumption that the judicial function of the elders and that of the judges described "in the D Code" are mutually exclusive (49). On the topic, see also Bruce Wells, "Competing or Complementary? Judges and Elders in Biblical and Neo-Babylonian Law," *ZABR* 16 (2010): 77–104.

31. For discussion of this punishment as "humiliation," see Bruce Wells, "Sex, Lies, and Virginal Rape: The Slandered Bride and False Accusation in Deuteronomy," *JBL* 124 (2005): 61–63.

32. Wells, "Competing or Complementary?," 102. Wells identifies fifteen laws in Deuteronomy that would have been preserved in an earlier collection: in addition to those profiled in this article, he includes Deut 19:4–5 + 11–12, 16–19a; 21:1–7, 15–17, 18–21aα; 22:13–21a, 22, 23–27, 28–29; 24:1–4aα, 5, 7bα; 25:1–3, 5–10, and 11–12. This characterization applies handily to Deut 25:5–10, given that the law deals with brothers who have apparently lost their father and live together on undivided land (Raymond Westbrook, *Property and the Family in Biblical Law*, JSOTSup 113 [Sheffield: JSOT Press, 1991], 77–80).

33. Rofé, *Deuteronomy*, 184. Locher presents a similar assessment of Deut 22:13–19 ("Deuteronomium 22, 13–21," 302).

34. A major exception to this rule is the Middle Assyrian Laws, which are much more

court transcripts; rather, they preserved only what were considered to be crucial data for the future. This is not to say that Deut 22:13–19 and 25:5–10 are lacking in details that belong to known Near Eastern trial records. Both include specific verdicts that are to be carried out and feature claims and counterclaims in direct speech. I suggest, however, that these elements can better be explained by rooting these texts and several others in a set of Israelite legal exercises that were developed for use in scribal education, akin to the SLFs. Several points support this proposal:

1. The ILFs are linked by a set of literary features and tropes that suggest either common origins or redaction with an eye toward likeness. The SLFs likewise include common features and literary flourishes (the "assembly at Nippur"; covering something with a cloth; the debate in the assembly) that can be explained in terms of common pedagogical origins.
2. The concept of law was clearly learned in the context of Israelite scribal education, as suggested by the numerous proverbs devoted to the perversion of justice and the problems of strife, not to mention adultery.[35] A logical extension of this early training would be exposure to exercises that could illustrate the proper execution of justice and/or present and solve legal conundrums.
3. The dramatic aspects of Deut 22:13–19 and 25:5–10 in particular, with the hard evidence of the bloody sheet in the former and the threefold "humiliation verdict" in the latter, resonate with elements in Adultery A: namely, the "hard evidence" of the adulterous bed and the threefold "humiliation verdict" of shaving the woman's genitals, piercing her nose, and parading her around the city.[36] Moreover, given that both

---

detailed and opaque in comparison with the Laws of Hammurabi and the other law collections. It is difficult to draw conclusions about how the Middle Assyrian Laws functioned in society, however, given that each tablet is available only in a single copy. As Westbrook points out, the copies are apparently neither inscriptions nor school texts; this may lend credence to the classification of them as a "legal library for judges" ("Biblical and Cuneiform Codes," 11, following E. F. Weidner, "Das Alter der mittelassyrischen Gesetztexte," *AfO* 17 [1937]: 46–54).

35. To name but a few, see Prov 12:17; 14:5, 25; 16:10, 29; 17:8, 14, 23; 18:5, 17; 19:5, 9, 28; 20:8; 21:6, 28; 23:33; 24:23, 28; 25:2; 26:17, 21; 29:9, 12, 14, 26; 31:8–9, 23, and so on. Proverbs are commonly thought to have formed an early stage of Israelite scribal education due to their pithy and didactic nature; this is supported by the fact that Sumerian proverbs were evidently learned at an early stage of scribal education. These proverbs were found in thematically grouped collections, and over twenty-five collections have been identified (Niek Veldhuis, "The Cuneiform Tablet as an Educational Tool," *Dutch Studies on Near Eastern Languages and Cultures* 2 [1996]: 11–26, here 20). Regarding the connection between Deuteronomy and wisdom literature, see Calum Carmichael, *The Laws of Deuteronomy* (Ithaca, NY: Cornell University Press, 1974).

36. Tikva Frymer-Kensky points to the ease with which the parents could manufacture

of these "verdicts" would have been carried out immediately, there is no practical reason why either one would have required written documentation.
4. Deuteronomy 21:15–17 (the man with two wives), 24:1–4 (the two-time divorcee), and 25:5–10 (the widow and the *levir*) all have a "stand-alone" quality that parallels the independent nature of the SLFs.[37]

Together these features suggest that these particular laws originated as mock cases that were learned at an advanced phase of Israelite scribal education. Such texts might have been studied as a means of helping scribes learn the conventions of writing trial records, though it is possible that they had a broader didactic and/or entertaining function, as may have been true for the SLFs. Whatever the case, a pedagogical *Sitz im Leben* would help explain how and why scribes came into contact with these texts in the first place and perhaps also how such texts ended up in Deuteronomy.

III. Incorporation of the Israelite Legal Fictions into Deuteronomy 12–26

It is now necessary to consider the editorial techniques that were used to incorporate the ILFs into an emergent work of Deuteronomy. Any discussion of this process must begin with Deut 16:18–20 + 17:2–13, two texts that stand out in their context for their preoccupation with the legal system.[38] Deuteronomy 16:18–20 prescribes the appointment of judges and scribes in all of the people's "gates" (בכל־שעריך) who can execute justice effectively (ושפטו את־העם משפט־צדק). These judges are advised to act fairly, without succumbing to bribes.[39] Deuteronomy 17:2–13 is then composed of two units. The former (vv. 2–7) prescribes a protocol for suspected cases of apostasy. If a man or woman "does what is evil" in the eyes of Yhwh

---

such evidence in the slandered bride case ("Law and Philosophy: The Case of Sex in the Bible," in *Women in the Hebrew Bible: A Reader*, ed. Alice Bach [London: Routledge, 1999], 293–302, here 296); this may be another factor that points to its fictitiousness.

37. The same is true for Deut 22:13–19, despite the fact that in its current form this unit is followed by an alternative scenario. The secondary nature of vv. 20–21 will be addressed in section IV.

38. This unit is generally called "Office-bearers of the Theocracy." Bernard Levinson dubs it one of the most problematic case studies available within the legal corpus, due to its "topic selection, sequencing, and ostensible redundancy" (*Deuteronomy and the Hermeneutics of Legal Innovation* [Oxford: Oxford University Press, 1997], 98).

39. For Otto, this unit represents a development of Exod 23:3, 6 that utilizes the authority of the Covenant Code for its own reform program, which includes the professionalization of judges (*Das Deuteronomium*, 147).

and follows other gods, one must investigate; if the allegations are true, the man or woman is to be stoned to death. Deuteronomy 17:6 indicates that capital punishment can be carried out only on the testimony of two or more witnesses. This process eliminates evil from the people's midst. The latter unit (vv. 8–13) then refers to cases that are too difficult to decide, presumably for the judges referenced in 16:18–20. The parties must go to the place that Yhwh has chosen and appear before the priests and judges who are adjudicating at the time. The claimants must follow the officials' verdict scrupulously, with punishment of death for disobedience. The unit concludes again with reference to the removal of evil and states that all the people "will hear and be afraid and no longer behave presumptuously" (וכל העם ישמעו ויראו ולא יזידון עוד).

Both the parallels between Deut 17:2–7 and chapter 13, a text that details three cases of apostasy in similar wording, and the disunity of 17:2–7 and vv. 8–13 prompt many to move 17:2–7 "back" to chapter 13.[40] It is noteworthy that the writers of the Temple Scroll insert the apostasy laws of Deut 13 and 17 after the laws on vows from Num 30.[41] As Bernard Levinson points out, however, the relocation of 17:2–7 in chapter 13 saddles the latter with two cases that treat apostasy by an individual (13:7–12 and 17:2–7).[42] While it is clear that 17:2–7 is related to the three cases of apostasy in chapter 13 and that, moreover, the unit lacks the conventions that mark 17:8–13, this need not warrant the removal of 17:2–7 from its current context. Rather, as I will demonstrate, links between Deut 17:2–7 and the ILFs indicate that this unit was designed especially to facilitate the integration of the ILFs into an extant work.[43]

Deuteronomy 17:2-7 begins with the possibility that a *man* or *woman* who has "done evil" might be found "in [the people's] midst, in one of

---

40. See discussion in Levinson, *Deuteronomy and the Hermeneutics*, 99–116. Levinson argues that vv. 2–7 are specifically designed to "work out the implications of centralization" on the judicial system and must not be detached from the verses that follow (100).

41. Levinson and Zahn, "Revelation Regained," 313.

42. See also Bruce Wells, *The Law of Testimony in the Pentateuchal Codes*, BZABR 4 (Wiesbaden: Harrassowitz, 2004), 86–94. Wells points to the debate regarding how to view Deut 17:2–7—as cultic or judicial—and concludes that the latter is more apt (86).

43. This suggestion works in the context of Gertz's assessment of Deut 16:21–17:7 as "eine spät-dtr Einfügung in 16,18 (+ 19f) und 17, 8–13" (*Die Gerichtsorganisation Israels*, 72). It is difficult to say to what degree the material in Deut 17:14–21:14 was already represented in such a collection, or whether some of it was either brought in or redacted along with the ILFs during this phase. The case(s) of the manslayer in 19:4–5 and 11–13 may have followed a process of development similar to that proposed for the ILFs in section IV, especially given the instruction to "sweep away" the innocent blood from Israel in 19:13. Deuteronomy 19:15–21 requires two witnesses, as in 17:6, and in both units the people/judges are instructed to "investigate well," suggesting a potential link between the two. These matters, however, belong to a larger discussion regarding the development of Deuteronomy and must await further consideration.

[their] *gates.*" Each of these referents—the man/woman, the act of evil, and the gates—is unique to Deut 17:2-7 in comparison with 13:2-19.[44] Gates appear repeatedly in the laws in question: 21:19; 22:15, 24; and 25:7.[45] Moreover, all of the laws in question pertain to men and women: throughout these cases, men take women as wives (21:15–17; 22:13; 24:1–4), refuse to do so (25:5–10), and lie with women (22:22, 23–24, 25–27, 28–29); and in 22:22, as in 17:2, a man and woman are "found" together.[46] The term *evil* surfaces in the case of the slandered bride in 22:14. The investigation conducted in 17:4 has counterparts in 22:13–19 and 25:5–10, where the elders follow up on claims of nonvirginity and noncompliance. The statement in 17:4 regarding the truth of the claim has echoes in 22:20 and 24:4. Moreover, not only is capital punishment prescribed throughout the laws in question (21:21; 22:21, 22, 24, and 25–27), but the specific procedure in 17:2–7 of *bringing out* the culprit to *the gate* and *stoning* him/her *to death* in order to *sweep out evil* occurs in 21:18–21, 22:20–21, and 22:23–24.

While some of these details may have originated in the ILFs (e.g., the gate, the man and woman, "evil"), others are likely interpolations into the ILFs inspired by Deut 17:2–7, given their close parallels in wording and harsh themes (e.g., bringing the culprit "out" and stoning him to death in 21:18-21, 22:20–21, and 22:23–24; "sweeping" the evil from the people's midst in 22:21, 22:22, and 22:24; the "abomination" in 24:4). The most salient example is 21:18–21, the case of the rebellious son. Not only does this case follow the protocol in 17:2–7 precisely, as Rofé observes, but it also mimics the style and terminology of the ILFs. Thus, it begins with the classic כי איש X לאיש formula that marks the other ILFs; it involves a set of parents, as in 22:13–19; the parents flog the son, as in 22:18; the parents "seize" the child, as in 22:28; and they bring him before the elders at the gate, as in 22:13–19 and 25:5–10.[47] In addition, as in 22:13–19 and 25:5–10, the plaintiffs' claim is reported both by the narrator and in direct speech.[48] This text thus works as a new and improved ILF, one with all of the classic

---

44. Levinson suggests that Deut 17:2-7 is a reworking of 13:2–19 (*Deuteronomy and the Hermeneutics*, 118–23); for further literature, see 120 n. 58.

45. The plural designation (versus the singular "gate" in the ILFs) works with the appointment of judges "in all of your gates" in Deut 16:18, as Levinson notes (*Deuteronomy and the Hermeneutics*, 131).

46. Otto sees Deut 22:13–21 and 24:1–4a as representing a frame with the same opening and notes that they are both linked by dislike of the wife and divorce; he further sees 21:15–17 and 25:5–10 as another frame involving brothers (*Das Deuteronomium*, 269–70).

47. Cf. Willis, who concludes that Deut 21:18–21aα is pre-Deuteronomic, in contrast to 13:7–12, which he identifies as Deuteronom(ist)ic (*Elders of the City*, 173). As Willis points out, there are parallels between the ordering of Deut 21:15–21 and LH 167–168: both follow a law pertaining to the division of property among two sons with a law pertaining to a man who wishes to remove his son from his house. While the observation is correct, this need not indicate the priority of Deut 21:18–21.

48. Pressler, *View of Women*, 4–5.

conventions of this genre but also infused with the themes of Deut 17:2–7. Together, these supplementations work to radically recast the small-scale disputes depicted in the ILFs as large-scale calamities threatening Israel and its relationship with Yhwh. The additional "cases" that feature execution by stoning—something arguably not present in any of the original ILFs—serve to hammer this point home. With this set of additions, not only were the old ILFs recast as "law," but adjudication itself was reenvisioned as somehow crucial to the maintenance of Israel's integrity. This phase was thus not a matter of combining an extant "family law" or "women's law" collection with cultic law but rather involved turning old legal exercises into laws with collective implications and severe consequences for Israel at large.[49] Given that these additions are more concerned with the maintenance of integrity than with cult centralization per se, it seems that they reflect a relatively late phase in the development of Deuteronomy, one that postdates those texts that are preoccupied with centralization and that apparently constitute the earliest "core" of the book.[50] In order to distinguish these additions from an early version of "Deuteronomy," I will classify them as post-Deuteronomic. Whether they represent a single hand or a series of successive and related additions is inconsequential in this context; the important point is that they appear to work toward the same end.

IV. The Post-Deuteronomic Production of Secondary Scenarios

The Near Eastern phenomenon of "making law" by multiplying scenarios is well known, as exemplified by the series of "eye for an eye" laws, best known from the Laws of Hammurabi. The law collections of the ancient Near East commonly feature clusters of laws with variations on a basic scenario, with different factors, such as the status of the individuals involved, the severity of the crime or injury, or the availability of witnesses, yielding different outcomes. By contrast, all of the SLFs and most of the ILFs (Deut 21:15–17, 24:1–4, 25:5–10, and even the "new" ILF, Deut

---

49. Cf. Otto, who sees these texts (including Deut 21:18–21) as forming an original collection of family law that was taken up by the Deuteronomic author and connected with blood-law and process-law (*Das Deuteronomium*, 271).

50. For discussion regarding the "core" of Deuteronomy, see Reinhard G. Kratz, *The Composition of the Narrative Books of the Old Testament*, trans. John Bowden (London: T&T Clark, 2005), 117–23 (= *Die Komposition der erzählenden Bücher des Alten Testaments*, Grundwissen der Bibelkritik, UTB 2157 [Göttingen: Vandenhoeck & Ruprecht, 2000]). Kratz identifies the following units as constituting the core/"Ur-Deuteronomy" (with secondary additions throughout): Deut 12:13–28; 14:22–29; 15:19–23; 16:16–17; 16:18–20; 17:8-13; 19:1–13; 19:15–21; and 21:1-9.

21:18–21) operate as independent episodes. Only two of the ILFs include multiple scenarios: Deut 22:13–21 + 22 and 22:23–29. It is noteworthy that these are also the only criminal cases among the ILFs. By extension, it is only in these two clusters that we find verdicts of capital punishment. Moreover, as noted above, language similar to that in Deut 17:2–7 pervades 22:20–21, 22 and 23–24; and both 22:20–21 and 22:23–24 involve bringing the culprits to a public place and stoning them to death.

There are two ways to account for these observations. First, it is possible that some of the secondary scenarios belong to an early redaction of the ILFs as a separate collection of laws. The scribe(s) would have encountered this material as a set and enhanced it with additions when he/they incorporated it into an extant version of Deuteronomy. Second, it is possible that these additional scenarios derive from the hands of post-Deuteronomic scribes, so that these individuals are solely responsible for rendering the ILFs into "law."[51] Certainly Deut 22:20–21 is widely recognized as an addition to 22:13-19. As Clemens Locher points out, the introduction to the law in v. 13 ("A man marries a woman ... then he hates her and makes false accusations against her ...") only suits the first scenario, not the second. This, combined with the fact that the style of the secondary scenario is altogether different and much shorter, indicates that Deut 22:20–21 is secondary.[52] By the same token, Deut 22:22 both includes the "evil" formula and uses an opening similar to 17:2, "If a man is found ..." (כי־ימצא איש), making it the only nonactive law among the ILFs. Moreover, while 22:22 does not prescribe stoning, its inclusion of double capital punishment, as is the case in 17:3, suggests either that the verse derives from the scribe responsible for 17:2–7 or that one of the two texts was composed to work with the other.[53] Deuteronomy 22:22 is also considerably shorter than the other ILFs. I would thus suggest that both Deut 22:20–21 and 22:22 reflect use of the "multiplication" convention by post-Deuteronomic scribes in order to supplement a detailed "model case" of slander with two casuistic laws of adultery that result in capital punishment.

Deuteronomy 22:23–29 may represent a similar phenomenon. The

---

51. Although Locher focuses only on Deut 22:13–21, my approach is in line with his remarks on 22:13–19 and 20–21: "Die Spannungen zwischen 22,13–19 und 22,20f. erklären sich ohne weiteres, wenn der erste Teil von einer solchen Vorlage abhängig, der zweite Teil dagegen nachträglicher Zusatz des 'Gesetzgeber' ist, der das Prozessprotokoll zu einem kasuistichen Gesetz umforte" ("Deuteronomium 22,13–21 vom Prozessprotokoll zum kasuistischen Gesetz," 303).

52. For discussion and literature, see Pressler, *View of Women*, 22; and Wells, "Sex, Lies, and the Slandered Bride," 42 n. 4.

53. On the late, exilic dating of Deut 22:22, see Georg Braulik, who sees Lev 20:10 as the *Vorlage* for this verse ("Weitere Beobachtungen zur Beziehung zwischen dem Heiligkeitsgesetz und Deuteronomium 19–25," in *Das Deuteronomium und seine Querbeziehungen*, ed. Timo Veijola, SESJ 62 [Helsinki: Finnischen Exegetischen Gesellschaft, 1966], 23–55, here 26).

three scenarios include a variety of factors that produce different outcomes: the first pertains to an engaged virgin in the city who allegedly did not cry out; the second, to the assault of an engaged virgin in the field; and the third, to the rape of an unengaged virgin.[54] Given the emphasis on evil and integrity in Deut 22:23–24, it appears that this first scenario represents a post-Deuteronomic contribution in the same vein as 17:2–7, 21:18-21, 22:20–21, and 22:22.[55] Deuteronomy 22:25–27, however, is not marked by the same post-Deuteronomic style and protocol. If the first half of 22:26 is identified as a *Fortschreibung* due to its redundant nature, it is possible to argue that an early form of 22:25–27 represents the core from which this series grew. This argument is not meant to dismiss the likely dependence of Deut 22:28–29 on MT Exod 22:15–16 (= LXX Exod 22:16–17), but the many links between Deut 22:28–29 and the preceding laws in 22:13–27 suggest that 22:28–29 was a late addition to the wider collection of illicit sex laws in this chapter. As such, the development of a "series" of assault laws arguably represents a later development.[56]

V. Conclusion

In taking stock of the place of SLFs in Old Babylonian scribal education, the possibility begins to emerge that certain laws (Deut 21:15–17, 22:13–19, 24:1–4, 25:5–10, and possibly *22:25–27) once served a similar function in Israelite scribal education. When this awareness is combined with other factors—the unique specificity of these laws in their wider context, their shared pre-Deuteronomic components, the parallels between these texts and certain literary/dramatic features in the SLFs, their limited quantity, and their very appearance in the book of Deuteronomy—the possibility that these texts had their origins in a set of legal exercises finds further support.[57] This hypothesis would help account both for the parallels that

---

54. On the use of the term *rape*, see Robert S. Kawashima, who argues that the apparent lack of women's rights in ancient Israel indicates that the notion of forcible rape did not exist "in biblical Israel's legal system" ("Could a Woman Say 'No' in Biblical Israel? On the Genealogy of Legal Status in Biblical Law and Literature," *AJS Review* 35 [2011]: 1–22, here 2).

55. Cf. Otto, *Das Deuteronomium*, 217. The notion that only the apodosis is secondary would require the existence and subsequent elimination of a pre-Deuteronomic apodosis. It is worth adding that v. 23a departs from the איש ... כי formula by opening instead with "If there is a girl, an engaged virgin, and a man finds her ...."

56. In a forthcoming article *JBL*, I argue for the priority of *Deut 22:25–27 in more detail, with emphasis on its unique display of Near Eastern legal reasoning in this unit ("Separating the Wheat from the Chaff: The Independent Logic of Deut 22:25-27"). Cf. Otto, however, who sees Deut 22:22a and 28–29 as "scholastically expanded" by 22:23–27 ("Aspects of Legal Reforms," 192).

57. On the likelihood that Deuteronomy was utilized in scribal education in the Persian period, see Karel van der Toorn, *Scribal Culture and the Making of the Hebrew Bible* (Cam-

these texts share with trial records and the ways in which they diverge. The different types of supplementations that I have identified above—the apostasy "introduction" in Deut 17:2–7; the secondary scenarios in 22:20–21, 22, 23–24, and 28–29; and the production of a new ILF in 21:18–21—appear to represent a unified redaction that was designed to adapt these exercises for new use as post-Deuteronomic "law." This involved taking the traditional Near Eastern convention of presenting legal clusters of multiple scenarios with different factors and putting it toward different ends. Rather than use this method to cover as much legal ground as possible, however, they cleverly employed it to re-present old quandaries as threats to the cultic order. In the process, they created a "law collection," but a law collection the likes of which had never been seen before in the ancient Near East.

In this case, the identification of these interrelated forms of supplementation sheds light on larger processes of "lawmaking" in ancient Israel. Not only did the Israelites/Judahites borrow and creatively adapt Near Eastern law, as is suggested by the numerous links between *mišpāṭîm* and cuneiform law, but they evidently also adapted the conventions of Near Eastern lawmaking for new use in the development of Deuteronomy. This proposed process of editorial intervention suggests that supplementations could be used to integrate old source material into an extant work, specifically with the purpose of putting that source toward decidedly new ends. It thus may be that elsewhere, clusters of supplementation in different forms, as with those surrounding the ILFs, could likewise point toward once-independent material that served different functions in other contexts.

Appendix

Israelite Legal Fictions (ILFs)

Unboxed material: "original" (or potentially original) ILFs
Boxed material: post-Deuteronomic additions

Deuteronomy 21:15–17

15 If a man has [כי־תהיין לאיש] two wives, one loved and the other hated, and both the loved one and hated one bear him sons, but the firstborn son

---

bridge: Harvard University Press, 2007], 101–2). Van der Toorn bases this conclusion on the large number of copies of Deuteronomy (in addition to Isaiah and Psalms) that were discovered at Qumran, in addition to the "Levitical signature" represented in each of these books. In the context of this argument, however, I envision an earlier (i.e., preexilic) pedagogical context for these particular laws.

belongs to the hated wife, **16** when he wills his property to his sons, he cannot treat the son of the loved wife as firstborn over his (actual) firstborn, the son of the hated wife. **17** He must recognize as firstborn the son of his hated wife and give him a double portion of all that he has, for he is the first of his strength. The right of the firstborn is his.

Deuteronomy 21:18-21

> **18** If a man has [כי יהיה לאיש] a stubborn and rebellious son who does not listen to his father and mother, and they flog him and he (still) does not listen to them, **19** his father and mother shall seize him and bring him to the elders of his city at the gate of his place. **20** And they shall say to the elders of his city, "This son of ours is stubborn and rebellious. He does not listen to us. He is a glutton and a drunkard." **21** And all the men of his city are to stone him to death. You must sweep out the evil from your midst. And all Israel will hear and be afraid.

Deuteronomy 22:13–22

13 If a man takes [כי־יקח איש] a wife and sleeps with her, and then he hates her **14** and makes up charges against her, and brings a bad name upon her, saying, "I took this woman, and when I approached her, I did not find evidence of virginity in her," **15** the father and mother of the young woman shall bring out the evidence of her virginity to the elders of the city at the gate. **16** And the father of the young woman shall say to the elders, "I gave my daughter to this man as wife, and (now) he hates her, **17** and here he has made up charges, saying, 'I did not find evidence of virginity in your daughter.' But this is the evidence of my daughter's virginity!" And they shall spread out the garment before the elders of the city. **18** Then the elders of that city shall take the man and flog him, **19** and they shall fine him a hundred shekels of silver and give that to the father of the young woman, because he has brought a bad name upon a virgin of Israel. And she shall remain his wife. He cannot send her out all of his days [לא־יוכל לשלחה כל־ימיו].

> **20** But if the charge proves true, if there is no evidence of the girl's virginity, **21** then the girl shall be brought out to the door of her father's house, and the men of her city shall stone her to death, for she did a disgraceful thing in Israel, whoring while in her father's house. Thus you will sweep away evil from your midst.
> **22** If a man is found sleeping with a married woman, both of them shall die—the man and the woman with whom he lay. And you shall sweep out the evil from your midst.

Deuteronomy 22:23–29

> 23 If there is an engaged virgin, and another man comes upon her in the city and lies with her, 24 you shall take out the two of them to the gate of that city and stone them to death—the girl because she did not cry out in the city, and the man because he has violated his fellow's wife. And you shall sweep out the evil from your midst.

25 But if the man finds the engaged girl in the field, and the man overpowers her and lies with her, only the man who lay with her shall die. 26 You shall do nothing to the girl, for she has done nothing deserving of death. For this is like the case of a man who rises up against his fellow and murders him. 27 He found her in the field and the engaged girl (may have) cried out, but no one saved her.

> 28 If a man finds [כי־ימצא איש] an unengaged virgin, and he seizes her and lies with her, and they are found, 29 then the man who lay with her must give the girl's father fifty shekels of silver, and she will become his wife. Because he violated her, he cannot send her out all of his days [לא־יוכל שלחה כל־ימיו].

Deuteronomy 24:1–4

1 If a man takes [כי־יקח איש] a wife and marries her, but then she falls out of his favor because he finds something indecent in her, and he writes her a certificate of divorce and puts it in her hand and sends her out from his house, and she goes out from his house, 2 and becomes another man's wife, 3 and the other man hates her and writes her a certificate of divorce and puts it in her hand and sends her out of *his* house, or if the other man who took her as his wife dies, 4 the first husband who sent her away cannot remarry her, after she has been unclean, for that is an abomination before Yhwh. And you shall not bring sin upon the land that Yhwh your God is giving to you as an inheritance.

Deuteronomy 25:5–10

5 If brothers dwell [כי־ישבו אחים] together and one of them dies and he had no son, the widow must not marry a foreign man outside [the clan]. Her brother-in-law shall come to her and take her as wife, and "brother-in-law" her. 6 And it will be that the firstborn that she bears will carry on the name of the dead brother so that his name will not be wiped out from Israel. 7 However, if a man does not want to marry his brother's wife, she shall go to the elders at the city gate and say, "My husband's brother

refuses to establish a name in Israel for his brother. He is not willing to 'brother-in-law' me." **8** The elders of his town will summon him and talk to him. And if he persists in saying, "I do not want to take her," **9** his brother's widow will approach him in the presence of the elders, remove one of his sandals from his foot, spit in his face, and say, "This is what is done to the man who will not build up the house of his brother." **10** And they will (henceforth) call his name in Israel "The House of the Withdrawn Sandal."

Supplementing Leviticus in the Second Temple Period: The Case of the Wood Offering in 4Q365 Fragment 23

CHRISTOPHE NIHAN
Université de Lausanne

I. 4Q365 and the Transmission of Leviticus in the Second Temple Period

Leviticus is commonly regarded as one of the most stable scriptures transmitted during the Second Temple period. This scholarly judgment is based on the comparison between the main textual forms of this book that have been preserved, namely, the MT, the SP, and the LXX, as well as the fragments of several copies of this book that were found in Qumran.[1] In general, the comparison between these textual forms suggests that Levit-

---

1. A brief note on the ancient versions of Leviticus is in order here. At least twelve copies of Leviticus in Hebrew from Qumran have been identified, most of which are, however, in a very fragmentary state. These Hebrew manuscripts include 1QpaleoLev-Num[a] and 1QpaleoLev[b]? (1Q3, published in DJD 1), 2QpaleoLev and 6QpaleoLev (2Q5, 2Q6, published in DJD 3), 4QExod-Lev[f], 4QLev-Num[a], 4QLev[b], 4QLev[c], 4QLev[d], 4QLev[e], 4QLev[g] (4Q17, 4Q23, 4Q24, 4Q25, 4Q26, 4Q26a, 4Q26b, published in DJD 12), as well as the paleo-Hebrew Leviticus scroll, 11Q paleoLev (11Q1), which was published in a separate volume by D. N. Freedman and K. A. Mathews, *The Paleo-Hebrew Leviticus Scroll (11QpaleoLev)* (Philadelphia: American Schools of Oriental Research; Winona Lake, IN: Eisenbrauns, 1985). Although it is not a copy of Leviticus proper, we may also include 4Qpap cryptA Text Quoting Leviticus A (4Q249[k], published in DJD 36). Additionally, fragments of two manuscripts of Leviticus in Greek from Cave 4 have also been identified, 4QLXXLev[a] and 4QpapLXXLev[b] (4Q119, 4Q120, published in DJD 9), as well as two small fragments of what appears to have been a targumic version of the book, 4QtgLev (4Q156, published in DJD 6). For a description of the Qumran evidence pertaining to Leviticus, see esp., P.W. Flint, "The Book of Leviticus in the Dead Sea Scrolls," in *The Book of Leviticus: Composition and Reception*, ed. Rolf Rendtorff and Robert A. Kugler, VTSup 93 (Leiden: Brill, 2003), 323–41; as well as Sarianna Metso, "Evidence from the Qumran Scrolls for the Scribal Transmission of Leviticus," in *Editing the Bible: Assessing the Task Past and Present*, ed. John S. Kloppenborg and Judith H. Newman, RBS 69 (Atlanta: Society of Biblical Literature, 2012), 67–79. One more piece of evidence is Schøyen

icus was transmitted with few significant variants. Additions and omissions of materials are limited in scope and usually comprise a few words.[2] Moreover, with only one partial exception, the comparison between these textual forms provides no evidence for the rearrangement of Leviticus materials, a phenomenon well documented for other pentateuchal books, especially Exodus or Numbers.[3] These and other observations have led scholars such as Sarianna Metso and Eugene Ulrich to conclude that the text of Leviticus in the Second Temple period, while not yet fully standardized, was nevertheless characterized by what Metso aptly terms "a modest number of predictable variants within [a] single edition."[4] Furthermore, according to Metso and Ulrich the greater stability and textual uniformity of Leviticus should be related to the cultic function of this book

---

MS 4611, which has not been published yet, but see provisionally E. Puech, "Un autre manuscrit du Lévitique," *RevQ* 21 (2003): 311–13.

Regarding the Greek text of Leviticus, see esp. John William Wevers, who concludes that the Old Greek (OG) of Leviticus is represented by Codex Alexandrinus (LXXA), Codex Vaticanus (LXXB), and one minuscule (MS 121) (*Text History of the Greek Leviticus*, AAWG.PH 3/153 [Göttingen: Vandenhoeck & Ruprecht, 1986]). A new Greek manuscript of Leviticus from the Schøyen collection (MS 2649), however, has recently been published by K. de Troyer in *Papyri Graecae Schøyen (PSchøyen): Essays and Texts in Honour of Martin Schøyen*, ed. Diletta Minutoli and Rosario Pintaudi, vol. 2 of *Papyri Graecae Schøyen (PSchøyen)*, Papyrologica Florentina 40 (Florence: Gonnelli, 2010), 7–68 and pls. 1–16. In addition, the evidence provided by the fragments of the two Greek manuscripts of Leviticus from Cave 4 (4QLXXLev[a] and 4QpapLXXLev[b]) may have been insufficiently considered. In the case of 4QLXXLev[a], see now the recent discussion by I. Himbaza, "What are the consequences if 4QLXXLev[a] contains earliest formulation of the Septuagint?" [sic], *Die Septuaginta–Orte und Intentionen: 5, Internationale Fachtagung veranstaltet von Septuaginta Deutsch (LXX.D), Wuppertal 24.–27. Juli 2014*, ed. Siegfried Kreuzer, Martin Meiser, and Marcus Sigismund, WUNT 361 (Tübingen: Mohr Siebeck, 2016), 294–308.

2. The most substantial addition is arguably represented by the plus preserved in Lev 17:4 in the SP, the LXX, and 4QLev[d]. See on this the recent and detailed discussion by David Andrew Teeter, *Scribal Laws: Exegetical Variation in the Textual Transmission of Biblical Law in the Second Temple Period*, FAT 92 (Tübingen: Mohr Siebeck, 2014), 76–94. One significant example of omission is preserved by 4QLev[b], where the portion of text corresponding to Lev 3:2–7 appears to be missing; however, this omission may simply reflect a scribal error caused by the similarity between vv. 2 and 8, as is often assumed.

3. The partial exception concerns frag. 1 of 11QpaleoLev, where, in the passage corresponding to Lev 18:27, the reference to the "disgusting things" (תועבת) committed by "the men of the land" is expanded with a clause referring to their expulsion from the land that is borrowed from Lev 20:23–24. In this instance, however, a distinctive sign (antisigma) was placed at the end of the clause borrowed from Lev 20. It appears, therefore, that the scribe who introduced this sign was well aware of the highly unusual character of this sort of textual rearrangement in the case of Leviticus. So this exception may arguably be viewed as confirming the general rule that the rearrangement of materials was normally avoided in the transmission of this book. One further exception to this trend is represented by manuscripts D and E of 4QRP (4Q366 and 4Q367); see n. 8 below.

4. S. Metso, "Evidence from the Qumran Scrolls," 70.

in the Second Temple period, as a scriptural "repertoire" of sorts for the various rituals performed by the priesthood.[5]

While there is much to be said for the view that Leviticus achieved textual stability earlier than other scriptures during the Second Temple period, there is nevertheless some evidence suggesting that the textual situation of Leviticus may, in fact, have been slightly more fluid and more complex. One such piece of evidence, in particular, concerns the text of Leviticus preserved in the five manuscripts known as "Reworked Pentateuch" (4Q158, 4Q364–367 = 4QRP^{a-e}).[6] While these manuscripts were initially classified by the editors as "parabiblical texts," this classification has been challenged in the past decade. There is now a broad agreement that these texts are better identified as preserving a distinct edition of the Pentateuch (a position also shared by the original editors, Emanuel Tov and Sidnie White).[7] Three of these manuscripts include portions of Leviticus

---

5. Sarianna Metso and Eugene Ulrich, "The Old Greek Translation of Leviticus," in Rendtorff and Kugler, *Book of Leviticus: Composition and Reception*, 247–68, here 267: "The Hebrew text tradition of Leviticus had basically achieved a uniform state, to judge from the extant sources, by the second half of the Second Temple period. Especially since this contrasts with the pluriform state of Exodus and Numbers, which display two or more literary editions, it is plausible to assume that the Jerusalem priesthood had kept a watchful eye on the text of Leviticus. From that perspective, however, the rationale would not have been textual concern for a 'standard text' of the scriptural book, but practical concern for clear uniform instructions for correct procedures in the traditional sacred rituals that were practiced in the temple and beyond."

6. For the edition of the text, see E. Tov and S. White, "4QReworked Pentateuch," in *Qumran Cave 4.VIII: Parabiblical Texts, Part 1*, ed. H. W. Attridge et al. in consultation with J. VanderKam, DJD 13(Oxford: Clarendon, 1994), 255–318. Initially, the editors considered the five manuscripts to be copies of a rewritten composition of the Pentateuch, and thus classified them as "4QReworked Pentateuch^{a-e}." More recent studies have shown, however, that these manuscripts cannot be copies of the same composition and should be regarded instead as five distinct compositions that share similar features with regard to both form and content. Accordingly, they should be reclassified as "4QReworked Pentateuch A–E." See George Brooke, "4Q158: Reworked Pentateuch^a or Reworked Pentateuch A?," *DSD* 8 (2001): 219–41; Molly M. Zahn, *Rethinking Rewritten Scripture: Composition and Exegesis in the 4QReworked Pentateuch Manuscripts*, STDJ 95 (Leiden: Brill, 2011).

7. See esp. Eugene Ulrich, "The Dead Sea Scrolls and the Biblical Text," in *The Dead Sea Scrolls after Fifty Years: A Comprehensive Assessment*, ed. Peter W. Flint and James C. VanderKam, 2 vols., STDJ 30 (Leiden: Brill, 1998–1999), 1:79–100; M. Segal, "4QReworked Pentateuch or 4QPentateuch," in *The Dead Sea Scrolls: Fifty Years after Their Discovery*, ed. Lawrence H. Schiffman, Emanuel Tov, and James C. VanderKam (Jerusalem: Israel Exploration Society and the Shrine of the Book, Israel Museum, 2000), 391–99; Brooke, "4Q158"; Emanuel Tov, "From 4QReworked Pentateuch to 4QPentateuch (?)," in *Authoritative Scriptures in Ancient Judaism*, ed. Mladen Popović, JSJSup 141 (Leiden: Brill, 2010), 73–91 (reversing his earlier position); Zahn, *Rethinking Rewritten Scripture*. Two related sets of observations, in particular, were decisive for this conclusion. First, the sort of rewriting involved in the five compositions comprising 4QRP does not differ in significant ways from the rewriting that can be observed in other ancient versions of scriptural texts, as is shown, for example, by the comparison between the MT and the LXX versions of biblical books such as 1 Kings, Jeremiah, or Esther

(4Q365, 366, and 367), and they often display significant differences from the text otherwise preserved in ancient versions of this book. In the context of this short essay, I will focus on one specific example, namely, 4Q365 frag. 23, which preserves a set of instructions for the wood offering.[8] This law is otherwise unattested in other versions of Leviticus, although it has parallels in the Temple Scroll as well as in one passage of Nehemiah (Neh 10:35). My discussion will focus on three issues in particular: first, the contents of the addition and the way in which it was introduced in Leviticus; second, the manner in which the addition was composed and its parallels with other biblical and nonbiblical traditions; and, third, its relationship to the development of the wood offering in the festal calendar of the Second Temple period. At the end, I will briefly comment on the significance of this legal supplement for the formation and the transmission of Leviticus in the Second Temple period.

II. The Wood Offering as a Supplement to the Festal Legislation of Leviticus

The text preserved on the fragment (4Q365 frag. 23) reads as follows:[9]

1 [בסו[כות תשבו שבעת ימים כול האזרח בישראל ישב בסוכות למ[ען ידע]ו דו[רותיכם]
2 כי[בס[וכות הושבתי את אבותיכם בהוציאי אותם מארץ מצר[י]ם אני יהוה אלוהיכ[ם]
3 [ ] [ ] וידבר מושה את מועדי יהוה אל בני ישראל
4 וידבר יהוה אל מושה לאמור צו את בני ישראל לאמור בבואכמה אל הארץ אשר
5 [א]נוכי נותן לכמה לנחלה וישבתם עליה לבטח תקריבו עצים עשׂים לעולה ולכול מלאכ[ת]
6 [הב]ית אשר תבנו לי בארץ לערוך אותם על מזבח העולה [ו]את העגל[י]ם[ ] [--]

(Tov, "From 4QReworked Pentateuch," 79–81). Second, as argued in particular by Molly Zahn, 4QRP does not evince some of the distinctive features that characterize prominent examples of rewritten (pentateuchal) compositions such as Jubilees or the Temple Scroll, for example, the introduction of a new narrative voice (such as that of the Angel of the Presence in Jubilees) or a new narrative setting.

8. The text of Leviticus preserved in a few fragments of 4Q366 and 4Q367 presents us with another significant phenomenon, because in three of these fragments (4Q366 frag. 2, 4Q367 frags. 2 and 3) this text has been rearranged in ways otherwise unattested in other Second Temple versions of this book. M. Segal suggested that 4Q367 would represent an excerpted text of Leviticus ("4QPentateuch," 395, 399). Yet, as noted by Tov ("From 4QReworked Pentateuch," 85), neither is this solution entirely satisfactory since there is evidence in at least one case that the text standing between two combined passages could be relocated elsewhere in the manuscript. Due to the highly fragmentary nature of these two manuscripts, it is difficult to provide a cogent explanation for this relocation of Leviticus materials in 4Q366 and 367. In any event, this scribal phenomenon is not attested in the case of 4Q365 (4QRP[c]), which is the focus of the present essay.

9. Tov and White, "4Q365," 290–93 with pl. XXVIII. The translation provided here is my own, although it differs only slightly from the one initially offered by Tov and White.

Supplementing Leviticus in the Second Temple Period 187

7 [ ]ם[לפסחים ולשלמים ולתודות ולנדבות ולעולות דבר יום] ביומו [--]
8 [--]ל[ ] ל[ ] ל[ ]מים ולד[ל]תות ולכול מלאכת הבית יקרי]בו [--]
9 [-- מ]ועד היצהר יקריבו את העצים שנים [שנים --]
10 [--]י המקריבים ביום הריש[ו]ן לוי [--]
11 [-- ראו]בן ושמעון וב[יום הרב]יעי [--]
12 [--]ל[--]

1 You shall dwell in [boo]ths for seven days: every native in Israel shall dwell in booths, so [that] your ge[nerations] [will kno]w
2 that I made your fathers dwell in [bo]oths when I brought them from the land of Eg[y]pt: I am Yhwh, your go[d].
3 [ ] And (thus) Moses declared the festivals of Yhwh to the Israelites.
4 Yhwh spoke to Moses: Command the Israelites as follows: When you enter into the land that
5 I am giving to you for an inheritance, and you dwell upon it securely, you shall bring wood for a burnt offering and for all the wor[k] of
6 [the h]ouse which you will build for me in the land, arranging it upon the altar of burnt offerings, and the calv[es
7 [ ]m for passover sacrifices, for peace offerings, for thank offerings, for freewill offerings and for whole burnt offerings, daily [
8 [ ] and for the doors and for all the work of the house the[y] shall br[ing
9 [ ] the [fe]stival of new oil. They will bring wood two [
10] the ones who bring on the fir[st] day, Levi [
11 Reu]ben and Simeon [and on t]he fou[rth] day [
12]l[

The fragment begins in lines 1–3 with a text that corresponds to Lev 23:42–44, the final instructions for the celebration of Sukkot, which conclude the festal calendar of Lev 23.[10] The text continues in line 4 with a new divine address to Moses, which reproduces for its part Lev 24:1–2a. But instead of introducing the command to bring oil for the luminary as in Lev 24:1–4, the following lines of the fragment provide an instruction for the bringing of wood to the temple (הבית). Although the description of the ceremony is only partly preserved, several details are clear. Lines 5–8 describe the use to which the wood is put: it is employed for the burning of various sacrifices, enumerated in lines 6–7, as well as for "all the work

---

10. The fragment shows only one significant variant from the text of Lev 23:42–44 preserved in the MT and the LXX: in line 2 it reads הושבתי את אבותיכם, "I made your *fathers* dwell," instead of "I made the Israelites (את־בני ישראל) dwell," as in the MT and the LXX. Additionally, line 1 of the fragment reads כל־האזרח בישראל ישב בסכת, with the verb in the singular, whereas the corresponding passage in Lev 23:42b has the verb in the plural (ישבו).

of the house" (כול מלאכת הבית, lines 5–6 and 8), which presumably refers here to the repair of various wooden structures of the temple such as the "doors" (ד[ל]תות) mentioned in line 8.[11] Lines 9–11 apparently refer to the bringing of the wood by the Israelite tribes in the course of a ceremony extending over several days, since line 10 mentions the "first day" and line 11 the "fourth day."

Because the fragment is badly damaged at this point, it is difficult to be more explicit about the nature of this ceremony. Nevertheless, the statement found at the end of line 9, יקריבו את העצים שנים, "they will bring wood two [...]," as well as the joint reference to Reuben and Simeon in line 11, may be taken to indicate that the wood is to be brought by two different tribes every day (with Levi and another tribe on the first day, and Reuben and Simeon on the fourth), in which case the text would envision a ceremony extending over six consecutive days. What seems clear, at any rate, is that the bringing of wood to the temple is expected to take place at a fixed point in the year, and not randomly. This conclusion is further supported by the connection established in line 9 between the bringing of wood to the temple and the festival of new oil (מועד היצהר). It is unlikely that the text of 4Q365 23, which focuses on the wood offering, provided further details about the festival of new oil.[12] Rather, it seems that the mention of this festival here serves as a chronological marker for the celebration involving the bringing of wood to the sanctuary. This conclusion, in turn, implies that we should classify this fragment as an instruction for the offering of wood (*not* for the offering of wood and oil, as has sometimes been suggested). Although the technical term קרבן does not occur in the extant fragment, the nature of the description as well as some of the terminology used—especially the verb קרב in lines 5 and 8—strongly support the notion that the bringing of wood is conceived of here as an offering. This conclusion is also consistent with two passages of Nehemiah, 10:35 and 13:31, which may represent the earliest evidence for this type of offering and which already reference it as קרבן העצים or "wood offering."[13]

---

11. This is the general understanding of the phrase "all the work of the house" in this fragment; compare, e.g., Cana Werman, "The Wood-Offering: The Convoluted Evolution of a Halakhah in Qumran and Rabbinic Law," in *New Perspectives on Old Texts: Proceedings of the Tenth International Symposium of the Orion Center for the Study of the Dead Sea Scrolls and Associated Literature, 9–11 January, 2005*, ed. Esther G. Chazon and Betsy Halpern-Amaru, STDJ 88 (Leiden: Brill, 2010), 151–81, here 157.

12. As pointed out, in particular, by Zahn, *Rethinking Rewritten Scripture*, 108 with n. 75. Zahn remarks that the mention of the festival of new oil in 4Q365 frag. 23 "makes it sound like this feast has already been discussed," which supports the suggestion that a description of the provision of oil was located elsewhere in 4Q365.

13. I am grateful to Marc Brettler for drawing my attention to this issue during the discussion of an earlier draft of this paper at the Brown symposium in May 2016. In the Priestly texts of the Pentateuch, the term קרבן primarily refers to animals or cereals brought to be sacrificed on the altar (e.g., Lev 1:2; 2:1; 3:1; etc.). Occasionally, however, it may also include

Supplementing Leviticus in the Second Temple Period 189

The obligation to bring wood to the temple is unparalleled in the other manuscripts of Leviticus, although a similar instruction may already have been known by the author of Neh 10:31–40 (more on this below). It is difficult to understand how and why this passage would have been omitted from all the other versions of Leviticus; in all likelihood, therefore, it represents a supplement to the festal legislation of this book.[14] This conclusion is also supported by the placement of this offering after the festal legislation of Lev 23. As noted above, the reference to the festival of new oil (מועד היצהר) in line 9 appears to indicate that the scribe who composed 4Q365 envisioned the wood offering as taking place at a fixed point in the year, even though no date is effectively preserved for this festival in the extant text of the fragment. The fact that this offering was not introduced in the festal legislation of Lev 23, as one would expect, but was appended to it *after* the subscription in Lev 23:44 (reproduced in line 3 of 4Q365 23), corroborates the view that the offering of wood described in 4Q365 is not integral to the festal legislation of Leviticus but was introduced at a later stage.[15] Finally, this conclusion is likewise consistent with the observation that the formulation of this fragment shows some features that are distinctive of Late Biblical Hebrew, such as the tendency toward plene spellings,[16] or the introduction of some late forms and idioms.[17]

---

sacred donations to the temple; compare, e.g., Num 31:50. In Num 7, both uses of the term (for sacrifices and for sacred donations) stand side by side. Hence, the fact that the wood is not a sacrifice proper but is intended for the maintenance of the altar fire and the repair of the sanctuary does not preclude that this donation could be classified as a קרבן, as is already the case in Neh 10:35 and 13:31. On the relationship between 4Q365 frag. 23 and Nehemiah, see below.

14. In theory, if we assume that the instruction for the wood offering was followed in 4Q365 by the command to bring oil for the luminary (= Lev 24:2b–4), and that this command was introduced by the repetition of the divine instruction to Moses corresponding to Lev 24:1–2a, we could hypothesize that the instruction for the wood offering was omitted as the result of parablepsis. Given the fact, however, that the instruction for the wood offering is missing in all the other manuscripts of Leviticus, this reconstruction seems rather implausible.

15. A similar point has already been made by Zahn, *Rethinking Rewritten Scripture*, 108. By contrast, the instructions found in Lev 24:1–9, following the subscription in 23:44, concern not annual festivals but other types of donations to the temple brought during the year. Note, in addition, that according to the calendrical document 4Q327 the festival of new oil, with which the wood offering is already connected in 4Q365 frag. 23 (see line 9), took place on the twenty-second day of the sixth month. Therefore, if the wood offering was an integral part of the festal legislation of Leviticus, it should arguably have been mentioned before the Feast of Sukkot (beginning on the fifteenth day of the seventh month), and not after it.

16. E.g., סוכות (consistently written with two *matres lectionis*) in lines 1 and 2 instead of סכת or סכות in 23:42, 43 MT; אלוהיכם (line 2) instead of אלהיכם in 23:43 MT; מועדי in line 3 instead of מעדי in 23:44 MT; etc.

17. In particular, note the form לכמה in line 5 (instead of the classical form לכם), as well as the reference in line 7 to the פסחים (Passover sacrifices); this idiom is never found in the Pentateuch but occurs for the first time in Chronicles: see 2 Chr 30:17; 35:7, 8, 9.

The placement of the instruction for the wood offering after the festal legislation of Lev 23 raises further questions regarding the relationship between this legal supplement and the materials comprising Lev 24:1–9, some of which are difficult to answer given the fragmentary nature of 4Q365.[18] It seems at least likely that the connection between the wood offering and the festival of new oil mentioned in line 9 explains why this legal supplement was introduced after the text corresponding to Lev 24:1–2a, since in the other Leviticus manuscripts Lev 24:1–2a is already followed by the command to bring "oil made of pure olives" (שמן זית זך) to the sanctuary (24:2b).[19] In addition, the fact that the wood offering was introduced in 4Q365 in place of the material corresponding to Lev 24:2b–4 may suggest that the scribe responsible for this addition identified the command to bring oil for the luminary as a legal precedent of sorts for the communal obligation to provide wood for the sanctuary. Whether the command to bring oil found in Lev 24:2b–4 was preserved in 4Q365—in which case it presumably followed the instruction for the wood offering—or whether it was replaced by new instructions related to the festival of new oil is, however, impossible to know. In any event, the fact that the author of 4Q365 reused Lev 24:1–2a to introduce the instruction of the wood offering indicates that this legal supplement, while appended to the festal legislation of Lev 23, was nevertheless considered to enjoy a degree of authority similar to that of the other feasts divinely ordained to Moses in Leviticus, even though its relationship to both the festal calendar in Lev 23 and the additional instructions in Lev 24:1–9 remains somewhat unclear due to the fragmentary nature of 4Q365 at this point.

III. The Composition of the Legal Supplement

Having clarified the way in which the legal supplement comprising the wood offering was added to the version of Leviticus represented by 4Q365, we may now look more closely at the way in which this supplement was composed. The editors of this fragment, Tov and White, already pointed out that the fragment is exceptional within 4Q365—and even within the Reworked Pentateuch manuscripts in general—for the way in which it introduces new, nonbiblical material into the legislation of the Pentateuch.[20] While other significant additions are preserved in 4Q365,

---

18. On the material preserved in Lev 24:1–9 as an appendix of sorts to the festal legislation of Lev 23, see my discussion in *From Priestly Torah to Pentateuch: A Study in the Composition of Leviticus*, FAT 2/25 (Tübingen: Mohr Siebeck, 2007), 511–12. On the relationship between 4Q365 frag. 23 and Lev 24:1–9, see also the brief remarks by J. Milgrom, "Qumran's Biblical Hermeneutics: The Case of the Wood Offering," *RQ* 16 (1994): 449–56, here 454.

19. As argued, in particular, by Zahn *Rethinking Rewritten Scripture*, 108.

20. Tov and White, "4Q365," 293.

such additions are usually based on a motif already found in the Pentateuch, which they develop and amplify.[21] This observation is correct on the topical level, since the obligation to bring wood to the sanctuary is unparalleled in any other version of the Pentateuch (although, as we will see below, the description of 4Q365 23 has a close parallel in the Temple Scroll). At the same time, however, the issue is more complex because the wood offering in this fragment is composed with terminology that effectively connects this legal supplement with various texts in the Pentateuch as well as in other scriptural traditions. This question therefore deserves a brief reexamination.[22]

The influence of other scriptural traditions is particularly clear in the opening lines of the fragment. As noted above, lines 1–3 reproduce Lev 23:42–44 with almost no substantial changes. Lines 4–5, for their part, reproduce Lev 24:1–2a but combine this passage with a long temporal clause that precedes the instruction for the wood offering proper:

בבואכמה אל הארץ אשר אנוכי נותן לכמה לנחלה וישבתם עליה לבטח
When you enter into the land that I am giving to you for an inheritance, and you dwell upon it securely ...

This temporal clause has no equivalent in Lev 24:1–4 but is clearly reminiscent of the phraseology used in other parts of the Pentateuch. Specifically, various authors have suggested that the first part of this clause has its closest equivalent in Deut 26:1.[23] While this parallel is certainly significant, the matter is in fact more complex. The designation of the land as נחלה ("inheritance") is typical of Deuteronomy (whereas it is never found in Leviticus)[24] and therefore indisputably supports the claim that the for-

---

21. A case in point is the Song of Miriam preserved in 4Q365 frag. 6, which expands on the short notice found in Exod 15:21. On this, see G. Brooke, "Power to the Powerless: A Long-Lost Song of Miriam," *BAR* 20 (1994): 62–65.

22. Although this point has often been noted by scholars, there are still few comprehensive discussions about the reuse of scriptural language in 4Q365 frag. 23. See esp. David Carr, "Method in Determination of Direction of Dependence: An Empirical Test of Criteria Applied to Exodus 34,11–26 and Its Parallels," in *Gottes Volk am Sinai: Untersuchungen zu Ex 32–34 und Dtn 9–10*, ed. Matthias Köckert and Erhard Blum, VWGTh 18 (Gütersloh: Kaiser, 2001), 107–40, here 117; as well as Zahn, *Rethinking Rewritten Scripture*, 102–8. Julia Rhyder also provides a detailed discussion of the main intertextual connections between 4Q365 frag. 23 and other scriptural traditions ("'The Temple Which You Will Build for Me in the Land,'" *DSD* 24 [2017]: 271–300).

23. See esp. Carr, "Method in Determination," 117; Zahn, *Rethinking Rewritten Scripture*, 103.

24. In addition to Deut 26:1, see esp. Deut 4:21; 15:4; 19:10; 24:4; 25:19, where we find the same formulation. References to the land as נחלה can also be found in Numbers, but not as part of the same formula (i.e., "the land that Yhwh, your god, has given to you for an inheritance").

mulation of 4Q365 23 has a passage such as Deut 26:1 in mind. The use of the first person singular, however, in the context of divine speeches referring to the gift of the land (with אני/אנכי followed by the participle of נתן) is not typical of Deuteronomy, since Deuteronomy almost exclusively refers to Yhwh indirectly in such contexts.[25] Instead, such usage is characteristic of Leviticus, and, moreover, it is already found in two passages, Lev 23:10 and 25:2, that form the immediate context of the festal legislation to which the law of the wood offering has been added. This observation suggests that the first part of the temporal clause found in lines 4–5 of 4Q365 23 should be identified as a deliberate conflation of Lev 23:10 + 25:2 with Deut 26:1.[26]

כי־תבאו אל־הארץ אשר אני נתן לכם (Lev 23:10 + 25:2)
כי־תבוא אל־הארץ אשר יהוה אלהיך נתן לך נחלה (Deut 26:1)
בבואכמה אל הארץ אשר אנוכי נותן לכמה לנחלה (5–4 ,23 4Q365)

The reference to Lev 23:10 and Deut 26:1 is particularly interesting because these two passages introduce the laws of the firstfruits of the land in Leviticus and Deuteronomy (see Lev 23:9–22 and Deut 26:1–11). This observation suggests that Lev 23:10 and Deut 26:1 were retained as the scriptural basis for the introduction of the wood offering in 4Q365 23 because the author of this text wanted to associate the offering of the wood with the offering of the firstfruits. Significantly, a similar connection with the firstfruits is suggested by one passage in Nehemiah (Neh 13:31), and it may also be implied by the Temple Scroll.[27]

The second part of the temporal clause found in 4Q365 23, 4–5, וישבתם

---

25. See the passages of Deuteronomy mentioned in the previous note. The only exception concerns Deut 32:49, 52, precisely a passage that is traditionally assigned to the "Priestly" portions of Deuteronomy.

26. From a redaction-critical perspective, the proximity of these three passages corresponds to the fact that Deut 26:1 was arguably the source for both Lev 23:10 and 25:2; see, e.g., Klaus Grünwaldt, *Das Heiligkeitsgesetz Leviticus 17–26: Ursprüngliche Gestalt, Tradition und Theologie*, BZAW 271 (Berlin: de Gruyter, 1999), 287–88. In addition, the fact that 4Q365 frag. 23 uses the verbal construction בבואכמה instead of the construction formed by בוא + כי yiqtol as in Lev 23:10; 25:2; and Deut 26:1, could possibly reflect the influence of Num 15:18, the only passage in the Hebrew Bible to preserve the same verbal construction followed by a reference to the entrance into the land (but not to the gift of the land by Yhwh). In this specific instance, however, it is difficult to decide whether the parallel is intentional or merely coincidental.

27. Nehemiah 13:31 mentions the joint reestablishment by Nehemiah of "the wood offering at its appointed times" (קרבן העצים בעתים מזמנות) and of the "firstfruits" (בכורים). The main copy of the Temple Scroll, 11Q19 (11QT^a), mentions the feast of the new oil as the last in a series of firstfruits festivals; the feast of the new oil is itself followed by a six-day festival (11Q19 XXIII), which may be identified with the feast of the wood offering. See on this below. For a general presentation of the firstfruits festivals in Temple Scroll, see Yigael Yadin, *The Temple Scroll*, 3 vols. (Jerusalem: Israel Exploration Society, 1977–1983), 1:99–122.

עליה לבטח, has a close parallel in Lev 25:18, 19 and arguably represents a further allusion to the jubilee legislation.²⁸ An alternative solution was recently argued by Zahn; for her, this clause corresponds in fact to Deut 12:9–11, which mentions the obligation for the Israelites to bring their offerings to the מקום, the central place, after Yhwh has delivered them from their enemies so that they can "dwell securely" in the land (וישבתם-בטח, cf. Deut 12:10). This explanation depends on her larger argument that 4Q365 23 refers shortly afterward to the building of the temple in the land (line 6: "the house which you will build for me in the land"), which she interprets as a reference to Deuteronomy's law of centralization.²⁹ There is arguably something correct to this view, inasmuch as Deuteronomy's law of centralization is the only tradition in the Pentateuch that provides detailed instructions for the post-wilderness cult. Nonetheless, there are also some difficulties with this argument.³⁰ To begin with, the formulation וישבתם עליה לבטח in 4Q365 23, 5 has a closer parallel in Lev 25:18, 19 than in Deut 12:10. As a matter of fact, within the pentateuchal traditions the use of the phrase לבטח (and not just בטח) with the verb ישב is unique to Leviticus.³¹ Second, the reference to the building of a sanctuary in the land in line 6 of 4Q365 23 shows no connection with Deuteronomy's law of centralization. While Deuteronomy refers to the divine "choice" (with the verb בחר) of a central "place" (מקום), 4Q365 23 does not use this language and mentions instead the building (בנה) of a "house" (בית).³² The use of the term בית to refer to a sanctuary in the land occurs in two passages of Exodus, 23:19 and 34:26, where this term is used in connection with the obligation for the Israelites to bring the "choicest firstfruits of your land" (ראשית בכורי אדמתך) to "the temple of Yhwh your god" (בית יהוה אלהיך). A more significant connection, however, is with the oracle of Nathan to David in 2 Sam 7, which refers to the temple of Jerusalem as the "house"

---

28. As noted, e.g., by Tov and White, "4Q365," 295; Carr, "Method of Determination," 117.

29. Zahn, *Rethinking Rewritten Scripture*, 103–4.

30. My discussion at this point is indebted to the recent and excellent reexamination of this issue by Rhyder, "Temple Which You Will Build," 283–95, even though my own argument occasionally differs from hers.

31. Furthermore, while the construction ישב + לבטח can be found in some passages of the Hebrew Bible outside of the Pentateuch, the specific construction used here in 4Q365 23, with ישב על + a reference to the land followed by לבטח, occurs exclusively in Lev 25:18, 19 as well as in one passage of Ezekiel (28:26).

32. Note, in addition, that the terms מקום and בית are not simply synonymous, since מקום in Deuteronomy appears to refer to a larger structure than just a temple. Some passages of Kings, which refer to Jerusalem as the city that was "chosen" by Yhwh, may even be taken to imply that, for the authors of Kings, the city as a whole, and not just the temple, was identified with the "place" chosen by Yhwh in Deuteronomy (see 1 Kgs 8:16, 44, 48; 11:32, 36; 14:21; and 2 Kgs 23:27).

(בית) which the king will build (בנה) "for me [Yhwh]" (2 Sam 7:5; cf. 7:13).³³ It is therefore possible that the somewhat unique reference to "the house which you will build for me in the land" is specifically intended, in 4Q365, to connect the cultic legislation of Leviticus with the tradition of the royal temple built in Jerusalem by Solomon.³⁴ In any event, 4Q365 23 arguably represents the first known attempt to connect the wilderness cultic legislation with the First Temple in the Pentateuch itself.³⁵ If it is accepted that 4Q365ª was, in fact, part of the same manuscript, then 4Q365 even contained detailed instructions for the building of this temple and the various rituals to be performed there.³⁶ A similar concern to introduce into the Torah instructions for the building of the temple is witnessed in the Temple Scroll, which arguably continues the scribal development of this theme in 4Q365.³⁷

While the influence of other scriptural traditions is particularly evident in the introduction to the wood offering (lines 4–6), a similar phenomenon can be observed in the description of the offering itself. In particular, as noted by Cana Werman, lines 9–11, referring to the tribes bringing the wood offering on several successive days, are reminiscent of the ceremony recounted in Num 7 describing the donations made by the tribal chieftains at the dedication of the tabernacle.³⁸ Despite some significant differences,³⁹ the obvious parallel between the ceremonies described in Num

---

33. I owe this observation to Saul Olyan, who pointed out this parallel in the discussion at the Brown symposium in May 2016.

34. This conclusion is consistent with Zahn's argument (*Rethinking Rewritten Scripture*, 104) that 4Q365 23 would further allude to 1 Kgs 5:5, a passage that describes the period in which Solomon was able to build the temple, with the following words: וישב יהודה וישראל לבטח. While the parallel may not be very strong, it certainly fits the overall argument presented here.

35. On this general issue, see now the comprehensive discussion by Rhyder, "Temple Which You Will Build."

36. On this question, see the recent reexamination of the manuscript and literary evidence by Sidnie White Crawford, "4QTemple? (4Q365a) Revisited," in *Prayer and Poetry in the Dead Sea Scrolls and Related Literature: Essays in Honor of Eileen Schuller on the Occasion of Her 65th Birthday*, ed. Jeremy Penner, Ken M. Penner and Cecilia Wassen, STDJ 98 (Leiden: Brill, 2012), 87–95. 4Q365ª frag. 2, in particular, preserves instructions for the day of firstfruits, which are followed in the next column by a description of the outer gates of the temple.

37. See esp. 11QT III–XIII and XXX–XLVI, where detailed divine commands, which are partly modeled after the commands given to Moses for the tabernacle in Exod 25–31, are now provided for the building of the temple in the land. Compare the comments already made by Yadin, *Temple Scroll*, 1:178–82.

38. Werman, "Wood-Offering," 157.

39. In particular, Num 7 describes a twelve-day ceremony during which each of the tribes presents its offering in turn, whereas 4Q365 23 apparently refers to the tribes presenting their offerings two by two. If we assume that 4Q365 23 has in view the twelve tribes (which seems logical), the ceremony would therefore extend over a set period of six days, instead of the twelve days mentioned in Num 7. Tentatively, one may wonder whether the

7 and 4Q365 23 makes it likely that the description of Num 7 served as a scriptural precedent for the ceremony of the wood offering in 4Q365. This conclusion is further supported by the observation that the verb קרב is already consistently used in Num 7 in connection with nonsacrifical offerings to the sanctuary, as is also the case with the wood offering in 4Q365 23 (see lines 5 and 8).[40] Another parallel with the cultic legislation of the Pentateuch concerns the expression לכול מלאכת הבית, which occurs twice in 4Q365 23 (lines 5–6 and 8). A similar expression is already used several times in the account of the building of the tabernacle in Exod 35–40; in two passages, specifically, it occurs in the context of the sacred donations that the builders receive from the Israelite community (Exod 36:3 and 38:24 MT).[41] This parallel is all the more significant since, as noted above, the wood offering in 4Q365 23 serves not merely for the maintenance of the fire on the altar but also for the repairs of the temple. As such, the use of the expression לכול מלאכת הבית in 4Q365 23 points to the fact that the offering of wood to the temple by the Israelite tribes is somehow continuous with the previous donations of the Israelite community at the time when the tabernacle was built. Finally, the enumeration in line 7 (לפסחים ולשלמים ולתודות ולנדבות ולעולות) is likewise reminiscent of similar lists enumerating the various types of sacrifices that may legitimately be burnt on the altar. The closest parallel appears to be with the lists found in Num 15, which already mention the whole burnt offering (עלה) and the peace offering (שלמים) in connection with the נדבה and the נדר, two categories of offerings related to vows. In 4Q365 23, this list has been supplemented with the תודה ("thank offering") and the Passover sacrifices.[42]

In conclusion, the previous discussion sheds some light on the scribal techniques used in the composition of 4Q365 23. While this fragment introduces a new legal topic—the wood offering—it does so by reusing several scriptural texts, arguably more than has been previously recognized. Three points, in particular, emerge from this reexamination of the evidence.

First, the analysis confirms the general view that the law of the wood

---

transformation from a twelve-day to a six-day ceremony might reflect the attempt to avoid having one of the tribes bringing its offering of wood on the Sabbath.

40. For this nonsacrificial use of קרב in Num 7, see esp. 7:3, 10, 11, 12, 18, 19; and compare also the repeated use, in this chapter, of the term קרבן to refer to both sacrificial and nonsacrificial offerings for the tabernacle. By contrast, other passages of the Priestly legislation referring to sacred donations to the sanctuary, such as the description of the תרומה in Exod 25:2–7 and Exod 35, do not use this verb.

41. This point is aptly noted by Rhyder, "Temple Which You Will Build," 287.

42. The addition of the thank offering, in particular, is logical since in the law of Lev 7:11–21 the תודה and the נדבה are already presented as two subcategories of the שלמים. The reason why 4Q365 23, 7 enumerates the whole burnt offering at the end of the list, rather than at the beginning as is usually the case, escapes me entirely.

offering in 4Q365 23 has been introduced in lines 4–5 by drawing on various passages in Leviticus and Deuteronomy. The relationship between these two pentateuchal sources in 4Q365 23, however, needs to be reevaluated. A clear case of conflation between Leviticus and Deuteronomy is represented by the first part of the temporal clause introducing the wood offering ("When you enter into the land that I am giving to you for an inheritance"), which combines Lev 23:10 and 25:2 with Deut 26:1. This phenomenon may be viewed as a further example of the general trend in pre-Samaritan manuscripts to align Leviticus and Numbers with Deuteronomy where possible.[43] At the same time, however, the previous analysis also shows that references to Deuteronomy are limited to Deut 26:1, and that the main scriptural references are in fact borrowed from the festal legislation in Lev 23–25[44]—a point that has been insufficiently recognized in the discussion so far.

Second, the previous analysis highlights the fact that the reuse of scriptural traditions in 4Q365 23 is not limited to the introduction of the law of the wood offering in lines 4–5, as has sometimes been assumed, but likewise characterizes the contents of this law in the following lines. While the discussion of this issue is complicated by the fact that the fragment is seriously damaged from line 8 onward, there is at least some evidence suggesting that the description of the wood offering in 4Q365 was influenced by the previous descriptions found in Exod 35–40 (the building of the tabernacle) as well as in Num 7 (the offerings of the tribal chieftains at the dedication of the tabernacle). Both texts arguably served as a legal precedent for the new ritual instructions presented in this fragment.

Third, and most important, the analysis suggests that the selection of scriptural references in 4Q365 23 is not random but strategic and that it points to some significant associations between the wood offering and other offerings. In particular, as noted above, the combination of Lev 23:10 and Deut 26:1 in lines 4–5 suggests a connection between the wood offering and the firstfruits festival, which seems to be similarly implied in Nehemiah and the Temple Scroll.[45] The connections with Exod 35–40 and Num 7, for their part, suggest that the obligation for the community

---

43. As observed, in particular, by Sidnie White Crawford, "The Pentateuch as Found in the Pre-Samaritan Texts and 4QReworked Pentateuch," in *Changes in Scripture: Rewriting and Interpreting Authoritative Traditions in the Second Temple Period*, ed. Hanne von Weissenberg, Juha Pakkala, and Marko Marttila, BZAW 419 (Berlin: de Gruyter, 2011), 123–36, here 123–24.

44. Namely, Lev 24:1-2a; 23:10 + 25:2; 25:18-19. See above. This conclusion is consistent with the argument developed by Rhyder ("Temple Which You Will Build," 290.

45. Additionally, the decision to introduce the law of the wood offering after Lev 24:1–2a may similarly serve to highlight the connection between the wood offering and the obligation for the Israelites to bring oil to the sanctuary (Lev 24:1–4). This connection is itself consistent with the reference to the feast of the new oil in line 9 of 4Q365 23 and is further supported by the Temple Scroll (see below).

to bring wood to the sanctuary is somehow continuous with the earlier situation of the wilderness community, which was likewise obligated to contribute to the tabernacle at the time of its building (Exod 35–40) and its dedication (Num 7). Finally, the reference to "the house which you will build for me" is unique in the Pentateuch and apparently serves to link the wood offering with the situation of the community *post* wilderness. The closest parallel for this expression, as noted above, is in 2 Sam 7, which may suggest a connection with the royal temple of Jerusalem specifically.

IV. The Origins of the Wood Offering in 4Q365

While the wood offering is not mentioned in any other manuscript of the Pentateuch, a similar ceremony is known from other ancient Jewish sources. A comprehensive discussion of the origins of the wood offering and its development is beyond the scope of this short essay. In what follows, I will limit myself to a few comments regarding the way in which other relevant materials shed some light on the origins of the wood offering in 4Q365 specifically.[46]

A regular offering of wood to the temple in the context of a festival is mentioned in Josephus, *J.W.* 2.17.6 §425, where it is designated as ξυλοφόριον, "the [feast of] wood-carrying." The wood offering is mentioned also in some passages in rabbinic literature (Megillat Ta'anit 4:5, in particular).[47] While these sources raise several interpretive issues, they appear to document the fact that the wood offering was well known by the end of the Second Temple period. For the earlier period, apart from 4Q365, our main evidence is provided by two passages from Nehemiah (10:35 and 13:31), as well as by some passages from the Temple Scroll.[48] The main copy of the Temple Scroll, 11Q19 (11QTª), mentions the wood offering at the end of a list of feast days upon which the tithe may be eaten (XLIII, 3–4). A further reference to the wood offering is found in another copy of the Temple Scroll (11Q20 VI = frag. 10e), which appears to describe a ceremony similar to the one mentioned in 4Q365 23, 9–11 since the wood is to be brought by the twelve tribes on consecutive days.[49] Moreover, it is pos-

---

46. For a comprehensive discussion of the origins and development of the wood offering in the Second Temple period and beyond, see Werman, "Wood Offering." Some aspects of this reconstruction are questionable in my view, but this issue cannot be addressed here.

47. For the wood offering in rabbinic literature, see esp. Werman, "Wood Offering," 167–74.

48. In addition, one passage of Jubilees, chapter 21, refers to the types of wood that are appropriate to offer for the burning of sacrifices.

49. The parallel between 4Q365 23 and this fragment of 11Q20 (11QTᵇ) has been noted by various authors; see Tov and White, "4Q365," 293, as well as Zahn, *Rethinking Rewritten Scripture*, 105–6.

sible that the ceremony mentioned in this small fragment belongs to the description of the six-day festival following the feast of new oil described in 11Q19 (11QT^a) XXIII, which should then be identified with the festival of wood offering.[50] If this reconstruction is valid (and there are some reasons to believe it is), it would provide further confirmation that 4Q365 23 and the Temple Scroll envision a similar festival taking place shortly after the feast of new oil and extending over the same period of six consecutive days, during which the twelve tribes—two tribes per day—were to bring wood to the temple.[51]

The references to the wood offering in Nehemiah and their potential implications for the origins of 4Q365 23 have been the subject of much scholarly discussion lately, and therefore deserve a longer discussion. In Neh 13, Nehemiah claims that, along with various reforms during his second stay in Jerusalem, he established (or reestablished?) the service of the Levites (v. 30) together with the wood offering (קרבן העצים) and the offering of the firstfruits (v. 31). If this passage is considered to be part of Nehemiah's "memoir" (which some scholars, however, would question), it may indicate that the wood offering was already known in the Persian period, although the details of this ceremony remain impossible to reconstruct on the basis of this single mention. Nevertheless, the fact that the reference to the wood offering in v. 31 is followed by the mention בעתים מזמנות, "at their appointed times" (plural) seems to indicate that this offering was not yet part of a single annual festival (as in both 4Q365 and the Temple Scroll) but was brought at different times in the year. The most interesting piece of evidence for the origins of the legislation preserved in 4Q365 23, however, is provided by another passage, Neh 10:35, which already mentions the wood offering in connection with the Mosaic law.

---

50. For this view, see Yadin, *Temple Scroll*, 1:222–24. This reconstruction has now been accepted by various authors; compare, e.g., Werman, "Wood-Offering," 158–59; Zahn, *Rethinking Rewritten Scripture*, 105–6. It is supported by the observation that the small fragment of 11Q20 (11QT^b) VI appears to fit into the lacuna at the top of column XXIII in 11Q19 (11QT^a); in particular, the words עזים שנים, "two goats," in 11QT^b overlap with line 4 of 11QT^a XXIII.

51. The parallel between 4Q365 and 11QT^a XXIII is all the more significant because the extant order for the twelve tribes that is preserved in these two documents appears to be identical, whereas it is not attested elsewhere in ancient Jewish traditions (as noted by Tov and White, "4Q365," 293).

Neh 10:35[52]

והגורלות הפלנו על־קרבן העצים הכהנים הלוים והעם להביא לבית אלהינו לבית־
אבתינו לעתים מזמנים שנה בשנה לבער על־מזבח יהוה אלהינו ככתוב בתורה

We have also cast lots regarding the offering of wood [קרבן
העצים] — the priests, the Levites, and the people — to bring it to the
house of our god, by ancestral houses, at fixed times [לעתים מזמנים]
year by year, to burn upon the altar of Yhwh our god as it is written in the Torah [ככתוב בתורה].

This passage is part of a list of stipulations in Neh 10:31–40 enumerating various commitments made by the community, most of which concern
obligations toward the temple (see vv. 33–40). While most scholars agree
that Neh 10:35 is significant for its claim that the Torah prescribes the wood
offering, the interpretation of this motif remains a matter of debate. Some
authors have inferred from this passage that the legislation on the wood
offering preserved in 4Q365 23 was already part of the Pentateuch at the
time of Nehemiah.[53] Others, on the contrary, have argued that the reference
to the offering of wood "as it is written in the Torah" (ככתוב בתורה) has no
scriptural basis but reflects a strategy to justify a ritual innovation; later,
this innovation would have led to the introduction of the corresponding
legislation in the version of the Pentateuch preserved by 4Q365.[54] In my
view, both arguments are questionable.

---

52. My translation follows the MT. The Greek text of Neh 10:35 is largely similar. The main difference concerns the fact that the Greek text mentions that the priests, the Levites, and the people cast the lots "regarding the office of wood-carrying" (περὶ κλήρου ξυλοφορίας), instead of the "offering of wood" as in the MT. Whether this variant formulation may effectively reflect the practice known by the Greek translator of Nehemiah in the second (?) century BCE is difficult to determine, although this is certainly an intriguing possibility. For a view of the relationship between Neh 10 and 4Q365 23 similar to the one presented here, see also now Rhyder, "Temple Which You Will Build," 278–80.

53. For a maximal version of this argument, see Armin Lange who concludes on the basis of Neh 10:35 that 4Q365 would actually represent the version of the Pentateuch that was known to Nehemiah himself ("The Dead Sea Scrolls and the Date of the Final Stage of the Pentateuch," in *On Stone and Scroll: Essays in Honour of Graham Ivor Davies*, ed. James K. Aitken, Katharine J. Dell, and Brian A. Mastin, BZAW 420 [Berlin: de Gruyter, 2011], 287–304). For a similar argument, see also Milgrom, "Qumran's Biblical Hermeneutics," 449–56; as well as Hannah K. Harrington, "The Use of Leviticus in Ezra-Nehemiah," *JHebS* 13 (2013): 1–20, here 17–19, http://www.jhsonline.org/Articles/article_183.pdf.

54. For this argument, see esp. Sidnie White Crawford and Christopher A. Hoffmann, "A Note on 4Q365, Frg. 23 and Nehemiah 10:33–36," *RQ* 23 (2008): 429–30; Werman, "Wood-Offering," 151–53, 157–58; Zahn, *Rethinking Rewritten Scripture*, 107–8. Compare also Hindy Najman, "Torah of Moses: Pseudonymous Attribution in Second Temple Writings," in *The Interpretation of Scripture in Early Judaism and Christianity: Studies in Language and Tradition*, ed. Craig A. Evans, JSPSup 33, SSEJC 7 (Sheffield: Sheffield Academic, 2000), 202–16.

On the one hand, the notion that Neh 10:35 would be referring to a law identical to the one preserved in 4Q365 23 does not do justice to the many differences that can be observed between the two texts. In effect, the procedure described in Neh 10 is markedly distinct from the one referenced in 4Q365. Whereas 4Q365 apparently envisions the bringing of wood by the twelve tribes in the course of a six-day festival taking place after the feast of new oil (see above), Neh 10 refers to an entirely different procedure involving the casting of lots by the "ancestral houses" (בית אבות). The purpose of the casting of lots in this context is not entirely clear, but a likely assumption is that it serves to determine the order in which the ancestral houses were to bring their offering of wood to the temple of Jerusalem during the year. At any rate, in Neh 13:31 the reference to the offering of wood at "fixed" or "appointed" times (לעתים מזמנים) appears to imply several occasions in the year rather than a single, annual ceremony. Last but not least, there is also a significant difference regarding the use of the wood in both texts. In 4Q365, the purpose of the wood offering is for both the maintenance of the fire on the altar and the "work of the house," that is, the various repairs of the temple itself (4Q365 23, 5–6 and 8; see above). In Neh 10, by contrast, only the first usage is considered (compare the expression לבער על־מזבח). Taken together, these differences make it highly unlikely, in my opinion, that Neh 10:35 has in view the legislation preserved in 4Q365 23 specifically.

On the other hand, the notion that a passage such as Neh 10:35 would have provided the scriptural basis for the introduction of the law of the wood offering in 4Q365 likewise faces some significant difficulties. To begin with, the various attempts that have been offered to show that the formulation of 4Q365 23 is influenced by Neh 10 are unconvincing in my opinion.[55] The only significant parallel between the two texts is the fact that the verse preceding Neh 10:35 (v. 34) uses the expression כל מלאכת בית־אלהינו, whereas a similar expression, כול מלאכת הבית, occurs twice in connection with the wood offering in 4Q365 23 (lines 5–6 and 8).[56] As argued above, however, the expression כול מלאכת הבית in 4Q365 23 is probably borrowed from the building of the tabernacle in Exod 35–40; there is no need, therefore, to assume that it was taken from Neh 10:34. Besides, the context in which this expression is used in both texts is significantly different, since in Neh 10 this expression is not related to the wood offering. Apart from this specific instance, there is no lexical evidence to support the view that the formulation of the wood offering in 4Q365 is derived

---

55. Contrast the arguments presented by Crawford and Hoffmann, "A Note on 4Q365," as well as Werman, "Wood-Offering," 157–58.

56. For this observation, see especially Crawford and Hoffmann, "A Note on 4Q365," 429.

from Neh 10. Furthermore, if we assume that Neh 10 was the scriptural basis for the wood offering in 4Q365 23, it becomes difficult to understand why the technical phrase קרבן העצים never occurs in this fragment, since this phrase is already used both in Neh 10:35 and in 13:31 for the wood offering.

Besides the absence of any compelling connection between the two texts, there are also some larger issues with this reconstruction. To begin with, the notion that Neh 10:35 would have provided the scriptural basis for the law of the wood offering in 4Q365 assumes that Nehemiah was regarded as authoritative scripture by the author of this manuscript, although there is only limited evidence for Nehemiah's authority in the Second Temple period. Furthermore, the argument that the phrase ככתוב בתורה in Neh 10:35 would represent a scribal strategy for authorizing what was in fact a ritual innovation is also not without some difficulties. Elsewhere in Ezra, Nehemiah, and Chronicles, the phrase ככתוב בתורה (or one of its variants) usually has some sort of legal referent in the extant Mosaic traditions.[57] Additionally, the fact that all the other offerings mentioned in the immediate context of this passage (Neh 10:33–40) have a scriptural counterpart in the Pentateuch strongly suggests that this must also be the case for the wood offering mentioned in v. 35.[58] Alternatively, some scholars have proposed identifying the scriptural basis for Neh 10:35 in Lev 6:1–6, a law that mentions the kindling of wood on the altar as a daily obligation for the priests (see Lev 6:5).[59] While this possibility cannot be excluded, it remains something of a stretch to identify Lev 6:5 as the scriptural basis for Neh 10:35 since the topic is distinct—Lev 6:5 does not mention the obligation to bring wood to the temple, only to burn it on the altar—and there is no significant lexical connection with Neh 10. Therefore, it may be more helpful to consider the possibility that Neh 10:35 effectively refers, with the phrase ככתוב בתורה, to an actual instruction for the offering of wood to the temple that was associated with the authority of Moses. As the differences noted above suggest, this instruction cannot have been simply identical with the one preserved in 4Q365. Rather, Neh 10 and 4Q365 23 should be viewed as two separate witnesses to an expan-

---

57. See Ezra 3:2, 4; Neh 8:14, 15; 10:37; 13:1; 1 Chr 16:40; 2 Chr 23:18; 25:4; 30:5, 18; 31:3; 35:12, 26. This point was made previously by Milgrom, "Qumran's Biblical Hermeneutics," 455–56. The main exception would be Ezra 6:18; however, in this case it is likely that the reference is not to the division of the priests and the Levites into "classes" (which has no basis in the Pentateuch) but to the עבדה, which in Numbers is the technical term for the Levites' service in the sanctuary.

58. I am indebted to Julia Rhyder for this observation.

59. For this idea, see, e.g., Michael W. Duggan, *The Covenant Renewal in Ezra-Nehemiah (Neh 7:72b–10:40): An Exegetical, Literary, and Theological Study*, SBLDS 164 (Atlanta: Society of Biblical Literature, 2001), 281–82.

sionist version of the Pentateuch that included provisions for the offering of wood to the temple.

In short, attempts to identify a reference to the law of 4Q365 23 in Neh 10 or, alternatively, to derive 4Q365 23 from Neh 10, are problematic and unconvincing. While both texts refer to a Mosaic law concerning the offering of wood to the temple, they do not appear to be directly related. This point is consistent, in particular, with the absence of any significant connection between these texts. If this reconstruction of the evidence is correct, Neh 10:35 arguably represents the earliest known witness to an expansionist version of the Pentateuch that included provisions for the wood offering. 4Q365 23, for its part, appears to represent a separate version of this same legal tradition, which was not (yet) known to the author of Neh 10:31–40. Furthermore, the connections noted above between the wood offering in 4Q365 and in the Temple Scroll suggest that the version of the law of the wood offering known to the author of Temple Scroll was similar to (albeit not identical with) the one preserved in 4Q365. It is difficult to be more precise about the origins of the legal tradition underlying the wood offering in the Second Temple period, not the least because we cannot know with certainty when Neh 10:35 was composed. As various scholars have argued, the unit comprising Neh 10:31–40 is unlikely to have been part of Nehemiah's memoir; more likely, it represents a later supplement to the Nehemiah tradition, possibly from the late Persian or early Hellenistic period (fourth or third century BCE).[60] This date, according to the reconstruction proposed here, would then represent the *terminus ad quem* for the creation of an expansionist version of Leviticus in which the ritual legislation of this book was supplemented with an instruction for the offering of wood. As for 4Q365, the manuscript itself can be dated to the mid-first century BCE.[61] However, the parallels between 4Q365 23 and the Temple Scroll suggest that this version of the law of the wood offering may actually go back to the second century BCE, if not somewhat earlier.

---

60. See esp. the detailed discussion by T. Reinmuth, "Reform und Tora bei Nehemia: Neh 10,31–40 und die Autorisierung der Tora in der Perserzeit," *ZABR* 7 (2001): 287–317; and see also Jacob L. Wright, *Rebuilding Identity: The Nehemiah-Memoir and Its Earliest Readers*, BZAW 348 (Berlin: de Gruyter, 2004), 218–20. As noted by various scholars, the stipulations in Neh 10:31–40 appear to presuppose the account of chapter 13, and they are only loosely related to the contents of Nehemiah's prayer in chapter 9. It is disputed whether 10:31–40 is a literarily homogeneous composition or whether it is characterized by the presence of various expansions. My own view tends toward the first solution, but in any case even scholars who identify redactional growth in 10:31–40 assign v. 35 to the final stage in the formation of this material.

61. Brooke, "4Q158"; Crawford, "Pentateuch," 126.

V. Conclusion: 4Q365 23 and Legal Supplementation in the Second Temple Period

Some general conclusions regarding legal supplementation as a scribal phenomenon may be derived from the material surveyed in this short essay.

First, the law of the wood offering provides some important insights into the *mechanics* of legal supplementation in the Second Temple period. Contrary to other supplements in the Reworked Pentateuch manuscripts, the law of the wood offering in 4Q365 23 cannot be explained merely as an inner-scriptural development. More likely, this supplement reflects the growing importance of the wood offering during the Second Temple period, which is independently documented by other contemporaneous sources. It is clear from the law's content that it does not purport to describe or prescribe an actual practice; this is suggested, in particular, by the reference in lines 9–11 of the fragment to the Israelite tribes bringing their offering of wood to the temple. Rather, the instruction for the wood offering in 4Q365 is a *legal fiction*, seeking to provide a scriptural basis for an offering that was deemed important enough by some scribes to be appended to the festal legislation of Leviticus. The fact that this legal supplement was added to the festal legislation of Leviticus is only logical given its topic (the wood offering). Nevertheless, as I have mentioned at the outset of this essay, this scribal development is intriguing, as it challenges some of our current assumptions regarding the textual stability achieved by this book during the Second Temple period. In effect, 4Q365 23 points to the existence of an expansionist version of Leviticus that included provisions for the wood offering—and presumably for other festivals as well, especially the festival of new oil—and was circulated alongside the main copies of the book until the first century BCE (the date of the manuscript of 4Q365).[62] The parallels between the wood offering in 4Q365 and in the Temple Scroll suggest that this supplement was part of a broader legal tradition that gradually developed during the Second Temple period and may be reflected for the first time in a late addition to the book of Nehemiah (Neh 10:35). At any rate, 4Q365 23 documents the fact that even relatively stable scriptures such as Leviticus were susceptible of being revised and amplified during most of the Second Temple period in order to reflect new legal and ritual traditions such as the wood offering.

---

62. By contrast, the two Leviticus manuscripts found at Masada, Mas1a (first century CE) and Mas1b (around 50 BCE), which preserve a text virtually identical to Leviticus MT, may indicate that it is around this time that an attempt was made to establish a single, fully standardized edition of this book.

Second, the case of the wood offering in 4Q365 is significant also for the way in which it sheds light on the scribal *techniques* used in the composition of a legal supplement such as this. While the wood offering in 4Q365 23 is a new topic, the language used in this fragment to describe this offering is not. Specifically, the examination of this material shows that the law of the wood offering draws on several scriptural traditions, arguably more so than has been previously acknowledged. The introduction to the law (lines 4–5) takes up Lev 24:1–2a and combines it with various passages from Lev 23–25 (23:10 and 25:2, 18–19) as well as with Deut 26:1. The references to Lev 23–25 suggest a concern to highlight the continuity between the law of the wood offering and its scriptural context (the festal legislation of Leviticus), whereas the conflation of Lev 23:10 and 25:2 with Deut 26:1 arguably reflects a broader scribal trend in the pre-Samaritan versions of the Pentateuch to align Leviticus and Numbers with Deuteronomy wherever possible. The description of the law itself, from line 5 onward, also presents some substantial parallels with other passages of the Pentateuch, such as Exod 35–40 and Num 7. For ancient readers, the presence of such scriptural parallels would have significantly facilitated the recognition of the wood offering as a Mosaic law. In addition, as we have seen, the selection of scriptural materials in the composition of 4Q365 23 simultaneously points to significant associations between the wood offering and other key offerings in the Torah, especially the firstfruits (Lev 23:10 and Deut 26:1), the community's contribution to the building of the tabernacle (Exod 35–40), and the offerings for the dedication of the tabernacle (Num 7). These remarks suggest that the scriptural phraseology used in the composition of this legal supplement serves a twofold function: it authorizes the introduction of a new offering in the Torah, while simultaneously positioning this material within the Mosaic traditions about the Israelite cult.

Index of Passages

Hebrew Bible/ Old Testament

Genesis
- 12–36   70
- 18:17–23   60n20
- 20:9   77
- 34   117n23
- 34:25   70n2
- 37–50   69
- 37   69, 72, 72n12, 75, 79n43
- 37:28   72, 73, 73n14
- 37:28a   72, 73
- 37:28b   72
- 37:36   72, 72n11, 73, 73n14, 74
- 38   69, 69n1, 72, 81
- 39   xvi, xvii, 70, 71, 72, 73, 74, 74n20, 75n26, 76, 76n28, 77, 78, 78n37, 79, 79n46, 80, 80n48, 81
- 39:1–23   82–83
- 39:1–6   71, 77
- 39:1   72, 73, 73n14, 74, 75, 77, 81
- 39:2–3   77, 78, 78n37, 81
- 39:2   71, 74n19, 75, 78
- 39:3   71
- 39:4   71, 75n26, 77, 78
- 39:4a   75, 77, 81
- 39:4b   75n26, 77, 78
- 39:5   74n19, 75, 78, 78n37, 81
- 39:6   77, 78
- 39:7–20   71, 76, 77, 78, 81
- 39:7   77n34
- 39:8–9   76n30
- 39:9   79
- 39:12a   77n34
- 39:16   77n34
- 39:17a   77n34
- 39:19–20   71
- 39:20   77, 77n34
- 39:21–23   71, 77, 78, 78n37, 81
- 39:21   71, 78, 78n38
- 39:22–23   72
- 39:22   78, 78n38
- 39:23   71, 78, 78n38, 79
- 40   69, 71, 72, 75, 75n26, 76, 76n28, 77, 78, 80n48
- 40:1–5   83
- 40:1   81
- 40:1a   75, 76, 78
- 40:2–3a   81
- 40:2   75, 78
- 40:3–4   75
- 40:3   74, 75
- 40:3a   75, 78
- 40:3b   76, 78, 78n37
- 40:4   72, 74, 75
- 40:5   76n28
- 40:15   76n29, 79n43
- 41   69, 74
- 41:12   75
- 41:25–26   70
- 41:45   73
- 41:50   73
- 42–44   69
- 42   69
- 43   69
- 44:30–31   78
- 45:4   73
- 45:17–21   60n20
- 46   69, 70n1
- 46:20   73
- 47:13–26   70
- 48–49   69
- 48   70n1
- 49   70n1
- 50:24–25   70
- 50:24   70

Exodus
- 2:20–21   60n20
- 8:16–20   60n20
- 9:1–6   60n20
- 9:13–20   60n20
- 12:4   57
- 12:11   139, 139n67, 141, 141n73
- 14   136, 136n54, 137, 138
- 14:16   137, 140
- 14:21   137, 138, 140
- 15   136n54, 137, 138, 139
- 15:3   140
- 15:5   140
- 15:8   140
- 15:13   xvii, 136, 139
- 15:16   xvii, 136, 138, 139, 140
- 15:21   191n21
- 15:22   61
- 15:23   61
- 15:27   61
- 16   53, 54, 56, 58, 61, 62
- 16:1   61, 62
- 16:2–36   61
- 16:2–3   54
- 16:3   55, 64, 65, 66

Index of Passages

Exodus (*continued*)		18	62	62n29	23:10	192, 192n26,
16:4–5	54, 55, 56, 57,	18:21		112n14		196, 196n44,
	58, 59, 60, 65,	18:25		112n14		204
	66	21:2–6		xvi	23:42–44	187, 187n10,
16:4	57, 59, 60,	21:22–25		161n1		191
	60n18, 65, 66	22:15–16		161n1, 177	23:42	189n16
16:6–9	54	22:16–17 MT		177	23:42b	187n10
16:6–8	63, 64, 67	23:3		172n39	23:43	189n16
16:6–7	64, 65n34	23:6		172n39	23:44	189, 189n15,
16:6	64n33	23:19		193		189n16
16:6b–7	63	25–31		194n37	24:1–9	189n15, 190,
16:6b–7a	64	25:2–7		195n40		190n18
16:7	63	34:26		193	24:1–4	187, 191,
16:8	63, 64, 65,	35		195n40		196n45
	65n34	35–40		195, 196, 197,	24:1–2a	187, 189n14,
16:9–12	63			200, 204		190, 191,
16:9	55	36:3		195		196n44,
16:10	63	38:24		195		196n45, 204
16:11–12	54, 55, 56, 57,				24:2b–4	189n14, 190
	63	Leviticus			24:2b	190
16:12–13	64, 65	1:2		188n13	24:13	57n12
16:12	55, 63, 64,	2:1		188n13	25:2	192, 192n26,
	64n33, 65, 66	3:1		188n13		196, 196n44,
16:13–14	56	3:2–7		184n2		204
16:13	65, 66	3:2		184n2	25:18–19	196n44, 204
16:15	56, 57, 65, 66,	3:8		184n2	25:18	193, 193n31
	57	6:1–6		201	25:19	193, 193n31
16:16	58	6:2		60n18	26	140
16:17–18	57	6:5		201	26:31–35	143
16:19	57, 58	6:7		60n18	26:36	139
16:19	59	6:18		60n18		
16:20	59, 65, 66	7:1		60n18	Numbers	
16:21	65	7:7		60n18	5:29–30	60n18
16:22	57	7:11–21		195n42	6:13	60n18
16:23	57, 58,	7:11		60n18	6:31	60n18
	65, 66	11:46		60n18	7	189n13, 194,
16:24	58, 65, 66	12:7		60n18		194n39, 195,
16:25–26	59	13:59		60n18		195n40, 196,
16:25	59	14:2		60n18		197, 204
16:26–27	60	14:32		60n18	7:3	195n40
16:26	59	14:54		60n18	7:10	195n40
16:28	58, 59, 60,	14:57		60n18	7:11	195n40
	60n18	15:32		60n18	7:12	195n40
16:29	60	17:4		184n2	7:18	195n40
16:30	59	18:27		184n3	7:19	195n40
16:31–35	65	20		184n3	9:9	57n12
16:31	59, 60, 63	20:10		176n53	15	195
16:35	66, 67	20:23–24		184n3	15:18	192n26
16:35a	66, 66n39, 67	23–25		196, 204	15:35	57n12
16:35b	66, 66n39, 67	23		187, 189, 190,	19:14	60n18
17	138			190n18	19:21	60n18
17:1	61, 62	23:9–22		192	20	138

24:7	129, 130, 130n26	19:11–12	170n32	22:22a	161n1, 177n56
26:31	111n13	19:13	173n43	22:23–29	161, 169, 176, 177, 180
27:6	57n12, 58	19:15–21	173n43, 175n50	22:23–27	170n32, 177
27:11	58	19:16–19a	170n32	22:23–24	162, 174, 176, 177, 178
30	173	20:8	118n27		
31:14	112n14	21–25	161	22:23a	177n55
31:21	60n18	21:1–9	175n50	22:24	174
31:40	189n13	21:1–7	170n32	22:25–27	174, 177, 177n56
31:48	112n14	21:15–21	174n47		
		21:15–21a	161n1	22:25	161n1, 77
Deuteronomy		21:15–17	161, 169, 170, 170n29,	22:26	177
1:15	112n14			22:27	161n1
4:21	191n24		170n32, 172, 174, 174n46,	22:28–29	161n1, 162, 170n32, 174,
12–26	162n3, 172–75				
12:9–11	193		175, 177, 178–79		177, 177n56, 178
12:10	193, 175n50				
13	173	21:18–21	161, 162, 169n27,	22:29	170
13:2–19	174			24:1–2	170
13:2–9	174n44		170n32, 174, 174n47,	24:1–4	161, 169, 172, 174, 175, 177, 180
13:7–12	173, 174n47				
14:22–29	175n50		175n49, 176, 177, 178, 179		
15:4	191n24			24:1–4a	161n1, 170n32, 174n46
15:12–18	xvi	21:18–21a	174n47		
15:19–23	175n50	21:19	174	24:4	174, 191n24
16:3	139, 139n67	21:21	174	24:7b	170n32
16:8	174n45	22:13–27	177	25:1–3	170n32
16:16–17	175n50	22:13–22	179	25:5–10	161, 161n1, 169, 169n27, 170, 170n32, 171, 172, 174, 174n46, 175, 177, 81
16:18–20	172, 173, 175n50	22:13–21	161, 169, 169n26, 169n27, 170, 174n46, 176, 176n51		
16:18	173n43				
16:19	173n43				
16:21–17:7	173n43				
17	173	22:13–21a	161n1, 170n32	25:7	174
17:2–13	172	22:13–19	170, 170n33, 171, 172n37, 174, 176, 176n51, 177	25:11–12	170n32
17:2–7	xvii, 162, 172, 173, 173n40, 173n42, 174, 174n44, 175, 176, 177, 178			25:19	191n24
				26:1–11	192
				26:1	191, 191n24, 192, 192n26, 196, 204
		22:13	174, 176		
17:2	174, 176	22:14	174	28:26	151
17:3	176	22:15	174	28:53	98n28
17:4	174	22:19	169n26, 170, 174	28:61	98n28
17:6	173, 173n43	22:20–21	162, 172n37, 174, 176, 176n51, 177, 178	29:4	141n73
17:8–13	173, 173n43, 175n50			32:49	192n25
				32:52	192n25
17:14–21:14	173n43	22:21	174	34:4	70
19:1–13	175n50	22:22	161, 162, 170n32, 174, 176, 176n53, 177, 178		
19:4–5	170n32, 173n43			Joshua	
				17:2	111n13
19:10	191n24			24:32	70
19:11–13	173n43				

Index of Passages

Judges		6:33–35	111	8:1–21		120n30
3:12–15a	108	6:33	111	8:1–3		111n12, 113,
3:13	111	6:34	111, 112,			113n17
3:27–29	113n17		117n25, 118,	8:3a		113, 120
4:1–3	108		120	8:4–21		107
6:1–8:35	107–17	6:35	111, 113, 118	8:4–9		120
6:1–10	107–11	6:35a	111	8:4		106, 113,
6:1–2a	108, 109n8	6:35b	111			113n16
6:1b	108n7	6:36–40	111, 111n12,	8:5–9		113–14
6:2–6	106n3		117	8:8–9		114
6:2b–6a	108, 108n8,	7	107, 112, 115	8:10–13		114–15
	109n8	7:1	112, 112n15,	8:10–12		106, 114
6:2b	108n7		117n24	8:10		111, 114, 119,
6:3	111		112n14			120n30
6:3b	108n7	7:1b–8a	106	8:10a		120
6:5	119	7:1b–8b	111	8:11–12		118, 120n30
6:6b	106, 106n3,	7:1b	111, 112	8:11		107, 120
	108, 109n8	7:2–8a	117, 121	8:12		117
6:7–20	106n3	7:2–3	118, 119	8:13–16		120
6:7–10	xvi, 105, 106,	7:2	118	8:14–17		113–14
	107, 108, 110	7:3	118n26	8:17		114
6:7a	106n3	7:5–6	112n14	8:18–21		xvi, , 114–15,
6:10	106n3, 110	7:6	111, 112			116, 120n30,
6:11–24	106n3, 107–10	7:8b	112			121
6:11	106, 108,	7:9	111	8:18–21b		106
	109n8, 117n25	7:10–15	117	8:18–19		117n25
6:11a	106	7:11b–15	111, 119	8:22–27		xvi, 115,
6:12–16	109	7:12	106			115n20, 116
6:12–15	109	7:13–15a	112	8:22–24		73
6:12	109, 117	7:15	112	8:22		115
6:12a	108	7:16–22	106, 119, 120,	8:23		116
6:13–18	109	7:16–21	112n14	8:24–27		116, 117
6:13–15	117		112	8:25b–27a		120n30
6:13	109, 110	7:16–19	112	8:27		116, 117n25
6:14	109, 117	7:16–18	112	8:28–35		116–17
6:15	109, 117	7:17b	112, 120n29	8:28		xvi, 116,
6:16–18	109	7:18	111			117n23
6:17–24	117	7:19–22	112, 112n14,	8:29–31		117
6:19	106, 108	7:19	112n15	8:32–34		116
6:20	111n12		120n29	8:32		117n25
6:21–24	108	7:20	117	9		110
6:21	106	7:21–22	112	9:1		117n23
6:24–32	117n25	7:21	119	9:2		116
6:24	106, 109, 110	7:22	112	9:43		112n14
6:25–32	106n3, 110,	7:22a	106, 119, 120,	10		107
	117n23	7:22b	120n30	12:1–3		113, 113n17
6:26	110	7:23–8:3	112–13	20		121
6:27	110	7:23–25	111, 120n30	20:1		121
6:28	110	7:23	113, 120	20:4		121
6:31	110	7:24–25	113	24:2–4		xvi
6:33–7:22	111–12	7:24	120			
6:33–7:2	114	8	112			

Index of Passages

1 Samuel		2:9b	39, 40, 43, 44, 46	3:3	99
1–2	29			3:5	147n2
1:24–28	34	2:10	32, 33, 40, 41, 42, 43, 43n54, 44, 44n57, 47, 48	3:7	147n2
1:24–28a	35			9:7	134n45
1:24–28b	36			10:29	99
1:26	36			10:31	99
1:28	25, 28, 30, 34, 35, 36, 45, 47	2:10a	27, 28, 40, 42, 43, 44, 46	13:2	99
				13:11	99
1:28b	35, 36, 36n38, 46	2:10b	40, 41, 42, 43	14:24	99
		2:11	28, 34, 35, 36, 36n38, 45, 46	15:5	71n9
2	25, 43, 43n55, 44			15:9	99
		11:11	112n14	15:18	99
2:1–10	25, 35	13:2	112n14	15:24	99
2:1–3	28, 44, 45, 47	13:17	112n14	15:28	99
2:1–2	34, 36	22:7	112n14	17	103
2:1	25, 30, 36, 44, 45, 46	24:14	133	17:11	99
		29:2	112n14	17:13	134n45
2:1a	46			17:16	99
2:1b	44	**2 Samuel**		17:17	99
2:2–3	34, 44	7	193, 197	17:21	99
2:2	26, 30, 36, 41, 43n54, 44, 46, 47	7:5	194	17:23	134n45
		7:13	194	20:17	93, 98n28
		13	80n49	21	99, 100
2:3–8a	34	18:2	112n14	21:1–10	99
2:3	31, 43			21:3	99
2:3a	46	**1 Kings**		21:5	99
2:3b	46	5:5	194n34	21:6	99
2:4–8a	28, 44, 45, 47	8:16	193n32	21:10	134n45
2:4–6	32	8:44	193n32	21:11	99
2:4	26, 31, 43, 45, 46	8:48	193n32	21:16	99
		11:32	193n32	21:17	100
2:5	26, 31, 32, 47	11:36	193n32	23	103
2:5a	46	14:9	99	23:15	99
2:5b	45, 46	14:16	99	23:19	99
2:6	27, 46	14:21	193n32	23:26	99, 100
2:7	27, 32, 43, 46	15:26	99	23:27	193n32
2:8–10	34, 36	15:30	99	24–25	89, 98
2:8–9	40	15:34	99	24	89, 91, 93, 94–97, 99, 100, 101, 102, 102n35
2:8	32, 38	16:2	99		
2:8a	27, 39, 40, 46, 27	16:7	99		
		16:13	99		
2:8b–10	28, 34, 38n42, 45	16:19	99	24:1–2	98n28
		16:26	99	24:1	xvi, 98
2:8b	38, 38n42, 39, 40, 43, 44, 45, 46, 47	16:33	99	24:2–4	98, 98n28, 102
		18:3	71n9	24:2	98, 98n28, 134n45
		18:39	153, 153n20		
2:9–10	47	21:22	99	24:2b	98, 98n28
2:9	27, 32, 38, 40, 43n54, 45, 47, 48	22:53	99	24:3–4	89, 98, 99, 100
		22:54	99	24:3	98, 100
				24:5	xvi, 98, 99
2:9a	39, 40, 44, 46	**2 Kings**		24:8	95
2:9b–10	45	1:1	147n2	24:10	95

Index of Passages

2 Kings (continued)		1:1–4	143, 144	29:1–2	49	
24:12–16	95–96	3:2	201n57	29:1	49	
24:12	96, 97, 100	3:4	201n57	29:3–9a	49	
24:13–14	89, 89n5, 97, 98, 100, 102, 102n35	3:11	8	29:3b	49	
		6:18	201n57	29:9b	49	
		9:11	134n45	29:10–11	49	
24:13	93, 94, 96			33:8	23	
24:14	93, 96, 98	Nehemiah		33:9	23	
24:15–16	96	8:14	201n57	33:16	40	
24:15	96, 97, 100	8:15	201n57	72:18–19	8	
24:16	96	9	202n60	78	60n18, 151n14	
24:18–20	90	10	199n52, 200, 201, 202	78:15	137n61	
24:18	90			84:5	4, 12	
24:19–20	90	10:31–40	189, 199, 202, 202n60	90:2	49	
24:20b	90			92	18	
25	74n23, 89–92, 93, 94, 97, 100, 102, 102n35, 103	10:33–40	199, 201	93:1	49	
		10:34	200	93:2	49	
		10:35	186, 188, 189n13, 197, 198, 199, 199n52, 199n53, 200, 201, 202, 202n60, 203	93:3–4	49	
				93:5a	49	
25:1–2	90			93:5b	49	
25:3	90			97:1	49	
25:9	91			97:2	49	
25:10	91			97:2a	49	
25:11–12	97n26			97:3–5	49	
25:11	91, 93	10:37	201n57	97:6a	49	
25:12	91, 92	13	198, 202n60	97:6b	49	
25:13–17	91, 92, 93, 94	13:1	201n57	97:7b	49	
25:13	91	13:30	198	97:8	49	
25:16	91	13:31	188, 189n13, 192, 192n27, 197, 198, 200, 201	97:9	49	
25:18–21	91			97:10–12	49	
25:22–26	91			99:5	8	
25:27–30	91			99:9	8	
		31:3	201n57	100	24	
1 Chronicles		35:12	201n57	104:1a	49	
16:40	201n57	35:26	201n57	104:1b	49	
				104:2a	49	
2 Chronicles		Psalms		104:2b	49	
23:18	201n57	3:8	15n55	104:3–4	49	
25:4	201n57	6	19	104:5–9	49	
30:5	201n57	6:1	19	104:10a	49	
30:17	189n17	6:2–9a	19	104:10b–12	49	
30:18	201n57	6:9a	19	104:13a	49	
35:7	189n17	6:9b–11	19, 20	104:13b	49	
35:8	189n17	6:11	20	104:14a	49	
35:9	189n17	18	44n57	104:14b	49	
36:21–22	141, 143, 143, 144	18:4–20	44n57	104:15	49	
		18:21–32	44n57	104:16–19	49	
36:21	143	18:30–50	44n57	104:20–24a	49	
36:22	143	18:33–51	44n57	104:24b	49	
		18:51	44n57	104:24c	49	
Ezra		19:8	49	104:25a	49	
1:1	141, 143	22:18	147n2	104:25b	49	

Index of Passages

Reference	Page(s)
104:26a	49
104:26b	49
104:27–29a	49
104:29b	49
104:30–31	49
104:32–33	49
104:34	49
104:35	49
112:8	147n2
112:8 (LXX)	32
113:8	32
115:18	4, 12
118	24
118:1–4	49
118:6–13	49
118:14	49
118:15–16	49
118:15b	49
118:17–19	49
118:20	49
118:21	49
118:22–27	49
118:28	49
118:29	49
135	24
136	17, 22, 24
144:15	4, 12
145	xvi, 3, 4, 12, 13, 15, 18, 19, 20, 22, 53, 65
145:1	6, 7, 8, 10, 10n35, 12, 23
145:2–21	8–12
145:2	9, 10, 23
145:4	10
145:5	10n31
145:12	23
145:13	23
145:14	23
145:17b	10
145:18	9, 11
145:21	9, 10, 11, 23
146:8	23
146:9	23
146:10	23
148	24
148:1–13	24
148:5	23
148:6	23
148:13	24
148:14	23, 24
149	24
149:1–9	24
149:1	24
149:9	23, 24
151 (LXX)	24

Proverbs

Reference	Page(s)
2:8	32, 39
7:13	80
7:16	80
7:18	80
7:19	80
7:21	80
7:23	80
7:24	80
7:25	80
7:26	80
7:27	80
12:17	171n35
14:5	171n35
14:25	171n35
16:10	171n35
16:29	171n35
17:8	171n35
17:14	171n35
17:23	171n35
18:5	171n35
18:17	171n35
19:5	171n35
19:28	171n35
20:8	171n35
21:6	171n35
21:28	171n35
23:33	171n35
24:23	171n35
24:28	171n35
25:2	171n35
26:17	171n35
26:21	171n35
29:9	171n35
29:12	171n35
29:14	171n35
29:26	171n35
31:8–9	171n35
31:23	171n35

Qoheleth

Reference	Page(s)
7:2	79n42
8:4	79n42

Isaiah

Reference	Page(s)
1	154n23
1:2	147n2, 154n23
1:10	154n23
1:27–28	154
1:27	154
1:28	xvi, xvii, 153, 154, 154n23, 156
1:31	154n23
6:22–23	157
11	141, 141n73
11:11–16	140, 141, 141n72
11:15	140, 141n73
11:16	126, 140, 145
13:9	132n37
14	131n29
14:4a	131
14:4b–21	131, 131n31
14:11	155, 155n25, 156
14:13	131, 131n31
14:25	131
16:22	153
22:15	71n9
39:6	132n37
40–66	141
40–55	135, 135n49, 149n5, 153
40:1	150, 150n9
40:5	153, 156n28
41:21	xvii, 136
43:1–7	138
43:1–4	136, 136n56, 138, 139
43:1–3a	137n56
43:1	136, 137, 138, 138n63
43:2	138
43:5–7	138, 138n63, 139
43:5	138, 138n63
43:6	138
46:8	154
43:16–21	135, 136n54, 137, 138
43:16–17	135
43:16	136
43:17	136
43:18–21	136
43:18	133, 136, 151n12
43:19–20	136
43:19	136

Index of Passages

Isaiah (continued)		66:18–21	xvi, 150, 150, 152, 156, 157	13:20–22	102
43:21	136, 137	66:18	156n28	15:4	99
48	137n61	66:19	156n28	15:9	32
48:20–21	137	66:20	157n29	16:14	132n37
48:20	137	66:22–24	149n5, 155n27	18:7	98n28
48:21	137, 137n60, 137n61, 138	66:22–23	xvi, 150, 152, 155, 155n26, 155n27, 156	19:6	132n37
				22:23	131n30
49:26	153, 153n19			23:5	132n37
50:1	154n22			23:7	132n37
51:9–11	138, 139	66:22	155n26, 156n27	24	101, 102
51:9–10a	138, 139			24:6–7	101
51:10a	139	66:23–24	153n20	25:11–13	141
51:10b–11	139, 139n65	66:23	151, 152, 153, 155, 155n26, 155–56n27, 156n28, 157n29	25:11–12	143
51:10b	139			25:12	143
52:7–10	139			25:4	134n45
51:12	139n65			26:5	134n45
52:11–12	139, 140			27–29	97
52:11	139	66:24	xvi, xvii, 147, 147n2, 148, 148n2, 149, 149n4, 151, 151n13, 152, 153, 154, 154n22, 155, 155–56n27, 155n25, 155n26, 156, 156n28, 157	27–28	101
52:12	139, 154			27:19–21	95
56–66	149, 149n5			29	143
63–64	140			29:1	143
63:11–14	140			29:10	141, 142, 143
63:11	140			29:14	143
63:12	140			29:16–20	102
63:13	140			29:19	134n45
63:14	140			30:3	132n37
66	149, 152n15, 154n23, 156			31:27	132n37
				31:28	98n28
				31:31	132n37
66:4–14	149n5	Jeremiah		31:38	132n37
66:5	154n23	1:10	98n28	32	101
66:7–14	149n5	1:12	43n54	33:14	132n37
66:10–14	149n5	2:8	147n2	35:15	134n45
66:12–14	149, 149n5	2:29	147n2	36	xi
66:13–14	149, 150, 152, 153	6:22–23	131	36:32	xi
		6:22	131, 131n31	37–44	97
66:13	152	6:23	131	37–38	101
66:14	149n5, 149n7, 152, 156	7:25	134n45	39–40	74n23
		7:32	132n37	44:4	134n45\
66:15–24	xvi, 149n5	8–10	43	48:12	132n37
66:15–23	151, 156	8:7–9	43	49:2	132n37
66:15–21	149n5	8:9	43n54	51:47	132n37
66:15–16	xvi, xvii, 150, 151, 151n13, 152, 156, 157	9	43, 43n53, 43n55	51:52	132n37
		9:22–23	41, 43	51:56	31
66:15	149n5	9:22	41	52:6	90
66:16	151, 152n15, 154, 156n28	9:23	41	52:28–30	97n26
		9:24	132n37		
		10:1–16	43	Lamentations	
66:17	xvi, 150, 150n11, 151, 151n12, 156, 157	10:2	43n54	1:7–8	102
		10:6–7	43n54	Ezekiel	
				1:2	102
		10:10–13	43	6:3	129

Index of Passages

6:13	129	38:1–9	128, 129, 129n18, 132	9:20–23	144
7:10	132n37			9:24–27	141, 144n83
8:1	102	38:1	132	9:24–26	144
12:19	102	38:4	132n34	9:24	144
14:9	136	38:6–7	132n36	12:2	148, 148n2, 157
14:21–23	102	38:6	131n31		
14:23	136	38:8	129	**Hosea**	
15:1	136	38:15	131n31	7:13	147n2
15:8	102	38:16	133		
15:19	136	38:17	126, 132, 133, 134, 134n47, 145	**Amos**	
15:21	136			3:7	134n45
18:25	31			4:2	132n37
19:9	129	38:18–23	133	7:1	129, 130
20:2	102	38:18	133	8:11	132n37
21:12	132	39	128, 129n18, 132	9:13	132n37
23:12	132n34				
25–32	130, 132, 132n34	39:1–5	128, 128n13, 129, 129n17, 129n18, 131, 131n30	**Obadiah**	
				1:12	147n2
26:1	102			**Nahum**	
28:26	193n31			1	11n40
29:1	102	39:1b–5	129n18		
29:5	130, 131	39:2	129, 131, 131n31	**Zechariah**	
29:17	102			1:6	134n45
30:20	102	39:3	130, 131	1:7–8	141
30:22	130	39:4	129, 131, 131n28	1:12	141, 142
31:1	102			1:13–17	142
32:17	102	39:5	130, 131	1:16	142
33:21–29	102	39:7	128n13, 129n18, 132	4:6	40
33:21	102			7–8	142
33:28	129	39:8–10	132n36	8	143
34:13–14	129	39:8	132, 132n36, 133, 145	8:11–13	142
35:12	129			8:13	143
36:1	129	39:9–10	132n36	14:1	132n37
36:4	129	39:17–20	129n18		
36:8	129	39:17	129	**Malachi**	
36:16–23a	128, 128n13	39:23–29	128, 128n13, 128n14	3:4	133
36:16–22	127			3:19	132n37
36:16–23a	129	39:25–29	129n17		
36:20	128	40:1	102	**New Testament**	
36:22	xvii, 128	43:11–12	60		
36:23a	127, 127n10	44:5	60	**Mark**	
36:26–23a	128n14	44:23–24	58	2:21	5
37:18	133			9:43	148
37:22	129	**Daniel**		9:48	148
38–39	xvii, 126, 127, 127n8, 128, 129, 129n23, 130, 130n26, 131, 131n30, 132, 145	9	141, 141n75, 142n76, 144, 144n82, 144n84, 145	**Apocryphal/ Deuterocanonical Writings**	
			126, 141, 144, 144n86, 145		
38	128, 132	9:2			
38:1–3a	129n18	9:6	134n45	**Judith**	
		9:10	134n45	16:17	148

Index of Passages

Sirach		3	189, 189n16	Psalm 145	
7:17	148, 148n2	4–6	194	v. 1	6, 7, 8, 10n35
		4–5	191, 192, 196, 204	vv. 2–21	8–12
Pseudepigrapha		4	187	v. 2	9, 9n29
		5–8	187	v. 3	xvii, 9
Jubilees		5–6	188, 195, 200	v. 4	xvii, 10
21	197n48	5	188, 189n17, 193, 195	v. 5	10n31
40:12	74n20			v. 15	9, 9n29
		6–7	187	v. 16	9n30
Pseudo-Philo		6	193	v. 17b	10
Liber antiquitatum		7	189n17, 195, 195n42	v. 18	9, 11
biblicarum				v. 21	9, 10
63:4–5	148	8	188, 195, 196, 200		
				11QT^a. *See* 11Q19	
Testament of Joseph		9–11	188, 194, 197, 203		
18	74n20			11QT^b. *See* 11Q20	
		9	188, 189, 189n15, 190, 196n45		
Dead Sea Scrolls				**Josephus**	
				Jewish War	
1QH^a		10	188	2.17.6 §425	197
IX, 26	12n43	11	188		
				Rabbinic Writings	
1QIsa^a		4Q387 2		b. Ber.	
66:15	149n5	II, 3–4	141–42n72	4b	13
66:22–24	155n27				
		4QJudg^a	xvi, 105	Gen. Rab.	
4Q51 (4QSam^a)				86	74n22
	25, 29, 30, 31, 32, 33, 35, 36, 36n38, 37, 38n42, 39, 40, 41, 42, 42n49, 44, 48	4QSam^a	25, 38n42	Megillat Ta'anit	
				4:5	197
		11Q5. *See* 11QPs^a			
				Other Ancient Near	
		11Q19 (11QT^a)		**Eastern Writings**	
II, 15–35	25	III–XIII	194n37		
II, 26–31	41n47	XVII	15	Esarhaddon inscription	
II, 29–35	41	XXIII	192n27, 198, 198n51	Ep 10:2b–9a/	
II, 29	41			10:19–20	142n78
II, 30	41, 42	XXIII, 4	198n50		
II, 31	41	XXX–XLVI	194n37	Laws of Hammurabi	
II, 32	41	XLIII, 3–4	197	32	164
II, 33–34	41n47			129	167
II, 33	41, 42	11Q20 (11QT^b)		131	164n8
II, 34	41	VI	198n50	141–143	167
II, 35	41	VI	197, 197n49	148	164n8
				153	167
4Q365 frag. 23		11QpaleoLev		167–168	174n47
	xvi, xvii	18:27	184n3	238	164n8
1–12	186–87				
1–3	187, 191	11QPs^a	3, 4, 24	Mari	
1	187n10, 189n16	II, 6–16	23, 24	6 28	112n14
		XVI–XVII	23		
2	189n16	XXVI, 1–3	24		

Index of Passages 215

Middle Assyrian Laws	TAD (Textbook of Aramaic Documents from Ancient Egypt)	Laws of Ur-Namma
Tablet A 161, 161n1	A4.7–8 34	9 164n8
Neo-Babylonian Chronicles	Ur III Sumerian verdicts	**Other Greek Writings**
2–5 90n10	#5 164n8	Plutarch
5 94, 95	#6 164n8	Marius 10.5–6 120n29
Nippur Homicide Trial	#7 164n8	
9–10 165n12	24 164n8	
14 165n12		
PRU (Le palais royal d'Ugarit)	LAPO (Littératures anciennes du Proche-Orient)	
IV 17.59 112n14	17 573 112n14	
Shebna Inscription 71n9	Laws of Eshnunna	
	31 167	

Index of Subjects

a posteriori approach, to determine supplements, 106
a priori approach, to determine supplements, 106
abbreviations, 6, 7, 9, 14, 15
acrostics, 12, 15, 22
  purpose of, 11
Aejmelaeus, Anneli, on versions of Song of Hannah, 29
aides-memoire, biblical texts as, 9
army, portrayal in Gideon narrative supplements, 118, 119, 120
ashrei prayer, and supplementation, 12-13
authority, of prophets, 143

Baden, Joel, on lack of large-scale rewriting in the Pentateuch, 61, 62
Bata, in Egyptian tale of two brothers, 79, 80
battle cries, 120
biblicist additions. See inner-biblical exegesis
Bottéro, Jean, on the Code of Hammurabi, 163, 164

capital punishment, in Israelite legal fictions, 173, 174, 176
captain of the guard (in Joseph narrative), 74, 75
Chavel, Simeon, on oracular novella, 56
codas, and supplementation, 14, 18
complaint genre, 54, 55, 56, 57, 58, 59
composition history
  and blending of genres, 56, 57
  diachronic approaches to reconstructing, 106-7
  and lack of manuscript evidence, 53, 54
corpses, as eternally subject to worm and fire, 151, 155
corrections
  factual and pattern, 61, 62
  as supplementations, 14, 15, 16
Cross, Frank Moore
  on composition of Deuteronomistic History, 103
  text-critical explanations for variations in Song of Hannah, 28, 29

Dead Sea Scrolls, as evidence for textual supplementation, 21
Deuteronomist, as one or multiple authors, 87, 88, 89
Deuteronomistic History
  redactional supplementation in, 87, 88, 89
  single author for, 87, 88, 89
Diaskeuasten, role of, xiii
divine agency, in 2 Kings 25, 91
D'Orbiney Papyrus, and Egyptian tale of two brothers, 79
doxologies, and supplementation, 8
dreams, and dream interpretation (Joseph novella), 75-76

editing, external evidence of, 24
education, scribal, 166, 168, 171, 172, 177
Egyptian (Genesis 39:1), name and titles of, 72-75
Eichhorn, Johann Gottfried, on interpolation in text of Pentateuch, xii
elimination, to determine supplements, 106

Elkanah, role in different versions of
    Song of Hannah, 34-36
אלהים, in Joseph narrative, 70
errors, scribal correcting of, 9
Esarhaddon inscription, and seventy-year motif, 142
eunuch of Pharaoh, 74
Exodus 16
    compositional history of, 53-67
    supplements to base narrative, 64, 65, 66

family law/women's law, pre-Deuteronomic collection of, 161, 162, 175
fear, as theme of Gideon narrative supplements, 117-21
fire, unceasing, 151, 154, 155
fire and worms, connection with hell and final judgment in later biblical and postbiblical literature, 147, 148, 151, 152
Fishbane, Michael
    on Exodus 16 as legal exegesis, 56
    and inner-biblical exegesis, xv
Fortschreibung (literary continuation), 125, 126, 138, 145, 177
Four-Source Documentary Hypothesis, xii, xiii, xiv
Fragment Hypothesis, xii
frame, addition of, and supplementation, 7, 14, 18, 19, 34, 45

Genesis 39
    context, 71, 72
    supplementation in, 71-75, 78-79
genre(s)
    blending of, 56, 57, 61
    significance for composition history, 54, 55
genre conventions, violation of, 59
Gideon, portrayal in original story and in supplements, 117, 118, 121, 122
Gideon narrative supplements
    capture and execution of Midianite Kings, 114-15
    capture of Midianite captains, 112-13

Cisjordanian campaign, 111-12
destruction of Baal altar, 110
encounter with angel, 108-10
Gideon's ephod and royal aspirations, 115-16
introduction, 107-8
life after Gideon, 116-17
polemics against Transjordanian towns, 113-14
Gog, identification of, 129, 130, 131
golah-oriented redaction
    in 2 Kings 24, 97-103
    in Jeremiah and Ezekiel, 100–102
Graf, K. H., on supplements to biblical text, xii
grammatical errors, 60
Great Psalms Scroll, and supplementation in Psalm 145, 3-20
Greek Papyrus 967, 127
Gunkel, Hermann, and contributions of compilers of biblical texts, xiii, xiv

Hallo, William, on Sumerian legal texts, 165, 166
Hannah, role in different versions of Song of Hannah, 34-43
harmonization, and supplementation, 14, 16

Ilgen, Karl David, and Older Documentary Hypothesis, xii
inclusio, 10, 13, 18
inner-biblical exegesis, 125, 126, 139, 145
Israel, as nation-in-arms in Gideon narrative, 120, 121, 122
Israelite legal fictions (ILF), 162
    editorial techniques to incorporate into Deuteronomy, 172-75
    similarities with Sumerian legal fictions, 169, 170, 171, 172
    and Sumerian legal exercises, 162
    use in Deuteronomy, 162
    use in scribal education, 171, 172
itinerary genre, 54, 61, 62, 63

Jerusalem, conquest of, 89, 90, 91

218 Index of Subjects

Joseph, as model of loyalty and chastity, 80
Joseph and the Egyptian woman, as unified narrative, 76
Joseph narrative
   double supplementation in, 76-78, 79-81
   and Egyptian tale of two brothers, 79, 80
   parallel narratives in, 69, 70
   reconstruction of compositional layers in, 82, 83
   redaction history, 69, 70
   supplementation in, 69-83
   and validity of Documentary Hypothesis, 69

keyword associations, 43
kings, seizing of, 95
Kleinerman, Alexandra, on use of literary letters at Nippur, 166, 167
Kratz, Reinhard
   analysis of Gideon narrative, 106, 107
   on seventy-year motif, 142
Kuenen, Abraham, and Four-Source Documentary Hypothesis, xii, xiii
Kugel, James L., and inner-biblical exegesis, xv

law collections, Near Eastern, 162
lawmaking, by multiplying scenarios, 175–78
Laws of Eshnunna, 167, 168
Laws of Hammurabi, 162, 163, 164, 168, 169, 171, 175
legal fiction, 162, 203
legal questions, and oracular novellae, 58, 59
legal texts, Sumerian, 164, 165
Leviticus
   4Q365 as expansionist version of, 203
   ancient versions from Qumran, 183, 184
   in Second Temple Period, 183
   textual stability of, 183, 184, 185, 203

literary criticism, and textual supplementation, 49
literary development, as inner-biblical exegesis, 145
literary letters, Sumerian, use in scribal education, 166, 177

Manasseh, role in 2 Kings 24, 98, 99, 100
mechanical text loss, 48
Medanites, Midianites, and Ishmaelites, 72, 73
metrical considerations, and supplementation, 16
military units, divisions into, 112
model contracts, 166
Mowinckel, S., on supplementation in psalms, 19

Neo-Babylonian Chronicle 5, on Nebuchadnezzar's capture of Jerusalem, 94, 95
Neo-Documentarians, xiv
new exodus, in Isaiah, 134-41
new oil, festival of, 188, 198, 203
Newer Documentary Hypothesis. *See* Four-Source Documentary Hypothesis
Nippur Homicide Trial, 164, 165, 167
Noth, Martin
   and contributions of compilers of biblical texts, xiii, xiv
   on Deuteronomist as one author, 87, 88

Older Documentary Hypothesis, xii
oracular novella, 56, 57, 58, 59
orthographic expansions, 6
orthography
   and supplementation in Song of Hannah, 29, 30, 31, 32, 33, 47

parallelism, 9, 10
Perles, Felix, on abbreviations in Psalter, 15
perpetual worship, and unending punishment, 155
pesharim, Daniel 9 as precursor to, 145

Index of Subjects   219

plene spellings, for correct pronunciation, 13, 15
pluses and minuses, in text of Song of Hannah, 34-43, 47
Popper, Julius, on the Diaskeuasten, xiii
Potiphar, as personal name, 73, 74
prison, as place of punishment for crime, 71
prophecy, actualization in later texts, 134
prophetic books, theological interpretation in, 103
prophetic texts, quoted as authoritative scripture, 144, 145
Psalm(s)
  internal analysis based on external evidence, 49, 50
  rearrangement of, 24
  supplementation through additions from other psalms, 24
  textual and literary history of, 21-25
Psalm 145
  in Jewish liturgy, 4, 5
  in MT and 11QPs^a, 3-20
  nun-line missing in, 9, 10, 11, 16, 22, 65
Psalm 151, as addition to psalter, 24

reemplotment, 62, 63
refrains, 14, 17, 22
resumptive repetition, 63
Reworked Pentateuch (4QRP^{a-e}), Leviticus in, 185, 186
ritual instructions, and use of זאת תורת, 59, 60
Rofé, Alexander, on Isralite legal fictions as rooted in a women's law collection, 168
Roth, Martha, on Sumerian legal texts, 165, 166

Schmid, Konrad, and creativity of compilers of biblical texts, xiii
scribal errors
  in original writing, 33, 34
  and supplementation in Song of Hannah, 30, 31, 32, 33, 47

scribal technique, evidence from 4Q365, 204
scripturalization of texts, 139
scripture, emergence of, in the prophets, 145
second exodus motif, 134-41
Second Kings 24
  historical information in, 94, 95, 96, 97
  redactional reworking and theological interpretation in, 94-97
  supplementation in, 93-102
Second Kings 25, supplementation in, 89-92
Second Kings 24 and 25, discrepancies in accounts, 93, 94
seventy-year motif
  in 2 Chronicles, 143
  in Daniel, 144
  in Ezra, 143
  in Jeremiah, 141
shrinkage, 4
Song of Hannah
  external and internal evidence for supplementation, 46-50
  location in versions of biblical text, 34, 35
  reconstruction of literary and textual history of, 43-46
  versions of, 25
spurned wife motif, 76, 77, 79
Steck, Odil Hannes, on redaction history of prophets as biblical interpretation, 126
stylistic peculiarities, as evidence of supplementation, 78, 79
Sumerian legal fictions, 167, 168
  implications for study of Deuteronomy, 168-72
  parallels in Mesopotamian legal collections, 167, 168
Supplementary Hypothesis, xiii
supplementation
  and abbreviations, 6, 7, 9, 14, 15
  accidental, 11
  and authors' use of older materials, 106, 107
  based on parallel texts, 7, 8

Index of Subjects

supplementation (*continued*)
  at beginning and end of literary works, 11, 12, 18, 19
  to clarify ambiguities and syntax, 9, 16, 151, 152, 156, 157
  to contemporize a text, 12-13
  to correct errors, 9
  definition of, 5, 6, 62
  and doxologies, 8
  at end of book of Isaiah, 149-51, 156, 157
  to forge connections with other texts, 153, 154
  function of, xvi
  in Gideon account in Judges, 105, 107-17, 121, 122
  identification of, xvi
  to increase severity in legal cases, 175
  in invasion of Gog from Magog, 127-34
  legal, in Second Temple period, 203-4
  and literary genre, xvi
  metrical considerations, 7
  and new exodus in Isaiah, 134-41
  orthographic expansions as, 6
  in the Prophets, 126-45
  reasons for, 14-15, 48
  reconstructing stages of growth of texts, xvi
  and refrains, 14, 17, 22
  role in composition of Hebrew Bible, xv, xvi
  and seamless editorial work, 66, 67
  and seventy-year motif in Jeremiah, 141-45
  and stylistic peculiarities, 78, 79
  to transform a literary figure, 80, 81, 109, 118
  types of, 13, 14
  through use of theological motif, 134-41
  through use of words and idioms of earlier passages, 156

tale of two brothers (Egyptian), 79, 80

tetragrammaton
  in 2 Kings 25, 91
  avoidance of, 10
  as supplementation, 7
  use of, as indication of supplementation in Joseph narrative, 77
textual variants, need for external evidence, 33, 47
theological interpretation, as aim of supplementation, 81
tôrâ, and Pentateuchal sources, 59
Tov, Emanuel
  on autonomy of versions of Song of Hannah, 29
  on gloss and interpolation, 5
traditio and *traditum*, Prophets, 140, 141, 144, 145
trial records, and Laws of Hammurabi, 163, 164

Van Seters, John, on editors of biblical texts, xiv

war stories, role in composition of biblical literature, 114
water imagery, in second exodus motif, 136, 137, 138, 139
Wellhausen, Julius, and Four-Source Documentary Hypothesis, xii, xiii
Wette, M. L. de, on Jehovist reworking of Elohim source, xii
Williamson, H. G. M., on certainty of hearing motif, 19
wood offering
  composition as legal supplement, 190-97
  and festival of new oil, 188, 189, 190
  and firstfruits festival, 192, 193, 194, 196
  grammatical characteristics of, 189
  in Josephus, 197
  as legal fiction, 203
  in Nehemiah, 198, 199, 200, 201, 202, 203
  origins, 197-202
  in rabbinic literature, 197

scriptural traditions behind, 191–96
as supplement to festal legislation
    of Leviticus, 186-90
in Temple Scroll, 197, 198, 203
worm, undying, 151, 154, 155

Yehoash inscription, 11

Zedekiah, in 2 Kings 25, 90, 91
Zimmerli, Walther
    and analysis of prophetic writings, xv
    on literary supplementation in the Prophets, 125
זאת תורת, and ritual instructions, 59, 60